Play Better
CHESS

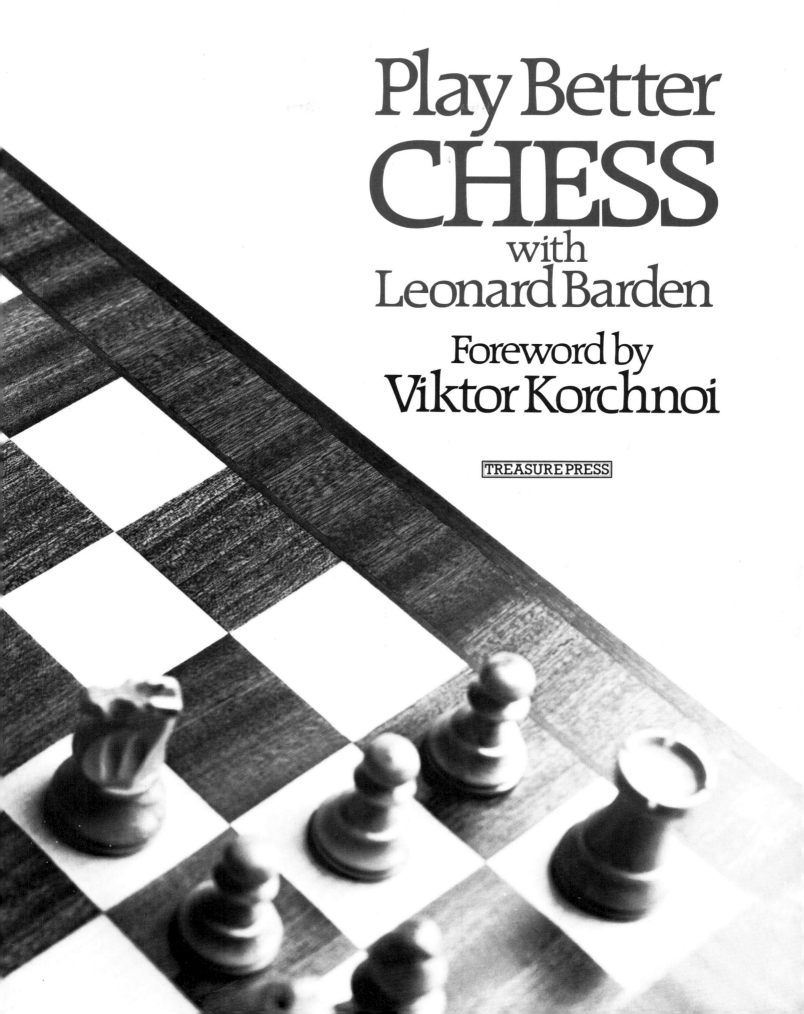

Play Better

CHESS

with
Leonard Barden

Foreword by
Viktor Korchnoi

TREASURE PRESS

CONTENTS

First published in Great Britain in 1980 by
Octopus Books Limited

This revised edition published in 1987 by
Treasure Press
59 Grosvenor Street
London W1

© 1980 Octopus Books Limited
©Revised Material 1987 Octopus Books Limited

ISBN 1 85051 231 0

Printed in Hong Kong

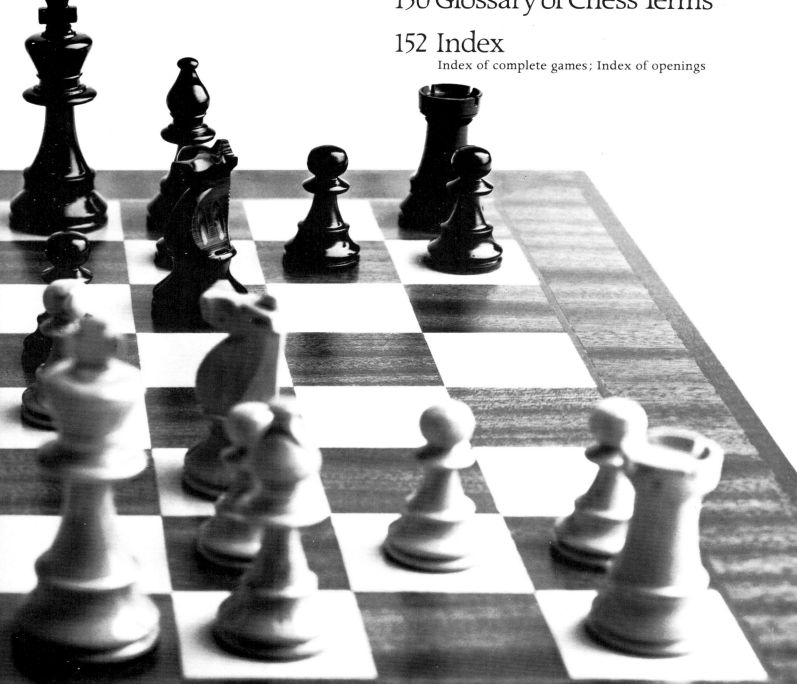

Foreword
by Viktor Korchnoi

Improving one's ability as a chess player is not an easy task. The physical development of muscles on arms or legs can be easily achieved by training with weights. Training will also help improve speed at running or swimming. But how much time and effort must be spent at chess to have any effect? Thousands of people play chess regularly but never improve their game at all.

At one time I studied the text-books of Lasker, Capablanca and Euwe. I admired Euwe's lectures for their consistent and logical approach, but I particularly remember Lasker's manual. He was a real optimist, writing that in just 120 hours he could teach a novice to such a high standard that he would be able to stand up to a master. I don't know how many players have followed Lasker's advice but, frankly, there is still a great distance between those who know how to avoid blunders and those who think independently, who can play openings, who appreciate the subtleties of chess strategy – I mean masters.

One does not have to be a grandmaster to tutor young chess players successfully. The ability to teach is something quite special. I never really managed to teach my own son to play chess. He would pester me to play, but I would point to a book on the shelf and say 'First, read this book and then we will play.' For a ten year old like him, chess was a game, like an electric train, but for me it is a profession, my work. I could not understand his attitude to chess, nor could he understand mine.

The task of a teacher is to discover talent in a pupil, to rouse his enthusiasm and only then to make him an expert by keeping him regularly occupied with new and increasingly complex problems. I would like to introduce the author of this book – well-known as a teacher of British juniors. In 1972 money was made available for chess education for junior players in London, and it was Leonard Barden who worked with them. In 1976 I had an opportunity to become an inspector of this 'kindergarten'. I played a simultaneous display with London schoolboys on 30 boards. The display lasted over seven hours and was exhausting, although enjoyable, work. I was held to a draw by no less than 11 players and lost to one. In 1979 Boris Spassky also put Leonard Barden's work to the test. Spassky won only 13 games, lost five and drew twelve.

Of Spassky's thirty opponents, three later became grandmasters, another ten are international masters or masters of the FIDE. And the player who beat me was Nigel Short.

I do not want to intrude into Leonard Barden's field of teaching, for in education he is a respected expert. But as a leading chess player I am often asked the same questions. At the risk of repeating the contents of this book, I will attempt to answer some of them.

Perhaps the main point which troubles the beginner is the extent to which ability will depend on natural talent. In an age where chess books and instruction are widely available, talent is not such a vital factor. The ability to work hard is more important. I know of several grandmasters with no specific talent for chess. One of them, Botvinnik, was World Champion for 15 years! To compensate for lack of talent, he possessed an exceptional capacity for work and an iron will.

So is studying chess useful and, if so, when should one begin? Clearly, it is not something to rush into headlong at any serious level. To play chess seriously can involve considerable stress, and chess can become a passion that interferes with other studies. But in moderate doses chess is generally useful. It is usual to begin at 10 or 12 years old and studies have shown that at that age chess develops perseverence, increases attentiveness, encourages the ability to think logically and teaches objectivity. Indeed, in some schools where chess has been introduced alongside other subjects, the level of achievement has been raised.

I am sometimes asked how to perfect one's game. Learning how the pieces move is a simple matter, but knowing this is no more than knowing a few words of a foreign language. You would be foolish to claim to be able to speak it. And, like a language, chess can be studied for a lifetime – there are always new things to learn. Not even World Champions can exhaust the possibilities.

If you have mastered the basic science of chess and want to take your ability further, it is a good idea to note down your games to analyze them later. You can do this with a friend or teacher, but better still by yourself. You should be really thorough and write a commentary on all your games, whether you have won or lost. In this way, you can investigate your own thought processes and discover the errors made by both you and your opponent.

It is more useful to play with a partner who is better than yourself. If he is much better, you will not understand why you lose. But if he is much weaker than you, the game will only serve to boost your ego. The occasional boost to the ego does have its value, however!

It is worthwhile studying a few games in detail – perhaps involving an opening that interests you or the style of a particular grandmaster. A memorized opening is a weapon you can use in practical play. And by imitating grandmasters you can bring yourself up to their level. Don't feel ashamed to copy the play of Capablanca or Fischer. They, champions of the world, began the same way.

It is only necessary to learn one or two openings, and perhaps some essential positions in the endgame. There is no point in endless learning of countless variations. What is important is the development of flair, the understanding of your chosen openings and a feeling for the delicacy of strategy.

Chess is both simple and complex. Armed with this knowledge, you are ready to proceed to develop your chess skill, with the help of Leonard Barden's splendid book.

Before You Start

Chess is a game for two people, played on a board of 64 squares coloured alternately light and dark. The light squares on the board are 'white' squares and the dark ones 'black'. Both you and your opponent may use all the squares during the game.

For play, the board is placed so that each player has a white square on his right at the end of the row nearest him (fig. 1). Remember 'White on the right' and you will never face the embarrassing moment common to many novices when an experienced player comes to look at the game and says scornfully 'You're playing with the board the wrong way round!'

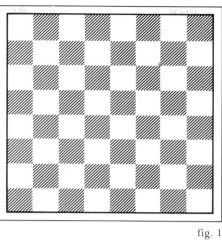

fig. 1

The line-up

At the start of the game, the chess pieces or men are placed on the board as shown in fig. 2 (illustrated).

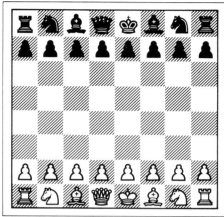

fig. 2

Each player has

1 king	2 bishops	2 rooks
1 queen	2 knights	8 pawns

You may only have one piece on a square at any time. Note that the white queen always starts on a white square and the black queen starts on a black square. White always moves first, then Black, then White again and so on until the end of the game.

Chess diagrams in this book are printed with White at the bottom of the board, moving up. This is usual in chess books as well as in magazine and newspaper articles about chess.

How to win and draw

The ultimate object of a chess game is to capture the king, or more precisely to force your opponent's king into a position where it is inescapably trapped – a situation called 'checkmate'. If it is no longer possible for either side to win, the game ends in a draw.

To win at chess, you must be more skilful than your opponent in moving and manoeuvring your pieces. Sometimes this may mean gaining an overwhelming material advantage so that checkmate of the enemy king becomes inevitable. On other occasions a strong player will sacrifice some of his men so that the other pieces can successfully attack the king.

Chess starting position. Note the white square in the bottom right-hand corner. The white queen always starts on the white square and the black queen on the black. With millions of ways to play the first few moves, novices should try to control central squares.

9

There are six types of chess piece, each with its own way of moving over the board. This probably derives from the ancient Indian game of Chaturanga, one of the precursors of modern chess, in which dice were thrown to determine which piece moved. Each of the six sides of the dice corresponded to a particular piece, so that if you threw a one you moved a pawn, two meant a horseman (the predecessor of the knight) could move, and so on.

Bishop and Rook moves

The bishop may move any number of squares along one diagonal in any one move. It cannot jump over other chessmen. A bishop moves on squares of one colour only, and each player has one bishop for black squares and the other for white squares (fig. 3). The rook can move any number of squares along one vertical column ('file') or horizontal row ('rank') in any one move. It moves on straight lines only, and cannot jump over other chessmen. The rook can land on both black and white squares (fig. 4).

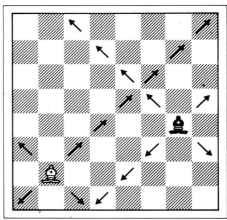

fig. 3

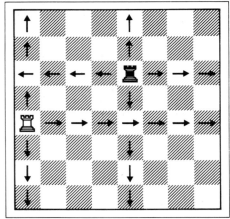

fig. 4

Captures

A chessplayer can choose whether or not to capture an enemy piece. You do not have to capture and there is no penalty for not capturing. You capture by taking the opponent's piece off the board and

moving your own man into its place. In fig. 5a White has the choice of capturing either the rook or the pawn with his bishop. The bishop cannot jump to the squares beyond the black men. The player of White may, if he wishes, make a non-

fig. 5a   fig. 5b

capturing move with the bishop, or decide to move a different piece.

In fig. 5b, White has taken the rook with his bishop and removed the captured rook from the board. This all counts as a single move.

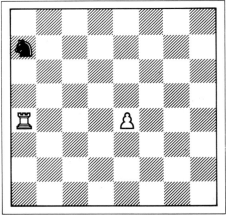

fig. 6

The white rook in fig. 6 can take the black knight but cannot go to the square beyond it. The rook cannot move to the square occupied by its own pawn, nor to the three squares beyond it.

Queen moves and captures

The queen is the most powerful of the chess pieces and can move like a bishop or a rook. The queen can move along diagonals, ranks or files, but must keep to one diagonal, rank or file on any one move. In fig. 7 the queen can move to any of the squares marked by crosses.

Fig. 8a shows a capturing move of the queen. She can either move like a bishop to capture the rook, or like a rook to capture the bishop. The queen has captured the bishop in fig. 8b – but watch out! Now it is Black's move and his rook

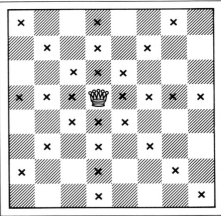

fig. 7

can take the powerful queen. It is important to keep pieces guarded when possible, so that if your opponent takes one of your pieces you can retaliate by capturing one of his.

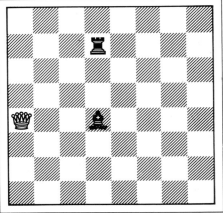

fig. 8a

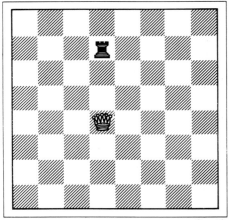

fig. 8b

Knight moves and captures

The knight moves differently from all the other chess pieces in that (a) it can jump over other pieces and (b) it does not move in a straight line. The knight's move is always L-shaped (fig. 9a). It goes either two squares up (or down) the board and then one square across, or alternatively two squares across and then one square up or down. If a piece of your own or your opponent's lies between the knight and its destination, the knight simply jumps over it. In fig. 9b the white knight can jump over either bishop.

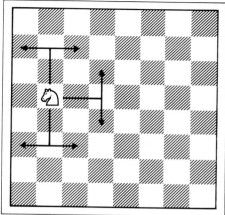

fig. 9a

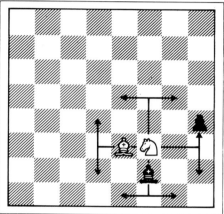

fig. 9b

The knight can jump over any piece in the path of its move without taking it. If you find its move a little hard to remember, note that it always travels from a white square to a black one or vice versa.

The knight captures any enemy man on the square where it lands. In fig. 9b, the white knight can capture the black pawn.

Pawn moves and captures

The pawn is unique among the chessmen in that it may move forwards only. Normally a pawn's advance is limited to one square at a time, but for its first move the pawn is allowed to move either one or two squares. The pawn is also the only man whose capturing move is different from its 'normal' move. Pawns can only capture enemy men which are one square diagonally ahead of them. The white pawn on the left of the board in fig. 10a has the option of moving one square or two for its first move. The two middle pairs of pawns block each other and none of them can move. Either of the pawns on the right can advance one square. The white pawn in fig. 10b has the option of capturing the knight or advancing to the

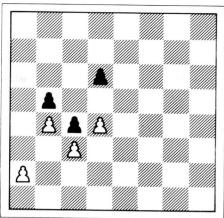

fig. 10a

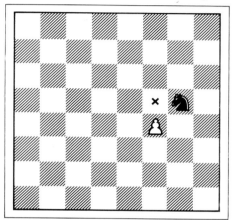

fig. 10b

square marked by a cross.

Pawn promotion

A pawn slowly inching its way up the board will normally be blocked or captured before it reaches the opposite side. But any pawn which does reach the far side is immediately promoted into a queen, rook, bishop or knight (but not a king) as the player wishes (fig. 11a).

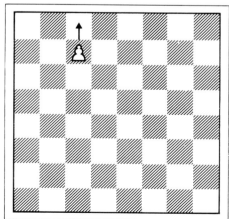

fig. 11a

Removing the pawn from the board and substituting the chosen piece is all part of one move. The player usually decides to promote the pawn into a queen because that is the strongest piece. The new queen

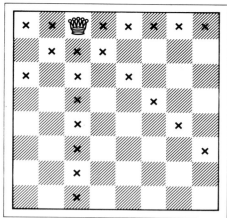

fig. 11b

can move to any of the squares marked with crosses on the next move (fig. 11b).

By promoting pawns it is possible to have two or more queens, or three or more knights, bishops and rooks. In theory, a player can have nine queens on the board – the original one and eight promoted pawns.

If the promoting pawn captures an opposing man on the pawn's final, promoting move, this still counts as part of the same move. If you need a second queen and your set has only one, use an upturned captured rook, a lump of sugar, or anything distinctive to hand.

King moves and captures

The king moves one square in any direction and it can generally capture opposing men in the same way as do other pieces. In fig. 12a the king can move to any of the starred squares while in fig. 12b the king can capture either the rook or the bishop.

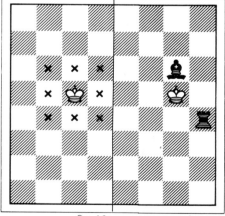

fig. 12a   fig. 12b

Check to the king!

The object of chess is to capture the king. When the king is attacked it is said to be 'in check' and it must get out of check immediately. Figs 13a and 13b show two examples of check. In both these positions the attacked king must move immediately to a square where it is not in check, that is, not being attacked by an opposing piece.

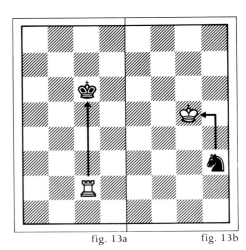

Getting out of check

You can escape from check in three ways: (a) by blocking your opponent's threat to your king (b) by capturing the checking piece or (c) by moving the king out of check. In fig. 15a Black can escape from check in any of the three ways.

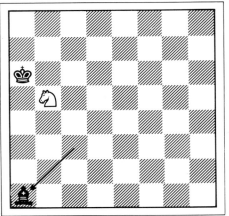

fig. 15a

fig. 16a

More on check

The king is never allowed to move into check, nor to stay in check. In fig. 14a the king can take the bishop or move one square diagonally north-east. All other moves would still leave the king in check and are not allowed under chess rules.

Kings cannot move to squares next to one another since this would effectively be a move into check (fig. 14b).

fig. 14a

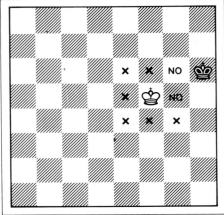

fig. 14b

fig. 15b

Black has captured the checking rook in fig. 15b with his bishop. He could also have escaped from check by interposing the bishop between the king and rook, by capturing the knight with the king, or by moving the king to one of the two other squares not attacked by the rook.

Discovered and double check

If White advances his pawn or moves his white-squared bishop, the black king is in check from one of the other white pieces – a discovered check (fig. 16a). Discovered checks can be strong because the moving piece has the chance to attack another opposing man.

If White moves his rook to either arrowed square in fig. 16b the black king is in check from both white pieces – a double check. It is impossible to meet a double check by interposition or capture, so the king has to move.

Checkmate

You have won the game when your opponent has no way to move out of check.

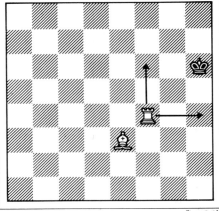

fig. 16b

The capture of the king on the next move is then inescapable and the king is checkmated.

Figs. 17a and 17b show two checkmates. In the first the black king is checked by the white queen. The queen cannot be captured because the king would then be in check from the rook – and there is no other way to escape from the queen check.

In the second example, the black king is in check from the white rook. It cannot retreat up the board because its escape squares are guarded by the white knight or bishop or blocked by the black rook. The black king cannot of course move next to the white king.

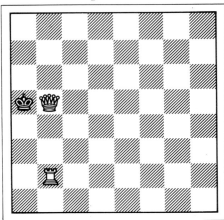

fig. 17a

fig. 17b

More checkmates

Checkmates occur most frequently with the loser's king on the edge or the side of the board. Figs 18a to 18d show typical checkmating (which experienced players call 'mating') finishes. In the first two, the black king is hemmed in by its own pawns and so has no escape square when attacked by the white rook or knight. The other diagrams show two white pieces combining for the final attack.

fig. 18a   fig. 18b

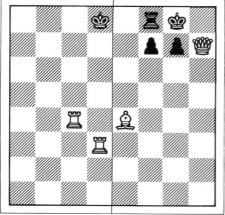

fig. 18c   fig. 18d

Draw by stalemate

Not all games end in checkmate. When a player is not in check, but has no legal move available, he is said to be stalemated, and the game ends in a draw.

fig. 19

The situation in fig. 19 is not checkmate – the black king is not even in check. But if the black king tries to move, it will either be in check from the white queen (not allowed) or directly next to the white king (also not allowed). If Black had another piece in the diagram it would not be stalemate because he could move that piece. It is only stalemate when the player on the move has no move at all he can make, and when his king is not in check.

Other ways to draw

If neither you nor your opponent has enough pieces to bring about a checkmate, the game ends in a draw. For instance, a lone king can never checkmate another lone king. A king and a bishop against a king, or a king and a knight against a king, are also situations where checkmate is impossible.

If your king can be continually checked but not checkmated by an opponent's piece or pieces, the position is a 'perpetual check' and the game is drawn.

In fig. 20a White's king and bishop cannot checkmate Black's lone king. If

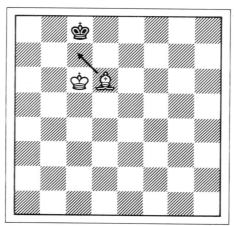

fig. 20a

fig. 20b

White plays the arrowed bishop move Black has no legal reply but is not in check, hence a draw by stalemate.

In fig. 20b White's queen keeps checking on the arrowed squares and Black's king cannot escape the checks. Black is ahead on pieces and would win if White did not give perpetual check.

Draws by agreement

If the material is even, with very few pieces left, and there is no reasonable chance of mating or promoting a pawn, the players generally agree to draw the game. One player says 'Draw?' and the other accepts his offer. Only a bad blunder in fig. 21 could permit a win for either side.

fig. 21

The scoring system for chess games in matches and tournaments is 1 point for a win, $\frac{1}{2}$ point for a draw, and 0 for a loss. There are very few draws among beginners, but the proportion gradually rises as the players become stronger. In tournaments and matches among grandmasters – the world's leading players – as many as two games in three may be drawn.

Two rare methods to reach a draw happen when the same position occurs three times with the same player to move each time; and when both players make 50 moves without taking anything or moving a pawn.

What are the pieces worth?

♟ 1 – but more if likely to become a queen ♙

♞ 3¼ ♘

♝ 3½ ♗

♜ 5 ♖

♛ 9 ♕

♚ No attacking value in the opening and middle stages of the game, when the king must be safeguarded from checkmate. However, when only a few pieces remain, attacking value rapidly increases up to 4 or 5 ♔

Usually, though by no means always, the stronger army wins a chess battle. Novices will find it useful to keep a point count of the pieces on the board. An advantage of two points or more (two pawns ahead, or rook against bishop or knight) is sufficient to win games between reasonably experienced players. In an endgame where few pieces remain, a one point lead may be enough. But you can afford to be ten or twenty points behind, or even more, if you are certain to checkmate your opponent's king.

Castling

Castling is a special move made by the king and the rook, before they have moved from their starting positions on the board.

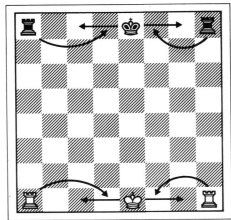

fig. 22

In castling, the king moves two squares in the direction of the rook. The rook then jumps over the king to the square immediately on the other side of the king. This all counts as a single move. Castling may be done once only by either player during a game. In castling, always move the king first.

Rules about castling

You are not allowed to castle
1 if there is any piece occupying a square between the king and rook.
2 if you are in check. If you get out of check without moving your king, then you can castle later in the game.
3 if your king has to cross a square where it would be in check.
4 if you have already moved your king, even if you later moved it back again.
5 if you finish up in check.
6 if the rook intended for castling has already moved during the game. If one rook has moved, you are still allowed to castle with the other rook.

fig. 23

The white king cannot castle on either side in fig. 23 because it would mean crossing a square where the black knight would give check. The black king cannot castle on the short side because he would be in check from the bishop, but he can castle on the long side even though the castling rook is attacked. The castling rook can jump from or through an attacked squares even though the king cannot do so.

Pawn takes en passant

The special pawn *en passant* ('in passing') capture is the least understood rule of chess. It ensures that a pawn advancing two squares on its initial move can still be captured by an opposing pawn on an adjacent file.
If the black pawn in fig. 24a advances one square, White can capture it. When the black pawn advances two squares, White's pawn can capture 'en passant' just as if the pawn had moved only one square. The capturing pawn has to be on the fifth square of a file, and the en passant capture can only be made if the opposing pawn advances two squares in one move. An en passant capture is optional, but can only be made on the move succeeding the captured pawn's two square advance as shown in figs. 24b and 24c.

fig. 24a

fig. 24b

fig. 24c

The moves summarized

Straight line ranks and files for the rooks; criss-cross diagonals for the bishops; the queen moves like a rook or bishop; L-shaped jumps (two up or down and one across, or two across and one up or down) for the knight; and one cautious square for the king. A pawn advances forward one or two squares on its first move, and one square at a time after that; it captures one square diagonally forward; and at the far end it is promoted.

Attacking the king is check, and attacking the king so that it cannot escape is checkmate. If you are pieces or pawns ahead you are on the way to a win if your king is safe. Remember the point count, and don't give away pieces for those of lesser value without a good reason.

Writing the moves

Every square on the board has its own unique combination of reference number and letter.

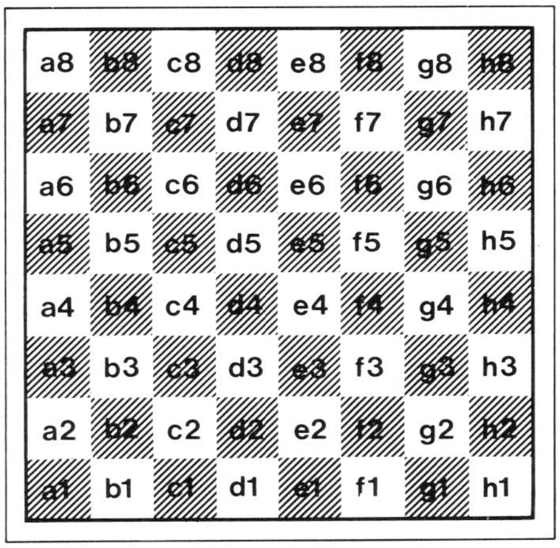

fig. 25

If the white bishop moves from c1 to g5 we can write this as Bc1-g5 or just Bg5. The letter B is used for the bishop, R for the rook, N for the knight, Q for the queen and K for the king. If there is no prefixing symbol, it means a pawn move.

A piece being played from one square to another constitutes one move. In writing the move the piece symbol comes first followed by the square of departure. The square of departure is linked to the square of arrival by a hyphen if the move is a non-capturing one. In condensed notation used in this book the departure square is omitted.

A capture is written with an *x* rather than a hyphen, so that Nxf7 means that a knight takes whatever man is on f7. Pawn captures are written giving the file from which the pawn starts and the square where it arrives, e.g. fxg6 means a pawn on the f file takes on the g6 square.

If both rooks or knights can move to the same square, the move actually played is indicated by the rank or file from which the piece departed. An example: White's rooks on a2 and f2 can both move to e2. If the a2 rook moves, it is written Rae2, if the f2 rook moves, it is written Rfe2.

If both pieces are on the same file a similar procedure is used. An example: White's rooks are on e7 and e1 and can both move to e5. If the e7 rook moves the notation is R7e5 and if the e1 rook moves it is described as R1e5.

Notations compared

1. e2-e4	e7-e5	1. e4	e5	1. P-K4	P-K4
2. Ng1-f3	Nb8-c6	2. Nf3	Nc6	2. N-KB3	N-QB3
3. Nb1-c3	Ng8-f6	3. Nc3	Nf6	3. N-B3	N-B3
4. Bf1-b5	Nc6-d4	4. Bb5	Nd4	4. B-N5	N-Q5
5. Nf3xd4	e5xd4	5. Nxd4	exd4	5. NxN	PxN
6. e4-e5	d4xc3	6. e5	dxc3	6. P-K5	PxN
7. e5xf6	c3xd2+	7. exf6	cxd2+	7. PxN	PxPch
8. Bc1xd2	Qd8xf6	8. Bxd2	Qxf6	8. BxP	QxP
9. 0-0	Bf8-e7	9. 0-0	Be7	9. 0-0	B-K2
10. Bd2-c3	Qf6-g5	10. Bc3	Qg5	10. B-B3	Q-N4
11. Rf1-e1	0-0	11. Re1	0-0	11. R-K1	0-0
12. Re1-e5	Qg5-f6	12. Re5	Qf6	12. R-K5	Q-B3
13. Bb5-d3	h7-h6	13. Bd3	h6	13. B-Q3	P-KR3
14. Qd1-g4	Qf6-h4	14. Qg4	Qh4	14. Q-N4	Q-R5
15. Qg4xg7+	Kg8xg7	15. Qxg7+	Kxg7	15. QxPch	KxQ
16. Re5-g5 mate		16. Rg5 mate (fig. 26)		16. R-N5 mate	

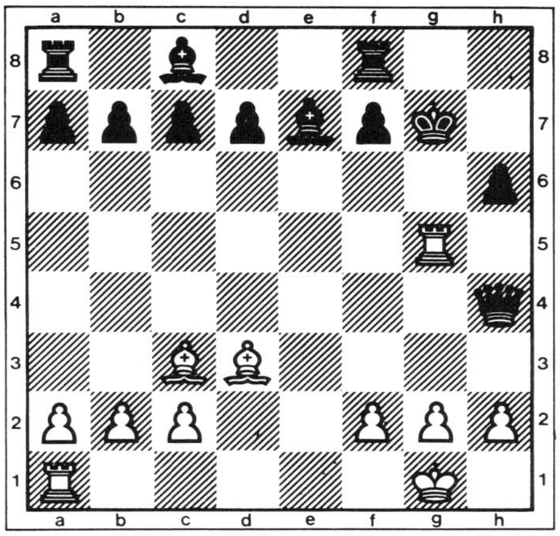

fig. 26

Notations compared

The notation just described is called the algebraic notation and is used in most countries of the world for chess publications. The descriptive system, in which each square is indicated by two combinations of letters and numbers depending upon whether White's or Black's move is being recorded, is favoured in English-speaking countries but is increasingly being replaced by the algebraic system.

The popular BBC2 Master Game chess tournament uses the algebraic system, and the International Chess Federation (FIDE) has announced that it will recognize only algebraic as an official notation from 1 January 1981 onwards.

For readers who are already familiar with descriptive notation but not with algebraic, the game above (Posch v Dorrer) is in full algebraic, condensed algebraic, and descriptive notation.

Summary of abbreviations

K (king) Q (queen) R (rook) B (bishop) N (knight) P (pawn) 0-0 Castles short (on the king's side of the board) 0-0-0 Castles long (on the queen's side of the board) + check — moves to × takes ep en passant ! good move !! brilliant move ? poor move ?? blunder !? prob-ably best ?! probably not best = promotes to, e.g. fxe8 = Q + means 'the f7 pawn takes a piece on e8, promotes to queen, and gives check'.

Rules of play

As well as the moves of the pieces, there are rules of behaviour during a game which also form part of the international laws of chess.

If you touch one of your pieces, you must move that piece if possible, while if you touch one of your opponent's pieces, you must capture that piece if you can. This rule is interpreted in a common-sense manner, and a player whose sleeve brushes against his tall king as his hand reaches out to move a pawn is not penalized.

If a piece is slightly dislodged from the centre of its square, and you want to replace it properly, you have to tell your opponent before you touch the piece. The conventional way to do this is to say 'J'adoube' ('I adjust') which allows you to make any necessary adjustments. Piece adjustments should only be made when it is your own turn to move.

Once you have moved a piece, placed it on a new square and let go of it, you cannot take the move back or put the piece on a different square. Novice players, worried about the touch-move rule, can often be seen to pick up a piece, put it hesitantly on a new square, then keep a finger on top while peering around the board to see if the move is safe. This isn't illegal, but it is bad manners and your hand blocks your own view of the board. If you suddenly notice you are making a mistake while the piece is still in your hand, replace it on its original square and think again. You must still move the piece you have touched, but at least there is a chance to find a better square for it.

If you castle, you have to either pick up your king first, or the king and rook together. If you touch the rook first you may have to move just the rook.

TOP TEN
Novice Pitfalls

Pitfall one – Scholar's mate

Almost every novice falls at least once for the Scholar's mate:

1. e4   e5
2. Bc4   Bc5
3. Qh5

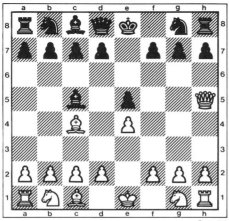

fig. 27

The beginner now decides to chase away the annoying white queen and plays **3. . . . Nf6?? 4. Qxf7 mate.** The checkmating queen is protected by the bishop, and the attacked black king has no escape.

Scholar's mate is the basic beginner's pitfall. White threatens instant checkmate by his queen capturing the pawn next to the black king, with the white queen guarded by the bishop. If Black knows how to meet this attack, he can gain the initiative.

How to avoid Scholar's mate

Black should play **3. . . . Qe7** in the diagram. Then 4. Qxf7+? Qxf7. 5. Bxf7+ Kxf7 leaves Black a bishop for a pawn ahead with a winning game. And 4. Bxf7+? Qxf7 5. Qxe5+ Qe7 6. Qh5+ Kd8 is little better.

If White answers **3. . . . Qe7** with 4. Nf3 then 4. . . . Nc6 5. Nc3 Nf6 and White's queen has its retreat cut off. If 6. Qh3 d5! and the black pawn, advancing to attack the white bishop, at the same time discloses an attack by the black bishop on the white queen. In that event, White's premature attack leads to decisive material gain for Black.

Pitfall two –
Scholar's rook fork

A variant of Scholar's mate, which also claims a large number of novice victims, is:

1.	e4	e5
2.	Bc4	Bc5
3.	Qh5	g6??

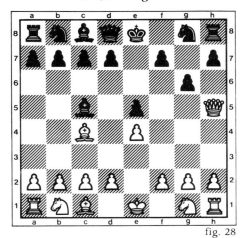

fig. 28

Black knows he must stop Scholar's mate, but hasn't learnt that he must protect his f7 pawn with his queen. So his 3. . . . g6?? is an instinctive forward defensive prod which White answers by **4. Qxe5+** and **5. Qxh8**, winning a rook and the game.

How to avoid Scholar's rook fork

There are two simpler ways to stop Scholar's mate attacks than in the solution to Pitfall One. Once White plays 2. Bc4 in a novice game, he telegraphs his intentions. So Black can counter at once by **2. . . . Nc6!** and if 3. Qh5 g6 (now the e5 pawn is protected by the knight) or if 3. Qf3 (again threatening Qxf7 mate) then Nf6.

If Black suspects a Scholar's mate is coming, he can take evasive action even on move 1. Simply, 1. e4 e6 2. Bc4? d5! controls the centre of the board and drives off the white bishop at once.

Pitfall three –
The weak f7 pawn

Another elementary attack which baffles many beginners occurs when White's knight and bishop combine to attack the f7 pawn. This pawn is the weakest defence point in the early stages of a game, protected as it is only by the king.

The pitfall runs:

1.	e4	e5
2.	Bc4	Nc6

Black stops Scholar's mate.

3.	Nf3	Nf6
4.	Ng5	

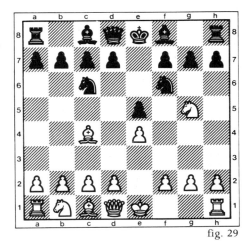

fig. 29

White threatens 5. Nxf7 with a 'fork' (a double attack against two pieces) of the black queen and rook. What should Black do? Certainly not 4. . . . Qe7? 5. Bxf7+ Kd8 6. Bb3 Ke8 7. d3 when White has won a pawn while Black has had to move his king and so cannot castle.

Also risky is 4. . . . d5 5. exd5 Nxd5? 6. d4! If then 6. . . . exd4 7. 0-0 Be7 8. Nxf7! Kxf7 9. Qf3+ Ke6 10. Re1+ and White has a crushing attack. If instead 6. . . . Nxd4 7. c3 wins one of the knights.

How to avoid
the weak f7 pawn

Black may be able to survive with absolutely correct play after 5. . . . Nxd5, but this particular game is not for novices. Instead meet 4. Ng5 with 4. . . . d5 5. exd5 Na5 6. Bb5+ c6, and though you will be a pawn down your pieces come into action quickly.

Pitfall four – The copycat trap

Copying your opponent's moves when you play Black may sound a plausible idea so what can go wrong? Sometimes, not very much. When White starts the game with a non-committal opening move – say 1. c4 or 1. Nf3 which are less forcing than 1. e4 – then Black may be able to mirror his opponent's plans for half-a-dozen moves without disaster.

However, if you try copycat chess when White opens with 1. e4, you could quickly be in trouble.

The pitfall goes:

1.	e4	e5
2.	Nf3	Nf6
3.	Nxe5	

A master game in progress. White pieces aim at the central squares, the clock indicates that it is White's turn to move.

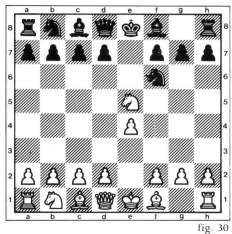

fig. 30

     3. . . .   **Nxe4**
     4. Qe2   **Nf6?**

Now Black notices that if 4. . . . Qe7 5. Qxe4, but that would be better than what happens.

     5.   **Nc6**

Discovering check from the white queen, while at the same time the knight threatens the black queen. White wins queen for knight.

How to avoid the copycat trap

Black should play **3. . . . d6!** first, chasing away the dangerous white knight. Only then should he recapture the lost pawn by 4. . . . Nxe4.

Pitfall five –
The back row mate

The novice who has held his own against an experienced opponent for many moves may finally be caught out by leaving his king behind a row of unmoved pawns. It's a common situation, and one to guard against.

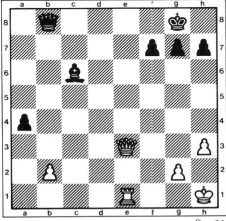

fig. 31

Here material is almost level. Black has a bishop and four pawns to White's rook and three pawns – just half a point down on the point count. Black sees a chance to restore the material balance. and seizes it without a final safety-first look round the board.

1. ...   Qxb2?
2. Qe8+! Bxe8
3. Rxe8 mate

How to avoid
the back row mate

Black should have played 1. ... h6! making an escape hole for his king. In the early and middle part of the game, pawn moves in the vicinity of the king can create serious weaknesses in the defences. In the late stages however, with few pieces left, it is important to provide against sudden raids on the back row.

Pitfall six –
The poisoned pawn

It is a famous chapter in chess lore that at the world championship match in Reykjavik Bobby Fischer captured Boris Spassky's b2 pawn with his queen and within a few moves found his queen trapped in ignominious fashion. There is also the story of the millionaire who left his fortune to his nephew on condition that he never took the b2 pawn with his queen.

This would be a useful hint for novices to remember, but in actual play there are few instances where one side has the chance to take off the b2 pawn with the queen. A more likely poisoned-pawn pitfall occurs where the queen greedily captures the d4 pawn like this:

1. e4   e6
2. d4   d5
3. e5   c5
4. c3   Nc6
5. Nf3   cxd4
6. cxd4   Qb6

Black is eyeing the d4 pawn and expects to build an attack against it by means of N(g8)e7 and Nf5,

7. Bd3

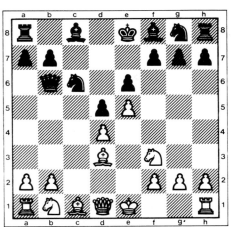
fig. 32

but White takes no notice, apparently leaving the d4 pawn to its fate.

7. ...   Nxd4??
8. Nxd4   Qxd4
9. Bb5+   Kd8
10. Qxd4 and wins

How to avoid
the poisoned pawn

Black should have played 7. ... Bd7, which prevents the white bishop on d3 moving away with check. Black would then be threatening to capture the pawn with no immediate danger.

Pitfall seven –
The Vienna push

Many chess novices become familiar with just one basic opening – a routine and stodgy development of the pieces on the lines of 1. e4 e5 2. Nf3 Nc6 3. Bc4 Bc5 4. d3 d6 and so on. Such players can be thrown mentally off balance when White does something different and unfamiliar as early as move two.

The 'something different' is 2. Nc3, known as the Vienna Game. White can follow up with a pawn advance which induces some 80–90 per cent of novices into a weak and panicky response.

1. e4   e5
2. Nc3   Nf6
3. f4

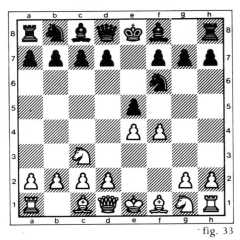
fig. 33

3. ...   exf4?
4. e5!   Qe7?

Black does not like the idea of retreating his knight back to g8, but the text is worse.

5. Qe2   Ng8
6. d4   d6?

Black should swallow his pride and play 6. ... Qd8.

7. Nd5   Qd8

If 7. ... Qe6 8. Nxc7+ wins the queen.

8. Nxc7+   Kd7

If 8. ... Qxc7 9. exd6+ wins the queen.

9. Nxa8 and wins.

How to avoid the Vienna push

Black should play 3. ... d5 4. fxe5 Nxe4. White can still stir up complications with 5. d3 (see page 110) but there is no question of a forced loss for Black.

Pitfall eight –
The hanging bishop

Novices like to develop bishops early. The more experienced player prefers in most cases to bring out the knights first, since the bishops have a greater variety of choice and it can pay to commit them late in the opening. But an early bishop move is not bad in itself.

What the novice must guard against when playing Black and developing his king's bishop (the one at f8) on the queen's side, is that the bishop may become unguarded and vulnerable to a white queen check.

An example of this kind of pitfall:

1. d4   Nf6
2. c4   e6
3. Nc3   Bb4
4. e3   d5
5. Nf3   b6??

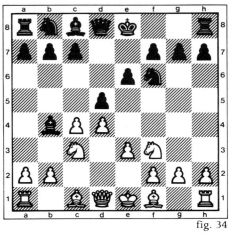
fig. 34

Black plans to put his bishop on a good square at b7.

6. Qa4+

and wins the bishop or (if 6. ... Nc6) the knight.

How to avoid
the hanging bishop

Black here set up the pitfall for himself. Before his 5. ... b6?? White's Qa4+ was no threat, as the black knight could interpose at c6 protected by the b pawn. Simplest for Black was 5. ... 0-0.

Pitfall nine – The pinned knight

Many novices, after a little experience with chess, settle on a routine opening, both for White and Black, bringing out the knights and bishops in the centre. This is an understandable choice for players lacking wide experience, but even this apparently harmless opening contains hidden pitfalls. Variants of one such snare catch many novices each year.

1.	e4	e5
2.	Nf3	Nc6
3.	Bc4	Bc5
4.	d3	d6
5.	Nc3	Nf6

So far there is complete symmetry, but remember pitfall four and the dangers of copycat chess.

6.	Bg5	0-0?

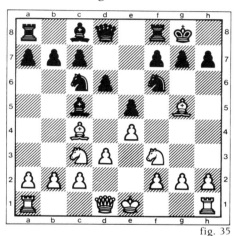

fig. 35

7. Nd5!

Black's knight is pinned against the queen and can be attacked by two white pieces. This weakness is made worse because the pawn front defending the king will be weakened.

7.	...	a6?
8.	Bxf6	gxf6
9.	Qd2	f5
10.	Qh6	

Threatening 11. Nf6+, winning the queen or mating by Qxh7.

10.	...	f6
11.	Nxf6+	Kh8
12.	Qxh7 mate	

How to avoid the pinned knight

Black should have played **6. . . . h6!** chasing away the attacking bishop and if 7. Bh4 g5. This pawn advance is safe while Black still has the option of long side castling, although too risky once the black king has castled short.

Black wasted a further move with the irrelevant 7. . . . a6. Instead he should play 7. . . . Be6 when, if 8. Bxf6 gxf6 9. Qd2 Bxd5. Then Black still has the inferior position because of his weakened pawns around the king, but he has avoided any early mate threats.

Pitfall ten – The master check

Some experts would include this final pitfall among the traps to catch experienced players which are described in Chapter 3. But this trap has now been in circulation since the year 1943 and has occurred so often and been described in print so many times that regular match and tournament competitors have little excuse for allowing it. Its great danger is to the novice, who takes up the Sicilian Defence 1. e4 c5, the most popular opening in chess, and is attracted to the 'Dragon' system where Black develops his bishop at g7, on the promising long diagonal from h8 to a1.

1.	e4	c5
2.	Nf3	d6
3.	d4	cxd4
4.	Nxd4	Nf6
5.	Nc3	g6
6.	f4	

This pawn advance is a signal that White is hoping to set the 'Levenfish trap' named after a Russian who popularized this opening. Usual moves are 6. Be2, 6. Be3 and 6. f3.

6.	...	Bg7

This natural move is already inferior. Somewhat better is Nc6.

7.	e5	dxe5?

A better practical chance is 7. . . . Nh5

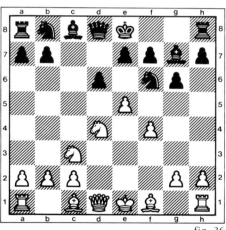

fig. 36

8.	Bb5+ (8. g4? Nxf4! 9. Bxf4 dxe5) Bd7

9. e6 fxe6 10. Nxe6 Bxc3+ 11. bxc3 Qc8 though a 1979 British Championship game J. Littlewood–Mestel showed this, too, as favourable for White. Play ended 12. Bxd7+ Kxd7 13. Ng5 Qc4 14. Rb1 Kc7 15. Rb4 Qxa2 16. Qe2 Nc6 17. Ne6+ Resigns. If 17. . . . Kc8 18. Rxb7! with mate in three if the rook is taken. Can you work out the mate?

8.	fxe5	Ng4?

8. . . . Nd5 also allows the unpleasant 9. Bb5+. Best, in a poor position, is 8. . . . Nfd7 9. e6 Nf6 10. exf7+ Kxf7.

9.	Bb5+	

setting Black a dilemma, for both Nd7 and Bd7 now lose a knight to 10. Qxg4. The best chance now is 9. . . . Nc6 10. Nxc6 Qxd1+ 11. Nxd1 Bd7, but in practice if Black reaches the position after 9. Bb5+ he looks round for a way to avoid losing material and thinks he has found it with . . .

9.	...	Kf8
10.	Ne6+	

and wins the queen.

How to avoid the master check

Black should play **6. . . . Nbd7!** This is the simplest way to a sound game while avoiding trappy lines. The game might continue 7. Nf3 Qc7 8. Bd3 Bg7 9. 0-0 0-0 10. Kh1 a6 11. a4 b6 12. Qe1 Bb7 13. Qh4 e5.

TOP TEN
Opening Traps

Opening traps are a more advanced form of novice pitfalls. Pitfalls are there for the player new to chess who has only a hazy idea of textbook moves and general strategy. It is possible, however, to fall into standard opening traps even after two or three years experience, and in positions with which a player thinks he is familiar.

The secret of a good opening trap is that the loser's moves should be natural and plausible. There may be only a small difference between the trap situation and one where the loser is adopting the classical tenets of the masters. But that difference is crucial, and it means quick victory or defeat.

Trap one – The master standby

When chess masters give simultaneous displays against 20 to 40 opponents at once, their usual plan is to win many games on technique. This means picking up a pawn or two, exchanging pieces, and simplifying into an endgame where the ultimate victory comes by promoting one of the extra pawns to queen. But how to win a pawn or two in the first place? One way is by a standard trap against a defensive set-up chosen by many average chess club members.

1. e4   e5
2. Nf3   Nc6
3. Bb5   d6

Many weaker players are less familiar with the Ruy Lopez 3. Bb5 than with 3. Bc4, and therefore choose what looks a solid defence eschewing tactical risks.

4. d4   Bd7
5. Nc3   Nf6
6. Qd3

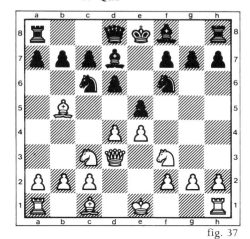
fig. 37

6. . . .   Be7?

Black continues to develop normally, but here this is a serious mistake.

7. Bxc6!   Bxc6
8. dxe5   dxe5
9. Nxe5

White has won an important pawn. The purpose of 6. Qd3 was to protect the e pawn so that Black cannot regain the lost material.

For maximum effect, such moves as 7. Bxc6 and 8. dxe5 should be made rapidly and with a flourish, to indicate to Black that he has blundered. Not infrequently players of Black become demoralized by the unexpected turn of events and continue 9. . . . Qxd3? 10. cxd3 0-0 11. Nxc6 bxc6 12. Ke2 when White has further assets to add to his extra pawn. He has weakened the black queen's side which can be pressurized by moves like f3, Be3, Rhc1 and Na4 when the pawns at c6 and c7 are vulnerable.

Attack formation against the Sicilian Defence is the most popular black opening. White prepares a queen side castling then a pawn storm on the black king. Only precise play keeps Black in the game.

How to avoid
the master standby

In place of 6. . . . Be7? Black should exchange pieces by 6. . . . Nxd4 7. Nxd4 exd4 8. Qxd4 Bxb5. Strictly speaking, White's 6. Qd3 is inaccurate and he should first play 6. Bxc6 and then 7. Qd3. The problem with that order of moves is that Black is more likely to notice the threat to his e5 pawn and to take measures to protect it – so White has to weigh up his opponent and decide whether to play it strictly by the book or to maximize the chances of the trap.

Trap two – Springing the Cambridge Springs

The Queen's Gambit Declined is a popular opening in club and social chess. One of Black's possible formations, an early queen development introduced at a 1904 US tournament at Cambridge Springs, contains a trap which always has a chance of success against opponents unfamiliar with this slightly offbeat line.

1.	d4	d5
2.	c4	e6
3.	Nc3	Nf6
4.	Bg5	Nbd7

Black already sets a trap: if White tries to win a pawn by 5. cxd5 exd5 6. Nxd5? Nxd5 7. Bxd8 Bb4+ 8. Qd2 Bxd2+ 9. Kxd2 Kxd8 Black has won a piece. Perhaps this looks too much like a trap, for it rarely occurs in practical play.

5.	e3	c6
6.	Nf3	Qa5

A logical move, for it removes the black queen from the pin by White's bishop and starts a counter-pin on White's knight.

7.	Nd2	Bb4
8.	Qc2	0-0

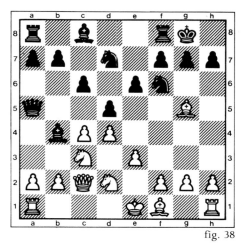

fig. 38

9. Bd3?

A natural developing move, which eyes Black's h7 pawn, but . . .

9. . . . dxc4

Black now wins a bishop after both 10. Nxc4 Qxg5 or 10. Bxf6 cxd3 attacking the queen.

There are several variants of this basic trap – for example if White plays 7. Bd3 (instead of 7. Nd2) Bb4 8. Qc2 Ne4 9. Rc1? (White should play 9. Bxe4) Nxg5 10. Nxg5 dxc4.

How to avoid
the Cambridge Springs

The simplest counter for White is to anticipate the Cambridge Springs once Black plays 5. . . . c6 and exchange pawns by 6. cxd5. Later on, White can still avoid material loss by 9. Bxf6 instead of 9. Bd3.

Trap three – Caro-Kann knights

A defence often preferred by solid and conservative players, but recently gaining in fashion as a weapon of counter-attack, is the Caro-Kann 1. e4 c6. It is almost routine to meet this defence by 2. d4 but in doing so White passes up the chance for a double trap which is well worth a try at club and social level.

1.	e4	c6
2.	Nc3	d5
3.	Nf3	dxe4

Pushing on the d pawn is not very good – 3. . . . d4 4. Ne2 c5 (d3 5. cxd3 Qxd3 6. Nc3 followed by 7. d4 and White controls the centre) 5. Ng3 Nc6 6. Bc4 e5 7. 0-0 followed by d3, Ne1 and f4 with attacking prospects for White.

If 3. . . . Nf6 4. e5 Ne4 (Nfd7 5. d4 and Black will soon have to advance c5 with loss of a move) 5. Ne2 and Black's knight is driven back by d3 with gain of time for White.

4. Nxe4

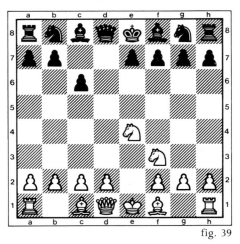

fig. 39

4. . . . Bf5

Another move here is 4. . . . Nd7, intending to play Ngf6 without allowing Black's pawns to be weakened. Then the trap is 5. Qe2 Ngf6?? 6. Nd6 mate! This trap has succeeded in a master tournament and world champion Alekhine once brought it off against four opponents who were in consultation.

5. Ng3 Bg6

6. h4 h6

to provide a retreat square for the bishop.

7. Ne5

In the usual order of moves with this variation, White has played d4 rather than Nf3 and so cannot bring his knight quickly into the attack. Now White threatens to weaken Black's pawns seriously by 8. Nxg6, so the bishop retreats.

7. . . . Bh7

8. Bc4

threatening 9. Bxf7 mate.

8.	. . .	e6
9.	Qh5	g6
10.	Qe2	Nf6

After countering two successive mate threats, Black is usually only too happy to snatch at what appears to be a breather with the chance to develop a piece by this knight move or by Nd7.

11.	Nxf7!	Kxf7
12.	Qxe6+	Kg7
13.	Qf7 mate	

This useful trap has occurred in a master tournament and has also enjoyed practical success at lower levels.

How to avoid the Caro-Kann knights

Black can avoid the main line trap by 4. . . . Nf6 or 4. . . . Bg4, and he can sidestep the trap in the note to 4. . . . Bf5 by playing Ndf6 or e6 instead of Ngf6.

Trap four – The Stonewall

The Stonewall Opening is considered a regular opening by many books, but it is really just a practical trap. White sets up an attacking formation which depends for its success on Black countering with conventional development rather than with moves designed to offset White's wall formation. It is inadvisable to try it against strong opponents, but at the lower levels of club chess and in friendly games it can prove a devastating weapon.

The Stonewall's name describes White's strategy. The first player sets up a wall of pawns in the centre, behind which he masses his pieces for a full-scale attack on Black's castled king.

A great advantage of the Stonewall in social chess or at the more modest levels of club play is that it is a system type of opening which can be prepared in a single evening, is easy to understand, and not likely to be forgotten when the player reaches the board. Admittedly there is a disadvantage when meeting stronger opponents. The stonewaller signals his intentions at an early stage and thus gives his opponent time to switch into a defensive formation designed to reduce the impact of White's wall.

So if your chess is of the friendly variety, in the club third or fourth team or in the minor or novice section of a weekend congress, the Stonewall attack/trap can prove a useful point scorer.

Higher up on the chess ladder I don't recommend it.

1. d4   d5
2. e3   Nf6

If Black brings his bishop into action by Bf5 White does best to abandon his projected wall formation and attack on the queen's side by c4, Nc3 and Qb3.

3. Bd3   e6
4. Nd2   c5
5. c3

a necessary precaution to prevent the bishop being chased off its good diagonal by c4.

5. ...   Nc6
6. f4

White's last move completes the wall of pawns on the black squares and gives the opening its name.

6. ...   Be7
7. Ngf3

It is technically more precise, but psychologically unnecessary, to play 7. Qe2 first – to stop Black setting up a wall in turn by 7. ... Ng4 8. Qe2 f5. But in a club or social game Black will rarely consider such a non-routine manoeuvre, and it is worth the slight risk of allowing it to gain an extra move for White's attack.

7. ...   0-0
8. Ne5

fig. 40

Now White's outpost knight, supported by the pawn wall, is ready to spearhead an attack against the black king.

8. ...   c4?
9. Bc2   Bd7
10. 0-0   b5
11. Rf3   a5
12. Rh3   b4?

Black reasons that he can advance on the queen's flank while White is attacking on the other side of the board, but in most such situations it is the threats to the king which are the more dangerous.

13. Bxh7+

Stonewall players have real chances of reaching this winning sacrifice against unprepared opponents.

13. ...   Nxh7
14. Qh5 and wins.

White threatens 15. Qxh7 mate; if the knight moves then 15. Qh8 mate; while if 14. ... Re8 there is mate in two by either 15. Qxh7+ or 15. Qxf7+.

How to avoid the Stonewall

Black can make White's attacking plan more difficult in the accompanying diagram by playing 8. ... g6! intending Ne8 and f6, driving away the attacking knight or forcing its exchange. But simplest of all, if you think your opponent plans a Stonewall, is to counter it on move 3 by 3. ... g6! and Bg7 when the white bishop 'bites on the granite' of a solidly defended king's position. If White's Stonewall attack does not succeed, he has a long-term strategic handicap in that his bishop on c1 remains blocked in by its own pawns.

Trap five –
The Vienna queen check

The Vienna queen check is a more advanced snare from the same opening as pitfall 7 – the Vienna push. It has two distinct advantages over many opening traps in that the Vienna is an unfashionable opening which will often be virgin territory to the opponent; while the move which sets up the trap appears a blunder due to White making two routine moves in an unusual order.

1.	e4	e5
2.	Nc3	Nf6
3.	f4	d5

For 3. . . . exf4? see pitfall 4.

4.	fxe5	Nxe4
5.	d3	

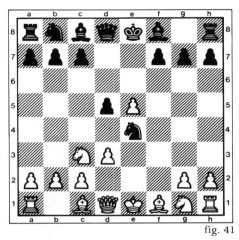

fig. 41

5.	. . .	Qh4+

It looks natural to 'punish' White for not preparing d3 by 5. Nf3. However, contrary to appearances, Black's queen check is a losing blunder.

6.	g3	Nxg3
7.	Nf3	Qh5
8.	Nxd5	

White counters the threat to his rook by a counter-threat to the black rook. If Black now defends his c7 pawn by Na6, Kd8 or Kd7, White wins the g3 knight by 9. Nf4 Qh6 10. Nh3.

8.	. . .	Nxh1
9.	Nxc7+	Kd8
10.	Nxa8	Be7
11.	Bg2	Bh4+
12.	Kf1	Nc6
13.	d4!	

Less good is 13. Bxh1 Nxe5; but after 13. d4 White remains at least a pawn up with the better position (Nf2 14. Qe1 and the black knight remains trapped).

How to avoid the
Vienna queen check

Black has two better plans in the diagram, **5. . . . Nxc3** 6. bxc3 d4 7. Nf3 Nc6 8. cxd4 Bb4+ simplifying, or **5. . . . Bb4** 6. dxe4 Qh4+ 7. Ke2 Bg4+ with complications. For these, see page 110.

Trap six –
The Blackmar pawn snatch

The Blackmar Gambit is one of the dashing by-products of chess opening theory which catches a goodly haul of victims in club and social play though it has few successes in master tournaments. Like most pawn sacrifice gambits, whose object is rapid piece development, it depends for its results on Black becoming too greedy and capturing irrelevant pawns.

1.	d4	d5
2.	e4	dxe4
3.	Nc3	Nf6
4.	f3	exf3

Black can decline the gambit by 4. . . . Bf5 or 4. . . . e3, but these enable White to gain a slight edge without risk and taking the pawn is best.

5.	Qxf3	

5. Nxf3 is a sounder line, but the capture with the queen poses the question of whether Black really knows the opening. If he does not, he may be swept off the board.

5.	. . .	Qxd4
6.	Be3	

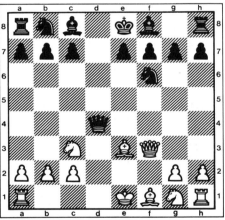

fig. 42

6.	. . .	Qb4?
7.	0-0-0	Bg4?
8.	Nb5!	e5

Black is already lost. If he tries to stop 9. Nxc7 mate by 8. . . . Na6 then 9. Qxb7 Qe4 (Rb8 10. Qxb8+) 10. Qxa6 Qxe3+ 11. Kb1 Bxd1 12. Qc6+ Kd8 13. Qxc7+ Ke8 14. Nd6+ Bxd6 15. Bb5+ wins.

9.	Nxc7+	Ke7
10.	Qxb7!	

This final coup closes the trap. If 10. . . . Qxb7 11. Bc5 mate, or if 10. . . . Qa5 11. Bc5+ Qxc5 12. Na6+ wins the queen.

How to avoid
the Blackmar Gambit

Black has chances to refute the gambit by 6. . . . Qg4 7. Qf2 e5 with the threat Bb4. A move later, 7. . . . c6 may still be a defence. If Black is completely unfamiliar with the gambit and wishes to duck all White's homework, he can transpose into completely different openings by 2. . . . e6 (French Defence) or 2. . . . c6 (Caro-Kann).

Trap Seven – The mazy Morra

The Morra Gambit (1. e4 c5 2. d4 cxd4 3. c3) has an attraction for many young players when they start to meet the fashionable Sicilian Defence. The Sicilian is the most analysed of all openings, and to choose the trappy Morra against it avoids the burning of much midnight oil. The gambit can certainly be defended, but isn't easy to counter at the board, and features trap variations which continue to claim victims in match and tournament chess.

1.	e4	c5
2.	d4	cxd4
3.	c3	dxc3
4.	Nxc3	Nc6

The plausible 4. . . . d6 5. Bc4 Nf6? fails to 6. e5! Qc7 (dxe5 7. Bxf7+ Kxf7 8. Qxd8) 7. Bb5+ Nfd7 8. Nd5 Qd8 (if Qa5+ 9. b4! Qxb5 9. Nc7+) 9. Qc2! and Black cannot avoid heavy material loss. If Nc6 10. Bxc6 bxc6 11. Qxc6 threatens both Nc7+ and Qxa8.

5.	Nf3	d6

Another apparently safe line which gets Black into difficulties is 5. . . . g6 6. Bc4 Bg7 7. e5! Qa5 8. 0-0 Nxe5 9. Nxe5 Bxe5 10. Nd5 e6 11. Re1 f6 12. Bb3 Kf7 13. Rxe5! fxe5 14. Qf3+ Ke8 15. Bh6 Nxh6 16. Qf6 and wins.

6.	Bc4	e6

Again 6. . . . Nf6? runs into trouble after 7. e5! and if dxe5 8. Qxd8+ Kxd8 (Nxd8 9. Nb5) 9. Ng5 Kc7 10. Nxf7 Rg8 11. Nb5+ Kb8 12. Nxe5 Nxe5 13. Bxg8 Nxg8 14. Bf4 and wins, or if here 7. . . . Ng4 8. e6 Bxe6 9. Bxe6 fxe6 10. Ng5 Nf6 11. 0-0 Qd7 12. Re1 e5 13. Qb3 d5 14. f4 e6 15. fxe5 with advantage.

7.	0-0	Nf6
8.	Qe2	

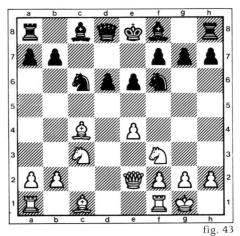
fig. 43

8. ...   a6?

This last is a plausible move, since it is normal in the Sicilian Defence for Black to advance his queen's side pawns. The pawn move also allows the black queen to go to c7 without risking harassment by 9. Nb5. Nevertheless a6 is a mistake which falls into another of the mazy Morra's traps.

| 9. | Rd1 | Qc7 |
| 10. | Bf4 | Be7 |

If 10. ... e5 11. Nd5 Nxd5 12. exd5 Be7 13. dxc6 exf4 14. cxb7 Bxb7 15. Rac1 with fine open lines for White's pieces.

If 10. ... Ne5 11. Bxe5 dxe5 12. Rac1 Bd7 13. Bxe6! Bxe6 14. Nd5 Qb8 15. Nc7+ Ke7 16. Qd2 with a winning attack against Black's exposed king.

| 11. | Rac1 | 0-0 |
| 12. | Bb3 | Rd8 |

If 12. ... e5 then again 13. Nd5! with advantage.

13. Nd5!

This is a typical idea in the Morra Gambit – White takes advantage of the concealed attack along the c file by his rook against the black queen to regain the gambit pawn with advantage after a temporary knight sacrifice.

13.	...	exd5
14.	exd5	h6
15.	dxc6	dxc6
16.	Nd4	Bd7
17.	Nxc6!	Bxc6
18.	Ba4	

followed by R or Bxc6 with a distinct advantage for White: he has two bishops against bishop and knight, while the isolated black d pawn and especially the a pawn are targets for the white pieces.

How to avoid the Morra Gambit

A better defence to the Morra Gambit from the diagram is **8. ... Be7** and 0-0. But many players who adopt this gambit do so regularly and know its nuances and subtleties even when Black defends well. This also applies to declining the gambit by 3. ... Nf6 or 3. ... d5. Therefore I recommend club players confronted with the Morra Gambit to sidestep it by 3. ...

g6 4. cxd4 d5 5. exd5 Nf6, when Black regains his pawn with a reasonable game and – most important – the gambiteer is diverted from the lines he knows well.

Trap eight – The anti-dragon

At the average club player level, few opening traps have enjoyed such consistent success as the special anti-Dragon attack employed against the Sicilian Defence. The Dragon (named because Black's pawn formation d6-e7-f7-g6-h7 has a vague resemblance to the outline of the mythical beast) is one of Black's most popular systems, but it can blow up in its owner's face if even one or two moves are too slow or inaccurate.

Such inaccuracies give White the chance to carry out a standard system which has brought success in hundreds of games. It is easy to understand, to remember, and carry out, and the Anti-Dragon can therefore be recommended as a very good trap for club play and in the lower sections of weekend congresses.

1.	e4	c5
2.	Nf3	d6
3.	d4	cxd4
4.	Nxd4	Nf6
5.	Nc3	g6
6.	Be3	Bg7
7.	f3	Nc6
8.	Qd2	0-0
9.	Bc4	Bd7
10.	Bb3	

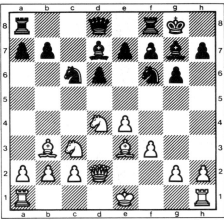
fig. 44

Here 10. 0-0-0 is the more usual move, but the immediate bishop retreat has in practice often caused Black to go wrong.

10. ...   Qc7?

One of several plausible but inferior moves in this critical position. Another example from actual play is 10. ... Na5? 11. Bh6 Rc8 12. Bxg7 Kxg7 13. h4 Nc4 14. Bxc4 Rxc4 15. h5! e5 16. N4e2 Nxh5 17. g4 Nf6 18. Qh6+ Kg8 19. g5 Nh5 20. Rxh5! gxh5 21. Nd5 f5 22. g6 hxg6 23. Qxg6+ Kh8 24. 0-0-0 Resigns, for White's rook will join in the attack at g1 or h1 with decisive effect. Also frequently

played, but weak, is 10. ... a6? when White continues as in the column.

11.	h4	Ne5
12.	Bh6	Nc4
13.	Bxc4	Qxc4
14.	Bxg7	Kxg7
15.	h5!	

It is an important part of the Anti-Dragon trap that this advance should be played at once and not delayed until White has pushed g4. If now 15. ... Nxh5 16. g4 Nf6 17. Qh6+ Kg8 18. Nd5 Rfe8 19. g5 Nh5 20. Rxh5 gxh5 21. Nf6+ exf6 22. gxf6 and mates.

15.	...	Kg8
16.	0-0-0	Rac8
17.	Qh6	b5
18.	g4!	e5

If 18. ... e6 19. Qg5 Ne8 20. Qe7 followed by 21. hxg6 wins.

19.	g5	Nxh5
20.	Rxh5	gxh5
21.	Nd5	f5
22.	g6	Resigns.

The finish is similar to the note to Black's 10th move: 22. ... hxg6 23. Qxg6+ Kh8 24. Qxh5+ Kg7 25. Rg1 mate.

How to avoid the anti-dragon

Black has two reasonable plans at move 10: the simplifying **10. ... Nxd4** 11. Bxd4 b5 (when White should continue by 12. h4 a5 13. a4) and **10. ... Rc8** 11. Bb3 Ne5 when White continues 12. 0-0-0 with complicated play. This main line of the Anti-Dragon system can also be reached with 10. 0-0-0, but by adopting the less familiar 10. Bb3 White takes little risk while giving Black the chance to go badly wrong on move 10.

Trap nine – Pieces beat the queen

Judging by the point count table on page 14, three pieces (two knights and a bishop or two bishops and a knight) should prove stronger than a queen. And so it usually happens in practice, except on a minority of occasions when there is some tactical chance favouring the player with the queen or else when the queen has freedom of action to capture pawns.

One good example of putting the value of three pieces against the queen to practical use occurs in a promising counter to the Pirc Defence (1. e4 d6) and the Modern Defence (1. e4 g6). These popular systems are often played in contemporary tournaments. Black can and should avoid the queen v pieces situation, but White's strategy has brought good results even when Black has avoided the trap.

1.	e4	g6
2.	d4	Bg7
3.	Nc3	d6
4.	Bc4	Nf6
5.	Qe2	

This position can arise just the same if Black begins 1. ... d6 and continues

2. ... Nf6, 3. ... g6 and 4. ... Bg7.

5. ...   Nc6

If 5. ... e5 6. dxe5 dxe5 7. Bg5, and if 5. ... c6 6. e5 dxe5 7. fxe5 Nd5 8. Bd2 followed by 0-0-0, in both cases with good attacking chances for White. An inter-club game (R. Harman–O. Hill) went 5. ... 0-0 6. e5 dxe5 7. dxe5 Ne8 8. f4 c6 9. Nf3 Bg4 10. Be3 Bxf3? 11. Qxf3 Kh8? (weakens the f7 square) 12. Rd1 Qc7 13. Ne4 b6 14. Ng5 h6 16. 0-0 Qe7 17. Bxe6! fxe6 18. Nxe6 Rg8 19. f5! gxf5 20. Nxg7 Qxg7 21. Rxf5 Qh7 22. Rh5 Resigns.

6. e5

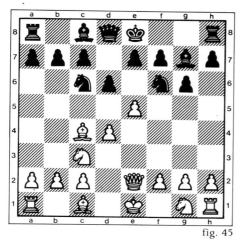

fig. 45

6. ...   Nxd4?

If 6. ... Ng4 a game Nigel Short–D. Sikkel, Jersey 1978, continued 7. e6! Nxd4 8. Qxg4 Nxc2+ 9. Kd1 Nxa1 10. exf7+ Kf8 11. Qh4 d5 12. Bd3 Be6 13. Nf3 Bxf7 14. Re1 d4 15. Bg5! Bf6 16. Ne4 Bxg5 17. Nexg5 Bxa2 18. Nxh7+ Kg8 19. Rxe7 Qxe7? (a better try is Bf7) 20. Qxe7 Rxh7 21. Qa3 Bd5 22. Qxa1 and White soon won with his extra piece.

Also insufficient is 6. ... Nh5 7. Bb5! dxe5 (Black's best chance is *7. ... 0-0 8. Bxc6 bxc6 9. g4 dxe5* with some compensation for the knight) 8. d5 0-0 (if *a6 9. dxc6 axb5 10. cxb7 Bxb7 11. Qxb5+ wins*) 9. dxc6 bxc6 10. Bxc6 Rb8 11. Qd1 Ba6 12. Qxd8 and White won on material (Regan–Shamkovich, New York 1978).

Upon the retreat 6. ... Nd7 there can follow 7. Nf3 dxe5? 8. Bxf7+! Kxf7 9. Ng5+ and wins.

7.	exf6!	Nxe2
8.	fxg7	Rg8
9.	Ngxe2	Rxg7
10.	Bh6	Rg8
11.	0-0-0	

This position has occurred several times in match and tournament chess because players with Black have been attracted by Black's two extra pawns in support of the queen. But practical play has shown that White can use his pieces to break down Black's pawn barricade, with good winning chances.

Possible continuations are: (a) 11. ... e5 12. h4 Be6 13. Bxe6 fxe6 14. Ne4 Kd7

15. Bg5 followed by Nf6+ or (b) 11. ... Be6 12. Bd3 Qd7 13. Nd4 0-0-0 14. Rhe1 Kb8 (*if Bf5 15. Bc4 e6 16. f3 intending g4*) 15. Bb5 c6 16. Ba4 b5 17. Nxe6 fxe6 18. Bb3 d5 19. Bf4+ Ka8 20. Ne4.

How to avoid this trap

Black can sidestep this opening by playing **4. ... Nc6** or **4. ... c6**, although White can then avoid well-analyzed variations by 4. ... Nc6 5. d5 Nd4 6. Nce2 or 4. ... c6 5. Bb3 Nf6 6. f4. (See also page 118.)

If Black reaches diagram 45 his best line is **6. ... Nd7** 7. Nf3 Nb6! 8. Bb3 0-0 9. Bf4 a5 10. a4 Bg4 11. 0-0-0 Qc8 12. Qe3 dxe5 13. dxe5 Be6 with a solid position (K. Arkell–Chandler, Manchester Benedictine 1979).

Trap ten – Catching the masters

Most opening traps find their victims among players in club matches and weekend congresses. Masters, better primed, usually know enough to sidestep and avoid them. But a trap in the Grunfeld Defence (where Black allows White a pawn centre then tries to undermine it with pieces) is unusual in that it bagged four masters in national and international play in under a year. It has the essential feature for all practical traps, namely that the opponent falls into it by making apparently natural and sensible moves.

1.	d4	Nf6
2.	c4	g6
3.	Nc3	d5
4.	cxd5	Nxd5
5.	g3	Bg7
6.	Bg2	Nb6
7.	Nf3	Nc6
8.	e3	0-0
9.	0-0	e5
10.	d5	Ne7
11.	e4	Bg4

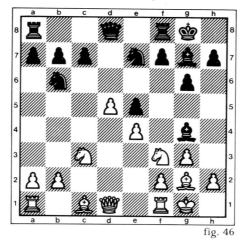

fig. 46

12. h3?

In the earlier moves, White has supported his centre pawns while Black has tried to blockade the d pawn and organize long-distance counterplay with bishops and knights. It is natural for White to try and eliminate the pin on his knight – but after 12. h3? the trap is sprung.

12.	...	Bxf3
13.	Bxf3	c6
14.	Qb3	

If 14. dxc6 Nxc6 and the black knight reaches the outpost square d4.

14.	...	cxd5
15.	Nxd5	Nbxd5
16.	exd5	Nf5
17.	Qxb7?	

17. Bg2 held out longer in Murray–Ribli, Reykjavik 1975: 17. ... Nd4 18. Qd3 f5 19. d6 Qxd6 20. Bxb7 Rad8 21. Bg2 f4 22. Be4 Qe6 23. Kh2 h5 24. b3 (*24. Bd2 Bh6 threatens fxg3+*) Kh8 25. Ba3 fxg3+ 26. Qxg3 Bh6 27. Qh4 Bf4+ 28. Kh1 Rf6 29. Rad1 g5 30. Resigns – the queen is lost.

17.	...	Nd4
18.	Bg2	Qd6!

Now there is no good defence to Black's threat to win the queen by Rfb8. In Lombard–Kirov and Sapi–Ribli, 1975, White resigned at once. In Gromek–Szymczak, 1975, White made the gesture 19. Bg5 f6 20. Rfc1 Rab8 21. Qxa7 Rf7 before he also gave up, faced with loss of queen or bishop.

How to avoid this trap

Since the natural 12. h3 turns out to be a losing mistake, White should try **12. Qb3** or **12. a4** – and much earlier in the opening he could transpose to another regular variation by 4. e4.

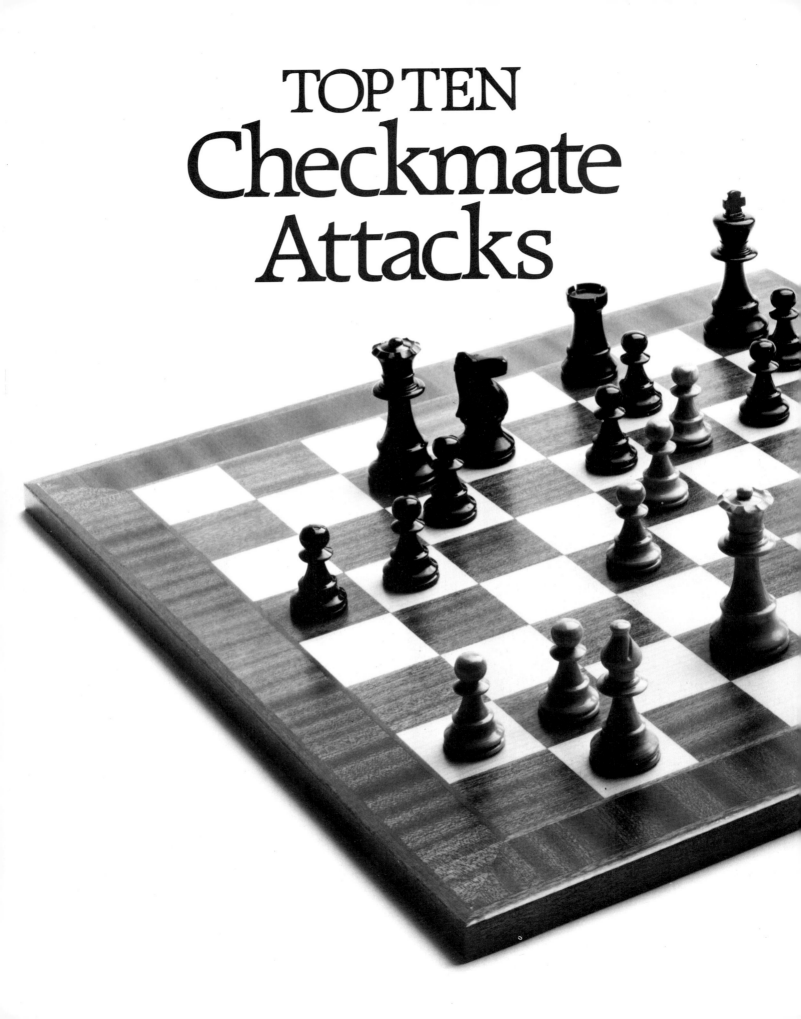

TOP TEN
Checkmate
Attacks

Checkmate on the chessboard is final – there is no recovery. And some types of mate and certain patterns of pieces crop up frequently at all levels of play. In novice chess they may occur in an elementary form, facilitated by poor defence; at the master and expert level, where both participants are alert to the implications of standard attacks, they have to be carefully prepared long in advance, and perhaps created by imaginative finesses and sacrifices.

It is no accident that almost all the attacks involve the queen, the most powerful chessboard piece, assisted by one or more lesser units. The secondary piece normally moves in first to control or occupy a key square near the enemy king, then the queen comes in for the kill.

The chess student who becomes familiar with the mechanics of these mating constellations is in possession of a reliable point scorer. Once the attacker has his combined forces lined up against the king, it is often impossible to find a defence.

Checkmate attack one – The f6 wedge

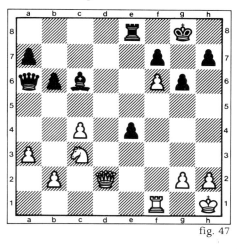

fig. 47

There are some middle games where one side plays for space on the queen's wing while his opponent has a free hand to organize an attack on the king. A strong attacking device in suitable positions is to advance the f pawn to f6 where it controls the g7 square and also acts as a wedge stopping defenders coming to aid the king.

The basic pattern: the white queen within range, no black piece available to guard g7. White wins by **1. Qh6** and **2. Qg7 mate**. If the black bishop was at c5 instead of c6, Black would have the defence Bf8 (fig. 47).

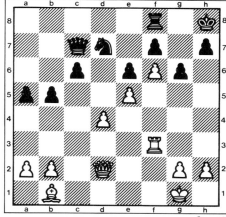

fig. 48

Here Black plans to defend both g7 and h7 against mate threats by 1. Qh6 Rg8 and if 2. Rh3 Nf8. White instead plays a brilliant but standard sacrifice from the f6 wedge: **1. Qh6 Rg8 2. Qxh7+! Kxh7 3. Rh3 mate.**

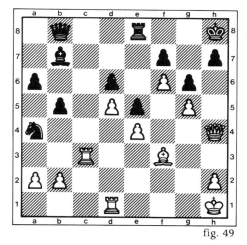

fig. 49

The game Szabo–Hartoch, Amsterdam 1972 illustrates a more complex position, but with exactly the same idea as in fig. 48: **1. Qh6 Rg8 2. Bg4 Nxc3 3. Rd3 Qf8 4. Qxh7+ Kxh7 5. Rh3+ Qh6 6. Rxh6 mate.**

The f6 wedge. The white pawn has penetrated to the heart of the black game and the pieces prepare a checkmate attack. In master chess Black tries to avoid such passive positions.

Checkmate attack two – The mating g6 pawn

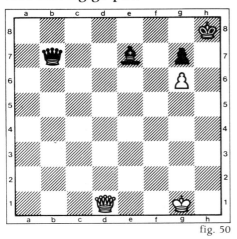

fig. 50

The basic pattern of this situation is the advanced pawn on g6, the queen within striking range and the black king unable to run far. White mates by **1. Qh5+ Kg8 2. Qh7+ Kf8 3. Qh8 mate.**

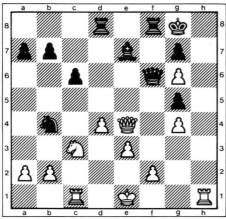

fig. 51

A more advanced example comes from a lightning game, at Hastings in 1948. There are many pieces on the board and Black, material ahead, threatens Qxf2+, but even at ten seconds a move White visualized the chance to force his queen to h7: **1. Rh8+ Kxh8 2. Qh1+ Kg8 3. Qh7 mate.**

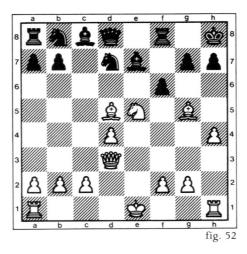

fig. 52

Here (J. Benjamin–G. Carter, London Amateur Championship 1975) we see White creating the g6 pawn several moves in advance. The key is the push with the h pawn to attack Black's castled position while the white knight waits at e5. Once the pawn can reach h5 the knight is sacrificed at g6 to set up the mating pattern.

For a sports parallel, imagine a long punt by a rugby full-back deep into the opposing team's 22, with the punter's three-quarter line following through in support. The 'sacrifice' of several attackers to tackling defenders matters not so long as there is a spare man to take the ball across the line.

Here the ball is the g6 pawn at move 14. The bishop (move 15) and the rook (17) are tackled but then the queen goes through to score the winning try by the right-hand post.

1. e4 e5 2. Nf3 Nf6 3. Bc4 Nxe4 4. Nc3 Nf6 5. Nxe5 d5 6. Bb3 Be7 7. d4 0-0 8. Bg5 c6 9. Qd3 Nfd7? 10. h4 f6 11. Nxd5! cxd5 12. Bxd5+ Kh8 (see fig. 52) **13. Ng6+! hxg6 14. h5! Qa5+ 15. c3 Qxd5 16. hxg6+ Kg8 17. Rh8+ Kxh8 18. Qh3+ Kg8 19. Qh7 mate.**

Checkmate attack three – Queen and bishop against h7

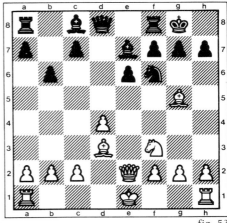

fig. 53

Before the king is castled, f7 is the most vulnerable square, as we saw in Scholar's Mate and other early attacks. After castling, the squares h7 and g7 (b7 and c7 in the case of long castling) are often protected only by the king and are thus prime targets for the checkmate attacker.

Fig. 53 is an example of a queen-bishop attack on h7 which arises from a useful opening trap: **1. e4 e6 2. d4 d5 3. Nc3 dxe4 4. Nxe4 Nd7 5. Nf3 Ngf6 6. Nxf6+ Nxf6 7. Bd3 Be7 8. Qe2 0-0 9. Bg5 b6? 10. Bxf6 Bxf6 11. Qe4** and if Black moves or protects his attacked rook then **12. Qxh7 mate.**

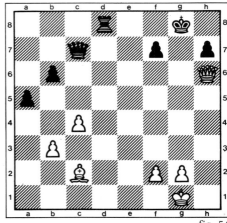

fig. 54

A useful manoeuvre to know is a device where the queen and bishop combine to attack first h7, then f7. Here the obvious 1. Qxh7+? allows the black king to escape, but White instead forces mate by **1. Bxh7+ Kh8 2. Bg6+ Kg8 3. Qh7+ Kf8 4. Qxf7 mate.**

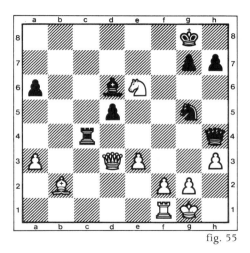

fig. 55

Example. Cochrane–Staunton, London 1842. Howard Staunton, the best player in the world at the time, knew all about the queen/bishop attack on h7 (in this case h2). He finished the game by **1. . . . Nxh3+! 2. gxh3 Rg4+! 3. hxg4 Qh2 mate.**

Checkmate attack four – The dark diagonals

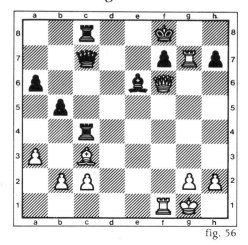

fig. 56

The dark-squared bishop lurking near the black king at f6 or h6, or further back along the open diagonal a1-h8, provides many opportunities for mating attacks in collaboration with the queen or other pieces. When Black is attacking, then there are equally good outposts for his light-squared bishop at f3 or h3, or any useful square on the a8-h1 diagonal.

Dark diagonal attacks are particularly strong when the opponent's bishop of the same colour has been captured or ex-changed. In the several popular defences where the black bishop is developed at g7, it rarely pays to exchange it for a white knight.

A basic pattern for a dark diagonal attack is: White mates by **1. Rg8+ Kxg8 2. Qg7** or **2. Qh8.**

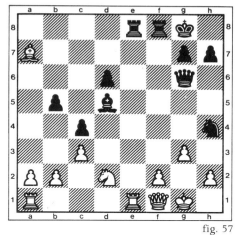

fig. 57

Example 1. Kupreychik–Romanishin, USSR championship 1976. Black has sacrificed a pawn for this promising attack on White's king, but the obvious Nf3+ allows Nxf3 and it is not easy for the light diagonal attack to break through. What Black really wants is to get his queen in front of the bishop as in the basic pattern: so he plays **1. . . . Qf7!** (attacking White's a7 bishop) **2. Rxe8 Nf3+! and White resigned.** If 3. Nxf3 Qxf3 4. Rxf8+ Kxf8 with no defence to Qh1 mate.

fig. 58

Example 2. I. D. Wells–G. Kenworthy, Cumbria v. Yorkshire 1978. Here it isn't clear how the dark diagonal bishop on c3 can get at the weak g7 square (protected only by Black's king) with other pieces in the way. The 14-year-old playing White settled the game with **1. Nd7! Qxd7** (if Nxd7 2. Rxg7+ Kf8 3. Qxh7 wins) **2. Bxf6 Be7** (if g6 3. Qxh7+! Kxh7 4. Rh3+ Kg8 5. Rh8 mate) **3. Rxg7+ Kf8 4. Rg8+ Resigns.** If Kxg8 5. Qg5+ and 6. Qg7 mate.

Checkmate attack five – Queen and knight

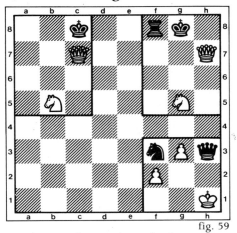

fig. 59

Figure 59 shows three basic patterns where queen and knight combine to mate a castled king.

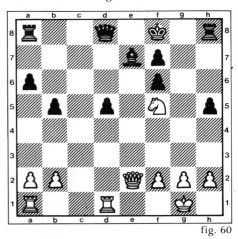

fig. 60

Example 1. Spassky–Avtonomov, Leningrad 1949. Boris Spassky, world champion to be, won this position as White (to move) at twelve years old by a combined queen and knight attack. He played **1. Rxd5! Qxd5 2. Qxe7+ Kg8 3. Qxf6 and Black resigned** as if Rh7 (to stop 4. Qg7 mate) 4. Ne7+ wins the queen.

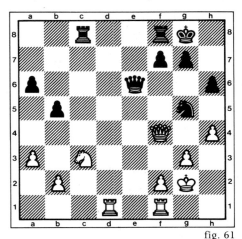

fig. 61

Example 2. Plachetka–Sveshnikov, Dubna 1979. An ideal position for a queen/knight mate except that the white queen is defending. So **1. . . . Rc4! 2. Qe3 Qh3+ 3. Kg1 Rxh4! 4. gxh4 Nf3+**. White has to give up his queen by 5. Qxf3 to avoid mate, and Black then wins easily on material.

Checkmate attack six – Back row mate

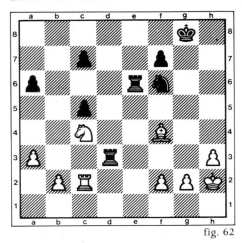

fig. 62

We have already seen an elementary example of a back row mate in Pitfall Five (page 19). But taking advantage of a cramped king on the back row is an important aspect of many mating devices. For example, all the basic queen and knight mates (fig. 59) show a back row king, although the distinctive feature of these positions is White's choice of attacking pieces.

A good player is on the alert for a mate any time the board is opened up and the enemy back row is unguarded or underprotected. Here (Simagin–Kholmov, Moscow 1966) White has made a bolthole for his king in the approved manner, but he is still short of flight squares and the back row is unguarded. White innocently took a pawn by **1. Bxc7? Ng4+! and resigned** because of 2. hxg4 Rh6+ 3. Kg1 Rd1 mate.

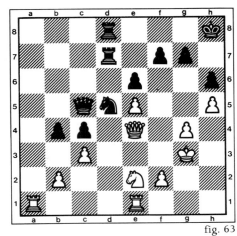

fig. 63

Example 1. Miles–Bennett, Totnes 1974. Missing a back row mate in this game cost £500. Gerald Bennett (Black, to move) was a point in front of his rival in the race for the £1,000 Cutty Sark Grand Prix as both experts hurried their moves to reach the time control. Black played **1. . . . bxc3 2. bxc3 Rb8 3. Reb1 Rxb1??** (expecting White to retake the rook with a drawn ending) **4. Ra8+** and Black is mated. Miles caught up with his rival by this game, and they shared the £1,000.

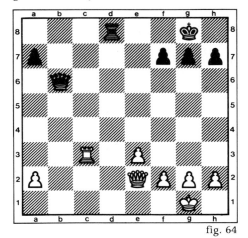

fig. 64

Example 2. Bernstein–Capablanca, St Petersburg 1914. A classic example of the back row mate. Both kings are vulnerable, e.g. if Black plays the obvious 1. . . . Qb1+ 2. Qf1 Rd1? 3. Rc8+ mates. Capa's startling solution was **1. . . . Qb2!** If 2. Qxb2 Rd1 mate. If 2. Qe1 Qxc3 3. Qxc3 Rd1+ mates. If 2. Rd3 Qb1+ 3. Qd1 Qxd1+ 4. Rxd1 Rxd1 mate.

John Nunn, individual gold medallist at the 1984 Salonika Olympics. England won silver to Russian gold in both 1984 and 1986.

Mathematician Dr Nunn says there's no direct link between his two interests: 'in maths you need to be right, in chess only more right than your opponent'.

fig. 65

Example 3. Tal–Olafsson, Las Palmas 1975. Ex-world champion Mikhail Tal is a famous tactician, but here he is on the receiving end. The key to the position is Black's potential back row mate Rd1. At present this is harmless because of Ne1 when the white queen guards the knight, while removing the knight by Bxf3 would be met by gxf3 when the white king has a hole. Black won brilliantly by combining the back row theme with a threat to the rook at e7: **1. . . . Rd1+ 2. Ne1 Qg5!! and Tal resigned**. If 3. Qxg5 Rxe1 mate, otherwise White loses the e7 rook.

Checkmate attack seven – Smothered mate

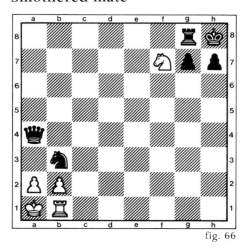

fig. 66

A king behind unmoved pawns and boxed in by his own defender on the rank can be a signal for a smothered mate attack by a knight. Here White's knight gives the most usual mate – at f7 – while the black knight can mate because the white pawn is pinned by the queen.

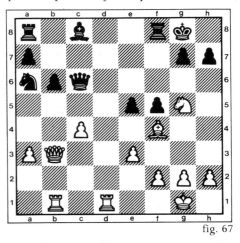

fig. 67

Example 1. Capablanca–Mattison, Carlsbad 1929. White to move. The great Capa's opponent resigned rather than allow this position! Why? Because of **1. c5+ Kh8 2. Nf7+ Kg8** (if Rxf7 3. Rd8+ with a back row mate) **3. Nh6+ Kh8 4. Qg8+! Rxg8 5. Nf7 mate.**

This form of the smothered mate with a queen sacrifice is known as Philidor's Legacy after the great eighteenth century chessplayer, musician and unofficial world champion of his time.

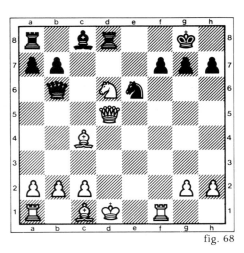

fig. 68

Example 2. Unzicker–Sarapu, Siegen 1970. White (to move) seems to have great difficulties despite being a bishop ahead, as Black threatens to win by Rxd6. But the game ended **1. Bf4! Nxf4 2. Qxf7+ Kh8 3. Qg8+ Rxg8 4. Nf7 mate.** White needed to visualize this possibility several moves before fig. 68 was reached.

Checkmate attack eight – Heavy piece attack

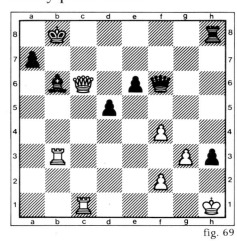

fig. 69

The basic pattern of this manoeuvre occurs with White's queen and rooks poised for attack while the black pieces are stranded on the other side of the board. White (to move) wins by opening up the black king and checking with queen and rook to force mate: **1. Rxb6+ axb6 2. Qxb6+ Ka8 3. Qa6+** (not 3. Ra1+?? Qxa1+) **Kb8 4. Rb1+ Kc7 5. Rb7+ Kc8 6. Qa8 mate.**

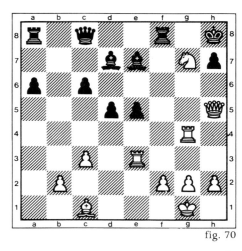

fig. 70

Example 1. Alekhine–Borochow, Hollywood 1932. With queen and both rooks all threatening the white king, it looks easy for White, but the obvious 1. Rh3 can be met by Bf5. Alekhine (playing a blindfold simultaneous exhibition) found **1. Ne6!** which blocks the line of Black's d7 bishop while removing the knight from the g file. Black resigned because of **1. .... Bxe6 2. Qxh7+ Kxh7 3. Rh3 mate.**

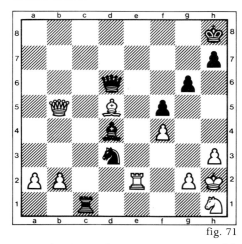

fig. 71

Example 2. Hübner–Petrosian, world championship interzonal, Biel 1976. This diagram (fig. 71) will go down in chess history as a remarkable grandmaster blunder where West Germany's best player had an easy win with a heavy piece attack but failed to see it.

Black's king is hopelessly exposed and ex-world champion Petrosian's last move Qd6 was a desperate attempt at bluff with a threat of his own. Hübner stared at the position and didn't hear even when the audience started to discuss the right move. He played 1. g3?? lost the game a few moves later, and with it a possible world title chance.

White can win by **1. Qe8+ Kg7 2. Re7+ Kh6** (Qxe7 stops mate but loses on material) **3. Qf8+ Kh5 4. Rxh7 mate.**

Checkmate attack nine – The Greek Gift

The sacrifice Bxh7+ was first worked out 300 years ago and has continued to claim victims ever since. Often called the 'Greek Gift' it can become possible when the white bishop is on the b1-h7 diagonal while the defending knight has left its best square at f6 and cannot return. A quick mate by queen and knight may follow; White may win by bringing his rook into the attack via the third rank. Sometimes the black king is driven round the board so hard that he has to give up decisive material to stave off mate.

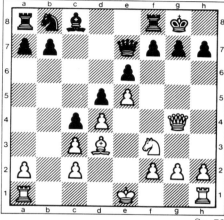

fig. 72

Example 1. The basic pattern can be seen from Yates–Marin, Hamburg 1930. The position was reached from the opening by **1. e4 e6 2. d4 d5 3. Nc3 Nf6 4. Bg5 Be7 5. e5 Ne4 6. Bxe7 Qxe7, 7. Qg4 0-0 8. Bd3 Nxc3? 9. bxc3 c5 10. Nf3 c4?** and now **11. Bxh7+ and Black resigned.** If 11. . . . Kxh7 12. Qh5+ Kg8 13. Ng5 and Black either has to surrender his queen or be mated by 13. . . . Rd8 14. Qh7+ Kf8 15. Qh8 mate. Declining the Greek Gift does not help: 11. . . . Kh8 12. Qh5 f5 13. Bg6+ Kg8 14. Qh7 mate.

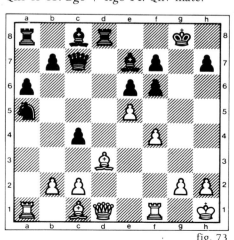

fig. 73

Example 2. P.G. Large–J.M. Ripley, Aaronson Masters 1978. White (to move)

sacrificed a knight to reach this position and, with bishop pinned against the queen, forced a spectacular win. The final checkmating position is nine moves deep, but White knew the Greek Gift idea and worked it out accurately: **1. Bxh7+ Kxh7 2. Qh5+ Kg8 3. Bd2!** (not 3. Rf3?? Rd1 mate) **Rxd2 4. Rf3 Rxg2** (hoping for 5. Kxg2 Qc6) **5. Rh3! Kf8 6. Qh8+ Rg8 7. Qxg8+ Kxg8 8. Rg1+ Kf8 9. Rh8 mate.**

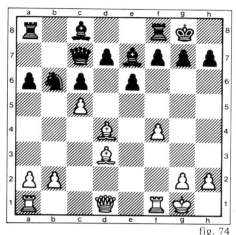

fig. 74

Example 3. Kuzmin–Sveshnikov, USSR championship 1973. Sometimes the Greek Gift sacrifice involves giving up both bishops. Here Black's pieces are cramped behind a row of pawns while his knight is far away exchanging on the queen's wing. White ignored the obvious capture of the knight and played **1. Bxh7+! Kxh7 2. Qh5+ Kg8 3. Bxg7!** Now White threatens 4. Qh8 mate, while 3. . . . f6 would be fatal because of 4. Qg6. So Black took the second bishop by **3. . . . Kxg7** and the game ended **4. Qg4+ Kh7 5. Rf3** threatening 6. Rh3. Black could stop the mate only by crippling material loss (5. . . . Qd8 6. Rh3+ Bh4 7. Rxh4+ Qxh4 8. Qxh4+) so resigned the hopeless position.

Checkmate attack ten – Rooks on the seventh

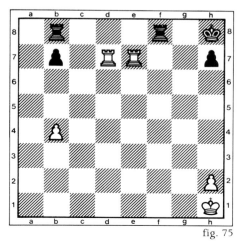

fig. 75

The basic pattern – the white rooks in command, the black king's flight barred by its own rook, and mate in two by **1. Rxh7+ Kg8 2. Rdg7 mate.**

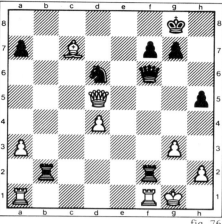

fig. 76

A more complex example has White offering a draw in this postal game position, suggesting 1. . . . Rg2+ 2. Qxg2 Rxg2+ 3. Kxg2 when White's pair of rooks balance Black's queen. But Black refused, played **1. . . . Qxd4!**, and White resigned. If **2. Qxd4 Rg2+ 3. Kh1 Rxh2+ 4. Kg1 Rbg2 mate.**

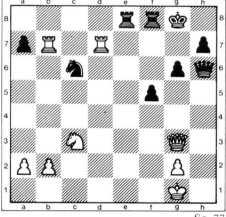

fig. 77

Chess is not just a matter of applying general principles – every position is liable to have its individual quirk. Here (Capablanca–Wohlbrecht, St Louis 1909) the great Capa, knowing about rooks on the seventh, casually played 1. Qg5. It brought an instant resignation when Black saw that if Qxg5 2. Rg7+ Kh8 3. Rxh7+ Kg8 4. Rbg7 mate. Capa graciously accepted the resignation, then pointed out **1. Qg5 Re1+ 2. Kf2 Rh1!** when Black can defend. Said Capa, 'I should have played **1. Nd1!** threatening Qb3+.'

TOP TEN Endgames

Ex-world champion Anatoly Karpov was once asked by a group of chess club players what they should do to improve their results. Karpov replied, 'I don't know what you do at the moment.' The club players said they played a lot of match games, and studied the openings. 'But the endgames not very much?' asked Karpov. 'Do the opposite – study endgames!'

Endgames are a weak spot for many players, largely due to the common practice in British team matches of stopping play somewhere between move 30 and move 45 and letting an expert adjudicator decide what ought to happen with best play. Not having to fight his own battle, and rarely making enough moves to reach a standard 'technical' endgame, the average club player pays little attention to it.

But times are changing, and more and more competitive chess is played at congresses where games continue to a finish. Even in inter-club chess, the trend is to require more moves before play is stopped for the adjudicator's verdict.

Thus endgames are becoming progressively more important.

Many endgame books list the nuances of slightly differing positions in knight, rook or queen endgames. Studying endgames this way is a great mistake as well as being both hard work and boring. Only when you reach a 'theoretical' ending across the board should you consult the reference books and compare your method of play with that of the masters. With that exception, concentrate on the basic principles emphasized in this chapter.

Endgame one – The active rook

Rook endgames are the most frequently met in endgames in practice, and the key principle is to maintain the rook as an

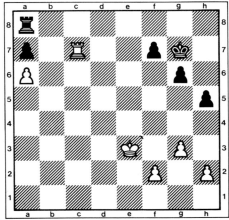

fig. 78

active piece ready to attack enemy pawns rather than passively defending your own pawns. The best active rook position is on the seventh row where it often attacks pawns and cuts off the enemy king on the back row. If your rook is passive, it frequently pays to sacrifice a pawn to establish the rook in a better position.

Fig. 78 shows a typical case of active against passive rook where White's rook attacks the a pawn while Black is tied down to defending it. If Black does nothing, White brings his king to b7 and captures the pawn with a simple win. Black's best chance to make it more difficult for his opponent is to give up the a pawn at once by **1. . . . Rb8 2. Rxa7 Rb3+ 3. Kd4 Ra3**. Black still loses, but there is more chance for White to go wrong.

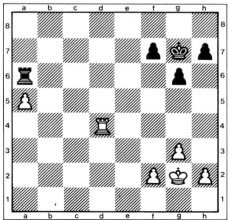

fig. 79

Example. Alekhine–Capablanca, 34th match game 1927. Another important active rook situation is behind an 'outside' passed pawn, distant from the

enemy king, with the opponent's rook forced to passively blockade the pawn. The classic endgame in fig. 79 decided the world championship in Alekhine's favour by **1. Ra4! Kf6 2. Kf3 Ke5 3. Ke3 h5 4. Kd3 Kd5 5. Kc3 Kc5 6. Ra2!** (this is the important 'zugzwang' – compulsion to move – technique; Black has no useful choice so must retreat and allow White's king an entry route) **Kb5 7. Kd4 Rd6+** (Rxa5 gives White an easily won pawn endgame) **8. Ke5 Re6+ 9. Kf4 Ka6 10. Kg5 Re5+ 11. Kh6 Rf5** and now the quickest win was **12. Kg7 Rf3 13. Rd2! Kxa5 14. Rd5+** and if Kb6 15. Rd6+ Kc5 16. Rf6 or if Kb4 15. Rd4+ Kc3 16. Rf4.

Note that the value of the rook supporting a passed pawn is less if the pawn is still in its own half of the board. If the white pawn in fig. 79 was at a4, a3, or a2, then the black rook blockader would be progressively more powerful. Its horizontal action along the rank would make it difficult for White to improve his king's position and would also give Black's king more opportunities to become an effective fighting piece.

Endgame two –
The active king

Look again at the point count for the pieces on page 14. The king's value rapidly increases when only a few men remain, and in an endgame the more active king can be decisive. The king is rarely in danger, and can usually be employed aggressively to attack the enemy pawns.

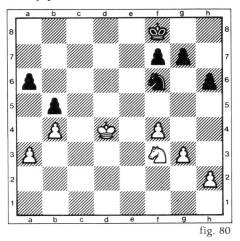

fig. 80

Fig. 80 is a basic example of how the more active king wins. Such a king is usually centralized like White's here so as to move rapidly to the scene of action. The action in fig. 80 is on the queen's side and White simply eats up the black pawns by Kc5-b6xa6. Black should have activated his own king earlier to keep the white monarch out of his position.

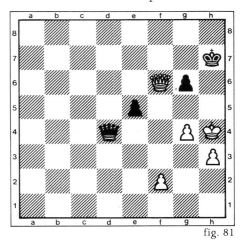

fig. 81

Example. Averbakh–Suetin, USSR championship 1954. Sometimes the active king is used to attack its opponent rather than win material. Here Black's king is corralled by the white queen, so by joining in the attack White's king forces mate. The game ended **1. Kg5! Qd2+ 2. f4! exf4** (the pawn endgame after 2. . . . . Qxf4+ 3. Qxf4 exf4 4. Kxf4 is a standard win since White's king can pressurize his rival into surrendering the g pawn) **3. Qf7+ Kh8 4. Kh6 Resigns**. If 4. . . . . f3+ 5. g5 parries the check, and mate by Qf8, Qg7 or Qh7 cannot be stopped.

Endgame three –
The outside passed pawn

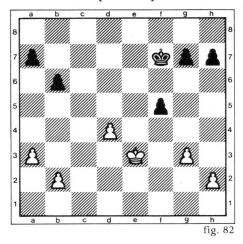

fig. 82

An outside passed pawn, that is a passed pawn far distant from the enemy king, is strong in all kinds of endgames (see the Alekhine–Capablanca rook ending, page 39. But when there are only king and pawns left, then such a pawn, actual or potential, is usually decisive.

Many inexperienced players are deceived in pawn endgames by believing that any passed pawn, wherever situated, is a great asset. But a passed pawn in the centre is often less effective than a majority of pawns on the flank which tie down the opponent's forces on one edge and open up the rest of the board to invasion.

Example 1. Evans–Reshevsky, US Championship 1969. Here White already has a passed pawn and Black only a potential one with a 3–2 king's side majority. But White's pawn is easily blockaded and indeed attacked by the black king, while the black majority advances smoothly. The game went **1. . . . . g5! 2. h4 h6 3. d5 Ke7 4. Kd4 Kd6 5. hxg5 hxg5 6. a4 a5 7. b3 g4! 8. Ke3** (if 8. Kc4 f4!) **9. gxf4 g3 and Black's outside passed pawn will queen) Kxd5** and Black won.

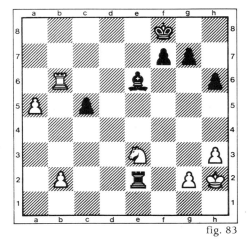

fig. 83

Example 2. Gulko–Dvoretsky, USSR championship 1975. In complex endings, a fast running passed pawn can clarify the result with dramatic effect. Think of this position as like a soccer match: while Boris Gulko (White, to move) sprints down the left wing with his pawn, Mark Dvoretsky's striker rook slips behind the sweeper knight and his midfield bishop gets ready for a cross by the far post. But the black forwards are stranded upfield and the outside pawn combines with White's striker rook to score: **1. a6!** (not 1. Nf1? Bd5 threatening Rxg2+) **Rxe3 2. Rb8+!** (not 2. a7? Bd5 draws) **Ke7 3. Rb7+ Resigns**. If 3. . . . . Kf6 4. a7 and the pawn scores the winning goal.

Israeli chess master Zilber, at the Hastings Premier, ponders the aggressive white queen. Note White's scoresheet to record moves. Hastings runs a promotion system enabling any good player to reach the grandmaster group.

Endgame four –
The pawn charge

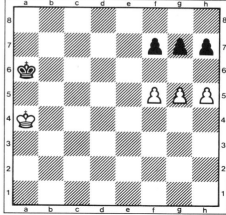

fig. 84

A classical type of breakthrough to queen can occur in a pure pawn endgame. It is well known, and opportunities for it occur rarely; but the practical player has to know it so as to be able to take measures against it well in advance. Here White wins by **1. g6!** and if hxg6 2. f6 gxf6 3. h6, or if fxg6 2. h6 gxh6 3. f6 and wins. It is virtually impossible to force this breakthrough: White's intentions are telegraphed as his pawns charge up the board and Black should put a stopper on the idea before it happens by a suitably timed . . . g6 or . . . h6.

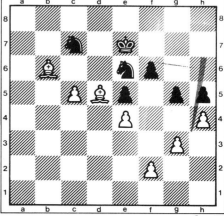

fig. 85

Example. Etmans–Tilstra, Holland 1967. More practical than the 3v3 classical pawn charge is a similar opportunity to break through in a 2v2 situation. Here White (to move) has a distant passed pawn and two bishops against two knights. The one distant passer cannot make much progress, so White creates another by **1. Bxc7! Nxc7 2. g4! hxg4 3. h5 Kf8 4. h6 Na6 5. c6 Nc7 6. Kg3** and, with Black's king and knight tied down to stopping the pawns, the white king is free to simply stroll up the board and eat up all the black pawns by Kxg4, Kf5, Kxf6 etc.

Endgame five – The one pawn win

A basic endgame which every player needs to know even at novice level is king and pawn against king. It can occur quite frequently if a game is played out. The four diagrams show the essentials.

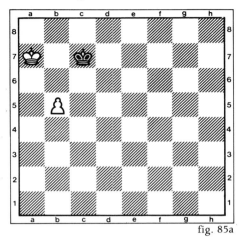

fig. 85a

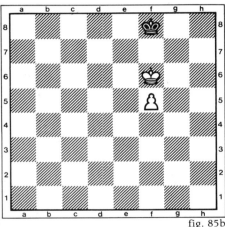

fig. 85b

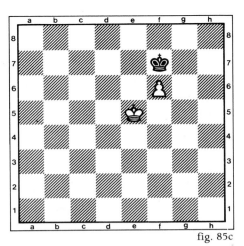

fig. 85c

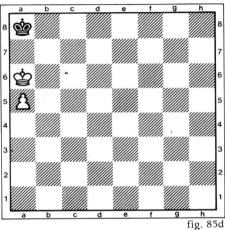

fig. 85d

Fig. 85a – an easy win for White. The K shepherds home the pawn via b6, b7 and b8 and Black can only watch.

Fig. 85b – another ideal position to aim for if you have the pawn. White wins, no matter whose turn it is to move. If it is Black's move then **1. . . . Kg8 2. Ke7** and White shepherds home the pawn as in (a). If it is White's move, then **1. Kg6 Kg8 2. f6 Kf8 3. f7 Ke7 4. Kg7** with another shepherd situation.

Fig. 85c – this is where most players go wrong. Black must go straight back by **1. . . . Kf8 2. Ke6** and now confront the white king by **2. . . . Ke8 3. f7+ Kf8 4. Kf6**, drawn by stalemate. If he plays instead **1. . . . Ke8?** then **2. Ke6 Kf8 3. f7 Kg7 4. Ke7** and White has reached the shepherd position.

Fig. 85d – an a pawn or an h pawn vastly improves the weaker side's drawing chances. Here White has an ideal situation akin to (b), but can make no progress. If **1. Kb6 Kb8 2. a6 Ka8 3. a7** is stalemate.

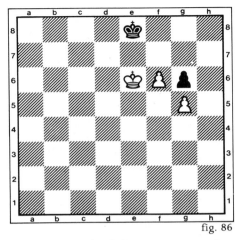

fig. 86

Example. Golombek–Pomar, London 1946. The technique of pawn promotion can be tricky and require tactical finessing, even in such a simple position as shown here. Play went **1. f7+ Kf8** and now **2. Kf6?** would be stalemate (fig. 85c). But the presence of another pair of pawns gives White a win by **2. Kd7! Kxf7 3.**

Kd6 Kf8 4. Ke6 Kg7 5. Ke7 Kh8 6. Kf6 Kh7 7. Kf7 Kh8 8. Kxg6 Kg8 (now White has reached fig. 85b) 9. Kh6 Kh8 10. g6 Kg8 11. g7 Kf7 12. Kh7 reaching the familiar shepherd situation and forcing Black to resign.

Endgame six –
The wrong colour rook pawn

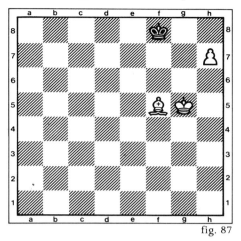

fig. 87

One of the unexpected endgame draws can occur when one player has a bishop and a rook pawn (a or h pawn) whose queening square is a different colour to that of the bishop. Then there is a real danger for the superior side that his opponent's king may be able to reach the queening square from which it can never be dislodged.

The board shows the basic drawing resource. Black simply plays 1. . . . Kg7 followed by 2. . . . Kh8 and White can only prevent the king oscillating ad infinitum between g7 and h8 at the price of allowing a draw by stalemate.

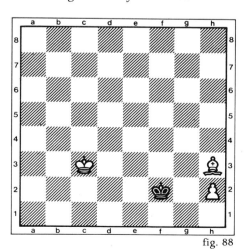

fig. 88

Despite the simplicity of Black's drawing plan, there are a few surprising exceptions to the wrong colour rook pawn ending. West German grandmaster Klaus Darga stumped players all round the world with this little ending 'For a long time, nobody found the solution,' claimed Darga. 'Everyone was beaten, whether in Havana, in Belgrade, in Tel Aviv or in Moscow. Even Tal and Spassky gave up, after they tried in vain for three-quarters of an hour to work it out'. The chess magazine editor who published the position after hearing Darga's story tried 1. Bg2. 'That's the same first move as Spassky played,' said Darga laughingly.

This story has probably gained in the telling – it's hard to credit that great players of the calibre of Tal and Spassky could fail to crack such a puzzle. Unusually, for the wrong colour rook pawn, White can manoeuvre his three men so as to stop Black getting to the corner square h8 in front of the pawn: 1. Bd7! Kf3 2. h4 Ke4 (if Kf4 3. Kd4! Kg3 4. h5 and the pawn has a straight run) 3. h5 Ke5 4. h6 Kf6 5. Be8! and the black king must move away, allowing 6. h7 and 7. h8 = Q.

Endgame seven –
The Zugzwang trick

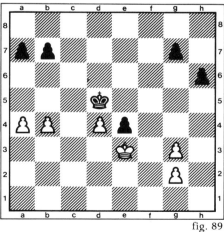

fig. 89

Knowledge of zugzwang – German for 'compulsion to move' – is essential for the chessplayer. Zugzwang crops up quite often in pawn endings when one or both kings attack or protect a pawn and the game is decided by who has to give way first. A tip for such endings: try to keep as many spare pawn moves in hand as possible, away from the scene of action. Often the player who uses up his pawn moves first will be 'in zugzwang' and compelled to make a losing king move.

Example 1. Popov–Dankov, Bulgaria

1978. Here the first player to move his king loses his central pawn and with it the game. White (to play) can easily go wrong by the routine 1. a5? h5! and White soon runs out of waiting moves. Instead he plays 1. g4! a6 (if g6 2. g5! hxg5 3. g4 or 1. . . . b6 2. b5) 2. a5 g6 3. g5! hxg5 4. g4 Kd6 5. Kxe4 Ke6 and Black resigned. After 6. d5+ the white king either shepherds his pawn home or penetrates the black position and eats up the pawns on either wing.

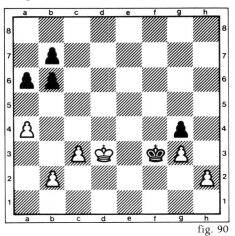

fig. 90

Example 2. N. Stone–G. Waddingham, national junior squad under-14 championship 1979. This is a critical zugzwang position, but White didn't realize it and, without much thought, played 1. b4?? b5! 2. a5 Kg2 3. Ke4 Kxh2 4. Kf4 Kh3 and White resigned. He has no spare moves left, is in zugzwang, and has to allow Black to win the g pawn and the game.

Instead 1. b3! keeping the spare move would have won: 1. . . . b5 2. a5 Kg2 3. Ke4 Kxh2 4. Kf4 Kh3 5. b4! and Black has to abandon the g pawn. Black could try 1. . . . a5 2. c4 b5 (hoping for 3. cxb5 b6) but then comes 3. axb5 b6 4. c5! and wins.

Endgame eight –
The bad bishop

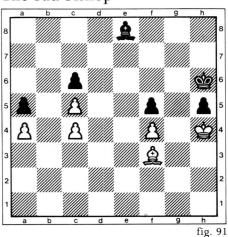

fig. 91

The 'bad' bishop is not a case of episcopal sinning, but merely describes a bishop whose mobility is seriously handicapped by its own pawns. These pawns offer targets for the combined action of the opposing king and bishop (or king and knight) which can often invade via squares of the colour not controlled by the bad bishop.

If you have the 'good bishop' whose action is not impeded by your own pawns, then you try to stop the inferior side making pawn breaks which might free the restricted bishop. Once the bad bishop player is tied down to passive defence then the player with the advantage can shift his attack from wing to wing until he breaks through.

Example 1 Schelfhout–Menchik, 1935. This is a typical bad bishop position. Three of Black's four pawns are on the same coloured squares as his bishop and, just as important, the white king and bishop can combine against them. Though White has doubled pawns and one of Black's pawns is passed this means little beside a classic bad bishop weakness.

The game ended quickly by 1. Bg2 Bd7 2. Bh1 Be8 3. Bf3 (zugzwang, now Black must unguard one of his pawns) Bd7 (if Bf7 4. Bxc6 Bxc4 5. Be8! and the c pawn advances) 4. Bxh5 Bc8 5. Be8 Bb7 6. Bd7 Kg6 7. Kg3 Kf6 8. Kf3 Kg6 9. Ke3 Kf6 10. Kd4 Ba8 11. Bc8 Ke7 12. Ke5 and wins easily.

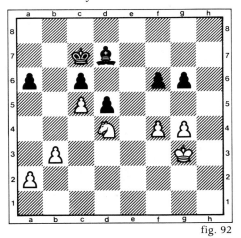

fig. 92

Example 2. Averbakh–Lilienthal, Moscow 1949. This is an example of winning with a knight against a bad bishop. Note that four of Black's five pawns are on white squares, restricting the bishop; the knight is ideally placed on a central black square whence it cannot be dislodged; and White's only real problem is how to create a route for his own king into the black camp. This explains White's first move 1. g5! after which Black has two choices:

if 1. . . . f5 2. Nf3 Be8 3. Ne5 Kd8 4. Kf3 Ke7 5. Ke3 Ke6 6. Kd4 Ke7 7. Nd3 Ke6 8. Nb4 a5 9. Nd3 Bd7 10. a4 Be8 11. b4 axb4 12. Nxb4 and White wins with his

a pawn;

if 1. . . . fxg5 2. fxg5 Bc8 3. Kf4 a5 4. Ke5 Bg4 5. Kf6 Bh5 6. Ke7 Bg4 7. a3 Bd1 8. Ne6+ Kb7 9. Kd6 Bxb3 10. Nd8+ Kc8 11. Nxc6 a4 12. Ne7+ and wins.

In both variations, what matters is not so much the individual moves, but the overall method by which White's K and N combine to squeeze the black K. The decisive material gain comes only when Black has no counterplay at all.

Endgame nine –
The Fischer/Karpov endgame

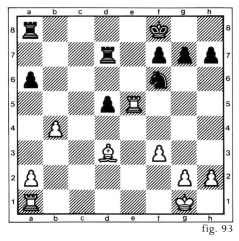

fig. 93

Both Bobby Fischer and Anatoly Karpov, en route to becoming world champions, proved particularly formidable in the endgame balance of rook, bishop and pawns against rook, knight and pawns. It was not the material itself which did the trick, but the ability of Bobby and Anatoly to create positions where the board was open, with good diagonals for the bishop which could be shown as superior to the knight.

The principles for playing the Fischer/Karpov endgame are partly those relevant to all good endgame play: activate your pieces, especially the king and rook; restrict the opponent's pieces, especially here the short-stepping knight; and look for opportunities to infiltrate the opponent's position with the king.

But there are also some special principles for the Fischer/Karpov endgame. You should avoid situations in which the knight can be swapped for the bishop to reach a rook endgame when the defender then often has good drawing chances; look instead for opportunities to eliminate the rooks when the B v. N endgame is clearly won. The attacker should use his rook to control important files and stop counterplay, and try to fix some of the defender's pawns on the same colour square as the bishop.

Such 'technical' endgames can take a long time to win, and this brings in another special factor: the stronger side must be alert for chances to make use of adjournment, when this will enable him to analyse the position in depth, and of adjudication, if the game is not continuing to a finish.

This is no endgame for novices: if you have not already had some years chess experience and become quite a strong player, then it is enough if you simply note the general principles and follow them as best you can. Afterwards try to find some of the games of the two champions and see how they tackled a similar position to yours.

The game Fischer–Petrosian, 7th match game, 1971, was one classic of this endgame type. Fischer's bishop controls the open board, he has a 2–1 queen's side majority, and Black's a pawn is weak. Further, the useful move f3 has deprived the black knight of a possible outpost square at e4 and cleared a path for the white king to advance rapidly towards the centre.

Fischer won by economical and precise play which made the game one of his most admired victories: **1. Rc1** (threat 2. Rc6) **Rd6 2. Rc7 Nd7 3. Re2 g6** (Black cannot move his knight because of 4. Ree7) **4. Kf2** (the king heads for the centre and an active position) **h5 5. f4 h4 6. Kf3 f5 7. Ke3 d4+** (otherwise comes 8. Kd4 and Black has no play at all) **8. Kd2 Nb6** (hoping to create a diversion by attacking the b pawn, but this gives White the chance to double rooks on the seventh rank) **9. R2e7 Nd5 10. Rf7+ Ke8 11. Rb7 Nxb4 12. Bc4 Resigns.** There is no answer to White's threats of 13. Rh7 and 13. Rxb4. (For the full game see page 77.)

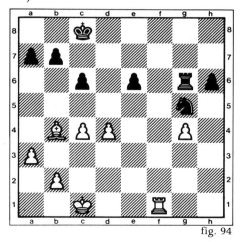
fig. 94

Example 2. Karpov–Pomar, Nice 1974. Anatoly Karpov, Fischer's successor as world champion, also made a speciality of this ending. The board shows an unusual example of the Fischer/Karpov endgame in that White plays for mate rather than win of material; but Karpov still keeps to the principle of using all his three pieces – king, rook and bishop – in the decisive attack.

1. Rf8+ Kc7 2. Ba5+! (forcing a

weakness, for if now 2. ... Kd6 3. Rd8+ Ke7 4. Ra8 a6 5. Ra7 and Black loses a key pawn) **b6 3. Bd2! Ne4 4. Bf4+ Kb7 5. Rf7+ Ka8** (not Ka6? 6. Bb8) **6. Rf8+ Kb7 7. b4** (starting to aim for mate, and reducing the chance of Black simplifying towards a draw by ... c5) **Rxg4 8. Rf7+ Ka8 9. Kc2** (remember the principle of the active king) **h5?** (Black either overlooks what is coming or feels despair about his position. 9. ... c5 is a tougher defence) **10. a4 h4 11. Kd3!** (driving away the knight and tightening the mating net) **Ng5 12. Rf8+ Kb7 13. Rb8+ Ka6 14. Bd2! Rg3+ 15. Kc2 Resigns.** White will mate, either by 16. b5+ or, if Black plays b5, by cxb5+.

Endgame ten –
Petrosian's endgame

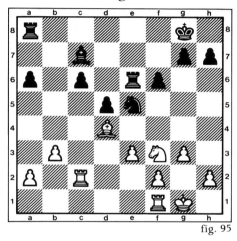
fig. 95

The converse of the Fischer/Karpov endgame is Petrosian's endgame, also a speciality of a world champion. On his way to the title, Petrosian won several games by the technique of enticing his opponent to advance pawns on one flank (h6 and g5 or a6 and b5–b4), then aiming for a position where these pawns would be fixed in a rigid chain with a bishop semi-immobilized behind it. Meanwhile, Petrosian's knight would occupy the holes created by the pawn advance, especially f5 on the king's side or c4 on the opposite flank.

Techniques to prepare for Petrosian's endgame include developing a bishop at g5 in front of a fianchettoed enemy bishop at g7, to encourage h6 and g5; and to advance an a or h pawn to a4/5 or h4/5, again to encourage the opposing b or g pawn to push forward.

Once the rigid pawn front is established, Petrosian and his imitators play for the endgame. They avoid giving the opponent any chance to exchange his restricted bishop, but willingly exchange other pieces when possible. Eventually, the knight and/or king will infiltrate along the squares of the opposite colour to the bad bishop and into the enemy camp.

Example 1. Petrosian–Belyavsky, USSR Championship 1973. Petrosian spots the way to his ending: **1. Bxe5!** (at first sight this is a mistake because Black can straighten out his pawn front by fxe5. However, then comes 2. e4! and either dxe4 3. Nd2 and Nxe4 or 2. ... d4 3. Ne1 followed by Nd3 accentuates the lack of scope of Black's B) **Bxe5 2. R1c1 Rc8 3. Rc5** (threat 4. Rxd5) **Rd6 4. R1c2 Kf7 5. Kf1** (the active king again!) **Ke6 6. Ne1 d4** (if Black awaits events, White switches his knight to b4 with decisive pressure against the weak pawns) **7. f4 d3 8. Rd2 Bb2 9. Rxd3** (avoiding the trap 9. Rxb2? d2) **Ra8 10. Rxd6+ Kxd6 11. Nd3 a5 12. Rc4 Ba3.**

The Petrosian ending has done its job: White is a pawn up, Black still has an inactive bishop and rook together with pawn weaknesses, while White's three pieces remain active and in control. The game finished **13. Ra4 Bc5 14. Nxc5 Kxc5 15. b4+ Kc4** (Kb5 16. Rxa5+ with a won pawn ending) **16. Rxa5 Rb8 17. a3 Kd3 18. Kf2 Rb7 19. Rc5 Ra7 20. Rxc6 Rxa3 21. Kf3 Resigns.**

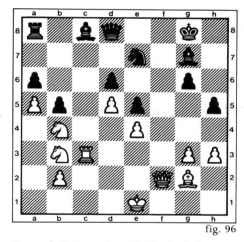
fig. 96

Example 2. Petrosian–Najdorf, Bled 1961. Petrosian's endgame can be created far in advance during the middle game.

Black's queen's side pawn advance has weakened the dark squares, the white knight has a useful outpost on b4, and the central pawn structure has left both black bishops with little scope. The key to the position is that after the exchange of queens White's rook and knights are already poised to pour into the badly defended dark squares: **1. Qb6! Qxb6 2. axb6 Rb8** (otherwise 3. b7 will win a piece) **3. Rc7 Bf8 4. Na5 Rxb6 5. N4c6 Nxc6 6. Nxc6 Resigns.** After 6. ... Bb7 7. Na5 Ba8 8. Rc8 Bb7 9. Rb8! White wins a piece, an eloquent demonstration of the weakness of the Petrosian endgame bad bishop trapped behind its pawn wall. (For another example, see page 69.)

The Fischer and Petrosian endgames are both important in expert chess. For further examples see *How to Play the Endgame in Chess.*

Test Your Chess IQ

Test board 1

Whatever your skill level at chess, you can obtain an idea of your natural aptitude for the game by looking at fig. 97 for ten seconds only and then setting up the position, as far as you can reconstruct it, on a chessboard.

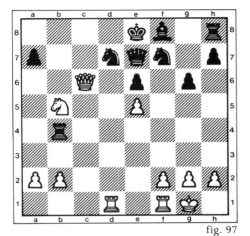

fig. 97

The position was shown in Holland to four chessplayers: to Dr Max Euwe, former world champion; to a chess master; to an expert and town champion; and to an average club player. Euwe easily dictated the position without a single mistake; the master added a pawn on c2. The local champion omitted the black bishop, transferred the rook on b4

Dutch psychologist Adrian de Groot's chess IQ test. Shown the position for a few seconds, former world champion Dr Max Euwe reconstructed it perfectly, but average players could only recall vague outlines.

to b8, misplaced or left out half a dozen pawns, and imagined an extra white bishop. The average player could only set up half a dozen of the pieces correctly, though he rightly judged within the seconds at his disposal that Black has a material plus.

Readers who succeed in reconstructing this position with fewer than four mistakes after ten seconds probably have

distinct natural gifts for chess visualization – not the only aspect of chess talent but an important one.

Dr Euwe, in his comments on the position, remarked that he always saw pieces in clusters rather than individually; for example he saw the entire cramped black king's position as a whole. It is clear from this experiment, set up by the psychologist Adrian de Groot, that great chessplayers have an outstanding ability to visualize the board. Possession of this faculty does not eliminate human error, and during his playing career Dr Euwe was noted for gross oversights.

Test board 2

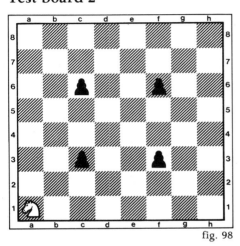

fig. 98

Fig. 98 can be treated both as a chess party game and as a serious test of skill. It can be tried by anyone who knows the moves of a knight and a pawn. You need a chess set and board, and a friend with a watch.

The object is to transfer the knight, making legal knight moves only, from a1 to a8, stopping en route at every square which is not occupied by or guarded by a black pawn. Thus the knight visits every square along the bottom row from a1 to h1, turns at h1 up to h2 then leftwards along the second row, and so on. The black pawns stay on their diagrammed squares and cannot be captured.

Add 10 seconds to your total time whenever the knight lands on a square occupied or controlled by a black pawn.

As an example, your first series of moves would be to move the knight from a1 to c2, to a3, and then to b1 – then you have to find a route to c1.

This little test measures quick sight of the board, flexible thinking patterns, and quick recall of patterns of play – all aspects of chess skill.

The test, and some others, were said in a German magazine to be used in evaluating new young talents in East Germany and Czechoslovakia. The claim that this test had shown up the future grandmasters Hort, Smejkal, Kavalek and Jansa at an early age in Prague was dis-

counted as great exaggeration by Hort, but in general this is a test where good players find their way round the board quickly. Among leading British men players, Jonathan Penrose, ten times national champion, took two minutes to complete the knight tour, Bill Hartston took three minutes, Raymond Keene four, Peter Clarke 4½ and myself five. Strong club players may take 5–10 minutes, and anyone who beats six minutes is likely to have above average chess talent.

Test board 3

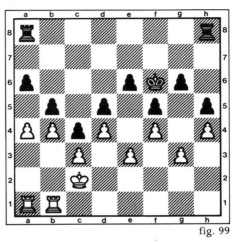

fig. 99

National chess coach Robert Wade has posed this simple test of endgame judgment at a number of junior tournaments. At the London under-10 championship none of the youngsters found the correct answer although their general standard of play was good for their age. Strategic planning is also involved in the puzzle, which is simply to decide the best way for White (to move) to improve his position.

The answers to this and the following five diagrams (figs. 99–104) are given at the end of this chapter.

Test board 4

This puzzle has the unique feature of five different verdicts given by players ranging from a beginner to a grandmaster: the test is to see how many of the moves in the five sections below you can fill in. Each of the blanks denotes a missing move. If there are two blanks after a move number, both a white and a black move have to be found.

(a) A novice watching this game thought that Black must win on material. Black's threat of 1. . . . cannot be stopped.

(b) His friend, an average club player, thought that White could allow the threat and win the game by 1. . . . . . . 2. . . . . . . 3. . . . . . . 4. . . . when White wins easily through his advantage on material.

(c) White looked at the position hard, then resigned the game. He was an expert player, and foresaw that after 1. . . ., which the second spectator anticipated,

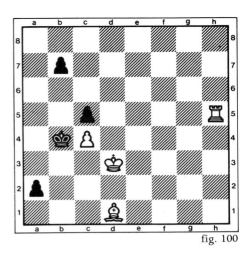

fig. 100

Black could reply 1. . . . 2. . . . . . . and if 3. . . . renewing the threat of the second move then 3. . . . and White no longer has any saving resource.

(d) Black, a stronger expert, accepted White's resignation. But then, to White's horror and the astonishment of the two kibitzers, he pointed out that after White's anticipated first moves of 1. . . . . . . White could improve his play dramatically by 2. . . . and after 2. . . . reply 3. . . . followed by 4. . . . winning on material.

(e) This game was played in 1914 and casually noticed by the Hungarian grandmaster Szabo 36 years later. Szabo pointed out that the spectators and both players had all been wrong in their assessment. Szabo said: 'After 1. . . . as given in the last variation, Black can improve on one of the previous lines of play with 1. . . . 2. . . . . . . 3. . . . . . . and White can only choose between 4. . . . and 4. . . .'.

If you fill in the blanks correctly, you will see why the spectators and players thought that White or Black won, what the grandmaster noticed which the lesser players overlooked, and the true result of the game with best play on both sides.

Test board 5

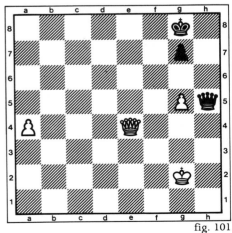

fig. 101

Petrosian–Gulko, USSR championship 1975. The ability to calculate moves ahead is not the most important item in a chessplayer's IQ. In many positions, a strong master or grandmaster simply 'feels' that the best move is the right choice, subconsciously weighing up the pros and cons of the numerous different factors.

But in the endgame, where many of the great champions like Capablanca, Fischer and Korchnoi have been at their best, you sometimes have to work out move sequences very precisely. Petrosian (White, to move) did so here, and it was the decisive game of the championship. It isn't easy, but a potential chess expert should be able to demonstrate a win in under five minutes, working just from the diagram without board and men.

Test board 6

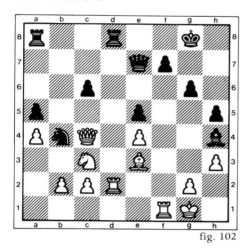

fig. 102

Grandmaster moves which perplex the ordinary player usually turn out to have a rational and explicable basis when examined closely. Occasionally, however, someone makes a move so deep that even fellow-masters would not consider it. When I demonstrated this position from the Karpov–Spassky match at two leading London chess clubs, it took in each case a full ten minutes for any of the 30-odd members present to spot Karpov's next move as White, and then only by desperate guessing after other more obvious possibilities had been discarded. The move and its idea were hailed in the Russian chess magazines as a world champion calibre plan.

The puzzle is to decide White's next move as well as the reasoning behind it. If you succeed on both counts and the game is not already known to you, then your strategic vision ranks anywhere between strong expert and grandmaster.

Test board 7

One of the rarest elements in the mental make-up of a great chess master is what the public calls 'genius' and the psychologist knows as creativity, flair or instinct for the unusual. Even outstanding players slightly below world championship class

may not possess this faculty to any marked degree.

As an illustration, look at this diagram from Furman–Smejkal (both strong grandmasters) played at Tallinn in 1971. Furman (White, to move) saw no serious prospect of halting Black's widely separated passed pawns with the short-stepping knight and, as a gesture before resignation, played **1. Ne4+ Kf3 2. Nxc5**. After **2. . . . a2 3. Nb3 Ke4 4. Kg2 Kd5 White resigned**, since the black king soon chases the knight away from the a pawn which then queens.

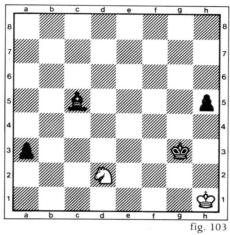

fig. 103

After the game, ex-world champion Tal, one of the most imaginative players in chess history, asked grandmaster Smejkal 'What would you have done after 1. Nb3?'. 'Why, a2 of course'. 'Then you would only have drawn.' Smejkal could not understand Tal's reasoning. If you can see what Tal meant in less than a minute, your chess equivalent of 'lateral thinking' is highly developed.

Test board 8

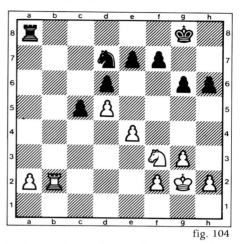

fig. 104

This position, with Black to move, is a test of long-term planning and general judgment. Five verdicts on the diagram were given by five different players: (a) 'Perhaps Black can draw if he plays well' (b) 'Black has a positional advantage' (c) 'White wins because of his outside a pawn which his king can support' (d) 'Black has a decisive advantage and wins material by force' (e) 'The position looks about equal, perhaps with a shade of advantage to Black'.

The verdicts come from a grandmaster (grading 240), an expert (grade 190), a county strength player (grade 170), and two club players, one slightly above average (grade 150) and one rather weak (grade 120). The puzzle is twofold: to decide which player gave which verdict, and to decide why the grandmaster's assessment was correct.

Test board solutions

Test Board 3: **1. Ra2!** (or 1. Ra3 or 1. Rb2), is best, planning to double rooks before exchanging the a pawn for the black b pawn. Black then has to remove his own rook from the a file to avoid losing a pawn, after which White exchanges pawns and infiltrates the black position with his rooks. He will then double rooks on the seventh rank and decide the game by mating threats to the black king.

Test Board 4: (a) **1. . . . a1=Q** (b) **1. Rh7 a1=Q 2. Rxb7+ Ka3 3. Ra7+ Kb2 4. Rxa1** (c) **1. Rh7 Ka5 2. Rxb7 Ka6 3. Rb8 Ka7** (d) **1. Rh7 Ka5 2. Rh8 a1=Q 3. Ra8+ and 4. Rxa1** (e) **1. Rh7 a1=Q 2. Rxb7+ Ka5 3. Ra7+ Kb4 4. Rxa1** (draw by stalemate) or **4. Rb7+** (perpetual check).

Test Board 5: **1. Qd5+** and if (a) Kf8 2. Qf3+ exchanges queens (b) Kh8 2. Qd8+ Kh7 3. Qd3+ transposes to (c). (c) Kh7 2. Qd3+ Kg8 3. Qb3+ Kh7 (Kf8 4. Qf3+) 4. Qh3 with a won pawn endgame.

Test Board 6: **1. Nb1!** plans to regroup

the knight via d2 to f3 where the extra pressure on Black's e5 pawn forces a decisive weakening of the pawn defences in front of Spassky's king. Play continued **1. Nb1 Qb7 2. Kh2 Kh7 3. c3 Na6 4. Re2 Rf8 5. Nd2 Bd8 6. Nf3 f6 7. Rd2** and Karpov's attack won in a few moves: **7. . . . Be7 8. Qe6 Rad8 9. Rxd8 Bxd8 10. Rd1 Nb8 11. Bc5 Rh8 12. Rxd8! Resigns**. If 12. . . . Rxd8 13. Be7 wins.

Test Board 7: **1. Nb3 a2? 2. Nc1!** draws. If 2. . . . a1=Q or R White is stalemated, if a1=N 3. Nb3! forces a draw and if a1=B Black has the wrong colour rook pawn shown on page 43.

Test Board 8: (a) above average club (b) expert (c) weak club (d) grandmaster (e) county strength. Grandmaster Walter Browne played Black and continued **1. . . . Ra4!** which wins an important pawn after **2. Nd2 Ne5 3. Kf1 Nd3 4. Rb7 Kf8** followed by Nc1 or Nb4 winning the a pawn. In the game, White gave up a pawn by 2. e5 but still lost.

Learn from the
Champions

Each of the great players of the past, and the leading grandmasters of today, has his individual approach to the technique and psychology of chess. Some aim to control events and reduce the risk-taking element in the game to a minimum, while others try to randomize the position and create scope for their flair in calculation or judgment. Some are purely interested in the game and its mechanisms, others play the man as much as the board.

One reliable method of improving your chess is to choose one of the great masters, replay and study a large number of his games, and try to use him as a model for your own style and chess-board tactics.

This chapter looks at 21 past and present champions and highlights their outstanding qualities.

Paul Morphy

1837–84

The 'pride and sorrow of chess', Morphy was a great player but his true status when compared with other champions remains an enigma even today, nearly 100 years after his death. Among all those recognized as best in the world for their time he had the shortest active career and he never met an opponent who threatened to beat him. His fame rests on fewer than 75 serious games plus a larger number of brilliant offhand victories.

Morphy was hailed as a prodigy at the age of 12 when he defeated the master Lowenthal, who was visiting Morphy's home city of New Orleans, in a series of friendly matches.

Then, in 1857, an event occurred which substantially advanced Morphy's name and career. This was the first American chess congress held in New York, and by good fortune it took place at a time when Morphy was technically ready for it. Similar strokes of fortune occurred in the careers of some later players, notably Lasker and Fischer.

The congress was staged as a series of knock-out matches, and Morphy out-classed his first three opponents before defeating Louis Paulsen 6–2 in the final. Paulsen later proved himself an excellent match player and a deep strategist, many of whose ideas in the openings were

The white knight on f5 outpost square is the key to the Ruy Lopez attack preferred by former world champion Anatoly Karpov (page 78). Capablanca and Fischer also favoured the Ruy Lopez.

taken up by grandmasters a century later. That Morphy could defeat this master of defence may be a better indication of his strength than his more highly praised victory over Anderssen.

Morphy's successes rested on his understanding of open positions, the need to develop pieces rapidly in the classical king's side openings and to take the initiative in an economical way without wasting moves. Generally, Morphy's contemporaries either attacked without the support of a sound development or played manoeuvre chess with wasted and irrelevant moves slowing down their plans. Morphy's economy of effort and means gives his best games an impression of simplicity and flow as he found the most accurate move at every stage.

Morphy's most famous victory was during the interval of an opera performance against two consulting dignitaries. It is the most celebrated and instructive friendly game of all time.

White: P. Morphy Black: Duke of Brunswick and Count Isouard

Philidor Defence
(Paris, 1858)

1. e4   e5
2. Nf3   d6
3. d4   Bg4?

This pin on the knight, indirectly controlling the centre, is good in many openings but here allows White a forced sequence gaining the advantage.

4. dxe5   Bxf3

4. ... dxe5 5. Qxd8+ and 6. Nxe5 wins a pawn.

5. Qxf3   dxe5
6. Bc4   Nf6?

Overlooking the threat – Qf6 or Qd7 is better.

7. Qb3!

Moving a piece, and particularly the queen, twice in the opening is usually contrary to sound play, but great champions know when to break general rules. Here White threatens both 8. Bxf7+ followed by 9. Qe6 mate and also 8. Qxb7.

7. ...   Qe7
8. Nc3

Stronger than 8. Qxb7 Qb4+ exchanging queens.

8. ...   c6
9. Bg5   b5?

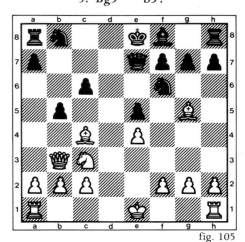

fig. 105

Note that White has been bringing his pieces into action as quickly as possible, while Black has made queen and pawn moves and exchanged off his developed bishop. Now White is already set up for a devastating sacrifice – Black should have played 9. ... Qc7.

10. Nxb5!   cxb5
11. Bxb5+   Nbd7
12. O-O-O   Rd8

Paul Morphy, the 'pride and sorrow of chess', beat all comers in a career of only three years.

13. Rxd7!   Rxd7
14. Rd1   Qe6

Now White could win simply by 15. Bxf6, but Morphy chooses the most artistic finish.

15. Bxd7+! Nxd7
16. Qb8+   Nxb8
17. Rd8 mate

Morphy travelled to Europe in 1858 and defeated all comers including an 8–3 margin over Anderssen, who had won the first international tournament at London 1851. The English champion, Staunton, ducked Morphy's attempts to arrange a match – wisely, for Staunton's best successes were in the 1840s and there is no doubt Morphy would have won. But after proving his supremacy over his contemporaries Morphy quickly lost interest in chess and his later life was marred by mental illness which left him a recluse, shunning the game for the 15 years before his death.

How would Morphy have performed against champions of later generations? Knowledge of opening play around 1860 was still rudimentary and Morphy would need an intensive course of modern theory to have any chance of competing with present-day masters. He would certainly have been able to absorb such information quickly, for he knew the theory of his time and one of his victories over Anderssen came through a prepared variation of the Ruy Lopez.

In his authoritative book *The Rating of Chessplayers Past and Present* (Batsford) which includes comparative performances of modern grandmasters and their predecessors, Professor Arpad Elo assesses

Morphy with a rating of 2690, sufficient in present-day terms to make him stronger than any player except the world champion and his challenger. I doubt this verdict, which depends on a small number of games and does not allow for Morphy's illness which would have affected his results in later life as it did with Rubinstein.

But the assessment makes it worthwhile examining the games of Morphy's match with Anderssen, another confirmed great player. Anderssen had not competed since 1851 and handicapped himself with inferior openings such as 1. a3 and the Centre Counter which provided Morphy's best win of the match.

White: P. Morphy. Black: A. Anderssen

Centre Counter (7th match game 1858)

1.	e4	d5
2.	exd5	Qxd5
3.	Nc3	Qa5
4.	d4	e5
5.	dxe5	Qxe5+
6.	Be2	Bb4
7.	Nf3	

Typical of Morphy's style – he has an advantage and sacrifices a pawn to increase his lead in development.

7.	...	Bxc3+
8.	bxc3	Qxc3+
9.	Bd2	Qc5
10.	Rb1	Nc6
11.	0-0	Nf6
12.	Bf4	

regaining the pawn but allowing simplifications. 12. Rb5 Qd6 13. Re1 0-0 14. Qc1, keeping up the pressure, was recommended later, and is more what would have been expected from Morphy.

12.	...	0-0
13.	Bxc7	Nd4
14.	Qxd4	Qxc7
15.	Bd3	

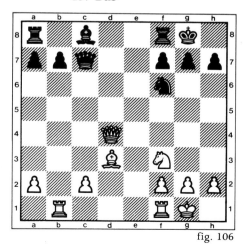

fig. 106

15.	...	Bg4?

This cannot be good since the bishop has to return miserably to c8 two moves later. 15. ... h6! (stopping White's next) 16. Qb4 b6 and if 17. Rfe1 Be6 would have

solved most of Black's problems.

16. Ng5!

Now Black's game is difficult because White threatens N or Bxh7 and also pressurizes the two Q-side pawns.

16.	...	Rfd8

If 16. ... Bh5 17. Ne4 Ng4 18. Ng3 b6 19. Rb5 wins, while moving the other rook to d8, which is positionally natural, loses a pawn to 17. Qxa7.

17.	Qb4	Bc8
18.	Rfe1	a5

If 18. ... h6 19. Re7 Rd7 20. Bh7+, but as played all Black's pawns are weak and are easy endgame victims to White's active rooks and minor pieces.

19.	Qe7	Qxe7
20.	Rxe7	Nd5
21.	Bxh7+	Kh8
22.	Rxf7	Nc3
23.	Re1	Nxa2
24.	Rf4	Ra6
25.	Bd3	Resigns

Anderssen's wry comment after his match defeat was, 'It is impossible to keep one's excellence in a little glass casket, like a jewel, to take it out whenever wanted. On the contrary, it can only be conserved by continuous and good practice.' In his later matches against Kolisch and Steinitz, Anderssen eschewed both 1. a3 and the Centre Counter and did much better.

As for Morphy, his last act before quitting tournament chess was to offer pawn and move odds to anyone in the world. There were no takers – an inconceivable event if any similar offer was made by an established grandmaster today. The nearest modern parallel was Fischer's offer to give knight odds to any woman player in the world, a proposal which he quickly abandoned when the Soviet chess authorities showed eagerness to match the women's world champion, Nona Gaprindashvili, against him for a substantial stake.

Wilhelm Steinitz
1836–1900

The first recognized world champion, Steinitz was a chess thinker and innovator whose insights into strategic and defensive play and the accumulation of small positional advantages were as great as were Morphy's contributions in open games. Whereas Morphy was an instinctive natural who taught by example rather than writing, Steinitz evolved his ideas gradually over a period of years, after a false start in which he tried to make his name by traditional gambits. By world championship standards, his play was not devoid of weaknesses and he lost many games by his stubborn loyalty to inferior lines despite previous defeats.

Steinitz was the youngest of a large Jewish family (a fact he liked to reveal

whenever Malthusian population control was discussed) and a cosmopolitan who was born in Prague, studied in Vienna, and settled in London. He had only fair success until some enterprising backers supported his 1866 challenge to Anderssen, who was again the recognized best player in the world following Morphy's retirement. Steinitz surprisingly won 8–6 and from then on was a consistent high prizewinner in the big tournaments of the 1870s and 1880s.

Steinitz expounded his theories in his chess column in *The Field* and his book *Modern Chess Instructor*. His basic approach was that the quick victories against weak defence shown in many games of Morphy and Anderssen were not possible if the opponent resisted simply, brought his own pieces into action quickly, and declined irrelevant pawn offers. Steinitz showed that against sound play it was incorrect to aim for rapid attacks and that instead you should build up your game quietly, looking for small advantages such as bishop against knight, play against doubled or isolated pawns, outpost squares, open files, a queen's side pawn majority, as well as seeking greater command of space.

His theory of defence was obstinate: he thought that if the defender could avoid structural weaknesses then his game would remain sound. Thus in a number of well-known Steinitz games he retreated forces to the back ranks solely to avoid pawn weaknesses. Another of his controversial ideas was that 'the king is a fighting piece' even in the middle game. From this he developed the Steinitz Gambit 1. e4 e5 2. Nc3 Nc6 3. f4 exf4 4. d4?! Qh4+ 5. Ke2, the idea being that in trying to mate the centralized white king Black will over-commit his own forces which can then be driven back with loss of time, e.g. the white knight at g1 comes to f3 with gain of tempo on the black queen.

Later generations have accorded these more controversial Steinitzian ideas a mixed reception. His favourite defence to the Evans Gambit brought him several heavy defeats against one of his contemporary rivals Tchigorin; but his idea for White against the Two Knights' Defence 1. e4 e5 2. Nf3 Nc6 3. Bc4 Nf6 4. Ng5 d5 5. exd5 Na5 6. Bb5+ c6 7. dxc6 bxc6 8. Be2 h6 9. Nh3 (instead of 9. Nf3 allowing the time-gaining 9. ... e4) was successfully taken up by Bobby Fischer and is now preferred to 9. Nf3 by several grandmasters.

Steinitz realized the importance of advanced knight outposts: he wrote that if he could establish a knight on d6 or e6, he could go to sleep and let the game win itself. He also showed later generations how to use a constriction motif when the opponent was handicapped by a 'bad' bishop locked in by its own pawns; the following game is a good example of this:

White: W. Steinitz. Black: A.G. Sellman

French Defence (match, 1885)

1. e4	e6
2. d4	d5
3. Nc3	Nf6
4. e5	Nfd7
5. f4	c5
6. dxc5	Bxc5
7. Nf3	a6

This and his tenth move already carry some strategical risk since they place pawns on light squares, handicapping the queen's bishop which is already hemmed in by the central pawn chain. Modern masters prefer 7. . . . Nc6 with the possibility of a more fluid game by a later . . . Qa5, . . . Qb6 or . . . f6.

8. Bd3	Nc6
9. Qe2	Nb4
10. Bd2	b5
11. Nd1	Nxd3+
12. cxd3	Qb6?

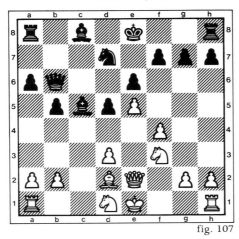

fig. 107

This is a serious positional mistake since White's next move immediately establishes control of the dark square and further restricts the bad bishop. Instead Black should play 12. . . . b4 intending a5 and Ba6.

13. b4!	Be7

If 13. . . . Bd4? 14. Rb1 threatening Nxd4 and Be3 winning the queen.

14. a3	f5?

This blocks the position, but further handicaps the bad bishop. A modern master would recognize the QB as Black's problem piece and try to look for chances to play . . . f6 and regroup the bishop via d7 and e8 to h5.

The move f5 also leaves the e pawn backward and vulnerable at a later stage to attacks from the white knights at d4 and g5 which will tie a black piece down to protection of the pawn.

15. Rc1	Bb7
16. Be3	

White's bishop has ample scope on the g1-a7 diagonal even though five of White's seven pawns are on dark squares.

16. . . .	Qd8

17. Nd4	Nf8
18. 0-0	h5?

Black fears the attacking g4, but this move places yet another pawn on a white square and means that g5 will be available as a white knight outpost if and when Black's dark-squared bishop is exchanged.

19. Nc3!

heading for a5, where the knight will strengthen White's overall bind and prepare for a piece invasion along the c file, the only open line.

19. . . .	Kf7
20. Nb1	g6
21. Nd2	Nd7

21. . . . a5 looks more logical, to try to gain some freedom before the knight settles on a5, but Steinitz was then ready to open up the game in his own favour by 22. Nxb5 axb4 23. axb4 Bxb4 24. Nd6+ Bxd6 25. exd6 Qxd6 26. Bd4 Rg8 27. Nf3 with great advantage due to control of the central and K-side dark squares.

22. N2b3	Rc8
23. Na5	Ba8
24. Rxc8	Qxc8
25. Rc1	Qb8
26. Qc2	Bd8
27. N5c6	

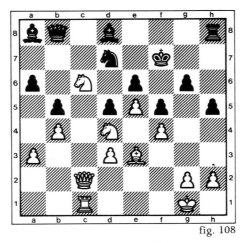

fig. 108

27. . . .	Qb7

On purely strategic grounds, Black would like nothing better than to exchange his dud bishop, but 27. . . . Bxc6 28. Qxc6 Nf8 29. Nxe6! Nxe6 30. Qd7+ Be7 31. Rc6 is hopeless. But as played Steinitz exchanges off Black's 'good' bishop and makes a decisive invasion on the dark squares.

28. Nxd8+	Rxd8
29. Qc7	Qb8
30. Bf2	

This threatens Bh4, so forcing the exchange of queens.

30. . . .	Qb6
31. Nf3	Qxc7
32. Rxc7	Ke8
33. Ng5	Nf8
34. Bc5	Nd7
35. Bd6!	**Resigns**

Black is in virtual zugzwang, with no

reasonable move left. If Rb8 36. Rxd7, or if Nb6 36. Re7+ Kf8 37. Nh7+ wins. Finally if d4 then 36. Nxe6 Rb8 37. Ng7+ Kd8 38. e6 and Black's game collapses.

Lasker, who succeeded Steinitz as world champion, said after beating him that 'the thinker was defeated by the player' and this has led to the belief that Steinitz succeeded only because of his advanced theories and had little understanding of psychological chess. Results, however, do not completely bear this out. Except when Steinitz was involved in defending his pet variations, he could be a shrewd observer of his opponent's state of mind and could tailor his play accordingly. Thus before starting his play-off against Blackburne at Vienna in 1873 he saw that the English grandmaster, who had gone in for a wild coffee-house style in his final round defeat from Rosenthal, was in a low state of morale for the tie-match. Steinitz therefore went in for trappy cut-and-thrust play and was rewarded when Blackburne replied poorly in both games.

In the first official world championship match, Steinitz–Zukertort, 1886, Steinitz began badly and was soon 1–4 down. But he kept his head as well as his title chances with a mixture of defensive and strategic chess which provoked Zukertort's nervous temperament into a succession of unsound and positionally weakening attacks. Steinitz finally ran out the champion by a score of $12\frac{1}{2}$–$7\frac{1}{2}$. The psychologically decisive game was the seventh which showed Zukertort as out of his depth in a subtle positional fight.

White: J.H. Zukertort. Black: W. Steinitz

Queen's Gambit Declined (7th match game 1886)

1. d4	d5
2. c4	e6
3. Nc3	Nf6
4. e3	c5
5. Nf3	Nc6
6. a3	dxc4
7. Bxc4	cxd4
8. exd4	Be7
9. 0-0	0-0

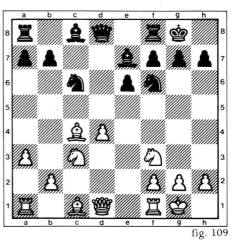

fig. 109

The plan of isolating White's central d pawn and then blockading and attacking it was hardly known in 1886 so it is small wonder that in the ensuing play Zukertort fails to find the optimum squares for his pieces. Best is 10. Re1, White has to combine the possibilities of lining up queen and bishop against h7 with opening up the centre by d5. Either way the likely best squares for the queen's bishop and queen's rook are g5 and d1, so that two of Zukertort's next three moves are inaccurate. However unlike a modern master, who would already be very familiar with fig. 109, Zukertort had little or no precedent to draw upon as the basis for his planning.

10.	Be3?	Bd7
11.	Qd3	Rc8
12.	Rac1?	Qa5
13.	Ba2	Rfd8
14.	Rfe1	Be8
15.	Bb1	g6
16.	Qe2	Bf8
17.	Rfd1	Bg7
18.	Ba2	Ne7
19.	Qd2?	

The only point of this seems to be the tactical idea 20. Nd5 Qxd2 21. Nxe7+ Kf8 22. Bxd2 Kxe7 23. Bb4+ Kd7 24. Ne5 mate – but this is easily prevented and White is left with his queen in an awkward position vis-a-vis the d8 rook. Superior is 19. Bg5, intending to meet Nf5 by 20. d5, after which White's piece formation would be similar to that favoured by modern masters on the white side of an isolated d pawn.

19.	...	Qa6
20.	Bg5	Nf5
21.	g4?	

This is an unsound move which weakens the white king's defences (see the later stages of the game) and precipitates a combination which Black intends anyway. 21. Qe1, still hoping for d5, was now best.

21.	...	Nxd4
22.	Nxd4	e5
23.	Nd5	Rxc1
24.	Qxc1	exd4
25.	Rxd4	Nxd5
26.	Rxd5	

If 26. Bxd8 Bxd4 27. Bxd5 Qe2! wins quickly.

26.	...	Rxd5
27.	Bxd5	Qe2
28.	h3	h6
29.	Bc4?	

This loses by force. White could not play 29. Bxh6? Bxh6 30. Qxh6 because of Qd1+, but 29. Be3 would fight on.

29.	...	Qf3
30.	Qe3	Qd1+
31.	Kh2	Bc6
32.	Be7	

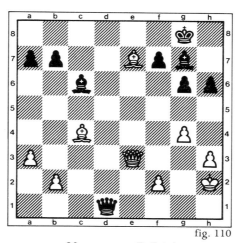

fig. 110

32.	...	Be5+!

An attractive finish. If 33. Qxe5 Qh1+ 34. Kg3 Qg2+ 35. Kh4 (35. Kf4 Qf3 mate) Qxf2+ 36. Qg3 g5+ wins the queen.

33.	f4	Bxf4+
34.	Qxf4	Qh1+
35.	Kg3	Qg1+
36.	Resigns	

And now if 36. Kh4 Qe1+ 37. Qg3 g5+ wins the queen.

Emanuel Lasker

1868–1941

Lasker lived in Berlin for most of his life but in old age emigrated first to Moscow then to New York. He was world champion for 27 years (1894–1921) and his chess longevity was exceptional: his first brilliancy was a double bishop sacrifice in 1889 and his last great achievement was third prize at Moscow 1936 when approaching 70.

Despite his many successes in tournaments and matches, his style has remained controversial and something of a mystery. One view of Lasker is that he was a fine strategist who added an extra tactical dimension to his play, combining this with superlative endgame ability. The alternative picture is of Lasker the fighter, playing the man as much as the board, deliberately accepting inferior but complex positions in order to build up the tension. However, he avoided strong opponents in matches and enjoyed phenomenal luck in critical games. There was even a suggestion that Lasker's partiality for strong cigars was a ploy to wear down the physical resistance of his opponents.

The truth is that no player could possibly remain world champion for so long or achieve such repeated tournament successes without an enormous measure of all-round skill. In most of his games, opponents were outplayed by Lasker's understanding of positional and strategic chess, which in many respects was well ahead of his time. His mastery of weak squares, outpost play, and switching the attack between two fronts was achieved long before Nimzovitch formulated these concepts in his classic primer *My System*. Lasker applied Steinitz's principles and refined them for the practical warfare of tournament and match chess.

Lasker possessed exceptional stamina and displayed a cool and pragmatic approach to his most critical games. His 'black magic' reputation arose because he proved himself a stronger and tougher personality than his opponent in some of the most critical games of his career – for example in his victory over Schlechter in the final game of their 1910 match which Lasker had to win to keep the world title; in his defeat of Capablanca at St Petersburg 1914 which gained first prize ahead of his main rival, and in the second game of his 1908 match with Tarrasch. In all of these wins Lasker demonstrated his skill in producing tension in opponents who were not playing their best.

His stamina is also evident from his good record in last round games and the frequency with which he overhauled rivals in the second half of a tournament –

'I have only two words, "check" and "mate",' said Tarrasch, left, but his enemy Lasker won.

for example at Hastings 1895 and the three St Petersburg tournaments of 1896, 1909 and 1914.

Lasker's stamina provides an important lesson for the ordinary club or social chessplayer or the ambitious youngster. In theory all chess games carry equal weight and a win in the first round has the same value as a victory at the end – but this is not so in practice. For instance, in Swiss System tournaments, players meet opponents with similar scores, and a poor start or a loss in the middle rounds can be compensated by wins over weaker opponents late in the tournament. Wins in the final rounds of a Swiss and especially in the last round in effect carry extra weight because they decide the prizes.

Lasker's career shows that he realized the importance of games towards the end in all-play-all tournaments. In the opening rounds of an event every player is fighting for an good result, but towards the end some will lose interest or confidence while others in contention for one of the top places may suffer from undue tension. In such a situation the strong and experienced player, accustomed to success, can use his superior technical skill or his tactical powers to pressure the opposition into mistakes. Thus one of Lasker's most important qualities, though one virtually unmentioned in all the many commentaries on his style and results, was his ability to pace himself during a long tournament or match.

The game shown here is from the final round of St Petersburg 1909, and while not one of Lasker's best known games, it exemplifies his cool competence.

White: Em. Lasker. Black: R. Teichmann

Ruy Lopez (St Petersburg 1909)

1.	e4	e5
2.	Nf3	Nc6
3.	Bb5	a6
4.	Ba4	Nf6
5.	0-0	Be7
6.	Qe2	

This is the Worrall Attack, later a favourite of Keres but at the time an unknown system. It illustrates Lasker's unpretentious approach to the openings – he disliked sharp and double-edged lines and preferred to aim for a fluid position with possibly a small advantage in space or mobile pieces, so giving him a base for the middle game and ending where he excelled. His opponent Teichmann was an expert on the favourite lines of the time with 6. Re1 or 6. d3 and his over-eager counter-attack on move 14 suggests that he was trying to 'punish' Lasker for his novel but still perfectly sound move.

6.	...	b5
7.	Bb3	d6
8.	c3	0-0
9.	d4	exd4
10.	cxd4	Bg4

11.	Rd1	d5
12.	e5	Ne4
13.	Nc3	Nxc3
14.	bxc3	f6?

This is a serious mistake which enables Lasker to gain a great advantage in space and hamstring the bishop. Correct is 14. ... Na5 first.

15.	h3	Bh5

15. ... Bxf3 16. Qxf3 loses a pawn, while 15. ... Be6 fails to 16. exf6 Rxf6 17. Bg5 Rg6 18. Bc2.

16.	g4	Bf7

16. ... Bg6 17. Nh4 is also good for White.

17.	e6	Bg6
18.	Nh4	Na5
19.	Nxg6	hxg6
20.	Bc2	f5

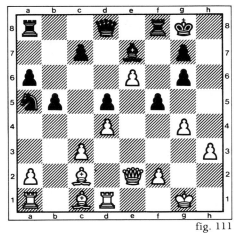

fig. 111

21. Kh1!

Lasker seizes on the winning idea of exchanging pawns on f5 and then attacking along the open g file.

21.	...	Bd6
22.	gxf5	Qh4
23.	Qf3	gxf5
24.	Rg1	

threatening both Bxf5 and Bg5.

24.	...	f4
25.	Rg4	Qh6
26.	e7!	Bxe7
27.	Bxf4	Qe6

and **Black resigned** without waiting for the finish 28. Rxg7+! Kxg7 29. Rg1+ and mates.

Lasker had an unequalled record in set matches, winning 19, drawing 2 and losing only to his successor as world champion Capablanca. This was partly due to his skill in choosing opponents, notoriously so in the period 1900–1914 when three times he took on the weaker Janowski who had a rich patron, while ducking the dangerous challengers Maroczy, Rubinstein and Capablanca. But the matches he did play showed his extraordinary skill in man-to-man combat, notably his 8–0 wins over Marshall and Janowski and his 6–0 victory over Blackburne.

Lasker was the first chess master to try seriously to establish the game as a profession; but ironically for a man who was a tough bargainer for high appearance fees, he was twice financially ruined, first by the inflation of the 1920s and then by the rise of the Nazis. Without these personal setbacks it is doubtful if he would have kept his career going for so long. In the late 1920s he began to take his mathematics studies seriously, received a doctorate for his work on abstract algebra, and was praised by Einstein; he dabbled in philosophy which he preferred to discuss rather than analyse chess.

In his simple approach to the openings Lasker established a model followed by some of his world title successors such as Capablanca, Petrosian and Karpov who also preferred a baseline approach in the early stages. We have already looked at his handling of the Ruy Lopez, and his treatment of the French Defence with White showed a preference for ideas like 1. e4 e6 2. d4 d5 3. Nc3 Bb4 4. Ne2 or 1. e4 e6 2. d4 d5 3. Nc3 Nf6 4. Bg5 Bb4 5. exd5 Qxd5 6. Bxf6 gxf6. One problem of such a non-bookish approach with the white pieces is how to meet the Sicilian Defence 1. e4 c5, the most double-edged and well analysed of all openings, but Lasker coped with that too in his later years. Playing the black pieces, he favoured simple rapid development with a minimum of pawn moves, as in the Lasker Defence to the Queen's Gambit 1. d4 d5 2. c4 e6 3. Nc3 Nf6 4. Bg5 Be7 5. e3 0-0 6. Nf3 h6 7. Bh4 Ne4, or as in this 'old-fashioned' defence to the Ruy Lopez which often served him well.

White: M. Porges. Black: Em. Lasker Ruy Lopez (Nuremberg 1896)

1.	e4	e5
2.	Nf3	Nc6
3.	Bb5	Nf6
4.	0-0	Nxe4
5.	d4	Be7

Modern theory prefers 5. ... Nd6 6. Bxc6 dxc6 7. dxe5 Nf5 8. Qxd8+ Kxd8 9. Nc3 h6 10. 0-0-0+ Ke8 when Black has good drawing chances despite his uncastled king.

6.	Qe2	Nd6
7.	Bxc6	bxc6
8.	dxe5	Nb7

Temporarily the knight is misplaced, but it can soon regroup via c5 to a good square at e6; while Black also intends to undermine the white centre by ... f6, opening up for his pair of bishops. Therefore White should now utilize his temporary development advantage by 9. Nc3 0-0 10. Nd4 Bc5 11. Rd1. The less forcing line in the game quickly concedes the initiative to Lasker.

9.	b3	0-0
10.	Bb2	d5
11.	exd6	cxd6
	e.p.	
12.	Nbd2	Re8
13.	Rfe1	Bd7
14.	Ne4?	

White should play 14. Qf1. By wasting time he allows Lasker an unchallenged pawn centre and the rest of the game is a model of how to use this type of advantage to create opportunities on both sides of the board.

    14. ...   **d5**
    15. N(4)d2

Both 15. Ng3 Bb4 and 15. Nc3 Ba3 win material for Black.

    15. ...   **Ba3**
    16. Be5   **f6**
    17. Qa6   **fxe5**
    18. Qxa3

18. Qxb7 allows e4 followed by Bb2.

    18. ...   **e4**
    19. Nd4   **Qf6!**

This is the key to the attack. White's queen is temporarily stranded far from the threatened K-side, so Black can now build up his attack rapidly. Note how the strong pawn at e4 deprives White of the normal defensive move Nf3.

    20. c3   **Rf8**
    21. f3

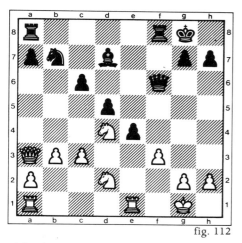

fig. 112

A further weakness, but if 21. Rf1 Qg5 22. Qc1 Bh3 wins rook for bishop.

    21. ...   **Qg5!**

Lasker handles this and the later attack most precisely. Now the d2 knight cannot move because of c5 followed by exf3, while if 22. Rad1 c5 23. Ne2 exf3 24. Nxf3 Rxf3.

    22. Qc1   **Nc5**
    23. Nf1   **Qg6**
    24. Re3   **Nd3**

This recalls Steinitz's motto that if you establish a knight at d3 or e3 the game wins itself – although it is not quite that simple. For the rest of the play Lasker's attack runs very smoothly.

    25. Qd1   **Nf4**
    26. Ng3   **h5**
    27. N4e2

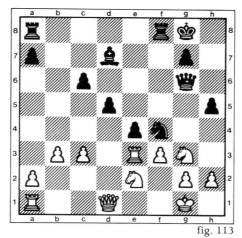

fig. 113

    27. ...   **Nxg2!**

A neat combination crowns Lasker's fine play and forces a mating finish.

    28. Kxg2   **exf3+**
    29. Rxf3   **Bh3+**
    30. Kxh3

or 30. Kf2 Bg4 31. Rxf8+ Rxf8+ 32. Ke3 h4 33. Nf1 Qe4+ 34. Kd2 Rf2 wins.

    30. ...   **Qg4+**
    31. Kg2   **Qxf3+**
    32. Kg1   **h4**
    33. Nh1   **Qe3+**
    34. Resigns

for if 34. Kg2 h3 mate.

Was Lasker the greatest chessplayer of them all as some commentators claim? Certainly – as is supported by Elo's historical ratings – he ranks in the top half-dozen world champions alongside Capablanca, Alekhine, Botvinnik, Fischer and probably Karpov. It is reasonable to suppose that the top grandmasters of today would be able to exploit Lasker's predictable opening repertoire more than did his contemporaries. Some of his wins from dubious positions would have been unlikely against players familiar with 'playing the man' and psychological chess. But his judgment of position and his analytical skill more than held their own against contemporary players in the 1930s; whether or not Lasker was the 'greatest' he ranks as the first of the moderns and as a supreme exponent of practical chess.

Harry Nelson Pillsbury 1872–1906

Pillsbury is one of the enigmas and might-have-beens of chess history. He won only one major first prize outright in his short career, but that was at Hastings 1895, the strongest event held up to his time. His feats of blindfold chess and memory are in a class of their own, and his best games including his last victory over Lasker have the stamp of a great artist.

Pillsbury learnt chess at Boston, Massachusetts late, at sixteen, which in our day would be considered a near-fatal obstacle to anyone's chances of becoming a strong grandmaster. But he developed rapidly and was only 22 when he scored his upset victory at Hastings ahead of Lasker, Steinitz, Tarrasch and Tchigorin.

In the following years Pillsbury was a consistently high international prize-winner without quite establishing himself as Lasker's natural challenger. He gained worldwide acclaim with his exhibitions of blindfold chess which included a then world record of 22 games at once. He gave blindfold performances of chess and draughts (checkers) while simultaneously taking part in a hand of whist.

Perhaps his most remarkable mental feat occurred when two professors gave him this list of words to memorize: Antiphlogistine, periosteum, takadiastase, plasmon, ambrosia, Threlkeld, streptococcus, staphylococcus, micrococcus, plasmodium, Mississippi, Freiheit, Philadelphia, Cincinnati, athletics, no war, Etchenberg, American, Russian, philosophy, Piet Potgelter's Rost, Salamagundi, Oomisellecootsi, Bangmanvate, Schlechter's Nek, Manzinyama, theosophy, catechism, and Madjesoomalops. Pillsbury looked at the list for a few minutes, repeated the words in the order given, and then in reverse order. He was able to recall the list the following day.

One of the chess curiosities of the late nineteenth century was the so-called 'automaton' AJEEB, a figure colourfully robed as a Moorish potentate which worked by levers and had in its interior a variety of gadgets and machinery which were supposed to enable it to play at master level. In fact a human expert was concealed in the interior and operated the levers. The trouble was that AJEEB's first owner and operator was a diminutive man who designed the machine to fit his own measurements. But he found it physically too tough a job – the air inside AJEEB's interior rapidly became stale and he became exhausted on hot summer days. Hence chess masters were engaged to sit inside AJEEB but they too found the physical conditions intolerable and there was a rapid turnover of staff.

Pillsbury took over the AJEEB assignment in 1890 and operated the machine, with breaks for international tournaments, till 1900, an incredible feat of endurance surpassing even his blindfold feats. But he was six foot tall and his muscles suffered badly in the machine's interior. It is said that Pillsbury drank up to a quart of whisky a day and that the alcohol relieved the physical pain. The challengers to AJEEB, and they were numerous, included the writer O. Henry, the actress Sarah Bernhardt and the baseball pitcher Christie Mathewson.

Many commentators and friends of Pillsbury believed that his blindfold and mnemonic feats took too much out of him and deprived him of his chances for the world title.

Pillsbury died at only 33, after a long illness. Maybe his drinking habits contributed, but the English grandmaster Blackburne (1841–1924), who was also a heavy whisky drinker, lived in good health to a ripe old age. It is also said that Pillsbury contracted a form of syphilis during the St Petersburg quadrangular of 1895–6 where at the half-way mark he led the four players with 6½ out of 9, including two wins over world champion Lasker, but collapsed in the second half where he scored only 1½ from 9 games. If Pillsbury's first-half results at St Petersburg are added to his score at Hastings, it is evident that he was of world championship stature at his peak. Like the other great American geniuses Morphy and Fischer, Pillsbury marred his own talent by not looking after himself.

Pillsbury was a deep and original player and his special system with the white pieces in the Queen's Gambit Declined can be effectively used by the club player of today. The basic concept is simple: White establishes his f3 knight at e5, supports it with f4, lines up his bishop on the b1-h7 diagonal, and then brings over queen and f1 rook to attack the black king. Until Pillsbury's time many grandmasters believed that a routine Queen's Gambit favoured Black

because of his majority of pawns on the queen's side. Dr Tarrasch, the leading theoretician of the time, held this view and when the new system defeated him at Hastings 1895 the effect of the Pillsbury Attack in chess was as revolutionary as the Fosbury Flop in the high jump. In this later game Pillsbury used his attack to win brilliantly.

White: H.N. Pillsbury. Black: S.R. Wolf

Queen's Gambit (Monte Carlo 1903)

1.	d4	d5
2.	c4	e6
3.	Nc3	Nf6
4.	Bg5	Be7
5.	e3	0-0
6.	Nf3	Nbd7
7.	Rc1	b6

As a result of Pillsbury, this move has been largely abandoned in favour of 7. . . . c6.

8.	cxd5	exd5

8. . . . Nxd5 loses a pawn to 9 Nxd5.

9.	Ne5	Bb7
10.	f4	a6
11.	Bd3	c5
12.	0-0	c4
13.	Bf5	b5
14.	Rf3!	

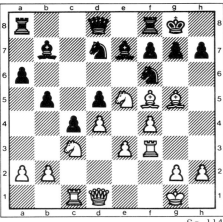

fig. 114

This is the key to the attack. White heads his pieces straight for the king's side to force weaknesses in the black defensive pawn front. For a modern refinement of this attack, see page 121.

14.	. . .	Re8
15.	Rh3	g6
16.	Bb1	Nxe5
17.	fxe5	Nd7
18.	Bxe7	Rxe7
19.	Qf3	Nf8
20.	Rf1	Qd7
21.	Qf6	b4?

White has a strong game, but Black could still defend with 21. . . . Re6. The weak pawn advance allows the knight to join the attack, for if 22. . . . Qxa4 23. Qxe7.

22.	Na4!	Qc7
23.	Nc5	Bc8
24.	Rh6	a5
25.	Rf4	Rb8

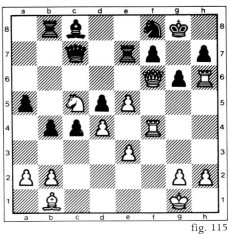

fig. 115

26. Bxg6!

The brilliant climax to Pillsbury's attack. Neither pawn can capture because of mate in one, while if 26. . . . Nxg6 27. Rxg6+ hxg6 28. Rh4 forces mate.

26.	. . .	Rb6
27.	Qxb6!	Nxg6
28.	Qf6	Re8

If 28. . . . Nxf4 29. exf4 followed by f5, Qg5+ and f6 with a mating attack.

29.	Rf1	Be6
30.	Qg5	Kh8
31.	Qh5	Nf8
32.	Nxe6	Rxe6
33.	Rxe6	Resigns

for if 33. . . . Nxe6 34. Rxf7.

Pillsbury's premature death makes it hard to assess his real standing in chess history. Elo gives him a rating for his best period of 2630, the equivalent of a world title candidate in present-day terms. More significantly, he had the best personal record against Lasker (5–5 with 4 draws) of any of the latter's rivals in the pre-1914 period, and his final victory, at Cambridge Springs 1904 when he was already a sick man, was one of his best, although the story often told about it and quoted below is patently untrue.

White: H.N. Pillsbury. Black: Em. Lasker

Queen's Gambit Declined (Cambridge Springs 1904)

1.	d4	d5
2.	c4	e6
3.	Nc3	Nf6
4.	Nf3	c5
5.	Bg5	cxd4
6.	Qxd4	Nc6
7.	Bxf6!	

In an earlier game Pillsbury–Lasker, St Petersburg 1895–6, Pillsbury played 7. Qh4?, castled long, and was crushed by a brilliant sacrificial attack. The story was that Pillsbury found 7.Bxf6 immediately after the St Petersburg game and patiently hoarded it for eight years until he got another chance to play it against Lasker. Unfortunately for this nice tale, there were three intervening games between the opponents where Pillsbury had White and didn't try to play his 'eight year move'. But certainly the knight capture is a big improvement: Black cannot allow 7. ... Nxd4 8. Bxd8 Nc2+ 9. Kd1 Nxa1 10. Bh4 when the a1 knight is trapped, and so has to allow the K-side to be permanently weakened.

7. ...	gxf6
8. Qh4	dxc4

8. ... d4 would be met by 9. 0-0-0.

9. Rd1	Bd7
10. e3	Ne5?

A further weakening of the pawn front, and perhaps one of Lasker's psychologically second-best moves which didn't come off. Better is 10. ... f5 11. Qxc4 Bg7 aiming to open lines for the pieces in compensation for the weakened pawn front.

11. Nxe5	fxe5
12. Qxc4	Qb6
13. Be2!	

sacrificing an unimportant pawn to bring all White's pieces into action against the black king.

13. ...	Qxb2
14. 0-0	Rc8
15. Qd3	Rc7
16. Ne4	Be7
17. Nd6+	Kf8

The king becomes a target on this square, as shown by White's moves 19–20; and yet there was nothing better. If 17. ... Bxd6 18. Qxd6 Qb6 19. Qxe5 0-0 20. Qg5+.

18. Nc4	Qb5

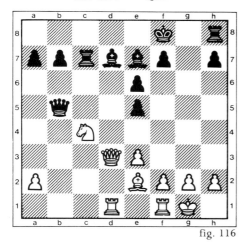

fig. 116

19. f4!	exf4
20. Qd4	

gaining a tempo to decisively strengthen the f file attack.

20. ...	f6
21. Qxf4	Qc5
22. Ne5	Be8
23. Ng4	f5
24. Qh6+	Kf7
25. Bc4!	Rc6

Not 25. ... Qxc4? 26. Ne5+.

26. Rxf5+!	

A clever sacrifice to wind up Pillsbury's convincing play. The point is not to win the queen for two rooks but to set up the position for White's queen and knight –

always a useful pair in attack – to combine for the final mate.

26. ...	Qxf5
27. Rf1	Qxf1+
28. Kxf1	Bd7
29. Qh5+	Kg8
30. Ne5	Resigns

José Raoul Capablanca 1888–1942

Capablanca was the finest natural chessplayer in the game's history. His genius in position play and subtle endgame skill inspired a legion of contemporaries and successors from Flohr and Smyslov to Fischer and Karpov. Uncharacteristically for chess, where compliments to rivals are often few and grudging, he gained full recognition from the other world champions who played and knew him. Euwe called him 'without peer in the endgame and in pure position play; as a tactician unsurpassable'; Botvinnik wrote that 'Capablanca was the greatest talent, he made the best impression on me of all the champions I have met'; Alekhine, though not on speaking terms with Capa for fifteen years, praised him as 'the greatest genius of chess. There will never be anyone to equal him'; while Lasker said 'I have known many chessplayers, but only one genius, Capablanca.'

Capablanca came first or second in 30 out of the 35 tournaments in which he played, and lost only 35 tournaments and match games out of a total 567 in his whole life. This included a period of eight years (1916–24) without a single defeat, while his overall loss ratio – around $5\frac{1}{2}$ per cent – was about half that of Lasker and Alekhine, and was matched in later times only by the peak periods of Fischer and Karpov.

Capa, as the chess world called him, was blessed by nature not only with extraordinary talent but with personal magnetism and charm. This made him a natural ambassador for Cuba, his native land, which appointed him a roving plenipotentiary to spread goodwill for his country through his chess exploits. Capa was brilliantly equipped for this function. He had an air of effortless superiority and confidence in his own genius, as well as being both elegant and handsome – an intellectual Valentino. Until Fischer came along half a century later Capa was the only chess grandmaster in the West whose name the public knew and would come to watch in large numbers. For decades he gave regular worldwide simultaneous tours, playing very fast and scoring high percentages even when the opposition was strong.

By chess standards, Capablanca was born with the proverbial silver spoon. He learnt the moves, self-taught, at four, and at twelve won a match with the champion of Havana. At eighteen, before playing a serious international event, he defeated the then US champion Marshall 8–1 in a match. On the strength of this result he was invited to the great international tournament at San Sebastian 1911. Dr

Capablanca 'the chess machine' at the zenith of his career, 1919. Unbeaten for several years, many rate him the greatest chess genius.

Bernstein, one of the established competitors, protested at the inclusion of this unknown and in storybook fashion Capa beat him brilliantly in the opening round.

Aiming to establish himself as Lasker's challenger, Capa then went on a whirlwind tour of Europe taking on leading masters in two-game mini-matches. He beat nearly all of them and the game shown here illustrates the Capa style of playing for the ending while being alert to every tactical chance.

White: J.R. Capablanca. Black: F. Dus-Chotimirsky

Ruy Lopez (St Petersburg 1913)

The opening was 1. e4 e5 2. Nf3 Nc6 3. Bb5 a6 4. Ba4 Nf6 5. 0-0 Be7 6. Re1 b5 7. Bb3 d6 8. c3 Na5 9. Bc2 c5 10. d4 Qc7 11. Nbd2 Nc6 12. Nf1

Modern theory prefers 12. h3 or 12. d5, avoiding the pin that follows.

12.	...	cxd4
13.	cxd4	Bg4
14.	d5	Nd4
15.	Bd3	0-0

15. ... Nh5! to play against the f4 square, would be good for Black. The openings were never Capa's strong point; he used to boast that he never read a chess book until he became a world title candidate.

16.	Be3	Rac8
17.	Bxd4	exd4
18.	a4	Qb6
19.	axb5	axb5
20.	h3	Bxf3
21.	Qxf3	Nd7
22.	Rec1	Nc5
23.	b4	Na4?

fig. 117

Aiming for the c3 square, Black overlooks Capa's tactical plan. Better was Nxd3 followed by Bf6.

24.	Rxc8	Rxc8
25.	e5!	

The point, gaining time for a king's side attack because if 25. ... dxe5 26. Qf5 attacking both the rook and the h7 pawn.

Average players should try to look out for such snap attacks whenever the opposing king position with unmoved pawns lacks a knight guard.

25.	...	g6
26.	e6	Rf8

or 26. ... fxe6 27. Qg4 threatening both Qxe6+ and Bxg6.

27.	Ng3	Qb7

Again if fxe6 28. Qg4, while f5 is met by 28. Bxf5! gxf5 29. Nxf5 with a winning attack.

28.	Nf5!	

Another fine move. If now gxf5 29. Qxf5, or if Kh8 29. Qe4.

28.	...	fxe6
29.	dxe6	Qc7
30.	Qc6!	

This is not just a flashy sacrifice (Qxc6? 31. Nxe7+ and 32. Nxc6). Capablanca is already planning ahead to the endgame and taking control of his e pawn's queening square.

30.	...	Qd8
31.	Nxe7+	Qxe7
32.	Bxb5	Nc3
33.	Qd7!	Qxd7
34.	Bxd7	Rb8
35.	e7	Kf7
36.	Re1	

36. e8=Q+ Rxe8 37. Bxe8+ Kxe8 38. Kf1 should also win, but the text is

Capablanca, left, and Lasker, Moscow 1925. Acclaimed as a hero in Russia Capa starred in the film Chess Fever *and may have played in the Kremlin.*

simpler. Black could resign now. The remaining moves were **36. . . . Re8 37. Bxe8+ Kxe8 38. Re6 d5 39. Kf1 Nb5 40. Ke2 Nc7 41. Re5 Na6 42. b5 Nb4 43. b6 d3+ 44. Kd2 Kd7 45. e8=Q+ Kd6 46. Qe7+ Kc6 47. Qxb4 Resigns.**

Lasker, sensing the risk to his title from this dangerous young rival, managed to avoid a match despite increasing public clamour for one until World War I temporarily ended chess activity. But when international play resumed the Havana Chess Club made a $20,000 offer which Lasker, impoverished by the war, accepted. He played the whole match listlessly and Capa became world champion by a margin of 4–0 with 10 draws in a series originally scheduled for 24 games.

Capablanca's easy success was followed by convincing victories at the big tournaments in London 1922 and New York 1927, while his challenger Alekhine was a distant runner-up in both events. Their title match at Buenos Aires lasted 34 games, the longest series in any world championship. At the end of it Alekhine was the surprise winner by 6–3 with 25 draws, Capa's legend of invincibility was tarnished, and the two men rapidly ceased to be on speaking terms. The conventional explanation for the result is that Capa, whose previous lifetime score against Alekhine was 8–0 with 7 draws, took his opponent too lightly, while Alekhine prepared with manic intensity. But in fact the match proved to be a mixture of dull, mostly short draws and decisive games marred by inaccuracies.

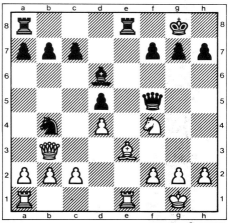

fig. 118

In the very first game Capa fell for a variation of the back row mate. Instead of 16. Nd3 Nxd3 17. Qxd3 when the endgame might be tenable despite doubled pawns, he played **16. Rac1?** overlooking **Nxc2 17. Rxc2 Qxf4!** winning a pawn because of 18. Bxf4 Rxe1 mate. Capa was never convinced by his defeat, and spent the rest of his life speaking of 'my title' and vainly arguing his right to a return. In 1936 he was first at Moscow and tied first at Nottingham, but could not re-establish his absolute supremacy of the

1920s. What he continued to show was his mastery and elegance of planning and his know-how in exchanging pieces. The most important lesson from Capablanca's games is the value of small advantages such as an active king, file control and superior pawn formation. The following game illustrates how to meet an opponent who tries to swap off all the pieces for an early draw.

White: E.D. Bogolyubov. Black: J.R. Capablanca

Queen's Indian Defence (Bad Kissingen 1928)

The opening moves were 1. d4 Nf6 2. c4 e6 3. Nf3 b6 4. Nc3 Bb7 5. Bg5 Be7 6. e3 Ne4 7. Bxe7 Qxe7 8. Nxe4 Bxe4 9. Nd2 Bb7 10. Be2 Qg5 11. Bf3 Bxf3 12. Qxf3 Nc6 13. Qg3 Qxg3 14. hxg3 Ke7.

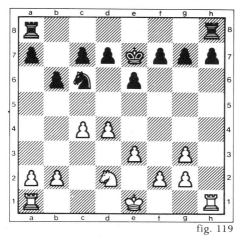

fig. 119

White's pacific intentions are clear, but he has fundamentally misunderstood the position. White's pawn centre, potentially valuable in the middle game, is here a target for a black pawn advance (a6 and b5) which will open lines of manoeuvre for the rooks and/or establish a knight outpost. Meanwhile White's own line-opening advance on the other wing by g4-g5 is easily stopped. Modern masters and strong players have learnt the techniques for such positions from Capa. Few today would diagnose fig. 119 as an easy draw.

15. g4	h6
16. a3	a6
17. Ke2	Rhb8!

preparing to meet 18. b4 by b5 19. c5 a5 opening up the a file with a useful outpost on a4. White chooses a different tack, but the result is only to switch Capa's target square to c4.

18. Ne4	b5
19. c5	d5!
20. cxd6	cxd6
	e.p.+
21. f4	Rc8
22. f5	

still trying to open lines for his own rooks, but Rhc1 was a better chance.

| 22. . . . | Na5 |
| 23. Kd3 | Nc4 |

| 24. Rab1 | d5 |
| 25. Nc3 | |

More obvious is 25. Nc5, but then e5! undermines the knight.

25. . . .	Rc6
26. fxe6	fxe6
27. g5	

Already a desperate measure: Black threatens both to double rooks on the c file and to attack the K-side pawns with Kf6-g5.

27. . . .	hxg5
28. Rh5	Kf6
29. Rh3	Rac8
30. Na2	a5
31. Rf3+	Kg6
32. g4	

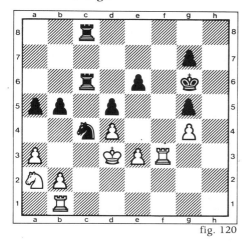

fig. 120

| 32. . . . | Nd6! |

A surprise resolution to the problem of finding a breakthrough method – for the rest of the game Black aims for mate. The immediate intention is Ne4, Rc2 and Rd2 mate.

33. Nc3	b4
34. axb4	axb4
35. Nd1	

or 35. Na2 Ne4 36. Nxb4 Rc4 37. Na2 Rc2 and wins.

35. . . .	Rc2
36. Rf2	b3
37. Ra1	Ne4
38. Re2	R8c6!

Putting White into near-zugzwang. If 39. Re1 Rd2 mate, or 39. Rxc2 Rxc2 mate, or 39. Nc3 Rxc3+.

| 39. Rb1 | e5! |

so that if 40. dxe5 R6c4 and Nc5 mate.

40. Ra1	R6c4
41. Ra5	Nc5+!
42. Resigns	

For if 42. dxc5 e4 mate – an attractively economical finish with such a small striking force.

Capablanca died in 1942 aged only 54 after a heart attack at the Manhattan Chess Club in New York. He is commemorated in his native Cuba by the annual Capablanca Memorial tournament, and his games will always be models for young players seeking to master the art of positional chess.

Alexander Alekhine *1892–1946*

Alekhine was one of the most original and tactically brilliant grandmasters of all time and, with the possible exception of Fischer, the most dedicated to chess. He had the hunger for achievement possessed by all great players. He spent five years preparing for his victory over Capablanca and his collections of his best games and book of the New York 1924 tournament are models of strategic appraisal and detailed, probing analysis. At the peak of his powers around 1930–34 he dominated his rivals and at San Remo 1930 and Bled 1931 finished respectively $3\frac{1}{2}$ and $5\frac{1}{2}$ points ahead of world class fields. His later years were clouded by excessive drinking and his wartime collaboration with the Nazis, but his legacy of beautiful games and his many contributions to chess theory make him one of the most interesting of the world champions.

Alekhine was born in Moscow of rich, aristocratic stock. His older brother Alexsei was also a chessplayer and, since boys were not allowed to attend chess clubs at that time, they developed their talent via postal chess. Alekhine was not a prodigy by the standards of Morphy or Capablanca but his game progressed rapidly during adolescence and by 15 he was winning matches with masters. By 1914, he was already third to Lasker and Capablanca in the great tournament at St Petersburg, but then came the war and revolution. He won the first Soviet championship in 1920 then left for the West and became a French citizen.

Alekhine is said to have been looking ahead to an eventual match with Capablanca even as early as 1914 and before Capa played Lasker. He won a series of big tournaments in the early and middle 1920s and gradually won attention, public acclaim and – most important – financial backing for a challenge to Capablanca. The charisma surrounding Alekhine came from his daring yet logical tactical play which was often based on exploiting his opponent's lagging development; his lucid and articulate annotations, and his driving personality were the perfect counterpoint to Capa's lazy elegance. He was particularly severe on the conventional strategists like Rubinstein and Tarrasch and this game is a typical win from his peak period.

White: A.K. Rubinstein. Black: Dr. A.A. Alekhine

Queen's Indian Defence (Semmering 1926)

1.	d4	Nf6
2.	c4	e6
3.	Nf3	b6
4.	g3	Bb7

5.	Bg2	Bb4+
6.	Nbd2	

Somewhat passive compared with 6. Bd2.

6.	. . .	0-0
7.	0-0	d5
8.	a3	Be7
9.	b4	c5

Typical Alekhine; when Black he liked a war of movement, opening up diagonals for bishops and creating chances against the white king. White's game is not yet inferior, but in sharpening the position Alekhine is also playing the man as well as the board. In his later years Rubinstein became liable to tactical oversights, and here more calculation is required than with a blocked pawn centre.

10.	bxc5	bxc5
11.	dxc5	Bxc5
12.	Bb2	

The bishop is exposed on this diagonal; an alternative is 12. Rb1 followed by Nb3, aiming to control d4 and c5.

12.	. . .	Nbd7
13.	Ne5	Nxe5
14.	Bxe5	Ng4
15.	Bc3	Rb8

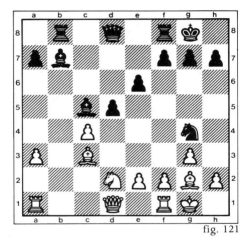

fig. 121

16. Rb1?

This routine move gives Alekhine the chance to switch the game into his beloved tactics. 16. cxd5! would still keep White well in contention, since Q or Bxd5 allows 17. e4 attacking the knight while 16. . . . exd5 17. Nb3 again gives black square counterplay.

16.	. . .	d4!
17.	Rxb7	Rxb7
18.	Bxb7	Nxf2!

This is the kind of tactical coup which gave Alekhine his reputation. The piece sacrifice is temporary and ensures Black the decisive advantage of a passed pawn on the seventh.

19.	Kxf2	dxc3+
20.	e3	cxd2
21.	Ke2	Qb8
22.	Bf3	Rd8
23.	Qb1	Qd6
24.	a4	f5
25.	Rd1	Bb4

26.	Qc2	Qc5
27.	Kf2	a5
28.	Be2	g5
29.	Bd3	f4!

Here **White overstepped the time limit**, but his position is resignable. A likely finish is 30. Bxh7+ Kh8 31. Qe4 Qxe3+ 32. Kg2 f3+ 33. Kh3 Qe2 34. Qg6 g4+ 35. Kh4 Be7+ 36. Kh5 Qxh2 mate.

After Alekhine won the world title from Capablanca his urge to dominate other players increased. Alekhine's peak was at San Remo 1930 where he scored 14 out of 15 yet still sweated for several hours in a heat-wave in the final round to win a rook ending a pawn up. At Bled 1931 his play was less convincing but he triumphed by $5\frac{1}{2}$ points and won this typical game against Flohr. The play seems to follow a positional course, but then comes a sudden tactical bolt from the blue which immediately decides the issue. Alekhine never specially sought such combinative traps but they occurred naturally as he increased pressure till the opposing defences broke.

White: Dr. A.A. Alekhine. Black: S. Flohr

Queen's Gambit Accepted (Bled 1931)

The opening moves were 1. d4 d5 2. c4 dxc4 3. Nf3 Nf6 4. e3 e6 5. Bxc4 c5 6. 0-0 Nc6 7. Qe2 a6 8. Rd1 b5 9. dxc5 Qc7 10. Bd3 Bxc5 11. a4 b4?

A positional error which gives White control of the useful b3 and c4 squares. Nowadays masters capture by 11. bxa4 to keep the pawn formation fluid rather than static.

12.	Nbd2	0-0
13.	Nb3	Be7
14.	e4	Nd7
15.	Be3	N7e5
16.	Nxe5	Nxe5
17.	Rac1	Qb8

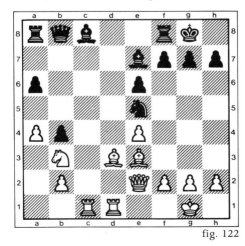

fig. 122

18. Bc5!

A standard manoeuvre to increase an advantage in a blocked position. The natural invasion points into the black camp are c7, c5 and a5, all dark squares; so White exchanges the piece which best guards these squares. There is also a good possibility of a further weakness: the black bishop at c8 is tied to the a pawn and to free that bishop Black may well have to advance the pawn to a5 where it becomes another dark square liability.

	18. ...	Bxc5
	19. Nxc5	Qb6
	20. Qh5	Nd7
	21. Be2	g6
	22. Qg5	Nxc5
	23. Rxc5	a5

An unwilling concession, but White threatened to split the Q-side pawns by a5.

24. h4

Another instructive feature of dark-square control; White intends h5-h6 to force g6 and consequent mate possibilities at g7.

	24. ...	Ba6
	25. Bf3	f6
	26. Qe3	Rad8
	27. Rxd8	Rxd8
	28. e5!	

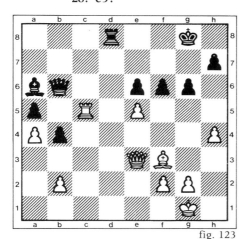

fig. 123

Apparently just further strengthening of the dark square control: if 28. .... fxe5 29. Qxe5 isolating Black's e pawn. But the move also sets an Alekhine trap.

	28. ...	f5??
	29. Rc8!	Resigns

Because d6 is no longer available to the black queen, Black loses at least a rook.

Alekhine's last great success in his peak period was at Zurich 1934, after which his results became more patchy. His drink problem became more acute, and affected his play and behaviour during his unexpected loss of the world title to Euwe in 1935. Shocked by defeat, he went into strict and abstemious training and regained the championship two years later.

He was still a difficult opponent for anyone. Botvinnik has described how, at Nottingham in 1936 when in complex positions, Alekhine would get up after making his move and start circling round and round the table like a kite. Playing Botvinnik, he kept up his kite imitation for twenty minutes while the latter fought inwardly to escape the psychological pressure. It was a vital game for both players, the first between the reigning Soviet champion and the White Russian emigré.

In his last years Alekhine was a leading participant in wartime Nazi tournaments and a series of anti-Semitic articles was published under his name. His play deteriorated further after 1943. When, in 1946, he accepted a title challenge from Botvinnik, few gave him any chance; but while preparing for the match, Alekhine died suddenly in Lisbon.

He played in 87 tournaments in his life, and won 62 of them – a record; after 1912 he was only once – at Nottingham 1936 – out of the top four in any event. If you like tactical chess and can also cope with strategy and positional play, Alekhine is an excellent chess hero.

Mikhail Botvinnik *1911–*

Botvinnik was the pioneer of the Russian domination of world chess which, the brief reign of Bobby Fischer apart, has lasted for most of the twentieth century. But, more important for the ordinary player, he was the first to treat chess as a science and a sport and to formulate a methodical training programme for competing in a major tournament.

This serious attitude to chess contrasted with Steinitz, who stuck to unsound openings after defeats, with Lasker and Capablanca, who rarely prepared for tournaments, and even with Alekhine, whose detailed planning for opponents was not matched by care for his own physical condition. The role of chess in Soviet society made Botvinnik's approach not only sensible for himself, a potential world champion, but for others. Lenin was a keen player, so was Krylenko, one of his lieutenants. Under their influence chess became an officially recognized Russian sport and masters had the opportunity to earn a state salary.

Botvinnik learned to play chess at twelve – late for a world champion. But at fourteen he beat Capablanca in a simultaneous and in 1927 he made his first appearance in the USSR championship. He graduated from Leningrad as an electrical engineer and kept up his scientific work even after winning the world title.

His big breakthrough came in the middle 1930s when he won two strong events at Moscow, then tied with Capablanca at Nottingham ahead of Alekhine, Lasker and other strong contenders. One of his first acts after this success was to put his name to a cable ghost-written by Krylenko thanking Stalin and the Soviet nation for their support. In the following years it became a prime goal of the USSR chess organization to secure for Botvinnik a chance at the world championship. When Alekhine died and left the title vacant, the World Chess Federation staged

Mikhail Botvinnik, first Soviet chess star. He twice regained the world title.

a match tournament from which Botvinnik emerged the clear victor over Smyslov, Keres, Reshevsky and Euwe.

Botvinnik was at his peak in the period before he won the world title, and during the limited chess activity of the war years and after. Although he kept the championship, with intermissions, from 1948 to 1963, he lost title matches to Smyslov and Tal before winning the return and only drew his 1951 series with Bronstein. After his 1963 defeat by Petrosian, and with the return match clause abolished, he abandoned title competition and gradually transferred his chess interests to two projects for the future: devising a successful chess computer program and discovering and teaching a future USSR world champion. The first project made only limited progress but the second was brilliantly successful. Both Anatoly Karpov and Gary Kasparov, who dominate chess in the 1980s, are pupils of Botvinnik.

Botvinnik's great strength as a player was his command of strategy, but it was not the clear-cut and endgame-orientated strategy of Capablanca. He liked complex positions with chances for both sides, relying on his ability in manoeuvre coupled with a sense of when to switch to endgames. Botvinnik was the specialist in the French Defence (1. e4 e6) and later the Caro-Kann (1. e4 c6) as Black, and in queen's side openings like the Nimzo-Indian (1. d4 Nf6 2. c4 e6 3. Nc3 Bb4) and Slav Defence Exchange (1. d4 d5 2. c4 c6 3. cxd5) as White. Two ideas often seen in his games are a sacrifice of rook for bishop or knight so as to create a mobile pawn centre and the effective use of a bishop at long distance in the late middle game after the exchange of several pieces. This last idea can be particularly useful for the average player.

White: M.M. Botvinnik. Black: O. Benkner

English Opening (Moscow 1956)

The opening moves were 1. c4 e5 2. g3 Nf6 3. Bg2 d5 4. cxd5 Nxd5 5. Nc3 Nb6 6. Nf3 Nc6 7. 0-0 Be7 8. a3 0-0?

Black's castling is premature; he should play 8. . . . a5 to stop White's Q-side pawn advance.

9.	b4	a6
10.	d3	Be6
11.	Ne4	h6?
12.	Bb2	f5?

Botvinnik writes that after Black's last two moves he is already lost because of the activity of White's b2 bishop on the long diagonal. Really Black misunderstood Botvinnik's strategy and thought that the e4 knight was heading for g5 rather than c5. In the next few moves Botvinnik makes sure of the pair of bishops and then masses his pieces in the centre ready for a decisive break with e4.

13.	Nc5	Bxc5

14.	bxc5	Nd7
15.	Rc1	Qe7
16.	Nh4	

threatening f4 to open up the centre and also attacking the g6 square which was weakened by 11. . . . h6.

16.	. . .	Qf7
17.	f4	exf4
18.	gxf4	Rad8
19.	Qe1	Bd5
20.	Bh3!	

Avoiding exchanges, and placing the bishop on a diagonal where its scope will gain immensely after the eventual e4.

20.	. . .	Ne7
21.	Qg3	g6

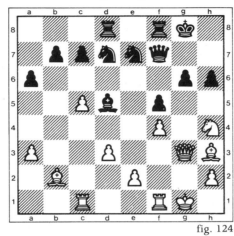

fig. 124

22.	e4!	

Botvinnik has prepared this advance admirably and now opens the game with decisive effect.

22.	. . .	fxe4
23.	dxe4	Bxe4
24.	Rce1	Qc4

Unfortunately for Black the natural 24. . . . Bd5 fails to 25. Rxe7 Qxe7 26. Qxg6+ followed by mate, but as played he loses two pieces for a rook and the white rook reaches the seventh rank with the deadly threat of Rg7+.

25.	Rxe4	Qxe4
26.	Re1	Qxf4
27.	Rxe7	Resigns

White: O. Neikirch. Black: M.M. Botvinnik

Sicilian Defence (Leipzig 1960)

The opening moves were 1. e4 c5 2. Nf3 Nc6 3. d4 cxd4 4. Nxd4 Nf6 5. Nc3 d6 6. Bc4 e6 7. Bb3 Be7 8. 0-0 0-0 9. Kh1.

The stronger move is 10. Be3. Botvinnik now chooses an economical method of starting counterplay, bringing his QN and QB into active positions with a minimum of pawn moves.

9.	. . .	Na5
10.	f4	b6
11.	e5	Ne8

It is dangerous to open up the position yet: if dxe5 12. fxe5 Nd7 13. Rxf7!

12.	Rf3	Nxb3
13.	Nc6	Qd7
14.	Nxe7+	Qxe7

15.	axb3	f6!

Botvinnik intends to bring the knight to d5 or f5 to support the long diagonal bishop. White should try to prevent this by 16. Qe2, because as played his own bishop is restricted by the f4 pawn.

16.	exd6?	Nxd6
17.	Rd3	Nf5
18.	Ra4	

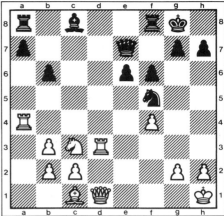

fig. 125

This is White's best chance – aiming to put R or N on e4 – but Botvinnik's next move continues his theme of white square play and makes sure that his bishop reaches its best diagonal.

18.	. . .	Qe8!

Mysterious at first sight, but quite logical. An immediate Bb7 would allow 19. Rd7.

19.	Ne4	b5
20.	Ra5?	

White still tries to attack, but here the rook proves fatally exposed. 20. Rb4 fails to a5, but he should try 20. Ra1.

20.	. . .	Bb7
21.	Nd6	

Or 21. Nc5 Bxg2+ 22. Kxg2 Qc6+.

21.	. . .	Nxd6
22.	Rxd6	Rd8!

threatening Qc6 and exposing White's back row.

23.	Qd2	Rxd6
24.	Qxd6	Qd8!

so that if 25. Qxd8 Rxd8 26. Be3 Rd1+ 27. Bg1 Rd2 wins.

25.	Qxe6+	Rf7
26.	Qe1	Re7!
27.	Resigns	

A pretty finish. Black's long-distance attack leaves White helpless, for if 27. Qg1 Qxa5, 27. Be3 Rxe3 or 27. Qd2 Rd7. The winner's powerful yet artistic play in this game is typical of Botvinnik at his best.

Samuel Reshevsky 1911–

Reshevsky, the greatest American player before the rise of Bobby Fischer, has established a record for chess longevity as a strong and active player which surpasses even Lasker. Born in Poland, he was touring Europe giving simultaneous displays at the age of eight and by the age of ten was already playing at the level of at least a national expert. 60 years later he is still a strong grand-master.

Reshevsky was the strongest Western player between 1945 and 1955 and his outstanding record in set matches would have given him a real chance against Botvinnik had he been able to challenge for the title. He was six times US champion and a regular high prize winner in the internationals of 1935–1960.

Reshevsky's special qualities as a player are his competitive resilience, his tactical skill, and his ability to survive time pressure. The three qualities go together. At the height of his career Reshevsky would get into severe clock trouble game after game and would then outplay his opponent even from dubious positions.

Reshevsky also became the world expert in utilizing the white side of symmetrical openings such as the English 1. c4 c5, as well as the small advantages from the Queen's Gambit Exchange Variation (1. d4 d5 2. c4 e6 3. Nc3 Nf6 4. Bg5 Nbd7 5. cxd5) and the Nimzo-Indian with 1. d4 Nf6 2. c4 e6 3. Nc3 Bb4 4. e3 c5 5. Ne2. He has been called the greatest player in boring positions and his technique of gradually grinding down an opponent after hours of patient manoeuvre has gained him disciples on the international circuit, e.g. Andersson and Hort.

In playing over the two Reshevsky games following, note how he is content to coast along with strategic play, aiming for a small advantage like the pair of bishops, and how quickly he switches to tactics when the chance comes.

White: S. Reshevsky. Black: J.H. Donner

Nimzo-Indian Defence (Santa Monica 1966)

The opening moves were 1. d4 Nf6 2. c4 e6 3. Nc3 Bb4 4. e3 c5 5. Bd3 d5 6. Nf3 0-0 7. 0-0 dxc4 8. Bxc4 Nbd7 9. Bd3 b6 10. a3 cxd4 11. exd4 Bxc3 12. bxc3 Bb7 13. Re1 Qc7 14. Bd2 Rfe8 15. Qe2 Rac8 16. Rac1 Bd5.

This is well-known opening strategy. Black has conceded the pair of bishops, and in return has play on the light squares and against White's hanging pawns at d4 and c4. Reshevsky probes his opponent's position and tries to gradually open the game for the bishops.

17. c4	Bb7
18. a4	Qc6
19. Bf4	Qxa4
20. Ra1	Qc6
21. Rxa7	Ra8
22. Rxa8	Rxa8
23. h3	

Reshevsky likes such waiting moves, tucking away an escape square for the king while Black decides how to commit himself.

| 23. ... | Ra3? |

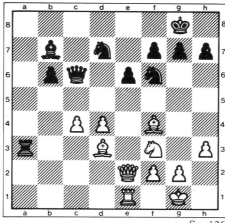
fig. 126

Donner ruefully commented later 'I would never have played this move if Reshevsky had not been in time trouble.'

24. d5!

Reshevsky's intuition in such positions is excellent. He had to see that the pawn sacrifice could be followed up by the bishop offer three moves later.

| 24. ... | exd5 |
| 25. cxd5 | Qxd5 |

or Nxd5 26. Bb5 Qe6 27. Qb2 winning material.

| 26. Bc4 | Qc5 |
| 27. Bxf7+! | Kxf7? |

Taken by surprise, Black misses the better defence Kh8!

| 28. Qe6+ | Kg6 |

not Kf8? 29. Bd6+

29. Bd6!

Every move is accurate despite having to be made within seconds. An immediate 29. Ne5+? Nxe5 30. Rxe5 would fail to Bc8.

| 29. ... | Qa5 |
| 30. Ne5+! | |

And here if 30. Nh4+? Kh5 31. Nf5 Black has Bxg2.

30. ...	Nxe5
31. Rxe5	Ra1+
32. Kh2	Qa8
33. Qf5+	Kf7
34. Re7+	Kg8
35. Be5	Re1
36. Rxg7+!	Resigns

White: A.J. Miles. Black: S. Reshevsky

Queen's Indian Defence (Lone Pine 1979)

The opening moves were 1. d4 Nf6 2. Nf3 b6 3. c4 e6 4. Bf4 Bb7 5. e3 Be7 6. h3 0-0 7. Nc3 d5 8. cxd5 Nxd5 9. Nxd5 Bxd5 10. Bd3 Bb4+ 11. Ke2 Bd6 12. Bxd6 cxd6 13. Qc2 h6.

The opening system with 4. Bf4 is a favourite with Miles – he has twice beaten Boris Spassky with it. Reshevsky counters by simple means, conceding White the edge in the centre but keeping open the chance of counterplay against the white king.

14. Rhc1 Bc6

If White could force an ending by Qc7, his centralized king would be an asset.

15. Qb3?

This underestimates Reshevsky's counterplay. More natural is 15. Be4, to swap bishops and/or force d5 fixing the central pawns and eliminating any danger to White's king.

15. ... Bb7

16. Rc3?

White could still recognize his error by 16. Qc2 encouraging Black to repeat moves.

16. ... Nd7

17. Rac1 e5!

Miles either underestimated this advance or missed Reshevsky's next move. Suddenly White's king in mid-board is a vulnerable target.

18. dxe5 Nc5!

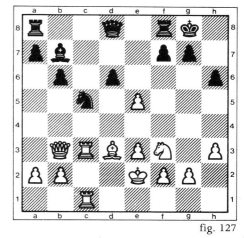
fig. 127

19. Qc2 dxe5

20. Bb5

Within a few moves, White's position has worsened from favourable to desperate. If 20. Nxe5 Qg5 followed by Qxg2 and White's king is wide open. If 20. e4 f5! again exposes the king further, while in any case Black threatens ... e4.

20. ...	a6
21. b4	axb5
22. bxc5	b4
23. Rb3	

If 23. Rc4 Ba6.

| 23. ... | bxc5 |
| 24. Qxc5? | |

blundering more material, but Reshevsky is a pawn up in the better position.

| 24. ... | Rc8 |
| 25. Resigns | |

If 25. Qxb4 Ba6+ Black wins a rook and soon mates.

Paul Keres *1916–75*

Born in Estonia, and becoming a Soviet citizen after that country was absorbed into the USSR, Keres was one of the unluckiest players in chess history in his attempts to win the world championship. From 1937 to 1965 he was always among the top three grandmasters yet the right to a title match continually narrowly eluded him. He won the Avro tournament 1938 ahead of Botvinnik, Alekhine and Capablanca, but the war put paid to the chance of a match with Alekhine. In the 1940s Keres found Botvinnik too good for him and in the candidates tournaments of the fifties and sixties he was runner-up four times consecutively. In 1959 he made a high score only to see Tal do still better and in 1962 a defeat right at the end put him behind Petrosian.

Keres was a fine chess stylist. A brilliant tactician in his younger years, he later developed an all-round game. His most trusted opening was 1. e4 and he won many elegant games with the Ruy Lopez as well as against the Sicilian and French Defence. Another of his specialities was in middle games with a central pawn majority against a queen's side pawn majority for the opponent, where Keres demonstrated the opportunities for a breakthrough on the d file or for a king's side attack.

White: P. Keres. Black: E. Geller Queen's Gambit, Semi-Tarrasch (match 1962)

The opening moves were **1. d4 Nf6 2. c4 e6 3. Nf3 d5 4. Nc3 c5 5. cxd5 Nxd5 6. e3 Nc6 7. Bc4 Nxc3 8. bxc3 Be7 9. 0-0 0-0 10. e4 b6 11. Bb2 Bb7 12. Qe2 Na5 13. Bd3 Rc8 14. Rad1 cxd4** (safer is Qc7) **15. cxd4.**

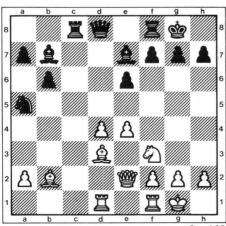

fig. 128

The lines of battle are drawn. White's bishops aim towards the black king, while Black hopes to gain play against the d pawn and along the c file. Geller's next move aims to exchange bishops by Bc3 and increase his chances to invade

the white camp with a rook, but White gets in first. The best move for Black is Bf6, aiming to entice e5 which would fix White's pawns.

15. . . .	**Bb4?**	
16. **d5!**	**exd5**	
17. **exd5**		

Now the bishop pair are a direct menace and White threatens to win a piece by 18. Qe4. If 17. . . . Bxd5 (Qxd5? 18. Bxh7+) 18. Qe5 f6 19. Qh5 h6 20. Qg6. If 17. . . . Re8 18. Ne5 again threatening Qh5, while if Geller continues his original plan by 17. . . . Bc3 then 18. Bxc3 Rxc3 19. Rfe1 and White controls both central files.

17. . . .	**Qe7**	
18. **Ne5**	**f6**	

18. . . . Bd6 would lose to a standard sacrifice: 19. Qh5 g6 20. Ng4! gxh5 21. Nh6 mate.

19. **Qh5**	**g6**	
20. **Nxg6!**	**hxg6**	
21. **Bxg6**	**Qg7**	

Keres' knight sacrifice has left the black king position in ruins with no time to organize a defence before White brings up decisive reinforcements. If 21. . . . Rc7 22. d6 Bxd6 23. Rd3 or 21. . . . Ba6 22. Bf5.

22. **Rd3**	**Bd6**	
23. **f4**	**Qh8**	
24. **Qg4**	**Bc5+**	
25. **Kh1**	**Rc7**	
26. **Bh7++!**		

so that if Kxh7 27. Rh3 mate.

26. . . .	**Kf7**	
27. **Qe6+**	**Kg7**	
28. **Rg3+**	**Resigns**	

White mates by 29. Qh3.

David Bronstein
1924–

Ukrainian-born Bronstein, one of the most creative and imaginative grandmasters, is a player whose style is difficult for experts, let alone lesser lights to copy. His games, like those of other great tacticians, show that all kinds of strange sacrifices and unusual positions are possible on the chessboard as long as a player keeps the initiative and control of events.

Bronstein nearly became world champion and would have done so with a little more steadiness and a little better endgame technique. Already recognized as one of the most promising younger Russians, he won the interzonal and candidates tournaments in 1948–50 to become Botvinnik's official challenger. Their title match took place in 1951 with Botvinnik completely out of practice after no tournaments since 1948, while his rival played incessantly not only in regular events but in blitz games in the Moscow clubs. After a fluctuating struggle, Bronstein was one up with two to play, but both his nerves and his endgame technique failed in the vital 23rd

out of 24 games. He and Schlechter (who drew with Lasker) are the only players to have challenged for the world title and tied the series.

Bronstein has had many tournament successes since 1951 without getting back to the very top. But his reputation rests more on his many remarkable games, which bear a special quality of genius. One of his pet openings was the King's Gambit 1. e4 e5 2. f4 which he adopted regularly despite criticism from Soviet colleagues (before the USSR v. USA match in 1946 Botvinnik warned him at the team meeting against playing this 'reckless' opening). Bronstein continued to play it, and his attractive collection of wins convinced others, notably Spassky, that the gambit should be rescued from its nineteenth-century museum.

White: D. Bronstein. Black: V. Panov

King's Gambit Declined (Moscow 1947)

The opening moves were 1. e4 e5 2. f4 Bc5 3. Nf3 d6 4. c3 Bg4? (known to be inferior to f5, Bb6 or Nf6, but Black wanted to avoid pre-analysed lines) 5. fxe5 dxe5 6. Qa4+! (releasing the pin without loss of time) Bd7 (not Qd7 7. Bb5 c6 8. Nxe5) 7. Qc2 Nc6 8. b4 Bd6 9. Bc4 Nf6 10. d3 Qe7 11. 0-0.

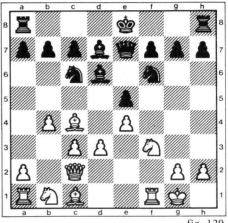

fig. 129

The attention which strong players give to opening analysis is often misunderstood. Here, after only eleven moves, Black is already in a dilemma because of his choice of an inferior line. If 11. . . . 0-0, then the pin 12. Bg5 is strong and cannot be relieved by 12. . . . h6 13. Bh4 g5 because of the sacrifice (which is often possible when the defender's dark-square bishop is not at e7 or g7) 14. Nxg5 hxg5 15. Bxg5. Castling long runs into a pawn storm as in the game, while 11. . . . h6 (to prepare short castling) is powerfully met by 12. Nh4.

11. . . .	**0-0-0**	
12. **a4**	**a5**	

Already weakening the pawns in front of the king, but otherwise White's attack makes rapid progress by a5 and b5.

13.	b5	Nb8
14.	Nbd2	Bg4
15.	Nb3	b6
16.	Be3	Nbd7
17.	Rae1	Be6
18.	Bxe6	Qxe6
19.	Kh1	

to keep the bishop on its best diagonal after Black plays Ng4.

19.	...	Qe7
20.	Nbd2	Ng4
21.	Bg1	h5
22.	Nc4	g5

Slightly better was h4-h3, to try and create a potential mate at g2. Now Bronstein breaks through by force.

23.	Nxd6+	cxd6
24.	Nd2	f6
25.	Nc4	Kb7
26.	Bxb6!	

This is the decisive sacrifice, which restores the mobility of White's pawn roller which Black temporarily stemmed at move 12.

26.	...	Nxb6
27.	Nxa5+	Kc7
28.	Nc6	Qe8
29.	a5	Nd7

Petrosian, left and Bronstein train with five-minute chess for the 1970 USSR v World Match. In blitz, the clocks are set five or ten minutes to the hour and the flagfall decides.

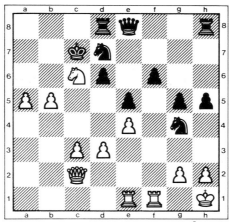

fig. 130

30. b6+! Kb7
A striking illustration of the power of a pawn roller against a bare king. If 30. ... Kxc6 31. Qa4+ Kb7 32. a6+ Kb8 33. Qc6 forces mate.
31. a6+! Kxb6
If Kxa6 32. Qa4+ Kb7 33. Qa7+ Kxc6 34. Qc7+ and mates. If Kxc6 32. Qa4+ Kxb6 33. Rb1+ Ka7 34. Qc6 Nc5 35. Rb7+ Ka8 36. Rd7+ Kb8 37. Qc7+ Ka8 38. Qa7 mate.
32. Rb1+
Black lost on time, but he could just as well have resigned. If Kc7 33. Rb7+ Kc8 34. Na7 mate.

Tigran Petrosian
1929–1984

Petrosian, an Armenian and world champion from 1963 to 1969, has often had a bad press from chess critics. He has been denounced as lacking fighting spirit, of making too many short draws, and of preferring a negative, defensive style. But no-one becomes world champion without great talent and skill, and Petrosian's chess has some highly instructive elements for average players.

Although a talented young player in his teens, he was no prodigy and rose to the top slowly and steadily. From the age of 24 he was a regular competitor in the world championship candidates but it was not until 1962 that he nosed into first place just in front of Keres and Geller. He reached a world title match in 1963 just as the years were catching up with Botvinnik, then aged 51, and Petrosian's patient strategy and better stamina proved decisive in the second half of the series.

Petrosian models his chess style on the tradition of Capablanca and Nimzovitch. The emphasis is on manoeuvre, on slow build-ups to control key squares, and on transition to marginally favourable endgames. He is accurate in calculation, and

likes simple positions where there are few or no accidental and random factors. He prefers to sacrifice for a clear-cut win rather than as a speculation like Tal or Bronstein. Rather than commit himself to a premature attack he will opt for a quiet spatial advantage where he can gradually squeeze his opponent's position until the decisive break can be made without risk.

This is a pragmatic, professional style, and it is notable that Petrosian was the first Soviet grandmaster to criticize the official ethic of the 'Soviet school' which claimed to prefer fighting, daring chess. He proved the value of his own approach when he defeated Spassky in the title match of 1966 though losing to the same opponent three years later. But the draw-back of Petrosian's style is that it tends to earn high places in tournaments rather than outright first prizes. In the opening and middle game he sometimes seems purely negative and spoiling, doing nothing and doing it well until his opponent loses patience and weakens his position.

The most useful aspects of Petrosian's chess for the ordinary player to follow are his constriction games, where the opponent's piece activity is gradually weakened and throttled, and his favourite endgame where a rook and an active knight triumph over a rook and a bishop made passive by its own pawns.

First, an example of constriction technique – a refined version of Nimzovitch's 'prophylaxis'. Petrosian's special treatment of blocked positions includes alternating and switching the attack between the wings, together with delayed castling. 'Castle if you will and if you must, but not just if you can' is good chess advice. Petrosian's logic is that in blocked positions the action and opening of lines – which spells danger for a king – takes place on the flanks. Therefore the usual procedure, where the king seeks safety away from the centre, is reversed. In this game, Petrosian castles only after the king's side is also blocked – and by then his forces are pouring into the enemy position on the other side of the board.

White: T. Petrosian. Black: J. Barendregt
Benoni Defence (Beverwijk 1960)
The opening moves were 1. c4 g6 2. d4 Bg7 3. Nc3 d6 4. e4 c5 5. d5 e5 6. Be2 Nh6 (Nf6 allows a favourite Petrosian opening system 7. Nf3 0-0 8. Bg5 h6 9. Bh4 g5 10. Bg3 when Black's many pawns on dark squares allow White's knights excellent play on light squares especially f5)

7. h4!
This is not really an attacking move, but a scheme to provoke weaknesses. If Black castles, 8. h5 is unpleasant, so Black tries for active play by pawn advances which leave gaps for Petrosian's knights.

7. ... f5

8. Bg5	Qb6
9. Rb1	Nf7
10. Bd2	

Retreating the bishop, but setting up another threat – a3 and b4. Black stops this at the price of more holes in his pawn front.

| 10. ... | a5 |
| 11. Nf3 | h6 |

Now Black hopes for f4 and g5 – Petrosian counters by a stopper move.

12. g3	Na6
13. a3	Qd8
14. Qc2	

threatening 15. h5 undermining the K-side pawns, and so provoking yet another weakness.

| 14. ... | h5 |
| 15. exf5 | gxf5 |

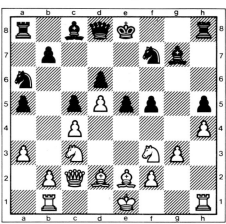
fig. 131

In a similar position, the British master Hugh Alexander once captured with the bishop and his opponent Botvinnik sank in a knight at e4 and made use of it to dominate the whole board. Bronstein made a comment afterwards that has gone down in chess lore: 'Every Russian schoolboy knows you have to capture with the pawn in such positions.' But here Black's game is so full of holes that the Petrosian knights now have a field day exploiting the weaknesses.

16. Ng5!	Qf6
17. Na4!	f4
18. Nb6	Bf5
19. Bd3	Bxd3
20. Qxd3	Rb8
21. Ne4	

Petrosian has achieved his main strategic objective. The exchange of white squared bishops has given his knight absolute control of the e4 square. White is now about to win a pawn, but more significant is the contrast between the active positions of the white knights and bishop and the hopeless lack of scope of Black's g7 bishop confronted by a wall of its own pawns on dark squares. This 'knight against bad bishop' theme is one of the most reliable winning methods in strategic chess.

| 21. ... | Qd8 |

| 22. Bxa5 | 0-0 |
| 23. Qd1! | f3 |

Loss of the h pawn would spell the rapid collapse of Black's pawn. But now the K-side is blocked and Petrosian can at last plan to castle.

24. b4	Nh6
25. Rb3	Ng4
26. 0-0	Bf6

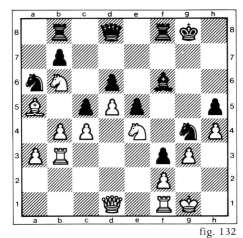
fig. 132

27. Qxf3!
Black was hoping to play Bxh4 and if gxh4 Qxh4 with mate at h2. Petrosian's neat counter-idea is 27. ... Bxh4 28. Qh1! Be7 29. Qxh5 Nf6 30. Qg6+ Kh8 31. Kg2 and it is Black who gets mated by Rh1.

27. ...	Qe7
28. Qf5	Rf7
29. Qxh5	Rg7
30. f3	

trapping the knight ...

30. ...	Bxh4
31. fxg4	Rh7
32. Qf5	

... and the bishop ...

| 32. ... | Resigns |

This is a good example of how a correct strategic approach can cause the quick collapse of the opposing position once the game is opened up.

Petrosian's skill in immobilizing his opponent's bishops is reflected in his choice of openings. The note to move 6 in the last game mentioned the 'Petrosian system' against the King's Indian, and he also favours openings such as the Sicilian Defence 1. e4 c5 and the English Opening 1. c4 where knight v. bishop situations often occur.

Petrosian's endgame target is often a rook and an active knight against rook and passive bishop. His techniques for exploiting it are to drive enemy pawns on one flank into a rigid, immobile formation on the same colour as the bishop on that side of the board. This usually means that as White he tries to lure Black's K-side pawns to dark squares and the Q-side pawns to light squares. He avoids giving the opponent any chance to exchange the handicapped bishop, but swaps off other pieces, especially the active bishop which is not restricted by the pawn chain. If all this is successful, Petrosian's king and knight can infiltrate the opposing position via squares of the opposite colour to the handicapped bishop.

All this may sound complex, but Petrosian's games often show the winning process to be almost automatic. Here is a classic example:

White: T. Petrosian. Black: S. Schweber

King's Indian Defence (Stockholm 1962)

The opening moves were 1. d4 Nf6 2. c4 g6 3. Nc3 Bg7 4. e4 d6 5. Be2 0-0 6. Bg5 h6 7. Be3 e5 8. d5 c6 9. h4 cxd5 10. cxd5 Nbd7 11. h5.
Petrosian's scheme is to entice the opponent to advance the K-side pawns and so create holes and limit the g7 bishop. Thus 6. Bg5 provokes h6 and g5 and when Black is reluctant to play the latter move then h4-h5 is an additional inducement to Black to advance his g pawn. Black's

Petrosian studies game analysis at home. When he became champion, Armenian fans invaded the Moscow stage and showered him with bouquets.

game is already difficult but he should now play Kh7 rather than weaken his pawns further.

11. ...	g5?
12. f3	a6
13. g4	b5

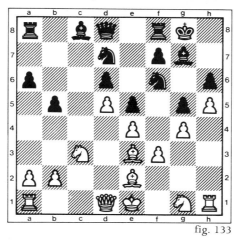

fig. 133

Now the V-chain of white pawns deprives Black of all serious counterplay, while White can prepare at leisure both to attack on the Q-side and to occupy the strong outpost square f5 with a knight.

I happened to be present at the Stockholm interzonal when this game was played and recall Petrosian's world-weary expression which mixed apparent contempt for his opponent's poor strategy with a sense that the game was pure routine. Petrosian often looks like that when he's winning.

14. a4
undermining the Q-side pawns and aiming to create white square outposts at c4 and b5. There is also a long-term thought for the endgame: if the position is simplified there may be queening possibilities with the advanced a and h pawns.

14. ...	b4
15. Nb1	a5
16. Nd2	Nc5
17. Bxc5!	

White exchanges his 'good' bishop (the one not restricted by his pawn chain) because he gets an additional Q-side weakness to attack and a potentially valuable passed d pawn.

17. ...	dxc5
18. Bb5	Bb7
19. Ne2	Ne8
20. Bxe8!	

Now the position is very blocked, and White has two bishops against two knights, the Petrosian endgame in its most favourable form. If White did not exchange, the black knight would reach the good blockading square d6.

20. ...	Rxe8
21. Nc4	Ba6
22. Qb3	Qf6
23. Rc1	Bf8
24. Ng3	

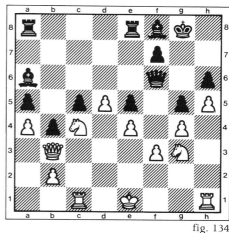

fig. 134

| 24. ... | Bc8 |

An admission of defeat. If 24. ... Bxc4 25. Rxc4 Bd6 White would break through systematically but surely as follows: (a) placing the knight on f5 and the king on e2 (b) placing the rooks on c2 and c1, the queen on d3 and the pawn on b3 and (c) advancing into the black camp by Qa6 or Qb5.

25. 0-0
Again late castling, as in the previous game.

25. ...	Rd8
26. Kg2	Ra7
27. Rf2	Kh7
28. R2c2	Qa6

Black is hamstrung and gives up the e pawn in a vain attempt to give his g7 bishop some freedom.

29. Nxe5	Rc7
30. Nc4	Bg7
31. Qd3	Kg8
32. Rd2	Re7
33. e5!	

returning the pawn to reach a winning endgame.

33. ...	Bxe5
34. Nxe5	Rxe5
35. Qxa6	Bxa6
36. Rxc5	Bc8

If Bb7 37. Nf5 Kh7 38. Rxa5 Rdxd5 39. R5xd5 Rxd5 40. Rxd5 Bxd5 41. a5 and the passed a pawn will win Black's bishop. This is a good example of Petrosian's long-term thinking (see the note to move 14). Petrosian thinks in constellations and long-term planning rather than individual moves; I have seen him during a post-mortem analyse an ending by moving his king straight from g1 to b8 – the intervening technical process of getting it there he considered pure routine.

37. Rxa5	f5
38. gxf5	Bxf5
39. Nxf5	Rxf5
40. Rb5	Rdf8
41. d6	Rxb5

If Rxf3 42. d7 wins a rook.

| 42. axb5 | Kf7 |
| 43. d7 | Resigns |

for if Rd8 44. b6 Ke7 45. b7 b3 46. Kg3 is zugzwang.

Viktor Korchnoi

1931–

Viktor Korchnoi captured the imagination of chess fans everywhere, and of many non-players besides, when, following his defection from the Soviet Union in 1976 and his publication of his insider's autobiography *Chess is My Life* (Batsford), he succeeded against all the odds at the age of 46 in becoming the world title challenger and in recovering against Karpov from 2–5 down to within one game of the championship.

Korchnoi is a man of great physical strength and nervous energy – you have to be to reach your peak at an age when most chess masters are settling for a lessened activity prior to retirement. But Korchnoi's talent, though marked even in his teens, took many years to reach full maturity.

It was 1954, at 23, before he won his first major tournament at Bucharest; and 1962, at 31, before he first reached the world title candidates. His breakthrough to the very top came in 1973–75 when he reached the candidates final against Karpov. Soviet officials clearly favoured the younger man and Korchnoi, an individualist increasingly frustrated by the mores of Soviet society, took the drastic step of leaving for the West.

The change in his lifestyle restored his energies, which he channelled into a burning desire to prove himself against his enemies in the USSR by taking the title. In the candidates matches of 1977 he defeated Petrosian, Polugaevsky and Spassky in impressive style and was within one game of beating Karpov for the world championship.

Korchnoi's acknowledged chess hero is Emanuel Lasker which makes his play full of dynamic movement and resourcefulness in difficult positions. This is not a style with which the ordinary player can cope easily and indeed many fellow-grandmasters admit they find Korchnoi's thought processes difficult to fathom. But one theme which is typically Korchnoi and which can be learnt from study of his games is his ability to combine the queen with minor pieces in an all-court attack. A good example of this Korchnoi approach is an unusual gambit opening which puts the opponent under sustained pressure and eventually cracks the defences.

White: V. Korchnoi. Black: M. Udovcic

French Defence (Leningrad 1967)

The opening moves were **1. d4 e6 2. e4 d5 3. Nd2 Nf6 4. e5 Nfd7 5. c3 c5 6. Ngf3** (normal is 6. Bd3; the text already has the pawn sacrifice in mind) **Nc6 7. Bd3 Qb6 8. 0-0 cxd4 9. cxd4 Nxd4 10. Nxd4 Qxd4 11. Nf3 Qb6 12. Qa4 Qb4 13. Qc2 h6?**

Best are Qc5 when White would continue in gambit style with 14. Qe2, or Nc5 (see page 94).

 14. Bd2 Qb6
 15. Rac1 Be7
 16. Qa4!

Now White is well on top, with the immediate threat of 17. Ba5 Qxb2 18. Bb5.

 16. ... Qd8
 17. Rc2 Kf8

A major concession; Black abandons castling. If instead 0-0 18. Qg4 f5 19. Qg6 with a powerful attack.

 18. Rfc1 Nb6
 19. Qg4 Bd7
 20. Ba5 Rc8
 21. Rxc8 Bxc8
 22. Bb4

In any gambit opening where the return is not immediate, the gambiteer has to keep up the pressure lest his opponent gradually consolidate the extra pawn. Here Korchnoi plans to cramp his opponent further by a4-a5 and also has some tactical ideas to keep the black king in the centre. He could also attack by h4-h5, and either way it is difficult for Black to counter the simultaneous pressure from both flanks.

 22. ... g6
 23. Qh4!

forcing another weakness; if Black could post his K at g7 and bring his h8 rook into play, he would be out of danger. But now the threat is 24. Bxg6.

 23. ... g5

Desperate measures, but the natural Bd7 is met by 24. Qf6 Rg8 25. Rc7 Qxc7 26. Qxe7+ Kg7 27. Qf6+ Kh7 28. Qxf7+ and wins.

 24. Nxg5

This takes advantage of the pin on the bishop. Black's last chance now to avoid losing by direct attack is Kg8 25. Bxe7 Qxe7 26. Nf3 although White then has a clearly superior ending – his bishop is more active than Black's and his rook threatens to reach the seventh rank.

 24. ... Ke8

fig. 135

 25. Bb5+

Starting a brilliant tactical finish – but the point for the average player to note is how all the white pieces combine with the queen in the attack and especially how the black king is caught in the crossfire from the bishops.

 25. ... Bd7
 26. Nxe6! fxe6

26. ... Bxh4 fails to 27. Ng7 mate, and Bxb5 to 27. Ng7+ Kf8 28. Nf5.

 27. Qh5+ Kf8
 28. Rc3!

Bringing the rook into action via the third rank is often a good device for finally breaking the defences of an exposed king. Black's best practical chance now is 28. ... Be8 but then 29. Bxe8 Qxe8 30. Qh4 (intending Qf6+, Rf3+ or Rc7) is a sure win.

 28. ... Rh7
 29. Qg6 Rg7
 30. Qxh6 Bxb5

Little better is Kg8 31. Rh3 Kf7 32. Qh5+.

 31. Rg3! Resigns

Korchnoi, left, and Karpov, final candidates match, Moscow 1974, watched by thousands of spectators. Korchnoi lost 3–2 with 19 draws; he later claimed Soviet officials arranged conditions to favour younger Karpov. When they met for world title in 1978, Karpov won 6–5 with 21 draws. A Soviet parapsychologist staring at Korchnoi caused new controversy.

Bent Larsen 1935–

Larsen, of Denmark, has been one of Europe's leading players for many years, and a regular though unlucky contender for the world championship. He has an unjustified reputation as a poor match player, caused mainly by well-known defeats by Spassky, who beat him heavily, and Fischer, who wiped him out 6–0.

Larsen frequently uses unconventional openings, not just for their surprise value, but because he believes they are basically sound and underestimated by other grandmasters. Thus he has revived or popularized the Bird Opening 1. f4, the Bishop's Opening 1. e4 e5 2. Bc4 and also what is now widely termed the Larsen Opening 1. b3.

Larsen's greatest strength is in the middle game and in his inventive approach which enables him to play aggressively for the win. He has said that he dislikes the standard professional tactic of playing for a win with White, a draw with Black; he doesn't mind the occasional loss if his draw percentage is lower than other contenders. There are more flank attacks in his games than in those of most grandmasters, and this is deliberate: the flank attack is less likely to lead to simplification and a draw; if it fails, there is time to regroup. But 'flank attacks' in Larsen games refer not to a crude pawn rush, but normally to combined operations with the heavy pieces. One of his favourite piece combinations is queen, knight and h pawn attacking a castled king; another is queen, rook, and a long-distance bishop.

White: S. Gligoric. Black: B. Larsen Nimzo-Indian Defence (Havana 1967)
The opening moves were 1. d4 Nf6 2. c4 e6 3. Nc3 Bb4 4. e3 b6 5. Bd3 Bb7 6. Nf3 Ne4 7. 0-0 f5 8. Bxe4? This obvious move is the cause of White's later troubles. Black's e4 pawn will not be so weak as it looks. Better is 8. Qc2.

8.	....	fxe4
9.	Nd2	Bxc3
10.	bxc3	0-0
11.	Qg4	Rf5!

The point, which Larsen had prepared before the game. Now if 12. Nxe4 h5, so White has to open up the centre to the benefit of Larsen's long diagonal bishop.

12.	d5	Rg5
13.	Qf4	exd5
14.	cxd5	Bxd5
15.	c4	Bc6

This is better than Bb7 because it allows the bishop and d pawn to protect each other while the knight comes into action at a6. Mutually protecting units on the chessboard spell good co-ordination.

16.	Nxe4	Rg6
17.	Bb2	Na6

Now White's Q-side pawns are split, while Black has chances of K-side attack.

It's not yet a winning position – White should defend by 18. Ng3.

18.	f3?	Nb4!

Eyeing the f pawn as much as the d3 square – for instance if 19. Rfd1 or Nf2 then Qe7 is strong.

19.	Bc3	Nd3

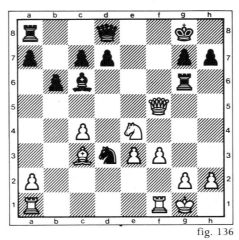

fig. 136

20.	Qf5	Qh4!

Before playing the queen here rather than the safe square e7 Larsen already foresaw the rook sacrifice at move 25 which decides the game. Without that resource, White's following play would weaken the black pawns and move his own king into safety.

21.	Nf6+	

21. Rad1 Nc5! 22. Nxc5 Rf8! also gives Black a decisive attack. Note how well Black's queen, rooks, and bishop combine against the white king – a trademark of Larsen's style at its best.

21.	....	gxf6
22.	Qxd3	Rh6

to stop White consolidating with Be1-g3.

23.	h3	Kf7

making room for the other rook. White's best chance now is the endgame 24. Qd4 Qxd4 25. exd4 but after Rh5! followed by Bb7-a6 his Q-side pawn on white squares are weak and Black has chances of making use of his own 4–3 pawn majority on that side. White of course has a 3–2 majority on the K-side, but it is the majority distant from the kings which carries most weight.

24.	Rf2?	Rg8
25.	Kf1	

trying to run to the Q-side.

25.	....	Rxg2!

the point, which White saw too late.

26.	Rxg2	Qxh3

Now White cannot stop all the three threats of Qxf3+, Bxf3 and Rg6. Originally White had planned to defend by 27. Kg1 but missed that after 27. .... Bxf3 the white Q defends the d7 pawn. It is worth noting for avoiding or inducing blunders that long diagonal moves backwards are among the hardest to visualize.

27.	e4	Rg6
28.	Resigns	

If 28. Qe2 Qh1+ wins.

Mikhail Tal 1936–

World champion 1960–61, the Latvian Mikhail Tal is regarded by many connoisseurs of chess as one of the most brilliant tactical geniuses in the game's history, Tal has remarkable powers of calculation, memory, and visualizing unusual positions. When he was a child of seven, he went to a lecture given by his father, a medical school professor, and repeated the lesson almost word-for-word when he got home that evening. Tal reached the world championship with a dazzling record of success: taking the USSR title in 1957 and 1958, he went on immediately to win the interzonal tournament, the Candidates, and the world title from Botvinnik. It was not only his results but his dashing style which captured public imagination, and his defeat by Botvinnik in their return match in 1961 caused a sense of shock. Only later was it revealed that Tal had played the match only a few weeks after coming out of hospital – a chronic kidney ailment has troubled him all through his playing career and prevented a longer reign at the very top.

Tal's appetite for chess exceeds that of any other grandmaster. He participates in post-mortems, reports for newspapers, annotates his games, and in between rounds and tournaments plays blitz chess at five minutes per game. He has been called the Paganini of chess, and his reputation for winning from even poor positions, plus his hypnotic stare at opponents, caused the American grandmaster Benko to don dark glasses before meeting Tal in a candidates tournament.

Tal's brilliant flair for combination can hardly be learnt by a strong master, let alone an average player. But there are some important lessons from his play: first, plunging the game into obscure complications will unsettle most opponents and a sacrificial attack in such conditions may work even if not objectively sound; second, as with Alekhine, a competitive will to win is of great importance; and third, practice and testing of variations in quick chess, frowned on by some experts, is a practical and rewarding method of training for bigger events.

The Tal game here ends with fireworks and sacrifices but is not one of his best known. I choose it because the type of attack – a breakthrough on the king's side against a half-open defence (1. .... c6 or 1. .... e6) is relatively easy to play and a case where the student can model his game on an attacking genius.

White: M. Tal. Black: B. Gurgenidze Caro-Kann Defence (USSR championship 1968–69)

1.	e4	c6
2.	d4	d5
3.	Nc3	b5

Petrosian watches Tal at Alekhine Memorial, Moscow 1971.

Unusual and inferior. The temporary threat to dislodge the white knight is easily stopped and the strategic result is too many black pawns on light squares.

    4. a3   dxe4
    5. Nxe4 Bf5

Logical, to exchange the potential 'bad bishop'.

    6. Bd3!

This type of gambit often occurs in similar positions. If 6. ... Qxd4 7. Nf3 and 8. Qe2 with good play for the pawn. Psychologically, Black's choice of a cautious defence like 1. ... c6 means he is unlikely to accept the gambit anyway, and the net result is White obtains a smoother development of his pieces than in more orthodox lines.

    6. ...   Bxe4
    7. Bxe4 Nf6
    8. Bd3   e6

White still offers the pawn and Black ignores it. But it is already difficult for Black to start counterplay; the normal idea in such positions ... c5 here fails to Bxb5+, and by the time Black has prepared this advance Tal is poised for a king's side attack.

    9. Nf3   Be7
   10. Qe2 Nbd7
   11. 0-0   0-0
   12. Re1 Re8
   13. Ne5

Another drawback to 3. ... b5; the c6 square is weak. However, Black's exchange of knights on the next move facilitates the attack and he should try 13. ... Rc8.

   13. ...   Nxe5?
   14. dxe5 Nd5
   15. Qg4   a5
   16. h4!

Already in a higher sense the winning move. Either the pawn advances to h6, with serious weakening of the black king's defences, or it is taken and White gets his rook to the h file with gain of tempo.

   16. ...   Bxh4
   17. g3   Be7
   18. Kg2

Already threatening 19. Bxh7+! Kxh7 20. Qh5+ Kg8 21. Rh1.

   18. ...   g6
   19. Rh1

Now the threat is 20. Rxh7! Kxh7 21. Qh5+ Kg8 22. Bxg6.

   19. ...   Bf8
   20. Bg5   Qc7

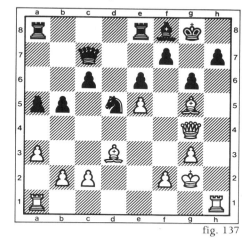

fig. 137

   21. Rxh7!

This sacrifice has been looming for several moves and it was probably almost a relief to Black to see it actually played. The rook still cannot be taken: 21. ... Kxh7 22. Rh1+ Kg8 23. Bf6 Nxf6 24. exf6 Qe5 25. Bxg6 Qxf6 26. Bh7+ and mate.

   21. ...   Qxe5
   22. Rxf7! Kxf7
   23. Bxg6+

The third sacrifice cannot be accepted because of 24. Bf4+ winning the queen.

   23. ...   Kg8
   24. Bxe8 Bg7

The bishop is still immune because of the discovered check.

   25. Bd7   Nc7
   26. Bxc6

Unusually for Tal, his combinative sequence ends not with a mate but with a simple gain of two pawns. The rest is easy.

   26. ...   Rf8
   27. Rd1   Qc5
   28. Bf3   Qxc2
   29. Rd7   Rf7
   30. Rd8+ Rf8
   31. Bf6   Qh7
   32. Be4   Qh6
   33. Bg5   Qh8
   34. Rd7   Resigns

for if 34. ... Rf7 35. Rxc7! Rxc7 36. Qxe6+ Kf8 (Rf7 37. Bg6) 37. Qd6+. This game shows that, contrary to popular belief, most of Tal's sacrificial attacks are based on logical positional ideas. The king's side brilliancy was the natural way to play the position once White had fixed Black's game in a permanent state of cramp with the pawn on e5.

73

Boris Spassky

1937–

Spassky wears world champion's laurel wreath and medal after beating Petrosian, 1969.

Spassky, from Leningrad, became chess's most famous and popular loser following his dignified manner of defeat in the world title match with Bobby Fischer at Reykjavik in 1972. He was noted as a boy prodigy in his early teens and the USSR chess federation awarded him the rare honour of selection for an international tournament abroad before he had played in the national championship final. This was at Bucharest in 1953, and Spassky made a storybook debut by defeating Smyslov, at that time the leading player in the world along with Botvinnik. The game is interesting not only for its circumstances but because it illustrated a plan which average players can also follow. White uses his two advanced pawns in the centre to bisect the black defenders, then uses his extra pieces available for king's side attack to score a decisive win.

White: B. Spassky. Black: V. Smyslov

Nimzo-Indian Defence (Bucharest 1953)

The opening moves were 1. d4 Nf6 2. c4 e6 3. Nc3 Bb4 4. Bg5 (the Leningrad system, much analysed in Spassky's home city and here making its international debut) h6 5. Bh4 c5 6. d5 d6 (nowadays this move is thought slightly passive, and Black prefers to react with the energetic 6. . . . b5!) 7. e3 exd5 8. cxd5 Nbd7. **9. Bb5**

An unusual but deeply judged move. It prevents Qa5 because of 10. Bxf6 and Black either loses pawns or has his pawn structure wrecked; and it prepares to meet a6 by Bxd7+ followed by Ne2 and a gradual build-up of White's forces in the

centre. However the simpler 9. Bd3 is now more popular.

9. . . .	0-0

Possibly Bxc3+ and then a6 is best.

10. Ne2	Ne5
11. 0-0	Ng6
12. Bg3	Nh5
13. Bd3	

Admitting that his bishop was misplaced; now White's new plan is to start a mobile K-side pawn roller without allowing too many exchanges.

13. . . .	Nxg3
14. Nxg3	Ne5
15. Be2	Bxc3
16. bxc3	Qh4
17. f4	Ng4
18. Bxg4	Bxg4
19. Qa4	

threatening 20. f5, so Black safeguards his bishop's retreat.

19. . . .	Bc8
20. e4	Qg4
21. Qc2	h5?

A weak move. Smyslov understandably feels obliged to attack his young opponent, but this advance lacks piece support and leaves Black's K-side full of holes. After the simple 21. . . . Bd7 and mobilizing the 3–2 Q-side pawn majority Black would be well in the game.

| 22. Rf2 | b5 |
| 23. e5! | |

While Smyslov tries to operate on both wings, Spassky makes the classical answer to a premature flank attack – a break in the centre.

23. . . .	h4
24. Nf1	Bf5
25. Qd2	

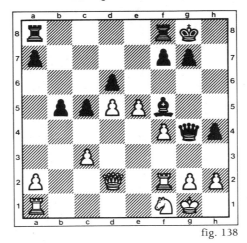

fig. 138

| 25. . . . | dxe5? |

A poor move which gives White a passed d pawn and opens the f file for White's attack. Best is 25. . . . Rad8. After this mistake Spassky brings off a fine tactical finish.

26. fxe5	Bg6
27. Re1	h3
28. d6	Be4
29. Ne3	Qe6
30. Rf4	Bxg2

not Qxe5 31. Ng4.

| 31. Nf5 | |

threatening Ne7+ followed by Rh4+ and so forcing the reply.

31. . . .	Rfe8
32. Re3	Rad8
33. Nxg7!	

A brilliant and decisive coup. If Kxg7 34. Rg3+ Kf8 35. Rxf7+! Kxf7 (Qxf7 36. Qh6+) 36. Qf4+ and mate next move.

| 33. . . . | Rxd6 |
| 34. Nxe6 | Resigns |

for if Rxd2 35. Rg3+ and mate next move.

Around the mid-1950s many expected Spassky soon to become world champion. But his nerves let him down in decisive games during the USSR championships of 1958 and 1961 which were also world title zonals. In a taped interview some years later, Boris described to me his feelings during his critical game with Tal in 1958 where both the USSR title and an interzonal place were at stake: 'The game was adjourned, and I had a good position; but I was very tired from analyzing and went to resume next morning unshaven. Normally before I played important games I tried to bathe, to put on a very good shirt and suit, and in general to look *comme il faut*. But this time I had analyzed incessantly and arrived at the board looking very dishevelled and fatigued. Then I was like a stubborn mule. I remember that Tal offered me a draw, but I refused. Then I felt my strength ebb away, and I lost the thread of the game. I in turn proposed a draw, but now Tal refused. When I resigned, there was a thunder of applause, but I was in a daze and hardly understood what was happening. I was certain the world went down; I felt there was something terribly wrong. After this game I went on the street and cried like a child.'

The personal crisis which enveloped Spassky around 1960 – he broke with his longtime trainer, was banned for a year from travel abroad for alleged misbehaviour at the student chess olympics, and divorced his first wife saying 'we were like bishops of opposite colours' – was resolved for a time when he took on a new coach, the calm and unemotional Bondarevsky. Spassky succeeded in winning through the world title eliminators for a match with Petrosian in 1966, but unexpectedly lost; he was still not quite mature enough to be world champion. But in 1969 he defeated Petrosian decisively in the final games of the match, the key victory coming with an example of the Spassky attacking style – control the centre, then launch the pieces on open lines – which we already saw in the previous game.

White: B. Spassky. Black: T. Petrosian

Sicilian Defence (19th match game 1969)

The opening moves were 1. e4 c5 2.

Nf3 d6 3. d4 cxd4 4. Nxd4 Nf6 5. Nc3 a6
6. Bg5 Nbd7 (usual and a little better is
e6) 7. Bc4 Qa5 8. Qd2 h6 9. Bxf6 Nxf6
10. 0-0-0 e6.

| | 11. Rhe1 | Be7? |

A fundamental mistake; Petrosian is
deceived by White's build-up along the
central files into believing that Spassky
does not plan a K-side attack. Better is Bd7
and 0-0-0.

	12. f4	0-0
	13. Bb3	Re8
	14. Kb1	

A normal move after castling queen's
side in a position where Black threatens
a counter-attack with pieces. Black has
to watch for the surprise Nd5! taking
advantage of his loose queen.

| | 14. ... | Bf8 |
| | 15. g4! | |

Switching the attack. Taking the pawn
opens the g file for White's pieces, but
Petrosian has little choice: if 15. ... b5
White continues strongly 16. g5 hxg5
17. fxg5 Nh5 18. g6.

| | 15. ... | Nxg4 |
| | 16. Qg2 | Nf6 |

If e5 17. Nf5 drives Black into defence.

| | 17. Rg1 | Bd7 |
| | 18. f5! | |

With control of the centre and poised
to attack the black K, Spassky opens all
the lines. Now the threat is 19. fxe6 fxe6
20. Nf5.

| | 18. ... | Kh8 |
| | 19. Rdf1 | Qd8 |

19. ... e5 would only provoke 20.
Ne6! fxe6 21. fxe6 intending Rxf6.

| | 20. fxe6 | fxe6 |

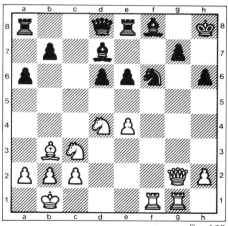

fig. 139

| | 21. e5! | |

Black's knight is partially tied to pre-
venting Rxf8+ and Qxg7 mate, and all
White's pieces are now ready for the
final assault. Spassky now breaks through
with a forced win.

| | 21. ... | dxe5 |
| | 22. Ne4 | Nh5 |

Not 22. ... Nxe4? 23. Rxf8+. Equally
22. ... exd4 23. Nxf6 Re7 24. Qg6 leads to
mate, and so does 22. ... exd4 23. Nxf6 g5
24. Qh3 Re7 25. Rxg5 Bg7 26. Rxg7.

| | 23. Qg6! | exd4 |

If 23. ... Nf4 24. Rxf4 exf4 25. Nf3 Qb6
26. Ne5 wins.

| | 24. Ng5! | Resigns |

If 24. ... hxg5 25. Qxh5+ Kg8 26. Qf7+
Kh7 27. Rf3! wins quickly. One of the
most attractive finishes in a world title
match.

When Spassky duly clinched the title,
chess fans expected a brave new era to
sweep away the arid style of Petrosian.
But they were generally disappointed:
Spassky found the title a burden and the
only memorable victory of his reign was
his win over Bobby Fischer of the US at
the chess olympics of 1970. When Fischer
finally qualified for the championship
match of 1972 and, after early threats to
withdraw, settled down to play, Spassky
often seemed gripped by a fatalistic
resignation to defeat. He lost the championship and also his favoured place in
Soviet society; eliminated from the next
two title series by Karpov and Korchnoi,
he settled with his French wife – his
third – near Paris. Now he represents
France in tournaments and continues to be
among the most popular grandmasters.

It sounds paradoxical to speak of a
world champion as a wasted talent, but
Spassky's natural gifts for chess were
such that he should have won the title
earlier in his life and kept it for a longer
period. There is a touch of laziness and a
touch of indecision in his intellectual
make-up; with the dedication to chess of
Alekhine or Tal, for example, Spassky
could have been one of the greatest
champions.

Bobby Fischer and Boris Spassky at the
'Match of the Century', USSR v World,
Belgrade 1970.

Bobby Fischer
1943–

The most controversial and quite possibly
the greatest player of all time, Robert J.
('Bobby') Fischer dominated his contemporaries and established himself as a
living legend before abandoning tournament and match play after winning the
world title from Spassky. Before that he
established the highest ever FIDE-Elo
rating of 2780 based on overall results;
he won successive candidates matches
against Taimanov and Larsen, both world
class grandmasters, by 6–0 and 6–0, and,
by a crude blunder and a default, he
effectively gave Spassky two games start
in the world championship before defeating him with some ease.

Fischer learnt the moves at six, but his
biggest break as a young chessplayer
came when his mother decided to settle
in Brooklyn. Chess life in New York, with
the thriving Manhattan and Marshall
clubs and many chess cafes, has proved a
stimulating environment for a number of
potential US grandmasters and Fischer
honed his game with incessant blitz games
combined with a study of Soviet chess
literature. The result of this hothouse
training, coupled with total neglect of
school work in favour of chess, was a
unique tournament result: Fischer was
men's champion of the United States at 14.

Probably at that time Fischer did not
realize how steep were the remaining
steps to the championship, at that time
held by the ageing Botvinnik, when he
qualified for the title candidates tournament at the first attempt and became the
youngest-ever grandmaster at 15. The
solid phalanx of Soviets easily outpaced
their less inexperienced rival in 1959 and

1962, and Fischer then successfully demanded that the system be changed from a tournament to a series of eliminating knock-out matches between the final eight challengers. It was under this system that he routed his rivals in 1971 and defeated Spassky the following year.

The general public will remember Bobby even more for his eccentricities and disputes than for his great play. His match with Reshevsky in 1961 ended in a scandal and a lawsuit, and he quit the 1967 interzonal when in the lead after a dispute about the playing schedule. He was only persuaded to fly to Iceland to meet Spassky when the British financier Jim Slater doubled the £50,000 purse; he was only persuaded not to walk out of the Spassky match by the personal intervention of US Foreign Secretary Henry Kissinger. And finally Fischer gave up his world championship without a fight when FIDE turned down his stipulation that his match with Karpov should be for the first to win ten games, the champion retaining his title at 9–9.

Fischer's financial demands were incredible. Both the projected match with Karpov and a comeback match with Gligoric in 1979, which also came to nothing, were for a million dollars or more. Despite claims that Fischer's figures benefited ordinary chess masters, there was an enormous contrast between these sums and those at stake in normal international tournaments. Then there were his increasingly finicky demands relating to light, spectator noise, and associated playing details. It is evident that Fischer finally reached a state where fear of defeat and fear of playing in public dominated his thinking. Indeed, it is difficult to see how anything other than victory over Kasparov or Karpov could enhance his legendary reputation. Perhaps straitened financial circumstances will one day force Fischer to play again, but more likely he will remain along with Morphy as the only other great master to have given up chess completely at the height of his fame.

What can the ordinary player learn from Bobby Fischer? First, will to win. Fischer's killer instinct meant that he continued to look for winning opportunities in positions which most masters would long ago have given up as drawn. His reply to a quick draw offer was 'Of course not'. It was physically difficult to play against him; his deep-set and hypnotic eyes and hawk-like face stared passionately at the board from which he rarely rose to look at other games. Fischer has long arms and fingers which he used to clutch opposing pieces when capturing, in the manner of a bird of prey. The will to win enabled him to finish ahead of opponents by record margins and a 100 per cent score was always on the cards. Only Alekhine had a similar fanaticism, but unlike Alekhine Fischer kept his

health in good shape as long as he was an active player.

Technically, Fischer had a deep knowledge of the sharp opening lines which he analyzed in depth before his tournaments; in simple positions his strategy was as pure and clear in reaching the objective as was Capablanca's. He used his opening knowledge especially well with the white pieces where he would typically gain the initiative and space control then use it energetically to drive his opponent into ever-deeper defence until resistance cracked. Between 1968 and 1970 he was in virtual retirement but when he emerged at the 'Match of the Century', where the USSR narrowly defeated a Rest of the World team, he at once played a game characteristic of his style at its best.

White: R.J. Fischer. Black: T. Petrosian

Caro-Kann Defence (Belgrade 1970)

1. e4	c6
2. d4	d5
3. exd5	cxd5
4. Bd3	

In his younger years Fischer had difficulty meeting the Caro-Kann and unsuccessfully used 2. Nc3 before switching to the attacking line 4. c4. Around 1970 he successfully ironed out one of the few weaknesses in his game by adopting a more varied and less stereotyped opening repertoire. He had played 4. Bd3 only once before and it obviously came as a surprise to Petrosian. The move is just simple piece development but provokes Black to a premature bid for the initiative.

4. ...	Nc6
5. c3	Nf6
6. Bf4	Bg4
7. Qb3	Na5?

As a result of the present game this feint at the queen has been abandoned in master chess in favour of the solid Qc8.

8. Qa4+	Bd7
9. Qc2	e6

Black's plan of Qb6 and Bb5 to exchange the white-squared bishops is refuted by Fischer's reply, so he should prefer a6 again intending Bb5.

10. Nf3	Qb6
11. a4!	Rc8

Now Black finds that if he goes hunting the advanced pawn by Qb3 then White has 12. Qe2 Bxa4? 13. Rxa4 Qxa4 14. Bb5+.

12. Nbd2	Nc6
13. Qb1	Nh5

Black intends another 'wing plan' which also fails. Fischer recommends g6.

14. Be3	h6

Petrosian's intention was f5 to block the position, but then comes 15. g4! fxg4 16. Ng5 Bd6 17. Bxh7 with a strong initiative. However Petrosian should have tried 14. ... Bd6! when 15. Bxh7 g6 16. Bxg6 fxg6 17. Qxg6+ Kd8 leads to an unclear position where Black would have counter-chances.

15. Ne5!

Once Fischer's knight is ensconced on this strong outpost square the game is strategically decided: Black's forces are effectively cut in two. Petrosian, of course, knew this but he had planned to play 15. Nxe5 16. dxe5 Bc5 overlooking until too late that 17. a5 Qc7 18. g4 wins the knight for insufficient compensation.

15. ...	Nf6
16. h3	Bd6
17. 0-0	Kf8

Already Petrosian is reduced to a desperate Steinitzian scheme of back rank defence. The normal 17. ... 0-0 would be easily met by 18. f4 followed by g4 and a pawn storm against the black king facilitated by the weakening 14. ... h6.

18. f4	Be8
19. Bf2	Qc7
20. Bh4	Ng8

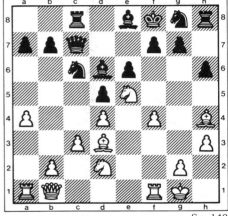

fig. 140

21. f5!

A classical break-through, using the combined force of white pieces to open up the black king. Note how even the distant queen at b1 plays an important role in the attack, eyeing the g6 square soon to become a target. Petrosian now chooses the best chance in such situations, exchanging off as many attacking men as possible.

21. ...	Nxe5
22. dxe5	Bxe5
23. fxe6	Bf6
24. exf7	Bxf7
25. Nf3	Bxh4

25. ... g5 wouldn't help because the white B comes back into action by f2-d4 and Black has only weakened his position further.

26. Nxh4	Nf6
27. Ng6+	

27. Bg6 to bring the queen rapidly into the attack might be more precise, but Fischer was always a strong believer in the value of bishop against knight on an open board.

27. ...	Bxg6
28. Bxg6	Ke7!

A desperately ingenious idea under

pressure – Black's king tries to escape the Q-side safety across the fire of Fischer's pieces.

        29. Qf5   Kd8
        30. Rae1   Qc5+
        31. Kh1   Rf8?

This loses in the middle game, whereas by 31. . . . Rc6 32. Qe5 Qd6 Petrosian could have lasted into Fischer's favourite endgame (33. Qxd6+ Rxd6) where rook(s) and active bishop on an open board are stronger than rook(s) and knight: White could continue then 34. Rf4 with further pressure on the weak pawns, but Black could still fight on. Note that 31. . . . Kc7 is met by 32. Qe5+ Qd6 33. Qe7+ winning at least a pawn.

        32. Qe5

Preparing to open the central files and cutting out the escape square c7. Black can't offer a queen swap by Qc7 because of 33. QxP ch! or 33. Rxf6! winning.

        32. . . .   Rc7

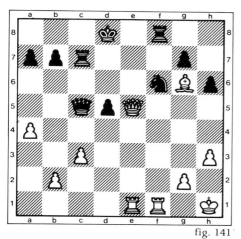

fig. 141

        33. b4!   Qc6
        34. c4!

The decisive line-opening. The black king is now exposed to an overwhelming attack from the combined white pieces.

        34. . . .   dxc4
        35. Bf5   Rff7
        36. Rd1+   Rfd7

If Nd7 37. Rfe1 is winning.

        37. Bxd7   Rxd7
        38. Qb8+   Ke7

or 38. . . . Qc8 39. Rxd7+ Nxd7 40. Qd6.

        39. Rde1+   Resigns

for if Kf7 40. Qe8 mate. As Petrosian resigned, two thousand chess fans in the hall erupted with applause.

Part of the reason for the immense public interest in Fischer was his ability to produce his best and most crowd-pleasing games on the most important occasions. This happened when he again met Petrosian the following year in Buenos Aires for the final eliminator in the world title series to challenge Boris Spassky. As Fischer went ahead in the match, global publicity increased, and crowds estimated at up to 10,000 daily besieged the playing hall for a glimpse of

the grandmasters. Fischer responded with one of the best games of his life, the final stages of which illustrate the strength of Fischer's favourite end-game: rook(s) and bishop on an open board outgunning rook(s) and knight.

White: R.J. Fischer. Black: T. Petrosian

Sicilian Defence (7th match game 1971)

The opening moves were 1. e4 c5 2. Nf3 e6 3. d4 cxd4 4. Nxd4 a6 5. Bd3 Nc6 6. Nxc6 bxc6 (better dxc6) 7. 0-0 d5 8. c4!

Illustrating another of Fischer's strengths. Studying chess constantly day and night, he had a magnificent armoury of innovations in a variety of openings. An earlier Spassky v. Petrosian game continued 8. Nd2 which is less effective.

        8. . . .   Nf6

8. . . . dxc4 9. Bxc4 Qxd1 10. Rxd1 is unappealing because of the weakness of Black's Q-side pawns, but Black could continue Nf6 11. Nc3 Bc5 12. Bg5 e5 with a better ending than he gets in the game.

        9. cxd5   cxd5
        10. exd5   exd5

Both Nxd5 11. Be4 and Qxd5 11. Nc3 are good for White since Black has no compensation for his pawn weaknesses.

        11. Nc3   Be7
        12. Qa4+!   Qd7?

Petrosian is dissatisfied with 12. . . . Bd7 13. Qd4 or 13. Qc2 and so plans to offer a positional sacrifice: 13. Bb5 axb5 14. Qxa8 0-0 15. Qa5 d4 16. Nxd4 Bb7 with attacking chances. But Fischer finds a clear line which gives him a lasting bind on the dark squares with his 2–1 queen's side pawn majority still in reserve.

        13. Re1!   Qxa4

Black is forced to exchange, thus bringing the white knight to an ideal square where it eyes the weak b6 and c5. Castling would lose a piece to 14. Qxd7.

        14. Nxa4   Be6
        15. Be3   0-0

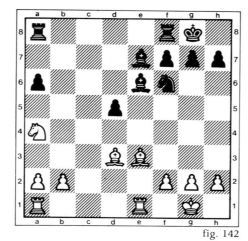

fig. 142

Slightly better would be Nd7 to contest the dark squares, but 16. f4 g6 17. Bd4 0-0 18. Rac1 is still a permanent bind

for White.

        16. Bc5!

An important move for the keen chess student. Elimination by exchange of the most active enemy minor piece is one of the keys to successful positional play. Here White exchanges off Black's dark-squared bishop, leaving him with the light-squared bishop restricted by the pawns on d5 and a6.

        16. . . .   Rfe8
        17. Bxe7   Rxe7
        18. b4!

Prevents . . . a5 and so fixes the weak a pawn firmly where it can be attacked by White's knight and bishop.

        18. . . .   Kf8
        19. Nc5   Bc8
        20. f3!

Another strong multi-purpose move which deprives the black knight of a possible e4 outpost, opens a route for the white king to advance smoothly to the d4 central square, and keeps Black firmly on the defensive. The best chance now is 20. . . . Nd7 so as at least to exchange or drive back the strong knight, but Petrosian instead tries to bring his bishop to b5 to neutralize the good-bad bishop situation.

        20. . . .   R7a7
        21. Re5   Bd7
        22. Nxd7+!

This move took all the watching grandmasters by surprise, but it is perfectly logical. White does not want to allow . . . b5 strengthening Black's defences, while 22. a4 would permit the defensive plan Bc6 and Nd7. So Fischer goes for the 'Fischer endgame' where his bishop is vastly more powerful than the black knight and where his rooks are active, Black's passive. The remaining play is also analyzed in the Fischer/Karpov endgame, page 44.

        22. . . .   Rxd7
        23. Rc1

Threatens 24. Rc6 increasing the pressure on the a pawn.

        23. . . .   Rd6
        24. Rc7   Nd7
        25. Re2

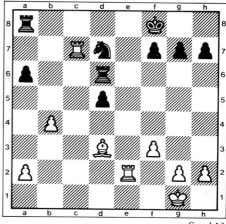

fig. 143

A classical position for the 'Fischer end-game'. While Black's rooks are tied to protecting his weak pawns, White's control the open files and one is on the seventh rank. Black's knight cannot move because of Ree7 while he cannot offer the exchange of a pair of rooks by Re8 because of Rxe8+ and Ra7 winning the a pawn. Thus Petrosian can only watch and wait while Fischer centralizes his king.

25.	. . .	g6
26.	Kf2	h5
27.	f4	h4?

Demoralized, Petrosian creates another weakness. A better defence is Nb6 28. R2e7 Rf6.

28. Kf3

threatening to pick up the pawn by Kg4 and so forcing the reply.

28.	. . .	f5
29.	Ke3	d4+
30.	Kd2	Nb6
31.	R2e7	Nd5
32.	Rf7+	Ke8
33.	Rcb7	Nxb4
34.	Bc4!	Resigns

There is a double threat: to take the knight or to win by 35. Rh7 Rf6 36. Rh8+ Rf8 37. Bf7+ Kd8 38. Rxf8 mate.

Anatoly Karpov

1951–

Karpov, world champion 1975 to 1985, is a player whose chess career advanced from learning the moves to winning the world title with scarcely a discernible setback. Karpov learnt chess at four, and though living far from the main Soviet centres, in the small town of Zlatoust in the Urals, he made rapid progress. At eleven he was a candidate master, and was given special tuition by Botvinnik. His first senior international victory, at 15, came about by accident; the Russians thought the invitation to Czechoslovakia was for a junior event. Thereafter Karpov went on to win the under-20 world championship, the grandmaster title, and a place in the 1972–75 series to decide Fischer's challenger. He succeeded at his first attempt, beating Spassky and Korchnoi and taking the title by default when Fischer refused to play.

Karpov's sustained record of first prizes in tournaments as world champion eclipsed his predecessors. His style is reminiscent of Capablanca, but in a more subtle way than Fischer. Unlike the American, he does not go all out in every game and with the black pieces he sometimes takes early draws. But with the exception of the final stages of his 1978 title defence against Korchnoi, when fatigue got on top of his play, Karpov has been one of the most difficult grand-masters ever to defeat. It is rare for him to lose more than one game in any event.

Karpov's old rival Victor Korchnoi has described the world champion as a computer-like cold fish, and to strangers he often gives an impression of detached aloofness. Slightly built, he looks too frail for the pressures of tournament chess, but his results show the opposite. As champion he has taken on the best players all over the world and clearly rates on a par with the greatest masters of the game – Lasker, Capablanca, Alekhine, Botvinnik and Fischer.

In his personal life, Karpov is a private man. He collects stamps, and wrote a thesis 'on problems of leisure activities' for Leningrad University. He was married in summer 1979 but his wife left him about the time that his title was under threat from Kasparov. Only Fischer and (so far) Kasparov have been bachelor world champions. In the USSR Karpov is a national hero and in 1978 he topped the poll for Soviet Sportsman of the Year following his victory over Korchnoi. He was personally decorated by President Brezhnev.

What can the ordinary player learn from the chess of Karpov? First, his skill with the Ruy Lopez. Like Capablanca and Fischer, for whom this opening was also a front line choice, Karpov is sensitive to its finesses and relies on it heavily to score a high percentage of points with the white pieces. It is useful in chess to have a repertoire of opening variations you know really well and which have a good chance of coming up in play. Karpov's approach to the Ruy Lopez involves what has been called his 'spider' technique. He aims at space control on the queen's side and piece play on the king's side, aiming to gradually deprive his opponent of useful squares, box the enemy pieces into a cramped position, and then break through on either flank. Often the result is that Karpov's pawn web controls the entire board. This game from the 1974 chess olympics illustrates Karpov's Ruy Lopez approach.

White: A. Karpov. Black: H. Westerinen

Opening: Ruy Lopez (Nice 1974)

The opening moves were 1. e4 e5 2. Nf3 Nc6 3. Bb5 a6 4. Ba4 d6.

Black chooses a strongpoint defence, aiming to keep his centre intact. Another game Karpov–Unzicker, Milan 1975, shows how Karpov counters one of the main lines of the opening: 4. . . . Nf6 5. 0-0 Be7 6. Re1 b5 7. Bb3 d6 8. c3 0-0 9. h3 Na5 10. Bc2 c5 11. d4 Qc7 12. Nbd2 Bd7 13. Nf1 Rfe8 14. d5 Nb7? (better Nc4 followed by Nb6–d7 to control the e5 square) 15. N3h2 g6 16. Ng3 c4 17. f4! exf4 18. Bxf4 Bf8? (he should try Bc8 and Nd7, still trying to hold e5) 19. Bg5! Be7 (or Bg7 20. Rf1) 20. Qd2 Bc8 21. Rf1 Nd7 22. Ng4, Resigns. The threat of Nh6+ wins at least a pawn with a continuing attack, so Black prefers to recognize that

Anatoly Karpov, reigning world champion. Continual brilliant tournament victories confirm him as the No 1.

his position has gone.

5. 0-0 Bd7 6. d4 Nf6 7. c3 Be7 8. Nbd2 0-0 9. Re1 Re8 10. Nf1 h6 11. Ng3 Bf8 12. Bd2 b5.

Black's strongpoint defence aims to keep his centre solid and intact. But this plan works better with b5 instead of Bd7, keeping the option of putting the QB at b7 and the KN at d7. Once committed to Bd7, the move b5 is illogical and Black should switch to a different strategy, opening the centre and freeing his game with piece exchanges after 9. . . . exd4 10. cxd4 Nb4.

13. Bc2!

Karpov has a good eye for little finesses. He saves a move on the routine 13. Bb3 Na5 because Black needs to regroup his knight in any case to mobilize his queen's side pieces.

13.	. . .	Na5
14.	b3	c5
15.	d5	Nh7
16.	h3	Be7
17.	Nf5	Nb7

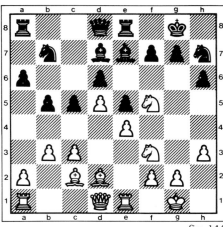

fig. 144

The white QN at f5 is on its best Ruy Lopez square for helping a king's side attack, but Black is solid in defence and experience shows that White can rarely break through on a single flank in this blocked opening system. Instead, Karpov takes advantage of the badly posted b7 knight and the absence of the black h7 knight from the queen's side to switch the action there.

18. a4!   bxa4
19. b4!

Another delicate chess dropshot. The obvious bxa4 would allow Na5-c4 with counterplay, whereas in the game the b7 knight remains a passenger till the end.

19. ...   a5
20. Bxa4   axb4
21. cxb4   Bf8

If 21. ... Bxa4 22. Rxa4 Rxa4 23. Qxa4 Qa8 24. Ra1 and White's queen or rook penetrates to the seventh row with a winning advantage.

22. Bc6!

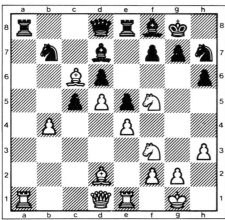

fig. 145

Typical of the positions Karpov likes to aim for. The strong b4 and d5 pawns, supported by minor pieces here and on moves 25–26, stop any counterplay and prepare the final attack on the a file. The rest of the game, to a Karpov, is a routine mopping-up.

The remaining moves were 22. ... Qc7 23. b5 Nf6 24. Qc2 Reb8 25. Ne3 Bc8 26. Nc4 Be7 27. b6 Qd8 28. Ra7 Nd7 29. Qa4 Rxa7 30. bxa7 Ra8 31. Qa6 Qc7 32. Bxd7 Qxd7 33. Nb6 Nd8 34. Qa1 Resigns. If 34. ... Qxa7 White wins a piece by 35. Qxa7 and 36. Nxc8, while if 34. Qb7 35. Nxa8 Qxa8 36. Rb1 and Black is hamstrung.

The second strength of Karpov which can be followed is his reliance on the endgame. In an interview in London in 1972, he was asked by a group of club players 'Can you advise us what we must do if we want to improve? We study openings a lot, we play a lot.' 'But endgames not very much?' he replied. 'Do the opposite – study endgames!'

Like his predecessor Fischer, Karpov is an expert in handling the endgame of

rook and bishop against rook and knight. But he is no dogmatist and can switch with equal facility to knight against bishop when that becomes appropriate. At Montreal in 1979, Karpov tied for first with Tal in one of the strongest tournaments ever held, with a prize fund of £50,000 and £12,500 for the winner. During this event Karpov played a game where he demonstrated first the superiority of bishop against knight, and then the advantage of knight against bishop.

White: B. Spassky. Black: A. Karpov Opening: Queen's Indian Defence (Montreal World Cup 1979)

The opening moves were 1. d4 Nf6 2. c4 e6 3. Nf3 b6 4. Bf4 Bb7 5. e3 Be7 6. Nc3? (Spassky had earlier twice lost to Tony Miles against this 4. Bf4 system, so decides to try it out for himself. Unfortunately he doesn't know it well enough – 6. h3 is necessary to preserve the bishop) Nh5! 7. Bg3 d6 8. Bd3 Nd7 9. 0-0 g6! Karpov's long-term strategy is based on his active e7 bishop. This piece will be transferred to the long black diagonal where it will have more future than any of White's minor pieces.

10. h3   Nxg3
11. fxg3   0-0
12. Rc1   Bf6
13. Rc2   Bg7
14. Rcf2   Qe7
15. Kh2   a6
16. Qe2   Rae8
17. Bb1   c6
18. a3   f5
19. e4

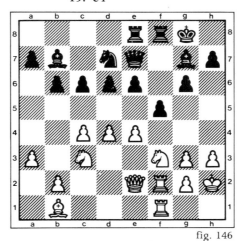

fig. 146

19. ...   c5!

This is the key move of Karpov's deep strategy, played just as White was hoping to gain space in the centre and keep the bishop pair under restraint. Now White is forced to exchange into Karpov's favourite endgame phase and the black bishops gain considerably more scope.

20. exf5   exf5
21. Qxe7   Rxe7
22. dxc5   bxc5
23. Rd1   Bxc3!

Another subtle move. The bishop pair

is abandoned, but the white Q-side pawns on the c and a files become weak and are targets for Black's rooks and minor pieces.

24. bxc3   Rf6
25. Rfd2   Re3
26. Ng1   Kf8!

This also had to be seen and assessed well in advance. Instead of defending the weak d pawn, Karpov gives it up and in return gets very active play for all his remaining pieces – including the centralized king.

27. Rxd6   Rxd6
28. Rxd6   Ke7
29. Rd3   Re1
30. Ba2   Rc1
31. Nf3

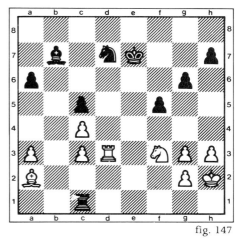

fig. 147

31. ...   Bxf3!

Karpov is still a pawn down but can make this exchange in the confidence that the R + B v. R + N ending is a clear win. The white bishop has no scope, his king is still out of play, and his rook is tied to passive defence of the Q-side pawns; on the other hand Black's rook, knight and king are all either poised to invade the white camp or are already doing so.

32. Rxf3   Ne5
33. Re3   Kf6
34. Bb3   a5
35. Ba4

Capitulation – White returns the pawn with 100 per cent interest in a vain attempt to get some play. Attempting to hold the material by 35. Ba2 or 35. a4 would fail to Rb1 and Rb2.

35. ...   Nxc4
36. Re8   Rxc3
37. Rc8   Ne3
38. Bb5   c4
39. Kg1   Rc2
40. Bc6   c3
41. Bf3   g5
42. g4   f4
43. Resigns

The passed c pawn will soon force the win of at least the bishop since the white king is unable to help the defence.

A third, and particularly important, lesson to be learnt from Anatoly Karpov's chess career is the great value of a serious and disciplined approach to chess study. The champion works at the game for at least a couple of hours a day even when he is not competing in a tournament, analysing the games of potential rivals, looking for opening improvements, and keeping in touch with new ideas.

Karpov has already played six matches for the world title and is still well under 40. He seems sure to be remembered as one of the all-time greats.

Tony Miles *1955–*

Tony Miles, Britain's first grandmaster, has inspired a generation of young British players to aim for individual and world team championships. He is a tough and successful young professional who plays almost continuously in tournaments all over the world, and he has an excellent track record against most of the leading Russians except for Karpov.

Miles learnt chess at five but developed rather slowly: even when he won the British under-14 championship in 1968 he did not gain instant recognition as a special talent. But when he became the leading player in the Midlands while still in his middle teens and won a junior international in France, the decision was taken that England should bid to stage the 1973 junior world chess championship so that Miles and another strong young player, Michael Stean, should have the optimum opportunity.

Miles won only the silver medal in that event behind the Russian Belyavsky; this followed a European junior championship where he was also second to the Russian, making Miles determined to win the gold medal the following year. In the junior world championship in Manila he was clearly the best player, decisively beating his Soviet opponent in a brilliant game, and winning both the championship and an automatic international master title.

It took Miles less than two years after the junior world championship to become a grandmaster. Then he declared that 'the only thing left is to have a go at Karpov', and in late 1977 he seemed on the brink of becoming established as the leading Western challenger.

But he was unwilling to cut back his active playing career to concentrate on the world title series, although he beat Karpov twice in individual games at Skara 1980 and BBC Master Game 1983. In 1986 Miles took on Kasparov in a non-title series, but lost by a crushing $\frac{1}{2}$–$5\frac{1}{2}$. His sad comment afterwards 'I thought I was playing a world champion, not a monster with 22 eyes who sees everything' has become part of chess lore.

What can the average player learn from Tony Miles? Above all, a practical approach to winning. In his early career

Miles liked to open 1. e4 and, as Black, used to play the sharp Dragon variation of the Sicilian defence with c5 and g6. But some heavy defeats against well-primed opponents convinced him that he should have a more positional repertoire whereby he could play for a win against slightly weaker opponents without too much risk. Standby openings for players who choose such a style are often the English 1. c4 and the non-commital 1. Nf3. Miles has been making increasing use of these moves and at the same time has been developing his own special ideas in the openings – for instance a queen's pawn system with Bf4 which twice helped him to beat Spassky.

Miles's first prize at Tilburg 1984 ranked as the finest ever British tournament result, judged by rating. The event was category 14 on the international scale, and his performance of 2770 was at world championship level. A little later John Nunn achieved a performance above 2800, though that was in the team olympics at Salonika.

At Tilburg Miles won with 8/11, a point and a half clear of his nearest rivals. He won five games in a row, defeating three Dutchmen and the world candidates Portisch and Smyslov. This victory was over his main rival for the status of No. 1 man in Western Europe.

White: A.J. Miles. Black: J. Timman
Opening: English (Interpolis Tilburg 1984)

The opening moves were 1. c4 e5 2. Nc3 Nf6 3. Nf3 Nc6 4. g3 d5 5. cxd5 Nxd5 6. Bg2 Nb6 7. 0–0 Be7 8. a3 Be6 9. d3 0–0 10. b4 f6 11. Ne4 Qd7.

Black's system of development, a Sicilian Defence, Dragon variation, in reverse, has conceded White a useful initiative. With the text, Black plans minor piece exchanges which he hopes will bring near equality.

12.	Bb2	a6
13.	Qc2	Bh3
14.	Nc5	Bxc5
15.	Bxh3	Qxh3
16.	Qb3+	Kh8
17.	bxc5	Nd7
18.	d4!	

Miles aims consistently to open up the long diagonal for his strong bishop towards the black king. Instead 18. Qxb7 Qe6 19. Qxc7 Nxc5 is unclear since White's queen lacks retreat squares.

18.	...	Rab8
19.	dxe5	N7xe5
20.	Nxe5	fxe5
21.	Rad1	Rf6
22.	f4!	Rxf4
23.	Rxf4	exf4
24.	Qf7	Rg8
25.	Rf1	Qg4

Miles's diagonal strategy has succeeded, based on the tactic 25. ... fxg3? 26. Qxg7+!

26.	Rxf4	Qg5

27.	Kg2	Qxc5
28.	Re4	Qf8

Material is reduced and Black is a pawn up, but the mate threat 29. Re8 is too strong.

29.	Qh5	Ne7
30.	Qg5	Ng6

Losing immediately, but if Nf5 31. Rf4 pins and wins, while if Nc6 31. Rh4 threatens Rxh7+ or Qg6.

31.	**Qxg6!**	**Resigns**

One year later, Miles tied first at Tilburg 1985 in a remarkable way. His start was poor, then he injured his back and played stomach down on a hospital massage table. He scored a series of wins, opponents petitioned against the table, and there was a compromise that they need not sit opposite Miles. One grandmaster treated the game like a simul, another played on a separate board, a third agreed a pre-arranged draw with farcical moves.

Another Miles technique is his ability to refute inferior opening play. International chess can mean up to ten hours tiring work a day, and most experts find it essential to have a number of shorter games with less mental effort. The simplest way to achieve this is by quick draws which often occur on the world circuit. But this means only half a point for each side, and the player aiming at a high place has to be able to defeat weaker opponents without excessive labour.

In the following game Miles' opponent makes a passive fifth move, conceding the centre to the white pawns and pieces. Many would be content to exploit this by a slow build-up, but Miles instead goes for a sharp gambit approach, sacrificing first a pawn and then a bishop. In return he gets a fine attack, the opponent's defences collapse quickly, and the grandmaster departs the board with his energy still fresh for the next round.

White: A.J. Miles. Black: E. Preissmann

Opening: Slav Defence (Haifa Olympiad 1976)

1.	d4	d5
2.	c4	c6
3.	Nf3	Nf6
4.	Nc3	dxc4
5.	a4	e6?

A poor move which hems in his queen's bishop just when this piece should be developed by Bf5 or Bg4.

6.	e3	Bb4
7.	Bxc4	Nbd7
8.	0-0	0-0
9.	Qb3!	

Forcefully attacking Black's weak e6 pawn as well as the bishop. Already there is a tactical trap, for 9. . . . Bd6 should be met by 10. Bxe6 fxe6 11. Qxe6+ and 12. Qxd6.

9.	. . .	Qe7
10.	e4!	Bxc3

Accepting the pawn sacrifice is risky, but otherwise White has a strong centre.

11.	bxc3	Nxe4
12.	Ba3	c5
13.	Rfe1	Nef6

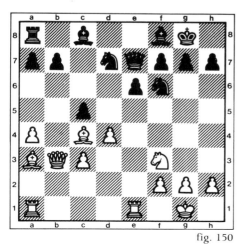

fig. 150

If 13. . . . Ndf6 14. Bd3 undermines the black knights and regains the c5 pawn with great advantage.

14. a5!

A subtle move whose significance Black fails to appreciate. Miles would like to sacrifice on e6, aiming to create a winning discovered check. But the immediate 14. Bxe6? fxe6 15. Rxe6 is met by Qf7 16. Ng5 c4! 17. Qxc4 Nb6! and the counter-attack on the white queen refutes the combination. Black does not see this at all and judging by his reply he thinks that 14. a5 is just a positional move aiming to gain queen's side space.

14.	. . .	Rb8?

Correct is h6, denying the white knight the g5 square.

15.	Bxe6!	fxe6
16.	Rxe6	Qf7
17.	Ng5	c4
18.	Qxc4	Nb6
19.	Qe2!	Qg6

Now 19. . . . Bxe6, aiming to get material compensation for the queen, is refuted by 20. Nxf7 Bxf7 21. axb6.

20.	Bxf8	Qxg5

Or 20. . . . Bxe6 21. Qxe6+ Kxf8 22. Qd6+ and 23. Qxb8 wins.

21.	Bd6	Resigns

For if 21. . . . Nbd7 22. Bxb8 Nxb8 23. Re8+ mates or wins material. This game was typical of Tony Miles, showing good strategic assessment backed by precise calculation of tricky variations.

The year 1980 brought a milestone in Miles's career: for the first time he beat world champion Karpov, and that in an opening so bizarre it was nameless. For some weeks the Russian chess magazines could not bring themselves to publish Black's first move.

White: A. Karpov. Black: A.J. Miles

Opening: Birmingham Defence (Skara 1980)

1. e4	a6

The round 1 pairings were announced before the tournament, and Miles, at home in Birmingham, decided on this rare defence to combat Karpov's command of orthodox theory. Its strategy of early queen's side play is an extension of 1. . . . b6 which Miles chose in an earlier encounter with the champion.

2. d4	b5
3. Nf3	

More forcing is 3. a4, but Karpov and some other great masters make a principle of taking no risks in the first round of an event.

3. . . .	Bb7
4. Bd3	Nf6
5. Qe2	e6
6. a4	c5
7. dxc5	

Again Karpov avoids an active line (7. c3) and Black's opening choice is vindicated.

7. . . .	Bxc5
8. N1d2	b4

9. e5	Nd5
10. Ne4	Be7
11. 0-0	Nc6
12. Bd2	Qc7
13. c4	bxc3 e.p.
14. Nxc3	Nxc3
15. Bxc3	Nb4
16. Bxb4	

By the simplest means, Black gains the advantage of the bishop pair, but otherwise his knight has a fine outpost at d5.

16. . . .	Bxb4
17. Rac1	Qb6
18. Be4	0-0
19. Ng5	h6
20. Bh7+?	

Fresh loss of time. White should prefer 20. Bxb7.

20. . . .	Kh8
21. Bb1	Be7

Not hxg5?? 22. Qh5+ mates.

22. Ne4	Rac8
23. Qd3?	

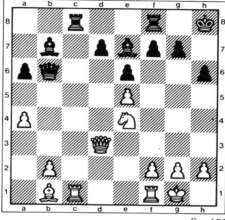

fig. 151

Hoping to attack h7, but this never materializes. Black now wins a pawn and already White gets a lost ending.

23. . . .	Rxc1
24. Rxc1	Qxb2
25. Re1	Qxe5
26. Qxd7	Bb4
27. Re3	Qd5
28. Qxd5	Bxd5

From now on the game is won. Miles plays the final stage accurately as his king, bishop pair and active rook force the world champion back. The remaining moves were **29. Nc3 Rc8 30. Ne2 g5 31. h4 Kg7 32. hxg5 hxg5 33. Bd3 a5 34. Rg3 Kf6 35. Rg4 Bd6 36. Kf1 Be5 37. Ke1 Rh8 38. f4 gxf4 39. Nxf4 Bc6 40. Ne2 Rh1 + 41. Kd2 Rh2 42. g3 Bf3 43. Rg8 Rg2 44. Ke1 Bxe2 45. Bxe2 Rxg3 46. Ra8 Bc7 and White resigned** as Black's two pawns will push through. This was only the second win this century by a British player against a reigning world champion.

Yasser Seirawan

1960–

Yasser Seirawan is the most successful of a new generation of young American players who have made their mark on the international scene. Born in Beirut, Yasser's family emigrated to California when he was a small boy and, inspired like many by the publicity for the Fischer–Spassky match, he started to take chess seriously when in his early teens.

Successes came quickly. In 1979 he won the junior world championship and achieved his first grandmaster norm at Lone Pine. He was joint US champion in 1981, outright winner in 1986. He defeated Korchnoi in 1980 (see below), Karpov in 1982, Kasparov at the 1986 olympics. His ambition is the world title itself, but so far his best placing is tenth in the 1986 candidates. The problem for Yasser, a man of wide interests with a zest for life in the full, is how to combine his professional ambitions without the obsessive drive of Bobby Fischer. Signs in the late 1980s were that he was succeeding as his status crept closer to the world top ten.

In complete contrast to Fischer, Yasser is one of nature's gentlemen and is a fine ambassador for the US at every tournament he attends. A few years ago he played at Hastings, England, and following that gave an exhibition against 25 young juniors at the London Evening Standard championships. He made sure to shake hands with each one before the game and had a pleasant word of commiseration or congratulation for all his opponents as they finished. One youngster had been eating a jam doughnut but nevertheless held out his hand at the end; Yasser looked at it, smiled, shut his eyes and shook the hand, spending the next round of play wiping his fingers clean.

What can be learnt from Yasser Seirawan's games is forceful position chess typical of the American style at its best. In the tradition of Pillsbury and Reshevsky, he plays mainly strategic openings. But whereas Pillsbury aimed for his own pre-analysed formations with Ne5 and f4 and Reshevsky liked the Queen's Gambit Declined Exchange variation where the white c4 pawn is swapped for the black d5 pawn, Seirawan's strategy is more complex.

His favourite is the English 1. c4 which is increasingly popular in master chess because of its flexible, non-committal qualities. Seirawan likes to use the English to gain space on the queen's side then outflank the defenders via the back rank or switching to the king's side. This is grand strategy if the concept works, and how well Seirawan handles it is demonstrated by this game which helped him win the world junior title.

White: Y. Seirawan. Black: G. Barbero

Opening: English (Junior World Championship 1979)

1.	c4	e5
2.	Nc3	Nf6
3.	Nf3	Nc6
4.	e3	Bb4
5.	Qc2	Bxc3

Unnecessarily premature, losing time. This exchange can wait till White forces it with a3.

6.	Qxc3	Qe7
7.	a3	a5
8.	b4!	

A mark of Yasser Seirawan's chess style. He advances on the Q-side as fast as possible, aided by a tactical nuance.

8.	. . .	axb4
9.	axb4	Rxa1
10.	Qxa1	e4

Yasser Seirawan at Hastings, 1980. The top US player, he has addressed Congress on the educational merits of chess and has also featured as a male pin-up in a magazine.

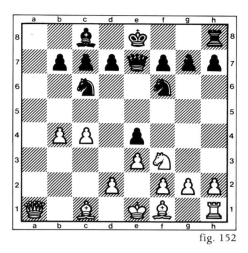

fig. 152

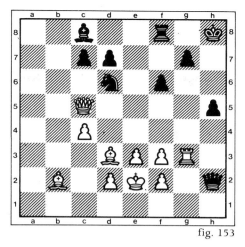

fig. 153

Both 10. . . . Qxb4 11. Nxe5 and 10. . . . Nxb4 11. Qxe5 are exchanges which clear the board of pawns and so increase the potential scope of the pair of bishops which Black casually conceded on move 5. With his actual move, Black aims to create weaknesses in the white king's side which his pieces can infiltrate, but another result of this approach is further opening of lines favouring White.

11. b5!
Creating more potential scope for the bishops, and completing the ultra-rapid demolition of Black's queen's side. In another half-dozen moves, the white queen is infiltrating the rear of Black's position.

11. . . .	exf3
12. bxc6	bxc6
13. gxf3	0-0
14. Bb2	Ne8

The threatened Rg1 followed by Bxf6 forces the knight to move, but Nh5 is more active.

15. Bd3   Qh4
This was Black's plan: given time, he will advance f5-f4 to open up the white king. But Seirawan's bishops are already directed for attack and in the next few moves Black's K-side comes under heavy pressure.

16. Ke2   c5
17. Qa8!
En route to the king's side. Backward diagonal retreats or captures by a queen or bishop are often hard to visualize in advance as many players have a mental block about such moves.

17. . . .   Nd6
Stopping Qe4, but White finds another way to transfer the queen to the other flank with gain of time.

18. Rg1!	f6
19. Qd5+	Kh8
20. Qxc5	Qxh2
21. Rg3!	

Shutting out the queen from protection of the threatened c7 pawn, and inducing the following fatal weakness.

21. . . .   h5?

22. Rxg7!
There are other ways to win – White could simply take the c pawn – but the move played is the most elegant and forcing. The average player is unlikely to be able to calculate such positions in advance but should not be deterred. Tactical vision is a matter of experience and training so the sensible policy if you don't see a clear win is to continue to increase the pressure or capture material – here by 22. Qxc7.

22. . . .	Kxg7
23. Qg5+	Kf7
24. Qxf6+	Ke8
25. Bg6+	Nf7
26. Be5!	

A fine, original conclusion. If the queen moves, 27. Bxc7 with unavoidable mate on d8.

26. . . .   Resigns
The important Wijk aan Zee international of 1980 showed that Seirawan would become America's greatest player since Fischer. He tied for first prize with three-time US champion Browne, reached the grandmaster score with three games to spare, and outplayed Korchnoi.

White: Y. Seirawan. Black: V. Korchnoi.

Opening: English (Wijk aan Zee 1980).
The opening moves were 1. c4 Nf6 2. Nc3 e6 3. e4 d5 4. e5 d4 5. exf6 dxc3 6. bxc3 Qxf6 7. d4 c5.
Book theory is one of Korchnoi's weaker points: 7. . . . b6 is superior.

8. Nf3	h6
9. Bd3!	

Intending the gambit 9. . . . Nc6 10. 0-0 with active piece play for the pawn.

9. . . .	cxd4
10. cxd4	Bb4+
11. Kf1!	

The king is safe here since it is White who has the initiative and attack.

11. . . .	Nc6
12. Bb2	Bc5
13. Bc2	0-0
14. Qd3	Rd8
15. Rd1	Kf8

16. Qe4	Bd6
17. h4!	

With ideas of g4-g5, Ng5, or h5 and Rh4.

17. . . .	Qf5
18. Qe2	Qa5
19. Bb3	Ne7
20. h5	b6
21. Qe4	Ba6
22. d5!	

Offering two pawns to open up all the lines against the black king.

22. . . .	exd5
23. Qh7	f6
24. Kg1	Bxc4
25. Rh4!	Bxb3
26. axb3	Kf7
27. Rg4	Rg8

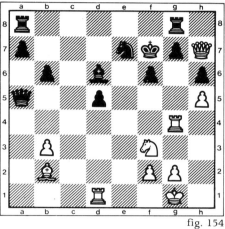

fig. 154

28. Re1!
The winning move. It cuts off the black king's escape, and threatens 29. Bxf6 Kxf6 30. Rg6+ or if 28. . . . Rad8 29. Ra1 followed by Rxa7.

28. . . .	d4
29. Rxd4	Be5
30. Rd7	Qxe1+

Korchnoi hopes to fight on with rook, bishop and pawn against queen, but the attack is too strong. The game ended 31. Nxe1 Bxb2 32. Nd3 Ba3 33. Nf4 Rgd8 34. Qg6+ Kg8 35. Qd3 Rxd7 36. Qxd7 Rc8 37. Kh2 Kf7 38. Ng6 Ra8 39. Nxe7 Resigns. If Bxe7 40. Qd5+ wins the rook.

Gary Kasparov

1963–

Kasparov is the youngest ever world chess champion, a player whose dynamic style, personal charisma and brilliant results have already made him a strong candidate to become the No. 1 of all time. He looks set to dominate the game well into the 1990s.

Kasparov's family name was Weinstein but they changed it, for it was rumoured that the Soviet authorities did not want their new star to sound Jewish. His early games at ages 10–11 already showed unusual gifts, so much so that I wrote an article in the 'Guardian' newspaper at that time predicting that Kasparov would be world champion in 1990.

Kasparov studied chess at the famous 'Botvinnik school' where Karpov also learnt from the ex-world champion. At 11, he scored well against the top Soviet grandmasters in a clock simultaneous match, and gave Karpov and Korchnoi a hard game. Then came a relative setback: he competed twice, at age 13 and 14, in the under-17 world championship but failed to win it. There was no news of him for some months, and it seemed possible that he was not fulfilling his promise.

But his achievements in 1978 provided the answer. First Kasparov won a strong Soviet invitation tournament, the Sokolsky Memorial; then he won a 64-man Swiss tournament against masters and grandmasters which qualified him directly for the final of the Soviet Championship. His debut caused an international stir: he scored 50 per cent and defeated Polugaevsky, a world title candidate, by an imaginative bishop sacrifice. As a result of this success, the USSR Chess Federation sent him to a strong grandmaster tournament at Banja Luka, Yugoslavia, in the summer of 1979, where, apart from the local champion, he was the only non-grandmaster.

Kasparov's score at Banja Luka outpaced even the early achievements of Spassky and Fischer. He led from the start, reaching the international master norm with five rounds to spare, won the tournament with three rounds in hand and achieved the grandmaster norm, which the World Chess Federation had raised, two rounds before the finish. His tournament performance was such that if repeated consistently it would already bracket him with Korchnoi as the leading contender for Karpov's throne.

Leading scores in this historic event were Kasparov (USSR) 11½ out of 15, Smejkal (Czech) and Andersson (Sweden) 9½, Petrosian (USSR) 9. In summer 1980 Kasparov won at Baku to become the world's youngest grandmaster.

When Kasparov was still an unknown, his mentor Botvinnik said that 'the future of chess lies in the hands of this boy'. Botvinnik's forecast and my own that Kasparov would be the 1990 champion were laughed at by the experts when they were made, but not so after Banja Luka. Kasparov, meanwhile, kept his feet on the ground. He admitted that he dreamt of the world title, but in the tradition of self-criticism favoured by Botvinnik said that he considered his weak points to be his defence and his play of simple positions. Botvinnik commented that even when only 10 he had been impressed by Kasparov's ability to quickly assess a number of complex variations, as well as by his desire to achieve perfection.

In the following years, Kasparov made what seemed his inevitable progress towards the highest world honours. He was USSR champion in 1981, won the interzonals, then defeated Belyavsky, Korchnoi and Smyslov in candidates matches to become the official title challenger.

Play began in his series against Anatoly Karpov in September 1984, victory going to the first man to win six games. Karpov quickly swept to a 4–0 lead as his younger opponent proved over-confident at the start then unable to adjust to defeats. Then Kasparov made a remarkable switch of match strategy. He began to settle for quick draws, aiming simply to spin out the contest well into the Russian winter in the hope of exploiting his superior physical condition.

A tedious series of 17 consecutive draws followed, a record for championship play and arousing the Moscow audience to slow handclaps and whistles of derision. At last Karpov won again, stretching his lead to 5–0 and apparently vindicating his patient approach.

Then the champion made what Kasparov later called 'a gross planning error'. Anatoly Karpov's dream as champion was always to prove himself on the same or a higher level than his great predecessor Bobby Fischer. Part of Fischer's legendary reputation rested on his 6–0 match victories over Taimanov and Larsen; now he, Karpov, also had a chance of 6–0.

So Karpov began to sit on his lead, just waiting for Kasparov to make a fatal slip. But the match was now into its fourth and fifth month, and Karpov's strength was ebbing. Kasparov got back to 5–1, then Karpov suddenly lost two games in a row for 5–3 after 48 games. The match was becoming an embarassment to the Soviet authorities, and play was transferred from the grand Hall of Columns to the Hotel Sport in the suburbs.

After 48 games Florencio Campomanes, President of the International Chess Federation (FIDE) took his controversial and unprecedented decision to annul the match. He made his announcement at a chaotic Moscow press conference where both Karpov and Kasparov declared they wanted to continue to play. Campomanes then led the grandmasters backstage for private discussions after which he confirmed his decision. K and K blamed each other, the chess world was aghast at what was seen as an arbitrary and false conclusion which many thought was made to rescue a tottering Karpov. Objectively, however, it was still much more likely that Karpov would win one game before Kasparov won three, and the defending champion played under a psychological burden in the next K v K series in 1985.

Kasparov recognised that he still had something to prove. He began a series of mini-matches against Western contenders for the world title, and showed brilliant form. In this game, an early knight raid dislocates the white position, then the white king is chased across the board into a mating net.

White: R. Hubner. Black: G. Kasparov

Opening: English (1st match game 1985)

1.	c4	e5
2.	Nc3	d6
3.	d4	exd4
4.	Qxd4	Nf6
5.	g3	Nc6
6.	Qd2	Be6
7.	Nd5	Ne5
8.	b3	Ne4
9.	Qe3	Nc5

Here the game really starts. White's rare opening system plans to control the centre at long distance via fianchettoed bishops, while Black harries with his knights. White's ninth improves on Qd4 of Taimanov–Smyslov, 1967, where Black gained time by a Nc6 attack on the white queen.

10.	Bb2	c6
11.	Nf4	Ng4
12.	Qd4	Ne4!

White's calm formation is suddenly wrecked. If 13. Qxe4? Qa5+ 14. Kd1 Nxf2+ wins the queen. So the white king has to run the other way, to a file which Kasparov can open for his rooks.

13.	Bh3	Qa5+
14.	Kf1	Ngxf2
15.	Bxe6	fxe6
16.	Nxe6	Kd7

Not Nxh1? 17. Qxe4 threatening both Nc7+ and Qxh1 – but now Black plans to strengthen his attack by Qf5.

17.	Nh3	Nxh3
18.	Qxe4	Re8
19.	Nc5+	Qxc5
20.	Qg4+	Kc7

21. Qxh3   Be7
22. Bxg7   Rhf8+!

At modest material cost, Kasparov has all his pieces trained on the white king.

23. Bxf8   Rxf8+
24. Ke1   Qf2+
25. Kd1   Qd4+
26. Kc2   Qe4+
27. Kd2   Bg5+
28. Kc3   Qe5+
29. Resigns

If 29. Kd3 Qe3+ or if 29. Kb4 Bd2+ 30. Ka3 Bc3 when White is soon mated.

In the first half of the 1985 title match, Karpov looked as if he might still fend off his challenger. It was now the best of 24 games, with Karpov keeping his crown if he could draw 12–12.

When the champion led 5½–4½ at nearly half-way and reached a level position in the next game, he looked well in control. Then he allowed a Kasparov brilliancy, and from that moment the odds favoured a new champion of the world.

White: G. Kasparov. Black: A. Karpov

Opening: Nimzo-Indian Defence (11th game 1985)

1. d4   Nf6
2. c4   e6
3. Nc3   Bb4
4. Nf3   0–0
5. Bg5   c5
6. e3   cxd4
7. exd4   h6
8. Bh4   d5
9. Rc1   dxc4
10. Bxc4 Nc6
11. 0–0   Be7
12. Re1   b6
13. a3   Bb7
14. Bg3

Here and in the next few moves, Kasparov expects too much from his central pawn push – more precise is 14. Ba2.

14. ...   Rc8
15. Ba2   Bd6
16. d5   Nxd5
17. Nxd5   Bxg3
18. hxg3   exd5
19. Bxd5   Qf6
20. Qa4   Rfd8
21. Rcd1   Rd7?

Karpov starts to relax, seeing no danger. Correct is Rc7.

22. Qg4   Rcd8?

Black should admit his error with R7d8, though 23. b4 gives White the initiative. Kasparov likes theatrical and flamboyant gestures. After Karpov's blunder, the challenger tugged at his collar and tie as if gasping for breath, swivelled his chair to stare into the audience, turned back to face Karpov, then pounced with his reply. Karpov sat shocked.

23. Qxd7!   Rxd7
24. Re8+   Kh7
25. Be4+   Resigns

For if g6 26. Rxd7 Ba6 27. Bxc6 Qxc6 28. Rxf7 mate.

In the second half of the match, Kasparov gradually took control and finished in the grand manner with a win in the final 24th game when Karpov himself was still trying to tie the series. FIDE rules provided for yet another K v K match, which Kasparov won in London and Leningrad despite losing three games in succession near the end.

Kasparov's recent chess career has been so dominated by his marathon against Karpov (at Brussels 1987 they contested their 100th game) that he has had too few opportunities to show his wonderful skills against slightly lesser opposition. But he won Brussels 1986

Gary Kasparov with one of his coaches, Sakharov. He was also taught by ex-world champion Botvinnik who said 'the future of chess is in the hands of this boy'.

convincingly, led the Soviet team to gold medals ahead of England's silver in the 1986 olympics, and defeated Miles by a remarkable 5½-½ margin.

The great strength of Gary Kasparov's chess style is that he keeps strategic control and only brings his tactical virtuosity into play at decisive moments. This unusual maturity, derived from his teacher Botvonnik, can be seen in one of his early games as a 16-year-old.

White: G. Kasparov. Black: M. Vukic

Opening: King's Indian Defence (Banja Luka 1979)

The opening moves were 1. c4 Nf6 2. Nc3 g6 3. d4 Bg7 4. e4 d6 5. Nf3 0–0 6. Be2 Bg4 7. Be3 Nfd7.

The opening is the Simagin variation, named after a late Russian grandmaster, which plans to attack th dark squares in the centre by Bxf3 and c5 or Nc6.

8. Ng1

Crossing Black's idea. The knight move is not new, but indicates Kasparov's preference for imposing his own strategy on the game rather than simply neutralizing his opponent's manoeuvres.

8. ...   Bxe2

9. Ngxe2   e5

This does not turn out well, and 9. ... c5 looks a better way of attacking the centre.

10. 0–0   a5
11. Qd2   Nc6
12. f3   exd4
13. Nxd4   Nc5

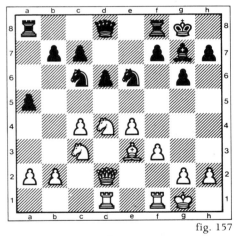

fig. 157

14. Rad1   Ne6

15. Ndb5!

A manoeuvre to note in similar positions – the knight outpost is strong because Black cannot easily dislodge it without losing his d pawn. In the next few moves Black prepares a cumbersome plan to drive off the annoying horse, but meanwhile Kasparov has time to build up a king's side attack.

15. Nxc6? or 15. Nxe6? would be basic strategical mistakes. White is ahead on space because of the c4 and e4 pawns which control the centre and the general rule is to aim for exchanges when you are cramped but avoid them if the opponent lacks room. Of course Black could have himself exchanged pieces by 13. ... Nxd4 on the previous move but that would incur another drawback. The black-squared bishops would almost certainly be exchanged after 14. Bxd4 Bxd4 15. Qxd4 and then White has good attacking chances based on Nd5 and f4-5-6, aiming eventually to create mating threats with the queen against g7.

15. ...   Re8
16. Qc1

Threatening to weaken the d pawn further by 17. c5, and so forcing the black queen to move away. Note that controlling a file with your rook opposite then enemy queen is generally a good technique even if several other men are between the rook and queen.

16. ...   Qb8
17. Bh6   Bh8
18. Nd5   Nb4
19. a3   Na6

At last Black is ready to kick away the annoying knight by c6, but his queen, QR and a6 knight are far from the king's side battlefield while Kasparov, with his superior space control, can easily switch his pieces between flanks. So White now aims to break through on the f line, which is the most promising to open up because his rook occupies it and his bishop controls f8.

20. f4!   c6

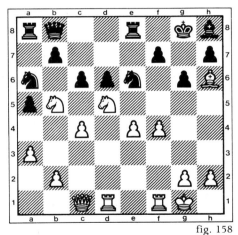

fig. 158

21. f5!

So that if Nec5 22. fxg6 hxg6 23. Qf4 with a winning attack, or if Nd8 22. fxg6 hxg6 23. Nf6+ Bxf6 24. Rxf6 cxb5 25. Qc3.

21. ...   cxd5
22. fxe6   Rxe6
23. exd5   Re7

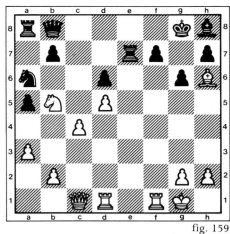

fig. 159

24. Bf4!

Now White's advantage becomes decisive, for if Be5 25. Bxe5 dxe5 26. d6 or here 25. ... Rxe5 26. Rf6.

24. ...   Rd7

25. Nxd6!

Winning a key pawn, for if Rxd6 26. c5 wins.

25. ...   Qd8
26. Nb5   Nc5
27. Qe3   b6
28. b4   axb4
29. axb4   Na6
30. Bg5   Qb8
31. d6   Nxb4
32. Be7   Qb7

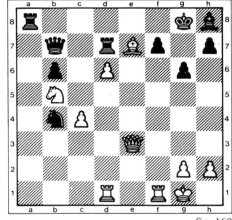

fig. 160

The d6 pawn cuts the black defenders in two. Now comes the final attack.

33. Rxf7!   Kxf7
34. Rf1+   Bf6

If 34. ... Kg7 35. Qe5+ forces mate.

35. Bxf6   Resigns

If 35. ... Kg8 36. Qe6+ Rf7 37. Be7 Raf8 38. Rxf7 Rxf7 39. d7 wins.

Nigel Short 1965–

In his early twenties, Nigel Short is already talked about as a young chess-player with a real chance of stopping the Russian master plan of the 1980s and the domination of world chess by Anatoly Karpov and Gary Kasparov. His achievements at the age of 14 were ahead of Kasparov's and comparable only with Fischer and Mecking, who were both national champions and qualifiers for the world title interzonal at that age. Nigel Short tied for the British men's championship at 14, though beaten on tie-break, and he obtained his first international master result a few months younger than did his great rivals.

One aspect of Nigel Short's chess which most surprises non-players is that he is a normal, friendly outgoing young man with none of the temperamental quirks which, due mainly to Fischer, people ascribe to all chess prodigies. Another surprise is that he is British — prodigies in music as well as chess tend to be Slavs, Jews or Latins.

Nigel has an instinctive natural grasp of chess principles which would have ensured his rapid development under any circumstances, but he was also lucky to be born into a family which did its utmost to help him in such vital practical matters as regular transport to matches and tournaments, and fortunate also to emerge coincidentally with a successful English programme to spot young talent.

At the age of nine, he was recommended for a place in a national junior squad coaching tournament, and as a result was able to play in a whole succession of events against older boys. Before the talent-spotting programme began, it was rare for British nine-year-olds to play outside their own age group, but now we emphasize the value of hard competition against older juniors as well as adults. By spring 1965, less than a year after joining the national squad, he competed successfully in the annual Jersey Open.

One of Nigel's early characteristics which set him apart from other talented juniors was his belief in his own ideas. At Jersey he lost a narrow rook ending and the referee, Peter Clarke, a master player suggested a different line. Nigel did not take this advice as gospel and demonstrated his own analysis. This would be a normal reaction from an adult expert but showed unusual self-confidence from a ten-year-old. By the time he was eleven, he had equalled or surpassed most of the other prodigies by qualifying for the British men's championship final, the youngest to perform such a feat. In the final he went further, and defeated Dr Jonathan Penrose, who had won the title a record ten times.

It is typical of chess prodigies that they concentrate on the strategical aspect of chess, can do the simple things well, and are strong in the endgame. How successfully Nigel mastered this approach is shown by the game which ensured his British Championship place. When Ludgate, the 1976 Irish champion, adopts a cramped formation, Nigel counters by the classical recipe of softening up the black defences by probing attacks (see the advance of White's KBP on moves 8–12) before going for a decisive break in the centre to open up the black king.

White: Nigel Short. Black: A.T. Ludgate

Opening: Modern Defence (British championship semi-finals, North-West England, zone 1977)

1.	e4	g6
2.	d4	Bg7
3.	Nc3	c6

Black hopes to switch to a Caro-Kann Defence (normally starting 1. e4 c6) if White now plays 4. Nf3, but Nigel likes to play positions with a space advantage and now plays to control the centre.

4.	Bc4	d6

More active is b5 followed by b4.

5.	Qf3!	

Played by many 11-year-olds, this move would simply denote a wish to give Scholar's Mate by Qxf7; but here it is part of White's plan to keep the Black game under restraint.

5.	...	e6
6.	Nge2	Ne7

Black is still playing passively; better d5.

7.	Bg5!	

To force weaknesses in the black pawn front.

7.	...	0–0
8.	h4!	

Aiming at restraint rather than mate. Quieter and more routine play would enable Black to counter by Kh8 followed by f5.

8.	...	f6
9.	Be3	d5

10. Bb3	Nd7
11. h5	g5
12. h6	Bh8
13. Qg3	

Nigel Short's only imprecision in this game. Black's knight now reaches f5 with gain of time so more accurate is 13. 0-0-0 at once.

13. ...	Nb6
14. 0-0-0	dxe4
15. Nxe4	Nf5
16. Qf3	Nxe3
17. fxe3	Nd5?

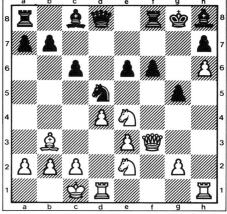

fig. 161

Here f5 18. Nc5 Qe7 intending . . . g4 gives Black some play and could cause White to regret his 13th.

18. Rh5!

This unusual move puts everything back in order for White. Black's counterplay is stopped, and White prepares to dislodge the d5 knight.

18. ...	Bd7
19. Nc5	b6
20. Nxd7	Qxd7
21. e4	Nc7
22. d5!	cxd5
23. exd5	Rad8

If 23. . . . exd5 24. Rxd5!

24. Nc3	Qe7
25. dxe6	Rxd1+
26. Qxd1	Re8
27. Nd5	Nxd5
28. Qxd5	Kf8

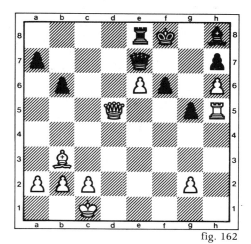

fig. 162

29. Rh1!

In conjunction with the previous diagram, this move reveals a refreshing freedom from dogma. Now it is right to bring back the rook and regroup for the final attack.

29. ...	Rd8
30. Qc4	f5
31. Rf1	f4
32. g3	Bd4
33. gxf4	Be3+
34. Kb1	Bxf4
35. Qc3	Kg8
36. Qg7+!	Qxg7
37. e7+	Resigns

A poor game by Black, but Nigel's direct logical play is reminiscent of the young Capablanca whose games influenced his style.

After his promising debut in the British Championship, Nigel Short's progress continued with few breaks. At the age of 12, in his first international event, the 1978 Aaronson Masters, he totalled 5½ out of 10 and only the top players could beat him. On his second appearance in the British Championship he finished in the top half and then he won in successive years the bronze and silver medals at the world under-17 championship where he was one of the youngest competitors. True he didn't win the gold medal, but neither did Kasparov.

For a while in late 1978 and early 1979 Nigel's progress slowed; then he suddenly progressed within a few months from national expert to international master strength. The organisers of the Geneva open invited him to Switzerland for the publicity. When, on his fourteenth birthday, he lost to grandmaster Nunn, few could have guessed what would follow, for he beat his next five Swiss opponents, and in the final round defeated France's No. 1 in the 1976 world team championship. Victory brought him a share of the first prize of 3,500 Swiss francs (about £1,000) with Nunn, and the decisive game once more had the hallmarks of the style of early Capablanca – clarity, rapid development, and a small combination to clinch the strategic advantage.

White: Nigel Short. Black: E. Preissmann
Opening: Ruy Lopez (Geneva 1979)
1. e4 e5 2. Nf3 Nc6 3. Bb5 f5 4. d3 fxe4 5. dxe4 Nf6 6. Qe2!

Black has chosen an unusual defence to Nigel's favourite Ruy Lopez (3. Bb5 f5 where 3. . . . a6 is normal) in the hope of catching him by surprise. Instead, he is himself surprised – the usual sixth move is Nc3 when Black has good play by Bb4. After the text Black has no good waiting move and has to lock in his f8 bishop.

6. ...	d6
7. Nc3	Bg4

Trying to make White lose time by capturing on f3 with the queen which has already moved, but the weakening of the

light squares is serious. Better is Be6.

8. h3	Bxf3
9. Qxf3	Be7
10. Qe2	a6

If 10. . . . 0-0 11. Bxc6 and 12. Qc4+ wins a pawn, while if 10. . . . Qd7 11. Nd5 is unpleasant to meet.

11. Bxc6+	bxc6
12. 0-0	c5
13. f4!	

This forcing move puts Black in a dilemma. 13. . . . exf4 14. Bxf4 0-0 15. e5 is good for White, but in trying to keep his pawn front intact Black risks rapid defeat.

13. ...	Nd7?
14. Qh5+	g6
15. Qg4	exf4
16. Bxf4	0-0
17. Qe6+?	

17. Bh6! wins quickly, for if Rxf1+ 18. Rxf1 White either invades by Qe6+ and Rf7, or if 18. . . . Nf8 19. Nd5 and Black is movebound.

17. ...	Kg7
18. Nd5	Bh4

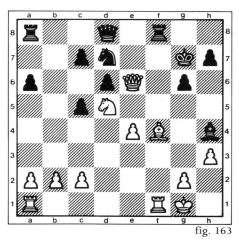

fig. 163

19. Nxc7!

Nigel demonstrates that White is still winning despite his slip a few moves earlier. This 'small combination' in Capablanca style leads to a forced sequence and to a decisive advantage for White.

19. ...	Qxc7
20. Bxd6	Qd8
21. Bxf8+	Nxf8
22. Qf7+	Kh8
23. Rad1	Qe7
24. Qd5	Ra7

Nigel Short became the world's youngest international master at 14, Hastings 1980. He was a grandmaster at 18, ranked in the world top ten at 21. Can he take Britain to the world title in the 1980s?

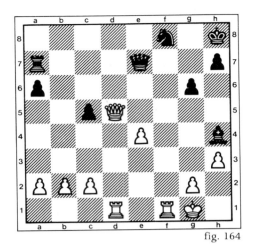

fig. 164

Apparently Black is just holding his game together, but . . .

    25. Qd8!

Decisive, for if Qxd8 26. Rxd8 Bxd8 27. Rxf8 + and 28. Rxd8.

25. ...	Kg7
26. Rxf8	Qxe4

Or Qxf8 27. Qxh4 wins.

27. Rg8 +	Kh6
28. Qf8 +	**Resigns**

After Kh5 comes 29. g4 + followed by Qxc5 + and Qxa7.

With its emphasis on space control and classical strategic play, Nigel's chess is in the tradition of Morphy, Capablanca, Fischer and Karpov rather than the more tactical, complex, psychologically-oriented and counterpunching style characteristic of Lasker, Tal and Korchnoi. Like most of the other classicists he favours 1. e4 and the Ruy Lopez as his standby opening with White, although when playing Black his speciality is the French Defence 1. e4 e6 which never found much favour with the other classicists. Capablanca and Karpov were sometimes rather negative with the black pieces, content to draw and reserve their major efforts for the games with White, while Short follows Korchnoi in using the Winawer variation of the French (1. e4 e6 2. d4 d5 3. Nc3 Bb4) as a counter-attack weapon.

At the ICL Hastings international of 1979–80, Nigel made a decisive breakthrough to prove his remarkable talent. He defeated four grandmasters including the tournament co-winner Andersson of Sweden and finished a prize-winner with 8 out of 15. It was not only his result, but the style of his wins which impressed all the experts. Here is his victory over a leading American GM.

White: Nigel Short. Black: P. Biyiasus (US)

Opening: Ruy Lopez (ICL Hastings, 1979–80)

The opening moves were 1. e4 e5 2. Nf3 Nc6 3. Bb5 a6 4. Ba4 d6 5. d4 b5 6. Bb3 Nxd4 7. Nxd4 exd4 8. c3.

This promising gambit incidentally avoids a trick worth knowing in club chess and so ancient as to be named the 'Noah's Ark Trap'. If 8. Qxd4? c5 9. Qd5 Be6 10. Qe6 + Bd7 11. Qd 5 c4 traps the bishop and wins.

8. ...	Bb7
9. cxd4	Nf6

9. ... Bxe4? 10. 0–0 followed by Re1 puts the bishop in a near-fatal pin.

10. f3	Be7

An immediate 10. ... c5 stops White consolidating his centre.

11. 0–0	0–0
12. Be3	c5
13. Nc3	Re8
14. Qe1	

Short's pawn centre shields his attacking piece build-up against the king.

14. ...	Bf8
15. Rd1	c4
16. Bc2	Nd7
17. d5	g6
18. Qg3	Qc7
19. a3	Bg7
20. f4	Nc5

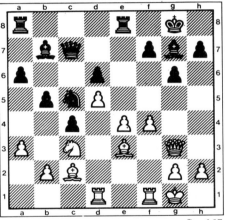

fig. 167

21. e5!

Strategically decisive. If 21. ... dxe5 22. f5! opens up the black king's defences. So the grandmaster tries to blunt the attack by exchanging one of the dangerous bishops.

21. ..	Nd3
22. Bxd3	cxd3
23. Rxd3	dxe5
24. f5!	Qc4
25. Rd2	Rad8
26. h4	a5

Not 26. ... Bxd5? 27. Rfd1 wins the bishop. With the text, Black hopes to undermine the centre and win the d pawn. He succeeds, but White's attack is too fast. Bc8 bringing an extra piece to defence is a better chance.

27. h5	Rd6
28. fxg6	fxg6
29. h6	Bf6
30. Bg5	Bxg5
31. Qxg5	

White is angling for one of two basic mates: back row (page 34) or pawn on h6 with queen on g7, a variant of the f6 pawn attack on page 31.

31. ...	b4
32. Nd1	Rxd5
33. Ne3	Qc5
34. Rdf2	

With terrible threats: Rf7, Qf6, Ng4–f6 + and Nxd5 are all in the air.

34. ...	R5d8
35. Ng4	Rf8
36. Nf6 +	Kh8
37. Ne4	Qd4
38. Qxe5 +	**Resigns**

The back row theme triumphs; logical finishes in chess always please.

Short's advance continued steadily through his teenage years. He won BBC2's televised Master Game at 15, qualified as a grandmaster at 18, and at 21 was firmly established in the world top ten.

Results in 1986 and 1987 gave him increasing prominence as the best Western hope to challenge Karpov and Kasparov. He beat the world champion at Brussels 1986, and in early 1987 won the strong grandmaster tournaments at Wijk aan Zee and Reykjavik in commanding style. London Docklands and Channel 4 combined to sponsor him for a six-game quickplay match against Kasparov at 25 minutes per player per game. Short did significantly better than most of Kasparov's opponents in mini-matches, losing only 2–4.

Short's brilliant run in early 1987 culminated in a brilliant game. White's strategy in opening up an apparently blocked position for his bishop pair, and his later dynamic tactics, are reminiscent of Bobby Fischer's celebrated first match game against Larsen.

White: Nigel Short. Black: J.H. Timman (Netherlands)

Opening: French Defence (IBM Reykjavik 1987)

    1. e4   e6

2. d4	d5
3. Nc3	Bb4
4. e5	c5
5. a3	Bxc3+
6. bxc3	Ne7
7. Nf3	Qa5
8. Qd2	Bd7
9. Rb1	

An unusual idea, designed indirectly to strengthen White's centre. Black's bishop is diverted to c6 and this stops a double attack by Black's knights on the d pawn.

9. ...	Bc6
10. Bd3	Nd7
11. 0–0	c4
12. Be2	h6
13. h4	

Another Short patent, which he also employed against Korchnoi in a slightly different position. The pawn audience neutralizes Black's possible ... g5 counterplay.

13. ...	0–0–0
14. Bd1	f5?

Here and next move Timman opens up e5 for Short's knight and concedes diagonals to the bishop pair. Instead Rdg8! main-taining the ... g5 option, would limit White's activity.

15. exf6	Nxf6?
16. Qe1	Ne4
17. Rb4	Rhf8
18. Ne5	Qc7
19. Bg4	Rf6
20. f3	Nd6
21. Bh3	Bd7
22. Rf2	Nf6
23. Rb1	Nf7
24. Nxd7	Qxd7
25. Bf4!	

The bishops erupt into action, and suddenly Black's king is caught in the crossfire. Here 25. ... Rxf4 fails to 26. Bxe6.

25. ...	g5
26. Re2!	Re8

If gxf4 27. Rxe6.

27. Bh2	gxh4
28. Qxh4	Ng5
29. Bg4	Qg7
30. Rde1	b6
31. Qh5	Qd7
32. f4!	

The elegant final attack flows naturally from White's earlier play.

32. ...	Ne4
33. Rxe4!	dxe4
34. d5	Nd8
35. Qe5	Rf5
36. dxe6	Qd2
37. Qxe4	Rd5
38. e7+	Kc7
39. f5+	Resigns

If Kb7 White has a winning choice of exd8=N+ or Rd1.

When Capablanca became Cuba's first world champion, Euwe won the title for Holland and Bobby Fischer defeated Spassky, the entire status of the game in their countries was raised. And in terms of world public interest a Western challenger means far more than an all-Soviet match betweeen the similarly named Karpov and Kasparov. It is likely that if you are a British reader buying this book in the late 1980's, it will be partly because your interest has been aroused by Britain's world title contender Nigel Short.

Winning Plans
for Black

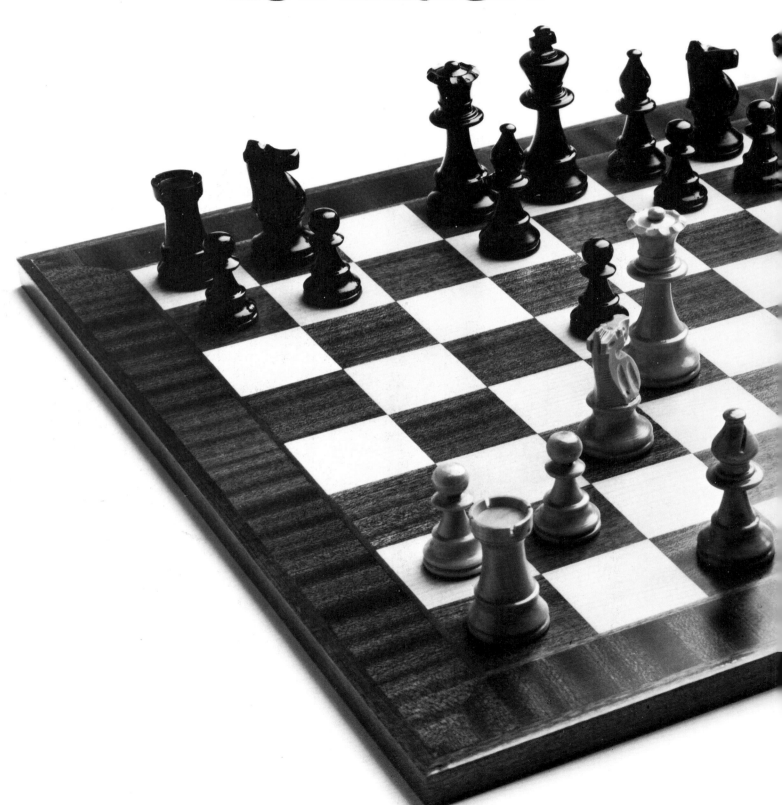

There is much to be said in favour of a novice chessplayer keeping to a narrow repertoire of solid openings to reduce the risk of quick disasters and enable him to build up his experience of middle games and endgames. But for the ambitious player who wants to win money prizes in congresses, and who aims to get into his club and county team and eventually to make his mark at national level, it is desirable to build up knowledge of a range of aggressive and currently popular formations. These can give a sub-stantial advantage against a less well-primed opponent even if he is a stronger player. It is particularly necessary in tournaments, where winning a prize requires a high percentage, to aim to do very well with the white pieces.

It is important, too, to be realistic about the openings in your repertoire. Check as far as possible in the literature (games collections, tournament bulletins, and your own observations from the score sheets at congresses) whether the opening has a good practical record. By this I mean it should score 65–70 per cent or more in a variety of over-the-board play, regardless of whether the system is assessed as strong and theoretically watertight by books and articles. You should be interested in winning, not just theoretical advantage. If you adopt a slightly unusual line regularly, you will not always have the supposedly best reply played against you. Opponents will either not know it and fear being 'out-booked', or be so impressed by your knowledge that they will duck into a less critical side-variant.

You should be prepared to play a chosen opening fairly regularly for at least one chess season. It takes time to get the feel of a new line of play and to be able to deal successfully using general principles with divergences from the analysis prepared at home. Recommended technique is that after each game with your repertoire opening you refresh your memory with the book references and try to find out where you and/or your opponent went wrong. Another valuable form of practice is to find a friend of similar chess strength and to play a succession of quick games on the clock (5–10 minutes per player per game) aimed principally at deepening your knowledge of your opening system.

Because White always starts the game, it is easier for him to prepare attacking, theoretical openings than for Black. Unless you are already a strong and experienced player, it is sensible to limit your Black repertoire, aiming to reach a solid and comfortable middle game. The strong player who knows a variety of openings can adopt a bolder, more varied approach. He can take on some of the sharp theoretical lines (for example the currently fashionable 1. e4 c5 2. Nf3 Nc6 3. d4 cxd4 4. Nxd4 Nf6 5. Nc3 e6 6. Ndb5 d6 7. Bf4 e5 8. Bg5 a6 on which there are already many articles and at least one book) knowing a lot of the theory and also being well prepared for

The Tarrasch Gambit (page 101). Black offers his d5 isolated pawn, and hopes to develop fast attacking play by forcing the exposed white queen to retreat with loss of time.

white alternatives between move 2 and move 6. The inexperienced player, however, should know at least a couple of black openings where the worst that can happen is a somewhat passive position.

Which of the openings do you choose? Paradoxically, it would be a disservice to readers of this book to recommend one in particular. Several books have gone into detail on one or two lines of play for Black, but their drawback is that White can also consult such literature and take appropriate counter-measures.

Thus in discussing a black repertoire I shall in most cases not analyse the openings in great detail. But it is possible to describe the type of play that results, and this may help readers decide on particular defences for their own repertoires.

The French Defence

The French Defence **1. e4 e6** has kept its reputation as a sound if slightly passive opening for a full century. In playing it, the best method is to avoid the main lines such as the Winawer 2. d4 d5 3. Nc3 Bb4 and to prefer an active plan which is less heavily analyzed.

I recommend two ideas. The first is 1. e4 e6 2. d4 c5 – a slightly inferior but still playable move. It has the advantage that it can lead to similar formations to the defence 1. d4 c5 which can also be adopted by those requiring a reasonable defence with a minimum of book. After 3. d5 (if 3. Nf3 then cxd4 is objectively best, transposing into one of the main lines of the Sicilian Defence 1. e4 c5, but in games between inexperienced players I recommend Black to continue 3. . . . d5 accepting a weak isolated queen's pawn by 4. exd5 exd5 5. Nc3 followed soon by dxc5 but gaining in return active piece play) exd5 4. exd5 d6 5. Nc3 Nf6 6. Nf3 Be7 7. Be2 0-0 8. 0-0 Na6, Black can follow up with the plan Nc7, Rb8, a6 and b5 to gain space on the queen's side.

The second, more conventional approach is **1. e4 e6 2. d4 d5** and now there are a number of possibilities which at any level Black has to know in some depth.

Before looking at these, it is worth noting the system 1. e4 e6 2. Nf3 d5 3. Nc3 (delaying d4), which has become popular in tournaments in recent years. Black's best answer is to open up the centre quickly by 3. . . . Nf6 4. e5 Nfd7 5. d4 c5 6. dxc5 Nc6 7. Bf4 Bxc5 8. Bd3 f6! not *0-0?* 9. *Bxh7+!* with a winning attack) 9. exf6 Nxf6 10. 0-0 0-0 e.g. 11. Ne5 Bd7 12. Nxc6 Bxc6 13. Qe2 Ne4! 14. g3 (better Bxe4) Nxf2! 15. Rxf2 Bxf2+ 16. Kxf2 (*16. Qxf2 e5*) Qb6+ 17. Kg2 e5 18. Qh5 h6 19. Bxe5 Qe3! 20. Qg6 Rf2+ and White resigns (Vogt–Farago, Kecskemet 1979).

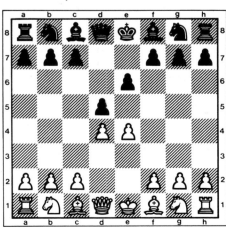

fig. 168

3. Nc3

The Exchange variation 3. **exd5 exd5** normally indicates that White is playing for a draw, though there have been some

modern attempts to infuse some life into the system. However Black can avoid symmetry by castling on the opposite side to White and then has good chances of achieving a lively game. Examples are:

(a) **4. Bd3 Nc6 5. Nf3 Bg4** followed by Qd7 and 0-0-0.

'b) **4. Bd3 Nc6 5. Ne2 Bd6 6. Nbc3** (*6. c3 Qh4!* with initiative) Nb4 7. Bb5+ c6 8. Ba4 Bg4 (prevents 9. Bf4 exchanging White's inferior bishop) followed soon by 0-0-0.

(c) **4. Nc3 Bb4 5. Qf3 Qe7+!** 6. Ne2 Nc6 7. Be3 Nf6 8. h3 Bxc3+! 9. bxc3 Ne4 and White's queen's side is weak.

(d) **4. Nc3 Bb4 5. Bd3 Nc6 6. a3 Bxc3+** 7. bxc3 Nf6 8. Bg5 Qe7+ 9. Ne2 Bd7 10. 0-0 h6 11. Bf4 0-0-0 12. c4 Be6 13. c5 g5! and Black's attack proved stronger in Miles–Short, British Championship 1979.

Another major plan is 3. Nd2. If then 3. . . . c5 4. exd5 Black is soon faced with an isolated queen's pawn which Korchnoi had difficulty in defending during his 1974 match with Karpov. This system is recommended for White and is analyzed later in the chapter. From the Black side I recommend two counters to 3. Nd2, one hardly analyzed at all and the other aiming to restrict White to a marginal plus. The hardly-analyzed plan is **3. Nd2 Ne7** 4. Ngf3 Ng6 (provoking White's reply: also possible is Nd7 followed by c5) 5. h4 c5 6. h5 Ne7 7. c3 cxd4 8. cxd4 Nbc6 9. Bb5 h6 10. 0-0 Bd7 11. Re1 Qb6 and, though cramped on the K-side, Black has counterplay in the centre and later castled queen's side (Plaskett–Taulbut, Lloyds Bank Masters 1979). Of course White has alternative plans to 5. h4 in straightforward development; but if the knight is not chased away Black can strike at the centre by f6.

A more conventional reply to 3. Nd2 is **3. . . . Nf6.**

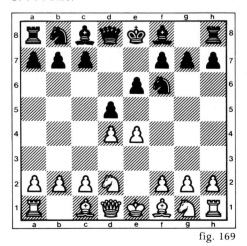

fig. 169

4. e5

If **4. Bd3 c5** 5. exd5 Nxd5 gives Black few problems.

4. . . .	**Nfd7**
5. Bd3	

5. f4 is a modern plan designed to build

a firm pawn base in the centre before a later advance on the K-side. One reasonable counter is c5 6. c3 Nc6 7. Ndf3 Qa5 8. Ne2 b5 9. Bd2 or 9. Be3 b4 opening lines for Black's pieces: if cxb4 Black retakes with the knight.

Also playable is the Korchnoi Gambit **5. Ngf3 c5** 6. c3 Nc6 7. Bd3 Qb6 8. 0-0 cxd4 9. cxd4 Nxd4 10. Nxd4 Qxd4 11. Nf3 Qb6 12. Qc2 (or *12. Qa4 Qb4 13. Qc2 Nc5*) Nc5 13. Be3 Bd7 14. Bxh7 Rc8 (Soltis–Root, Lone Pine 1979) when White has pressure but Black can hold the game with careful defence. For another example of the Korchnoi Gambit, see page 71.

5. . . .	**c5**
6. c3	**Nc6**
7. Ne2	**cxd4**
8. cxd4	**f6**

The other main alternative is 8. . . . Qb6 9. Nf3 f6 10. exf6 Nxf6 11. 0-0 Bd6 12. Bf4 Bxf4 13. Nxf4 Qxb2 14. Re1 0-0 15. Nxe6 with a slight edge for White.

9. exf6	**Qxf6**

Better than 9. . . . Nxf6 10. Nf3 Bd6 11. Bf4 when the exchange of bishops leaves Black with the inferior bishop and weak dark squares in the centre.

10. Nf3	

An alternative to 10. 0-0 when accepting the pawn by Nxd4 11. Nxd4 Qxd4 12. Nf3 Qf6 13. Bg5 allows White's pieces too much activity, but Black can decline the gambit safely by 10. . . . Bd6.

10. . . .	**Bb4+**

Black exchanges off his 'good' bishop, the one not restricted by his pawn front, with a view to gaining time for his later . . . e5 which will give scope for the other bishop.

11. Bd2	**Bxd2+**
12. Qxd2	**0-0**
13. 0-0	**e5**
14. dxe5	**Ndxe5**
15. Nxe5	**Qxe5**

White has a marginal advantage because of the isolated central pawn, but Black has free play for his pieces and in practice usually holds on comfortably.

The third important alternative to 3. Nc3 which Black needs to know is the direct advance **3. e5** setting up a pawn centre which Black must try to undermine or eliminate. Play generally continues:

3. . . .	**c5**

Also reasonable is 3. . . . **Ne7** (compare the similar idea 3. Nd2 Ne7 quoted earlier) 4. Nf3 (more flexible is *4. c3* to keep open the option of developing the knight at h3 or e2. On the other hand *4. Bd3* would allow c5 5. c3 Nec6 6. Ne2 cxd4 7. cxd4 Nb4! eliminating White's active bishop) b6 5. c3 Qd7 6. a4 a5 7. Na3 (more natural is *7. Nd2*) Ba6 8. Bxa6 Nxa6 9. 0-0 c6 10. Ne1 Nf5 and Black soon plays h5 and g6 with a solid light-square barricade (Kosten–Bednarski, Manchester Benedictine 1979).

4. c3	**Nc6**
5. Nf3	

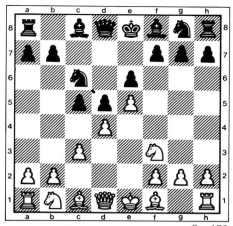

fig. 170

5. ...   Bd7

This innovation pioneered by Korchnoi and others is at least as good as the older moves **Qb6** and **Nge7** and carries less risk to Black of becoming embroiled in tactical gambits.

6. Be2

Other possibilities are (a) **6. Bd3** cxd4 7. cxd4 Rc8 and if 8. 0-0? Nb4 gains the bishop pair or (b) **6. dxc5** Bxc5 7. Bd3 f6 8. b4 Be7 9. b5 Nxe5 10. Nxe5 fxe5 11. Qh5+ Kf8 12. Qxe5 Bf6 13. Qd6+ Ne7 (Sveshnikov–Savon, Lvov 1978) when Black has a strong centre to compensate for moving his king.

6. ...   Nge7

A more active and double-edged plan is **6. ... f6** 7. 0-0 fxe5 8. dxe5 Qc7 9. Na3 (Hartston recommends *9. Re1* followed by c4) a6 (*Nxe5* is risky) 10. Bf4 Nh6! 11. Nc2 Nf7 12. c4 d4 13. Bd3 Be7 14. Qe2 g5 15. Bg3 0-0-0 16. b4 h5 with a strong attack for Black (Kupreychik–Gulko, USSR championship 1976).

7. Na3

Or **7. 0-0** Rc8 8. Re1 cxd4 9. cxd4 Nf5.

7. ...   cxd4
8. cxd4   Nf5
9. Nc2   Nb4
10. Ne3   Nxe3
11. fxe3   Be7

Better might be **11. ... a5** to stop the following advance.

12. a3   Nc6
13. b4

White has a slight advantage, but Black eventually won the game (Spassky–Korchnoi, match 1978).

The main line of the French Defence from which 3. exd5, 3. Nd2 and 3. e5 are variants is (**1. e4 e6 2. d4 d5**):

3. Nc3   Nf6

More fashionable, but too complex and highly analyzed from the ordinary player's viewpoint, is **3. ... Bb4**, the Winawer variation. The knight move can also start a promising counter-attack while Black can more easily lead the game into lines he knows well.

4. Bg5

4. Nfd7 5. f4 c5

A dangerous alternative is **4. e5** Nfd7 5. f4 c5 6. Nf3 Nc6 7. Be3 when Black's best is to exchange pieces and pawns on d4, then settle for Qb6 and a slightly inferior endgame. Instead the forcing line 7. ... Qb6 8. Na4 Qa5+ 9. c3 cxd4 10. b4 Nxb4 11. cxb4 Bxb4+ 12. Bd2 Bxd2+ 13. Nxd2 b6 14. Rb1 Ba6 turns out well for White by 15. Nb2! Bxd3 16. Nxd Nc5 17. Nf2 Na4 18. 0-0 Nc3 19. Qg4 0-0 20. Nf3 Rac8 21. Qh4 Qa4 22. Ng4 with a winning attack in Timman–Korchnoi, Brussels 1987.

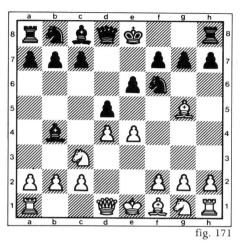

fig. 171

4. ...   Bb4

The McCutcheon variation (invented by a US amateur who played it successfully against Steinitz), launching a queen's side counter-attack with the intention of creating doubled pawns for White. Black has to defend carefully on the K-side, but the onus is on White to prove an advantage since exchanges usually give Black the better ending.

5. e5

If **5. exd5** Bxc3+ 6. bxc3 exd5 with similar play to line (c) of the Exchange variation. If **5. Bd3** h6 gains the pair of bishops.

5. ...   h6
6. Bd2

There are three important alternatives:
(a) **6. exf6** hxg5 7. fxg7 Rg8 8. h4 gxh4 9. Qh5 Qf6 10. Qxh4 Qxg7 and Black has safeguarded his two bishops.
(b) **6. Bh4** g5 7. Bg3 Ne4 8. Ne2 c5 9. a3 Bxc3+ 10. Nxc3 Qa5 11. Qd3 Nc6 and Black's Q-side initiative leaves him a comfortable game.
(c) **6. Be3** has become popular recently and requires careful defence: **6. ... Ne4 7. Qg4 Kf8** (moving the king is preferable here to 7. ... *g6*) 8. a3 and now:
(c1) **8. ... Ba5** 9. Nge2 c5 10. dxc5 Nc6 11. 0-0-0 or 11. b4 Nxc3 12. Nxc3 Nxe5 with unclear complications.
(c2) **8. ... Bxc3+** 9. bxc3 Nxc3 10. Bd3 c5 11. dxc5 Nc6 12. Nf3 d4! 13. Bxd4 Na4 14. c3 Qa5 (analysis by Cafferty) when Black will soon regain his pawn and complete his development.

6. ...   Bxc3
7. bxc3

As great a player as Fischer got an inferior position in a few moves as White in this opening: **7. Bxc3?** Ne4 8. Ba5 0-0 9. Bd3 Nc6 10. Bc3 Nxc3 11. bxc3 f6 (Fischer–Petrosian, Curaçao 1962) when White is handicapped by weak pawns.

7. ...   Ne4
8. Qg4   g6

In contrast to the note after 6. Be3, this now seems better than **Kf8**. Black has to be careful about White's advance h4-h5 and also of a bishop sacrifice at g6, but both can be parried and meanwhile Black can counter against White's Q-side.

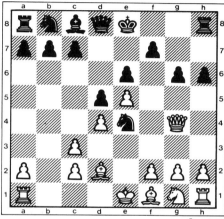

fig. 172

9. Bd3

White's most promising move. If:
(a) **9. Bc1** Nxc3 10. Bd3 c5 11. dxc5 Qa5 12. Bd2 Qa4! (Black offers the queen exchange to exploit White's weak pawns in the ending) 13. h3 (so that if *Qxg4? 14. hxg4* and Black's h pawn is weak) h5! 14. Qxa4 Nxa4 15. Bb5+ Bd7 16. Bxa4 Bxa4 17. Rb1 Nd7 18. Rxb7 Nxc5 19. Rc7 Na6 followed by 0-0 and Rfc8 and Black has an endgame edge.
(b) **9. h4** c5 10. Bd3 Nxd2 11. Kxd2 Nc6 12. Rh3 (*12. Nf3 Qa5 13. dxc5 Bd7* and White's tripled c pawns are weak) cxd4 13. cxd4 Qb6 14. Nf3 (the sacrifice *14. Ne2 Qb4+ 15. Kd1 Nxe5 16. Qf4 Nd7* followed by Ke7 and Qd6 is unsound) Bd7 15. Qf4 0-0-0! (*16. Qxf7 Nxd4*) with the initiative for Black.

9. ...   Nxd2
10. Kxd2   c5
11. Rb1

The best idea – White hopes that Black will swap pawns in the centre after which he can continue with the plan Nf3, Rhc1 and c4 opening up lines against the black king. If instead: **11. Nf3** Nc6 12. Qf4 cxd4 (Black can also play for a blocked, drawish position with *12. ... c4* as in the column, but not *12. ... Qc7? 13. Qf6* when White's Q invades on the dark squares)

95

13. cxd4 Bd7 14. h4 (*14. Rab1 Qa5+ 15. Ke2 b6*) Rc8 15. Qf6 Qa5+ and Black has enough central counterplay to meet White's K-side attack.

11. ...	**Nc6**
12. Nf3	**c4**

Black can also go for the more active but more risky **12. ... cxd4** 13. cxd4 Qa5+ 14. Ke2 b6 15. Qf4 Ba6 16. Rhc1 Rc8 17. Kf1 Qa3 (Matulovic–Zwetkoff, Varna 1965) when White can gambit a pawn at a2 or d3 for attacking chances.

13. Be2	**Qe7**
14. h4	**b6**
15. Qf4	**Bd7**
16. h5	**g5**

Similar positions occurred in some of Korchnoi's early games. Black's game is solid and he can even castle QR since the open b file is not enough on its own for White to mount a successful attack.

Gambit Defence

While recommending the French Defence as a solid standby against stronger opponents, it is not sufficient on its own as an answer to 1. e4. Unless your knowledge and feel for this opening is very good, playing it every time runs you into too many special counters prepared by opponents at home.

Against weaker players it is also particularly important to have some tactical, gambit counter-attacks which may be unsound but which can score quickly against imperfect defence. Many people reject inferior openings without even bothering to analyze them, so it is likely that your opponent will be unfamiliar with the resulting positions and will soon be playing on his own instead of remembering grandmaster analysis.

The sharp gambit nature of such counter-attacks means that hesitations or passive moves can quickly enable the 'unsound' system to blossom into a winning assault on the king. There is also the psychological angle to be considered: most amateurs believe that attacking chess wins. This may be so because so many published games are won by direct attacks, perhaps because the average amateur is a poor defender and gets flustered under pressure. Certainly at the lower levels of competitive chess attacking play makes an impression, and can easily induce a defeatist attitude in the opponent, thus lowering his resistance and making errors more likely.

The counter-attacks below are a selection of possible ideas which can disconcert a weaker opponent. Even more than in the French Defence, detailed knowledge of them will pay off and you are advised to consult other reference sources for any counter-attacks you decide to take up regularly.

Sicilian defence with 2 . . . Nf6

Worth a place in your repertoire because (a) after 1. e4 c5 2. Nf3 is normal for White and you are less likely than in other counter-attacks to have the frustration of finding the opponent doing something quite different (b) the defence is reputedly unsound but in practice is difficult to play for White.

The main line goes (1. e4 c5 2. Nf3) **Nf6** 3. e5 Nd5 4. Nc3 (from the White side 4. d4 cxd4 5. Qxd4 e6 6. Bc4 is more promising) e6.

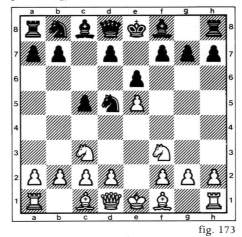

fig. 173

5. Nxd5

If **5. d4** or **5. Bc4**, Black plays 5. ... Nxc3 followed by ... d5 and develops easily against the weakened Q-side pawns. If **5. Ne4** f5 6. exf6 (the retreat 6. Nc3 is best, followed by Nc6 7. Nxd5 exd5 8. d4 d6 equalizing. In practice a weaker player is unlikely to think of moving his knight to e4 and then back again) Nxf6 with an open f file for counterplay, or here 6. Ng3 Nc6 7. b3 Qc7 8. Bb2 Nf4 and White's e pawn is weak.

5. ...	**exd5**
6. d4	**Nc6!**

Gambitting the d pawn for a complex attack.

7. dxc5	**Bxc5**
8. Qxd5	**d6!**

The older move is 8. ... Qb6 but then White has a direct and strong line in 9. Bc4 Bxf2+ 10. Ke2 0-0 11. Rf1 Bc5 12. Ng5 Nd4+ 13. Kd1 Ne6 14. Ne4 d6 15. exd6 Rd8 (*Bxd6? 16. Nxd6 Rd8 17. Bf4! Nxf4 18. Qxf7+ Kh8 19. Qg8+* with smothered mate, Unzicker–Sarapu, Siegen 1970) 16. Qh5 Bxd6 17. Bd3 f5 18. Nxd6! Qxd6 19. Qxf5 Qxh2 20. Qf7+ Kh8 21. Bg5 Rg8 22. Be3 with a winning attack (Pritchett–E. Gonzalez, Buenos Aires 1978).

9. exd6	**Qb6**

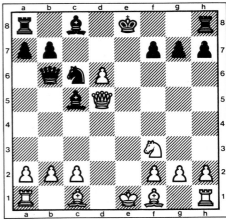

fig. 174

A promising position to have against a weaker opponent: White is temporarily two pawns up but likely to get worried by his exposed king and by the lack of a clear line of play.

Possibilities now are:

(a) **10. Qd2** 0-0 11. Bd3 Re8+ 12. Kf1 Bg4 and the lead in development is worth two pawns.

(b) **10. Be3** Qxb2 11. Qe4+ Be6 12. d7+ Kxd7 13. Rd1+ Kc8 14. Bxc5 Qc3+ and Qxc5.

(c) **10. Bd3** Bxf2+ 11. Ke2 Be6.

(d) **10. Qe4+** Be6 11. d7+ (or *11. Qh4 Bxd6 12. c3 Be7 13. Qg3 0-0-0* with attack) Kxd7 12. Be3 Bxe3 13. Rd1+ Kc7 14. fxe3 Qxb2 with unclear complications.

(e) **10. Bc4** Bxf2+ 11. Ke2 (*11. Kf1 0-0 12. d7? Bxd7 13. Qxd7 Rad8 14. Qg4 Rd1+*) 0-0 12. Rd1 Be6 13. Qe4 Rae8 14. Kf1 Bd7 (*Bd4 is also good*) 15. Qd5 (*not 15. Qf4? Re6 16. Qg5 Rf6 17. Qb5 Re8* with a winning attack, Parma–Pribyl 1974) Be6 16. Qe4 with level chances (analysis by Parma).

(f) **10. Bc4** Bxf2+ 11. Ke2 0-0 12. Rd1 Be6 13. Qb5 Nd4+ 14. Nxd4 Bxd4 15. Kf3 Bxc4 16. Qxc4 Bg1! 17. Kg3 Rac8 18. Qd3 Rfd8 (Smith–Regan, USA 1978) with unclear complications – in theory White is holding his own, in practice his insecure K is a problem.

Even if improvements are found in some of these lines, an inexperienced White player over the board is likely either to hang on to both pawns, allowing Black a winning lead in development, or to have the worrying position of his king stuck in mid-board at e2 or f1. Either way Black will have good practical chances.

Unsoundness pays

Another good example of a slightly unsound opening ideal for weaker opponents is the so-called Bulgarian variation of the Schliemann Defence, reached by **1. e4 e5 2. Nf3 Nc6 3. Bb5 f5**. For practical purposes I recommend **4. d3** as the best reply to the Schliemann (see the game Nigel Short v. Preissmann p. 88) but most players know the regular book move **4.**

Nc3 and prefer it since it develops another piece. Then the Bulgarian variation is introduced by **4. . . . Nf6.**

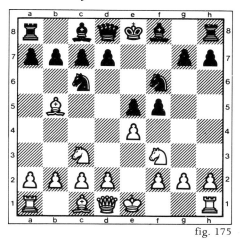

fig. 175

In an interesting experiment, the New York master and teacher Larry D. Evans recommended his students to play the Bulgarian variation exclusively against the Ruy Lopez and report results. He relates in *Chess Life and Review* that the unexpected move 4. . . . Nf6 proved a psychological blow and a few opponents replied **5. 0-0**, soon losing a piece to 5. . . . fxe4 6. Bxc6 dxc6 7. Nxe5 Qd4.

Most opponents put their trust in **5. d3**, which is here not so strong as in the Short–Preissmann game because White has already developed his QN and Black can reply 5. . . . fxe4 6. dxe4 Bb4. Soon many of the students reached a position like this diagram.

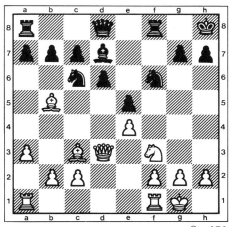

fig. 176

Here Black has a solid centre with both white bishops away from the critical action on the K-side. Black continues with Qe8 and then either Qg6 and Bh3 or Qh5 and Bg4. The pressure is increased further by focusing the knights on the outpost square f4: one knight goes via h5 and the other via d8-e6 or e7-g6. In due course the rooks will double on the f file and Black's attack is likely to become decisive. Note that it was important for Black to play Bb4xc3 since otherwise White could

create counterplay by bringing his knight to the strong square d5.

The best reply for White to the Bulgarian variation is (1. e4 e5 2. Nf3 Nc6 3. Bb5 f5 4. Nc3 Nf6) **5. exf5!** But many White players unfamiliar with the finesses of the opening remember that exf5 is bad on move 4 (because of 4. . . . e4 and White's attacked knight has no good square) but fail to realise that after 5. exf5 the black queen's diagonal is blocked and White can meet 5. . . . e4 strongly by 6. Ng5 or 6. Nh4.

Now after 5. exf5 play continues **5. . . . Bc5 6. 0-0 0-0.**

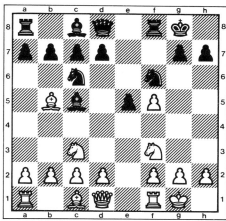

fig. 177

Here there are several plausible continuations but only one of them is a good one:

(a) **7. d3** d6 and Bf5 regaining the pawn with active play based on the attacking chances given by the open f file.

(b) **7. Re1** d6 with similar play.

(c) **7. Bxc6** dxc6 8. Nxe5 Bxf5 9. d3 Bd4! 10. Nc4 (*10. Nf3? Bg4* and White can only escape the pin by allowing the pawn which guards his defences to be wrecked) Ng4 (threat Nxf2!) **11. Ne3 Qh4.**

(c1) **12. Nxg4?** Bxg4 13. Qd2 Rae8 14. Ne4 (14. Qg5 Qxf2+!) Re5 and Rh5 with a winning attack.

(c2) **12. h3!** Nxe3 13. Bxe3 Bxe3 14. fxe3 Bxh3 15. gxh3 Qg6+ with perpetual check.

(d) **7. Nxe5! Nd4** (better than *Nxe5 8. d4*) **8. Nf3!**

It took several years of trial for masters to find this unexpectedly strong retreat as the answer to the Bulgarian variation, and an unprepared opponent is unlikely to find it. The more obvious **8. Ba4?** shuts White's B out from the K-side, and Black continues 8. . . . d5 9. d3 Bxf5 10. Bg5 Qd6 with a powerful attack.

After 8. Nf3 c6 9. Nxd4 Bxd4 10. Ba4 d5 11. Ne2 Bb6 12. d4 Bxf5 13. Bf4 (Unzicker–Nievergelt, Zurich 1959) Black is a pawn down and has to fight for a draw with the aid of bishops of opposite colours. But when Black plays 3. . . . f5 against an amateur opponent, the percentage risk of ending up in this position is small.

The Mestel Philidor

Philidor's Defence **1. e4 e5 2. Nf3 d6** still has the image of a defensive, second-rate opening. The immediate reaction of many players is 'maybe I can repeat Morphy's opera box game (see p. 52).' In 1975 the English master Jonathan Mestel revived an old counter-attacking variant of the Philidor which looks another good try against weaker opponents: **3. d4 f5!?**

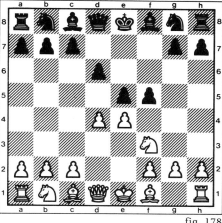

fig. 178

There are now four main possibilities:

(a) **4. exf5** e4 5. Ng5 Bxf5 6. Nc3 Nf6 7. f3 d5 8. fxe4 dxe4 9. Bc4 Qe7 10. Nf7 Rg8 and White's early attack may rebound.

(b) **4. Nc3**, usually given as good for White after Nf6 5. dxe5 or 4. . . . exd4 5. Qxd4 or 4. . . . fxe4 5. Nxe4 d5 6. Nxe5 dxe5 7. Qh5+ – but Black can instead play to hold his centre by 4. . . . Nc6.

(c) **4. dxe5** fxe4 5. Ng5 d5 6. c4 Bb4+ 7. Nc3 d4 8. a3 Bxc3+ 9. bxc3 e3 10. f4 c5 11. Bd3 Ne7 12. 0-0 Nbc6 13. Ne4 0-0 14. Nxc5 Nf5 15. Nb3 dxc3 16. Bxf5 Qxd1 with the better ending (van der Sterren–Mestel, junior world championship 1975).

(d) 4. Bc4

A frequent reaction in over-the-board play.

    4. . . .   exd4
    5. Ng5

If **5. exf5** d5 6. Bd3 Qe7+ 7. Be2 Bxf5 8. Nxd4 Bg4 9. f3 Bd7 10. 0-0 Nc6 11. Re1 0-0-0! 12. Nc3 Qh4 13. Nxc6 Bc5+ with a strong attack (Keller–Mestel, Berne 1975).

    5. . . .   Nh6
    6. 0-0

Weak is **6. Nxh7?** Ng4! (Mestel's improvement over the old theory move *Nxh7? 7. Qh5+*) 7. Nxf8 Kxf8 8. exf5 Qe7+ 9. Kf1 (*9. Qe2 Qxe2+* gives Black a good endgame) Bxf5 10. Qxd4 Nxh2+ 11. Rxh2 Rxh2 12. Be3 Qe4 13. Qxe4 Rh1+ 14. Ke2 Bxe4 and White resigned in Nurmi–Mestel, junior world championship 1975. He is the exchange down and can't develop his Q-side. The column move is a later improvement prepared by the Hungarians.

6. ...   Nc6

Though **6. ... fxe4** looks risky it may be better: 7. Qxd4 Nc6 8. Qxe4+ Qe7 followed by Bf5 and 0-0-0.

7. exf5   Bxf5
8. Re1+   Kd7
9. c3   Qf6
10. Qb3   Be7

Adorjan–Mestel, European team championship final 1976. Black's position is inferior, but he still has counterplay: 11. Ne6 Rab8 12. cxd4 Qh4 13. Nxg7 Nxd4 and White won only after an endgame of over 80 moves.

Defending 1. d4

In choosing a main line defence to 1. d4 the amateur player should again try to opt for a solid and reliable plan whose variations will not change much due to new theoretical discoveries. And as with defending 1. e4 it is important to have one or two sharp and tactically-orientated second-line systems which can be used against weaker opponents. I recommend as the main line plan the 'Old Benoni' **1. d4 c5 2. d5 d6**, which differs from the 'Modern Benoni' where Black only advances ... c5 when White has pushed c4. The Old Benoni has become unfashionable in recent years, but this seems to be because two of its main exponents, grandmasters Schmid and Szabo, are now less active in international chess.

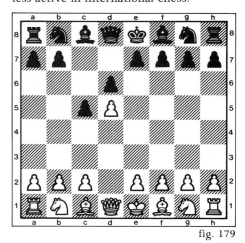
fig. 179

From the diagram play varies according to whether White advances e4 and tries to use the c4 square for a knight (line A) or transposes into more fashionable lines by the pawn move c4 (line B). In either case Black's plan is a Q-side pawn advance.

Line A   3. Nc3   g6
4. e4

Other moves are harmless, eg. **4. g3** Bg7 5. Bg2 Na6 6. e4 Nc7 7. Nf3? b5 8. 0-0 b4 with initiative (Jimenez–Penrose, Varna 1962).

4. ...   Nf6

Possibly more precise than **4. ... Bg7** 5. Bb5+ Nd7 (exchange of bishops favours White) 6. a4 Nf6 7. Nf3 when the f6 knight may be a little misplaced. However Tal–Benko, Bled 1959, continued 7. ... 0-0 8. 0-0 a6 9. Be2 Rb8 10. Re1 Ne8 11. Bf4 Nc7 12. Bf1 and now 12. ... b5 should equalize, while earlier Black could accelerate his Ne8-c7 regrouping and leave the possibility of counter-attack by ... f5.

5. Nf3   Bg7
6. Be2

Now **6. Bb5+** can be met by Nfd7 7. a4 Na6 8. 0-0 Nc7 9. Be2 0-0 10. Bf4 f5 11. exf5 Rxf5 with active counterplay (Larsen–Browne, USA 1972).

6. ...   Na6
7. 0-0   Nc7

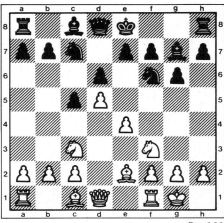
fig. 180

An important position because it, or similar positions, can occur not only after 1. d4 but from two other openings; from the Sicilian Defence after 1. e4 c5 2. Nf3 g6 3. d4 Bg7 4. d5 d6 5. Nc3 Nf6 6. Be2 Na6 7. 0-0 Nc7, and from the Pirc Defence after 1. e4 d6 2. d4 Nf6 3. Nc3 g6 4. Nf3 Bg7 5. Be2 0-0 6. 0-0 c5 7. d5 Na6. This last order of moves occurred in the famous final game of the Karpov–Korchnoi world title match of 1978 and the difference from the column is that Black has played 0-0 instead of Nc7. Korchnoi lost the game and because of this the Old Benoni is likely to have a poor reputation for a long time to come. That's your chance! Little-known openings which are better than their reputation are ideal surprise weapons.

8. a4

This is one of two logical plans. Here White hopes to restrain the black pawn advance long enough to infiltrate with his knight on the Q-side. The other plan is to play for a central push with an eventual e5. Since White in particular can still vary the order of his moves and switch from one line to another, the continuations appear as examples of play rather than definitive lines:

(a) **8. Bf4** 0-0 9. a4 b6 10. Re1 Rb7 11. Bc4 Nh5? 12. Bg5 Nf6 13. Qd3 and after Black's loss of time White is well on top (Karpov–Korchnoi, 32nd match game 1978). Better was 11. ... Qd7 or a6.

(b) **8. Bf4** 0-0 9. a4 Bg4 10. Qd2 a6 11. h3 Bxf3 12. Bxf3 Nd7 13. Be2 Rb8 14. Bh6 b5 15. axb5 axb5 16. Bxg7 Kxg7 17. b4 cxb4 (Speelman–Hartston, BBC Master Game 1976) 18. Qd4+ with a slight edge. Black could probably improve by 12. ... Rb8 at once.

(c) **8. Nd2** 0-0 9. a4 e6! 10. Nc4 Nfe8 11. Be3 b6 and Black easily holds the central pressure.

(d) **8. h3** 0-0 9. a4 a6 10. Bf4 b6 11. Re1 Bb7 12. Bc4 (Sosonko–Larsen, Menorca 1974) Qd7 13. e5 Nh5 14. Bh2 f5! gaining king's side space.

(e) **8. Re1** 0-0 9. a4 a6 10. Bg5 (*10. Bf4 Rb8 11. e5 Nfe8 12. a5 b5 13. axb6 Rxb6 14. Ra2 Rb4 with play on the b file and the central dark squares, Kottnauer–Keene, Hastings 1969*) h6 (also Bg4 is playable as in line b) 11. Bf4 (Spassky–Schmid, Varna 1962) when the routine 11. ... Bd7 12. Qd2 b5 allowed the breakthrough 13. e5! but Black should play 11. ... g5 12. Bg3 Nh5.

8. ...   a6
9. Nd2   Bd7

Black could also castle as in (c) above, but has this possibly better option of a fast Q-side counter.

10. Nc4   b5
11. e5

11. Nb6? is well met by 11. ... b4! 12. Nxa8 Qxa8 13. Nb1 Nxe4 when Black's powerful pawn chain and centre outweigh White's small material edge.

11. ...   dxe5
12. axb5   Nxb5

Simpler than **12. ... axb5** which is also playable.

13. Nxb5   Bxb5
14. Nxe5   Bxe2
15. Qxe2   Qxd5
16. Rxa6   Rxa6
17. Qxa6   0-0

The delayed castling has given Black time for freeing exchanges, and now the game is level (analysis to Botvinnik–Schmid, Leipzig 1960).

As can be seen from these examples, Black has several good plans available after the early moves in the Old Benoni. He can play for the advance ... b5, neutralize White's centre thrust by ... Bg4xf3, or put his QB at b7 and wait for a suitable moment for ... f5. Generally speaking the ... b5 Q-side pawn advance is the simplest plan for an amateur to adopt; Black only has to watch that White does not establish his knights on blockading squares (eg. a4 and c4) or break into the centre with e5 when Black is not ready to meet it.

Line B (after 1. d4 c5 2. d5 d6).
3. c4   Nf6
4. Nc3   g6

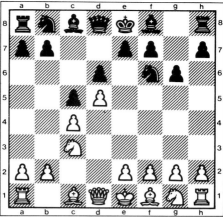

fig. 181

Thus the opening has now transposed into the King's Indian Defence, which is normally reached by the different move order 1. d4 Nf6 2. c4 g6 3. Nc3 Bg7. However, by reaching the diagram via the Old Benoni, Black rules out several popular variations where White leaves his pawn at d4 or only advances to d5 in reply to Black's . . . e5. In particular, the attacking lines with f3, intending a later g4/h4, are neutralized, since in the diagram 5. e4 Bg7 6. f3 0-0 7. Be3 or 7. Bg5 are met by 7. . . . e6 with an easy game for Black whose well-placed g7 bishop guarantees good counterplay after the opening of the e file.

Thus the significant lines Black will meet in practice are (a) systems where White plays g3 (b) systems where White plays Nf3 and Be2 (c) systems where White plays Be2 and Bg5 and (d) attacking lines with f4. We will look at each of these in turn.

(a) g3 systems

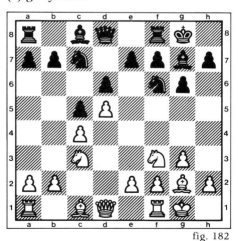

fig. 182

5.	Nf3	Bg7
6.	g3	0-0
7.	Bg2	Na6
8.	0-0	Nc7

Black's plan is clear: a6, Rb8, Bd7 if necessary, and the space-gaining . . . b5. White cannot really prevent this and tries to counter by a central advance and/or probing for Q-side knight outposts.

Ulf Andersson of Sweden on his way to joint first prize with Nunn, Hastings, 1980. Andersson is a great endgame specialist.

9. a4

Probably best, since White normally plays this irrespective of where he puts his pieces. Some other examples to show how Black should develop counterplay:

(a) **9. e4** (this natural advance weakens the d4 square which often becomes a target for Black's knights or KB later on) Rb8 10. a4 a6 11. Qe2 (better *11. a5 b5 12. axb6 e.p. Rxb6* though Black's rook has a good outpost at b4) b6 12. e5 Ne8 13. Bf4 b5 14. axb5 axb5 15. cxb5 Bd7 16. Rfe1 Nxb5 17. Nxb5 Bxb5 (Filip–Radulescu, Bucharest 1953) and Black stands well. He has pressure on the b file, and his remaining knight can eventually transfer to the d4 square from which White's 9. e4 kindly removed a potential defender.

(b) **9. h3 a6** 10. a4 Rb8 11. a5 Nd7 (here *11. . . . b5* is less good because of *12. axb6 e.p. Rxb6 13. Nd2!* followed by Nb3-a5) 12. Bd2 b5 13. axb6 e.p. Nxb6 14. b3 e6 15. dxe6 Nxe6 16. Ne1 (or *16. Rc1 d5*) a5 17. Ra3 Bd7 18. Nd5 Nxd5 19. Bxd5 Qf6 with a level game (Furman–Korchnoi, USSR championship 1955).

(c) **9. Nd2** Rb8 10. a4 b6 11. Nb5 (if *11. Qc2 a6 12. Nb3* then not *b5? 13 axb6 e.p. Rxb6 14. Na5* but *12. . . . e6!* switching from Q-side to centre to exploit the white knight's absence) Rb7 (not *11. . . . a6 12. Na7* and *13. Nc6*) 12. Rb1 a6 13. Nc3 b5 14. Nb3 bxc4! 15. Na5 Rb4 16. Nc6 Qd7 17. Nxb4 cxb4 18. Na2 a5 when Black's strong pawns compensate for his exchange sacrifice.

9.	. . .	Rb8
10.	Bf4	

Now White's intention is to use the bishop to pressure Black's d pawn and thus restrain an advance of the black e pawn, while the QR guards the b pawn against the attack down the b file.

10.	. . .	a6
11.	a5	b5
12.	axb6	Rxb6
	e.p.	

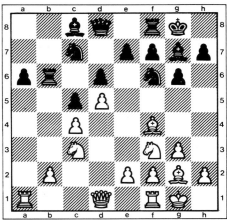

fig. 183

Now the chances are balanced: Black's game is sufficiently dynamic to ensure active counterplay. At the same time Black is forced to continue aggressively lest White obtain a restraining bind by Ra2, Qd2 and Bh6 neutralizing the strong bishop.

Play can continue:

(a) **13. Ra2 Re8** 14. b3 e5 15. dxe6 e.p. Nxe6 16. Na4 Nxf4 17. Nxb6 Qxb6 18. gxf4 Ne4 19. Qd3 (Korchnoi–Gligoric, Buenos Aires 1960) Bf5 20. Nh4 Nc3 regaining the lost material with equality.

(b) **13. b3 Bf5** 14. Ne1 (weaker is the decentralizing *14. Nh4 Bd7 15. Ra3 Qb8* when Black has strong pressure on the b file. Donner–Toran, Barcelona 1952) Qd7 15. Ra3 Bh3 16. Nd3 Bxg2 17. Kxg2 Nh5 18. Bd2 e6 19. e4 exd5 20. exd5 (Vukic–Tringov, Sarajevo 1967).

(b) Systems where White plays Nf3 and Be2

5.	Nf3	Bg7
6.	e4	0-0
7.	Be2	e6

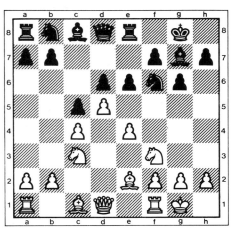

fig. 184

This is better than the previous **8. . . . exd5** 9. cxd5 transposing into a Modern Benoni formation where White has good possibilities of strengthening his bind by Nd2-c4. After Re8 Black has the positional threat of exd5 when White cannot retake with the c pawn and has to allow a symmetrical position where Black's

command of the e file gives him a comfortably level game.

White has several possibilities:

(a) **9. dxe6** Bxe6 10. Bf4 Nc6! 11. Bxd6 Qa5 is a promising pawn sacrifice, *e.g.* 12. Nd2 (*12. a3 Red8 13. b4 cxb4 14. axb4 Qxa1 15. Qxa1 Nxe4* is unclear) Red8 13. Nb3 (*13. e5 Ne8*) Qb6 14. Na4 Qb4 15. Nbxc5 Bxc4 16. Bxc5 Qxc4 and Black has the edge (Alburt–Kasparov, USSR 1978. In the game White first played Bg5 before Bf4 as in system (c) below so that Black had the extra move . . . h6.)

(b) **9. Qc2** (to retake on d5 with the c pawn) Na6 10. Re1 cxd5 11. cxd5 Nb4 12. Qb3 Bg4 13. a3 Bxf3 14. gxf3 Na6 15. Qxb7 Nc7 and Black has good compensation for a pawn in White's broken king side which he can exploit by Nh5-f4 (Kozma–Polugaevsky, Kislovodsk 1972).

(c) **9. Nd2** Na6 (White is waiting for . . . exd5, but Black can also wait) 10. Kh1 (or *10. Rb1 Nc7 11. a4 b6 12. f4* and now Black can safely exchange by *12. . . . exd5 13. cxd5 Ba6* with a level game, Spassky–Kavalek. IBM 1973) Nc7 11. a4 b6 12. f4 (*12. f3 Ba6*) exd5 13. cxd5 Ba6 (so that if White swaps bishops a black knight will reach a good outpost square at b4) 14. Re1 Bxe2 15. Rxe2 Ng4 16. h3 Qh4 17. Qf1 (Savon–Belyavsky, USSR championship 1974) Bd4 (threatening Nf2+ and perpetual check) 18. Qf3 Nf2+ 19. Kh2 f5 with at least a draw.

Thus, against the Be2/Nf3 system, the plan of holding up exd5 until Black can mount active counterplay with his pieces yields good results.

(c) Systems where White plays Be2 and Bg5

This, the Averbakh system named after a Russian grandmaster, is a popular approach in master chess. It aims at a small but permanent bind on the position which against inaccurate defence can lead to a favourable ending. The Averbakh is reached by (**1. d4 c5 2. d5 d6 3. c4 Nf6 4. Nc3 g6**) **5. e4 Bg7 6. Be2 0-0 7. Bg5.**

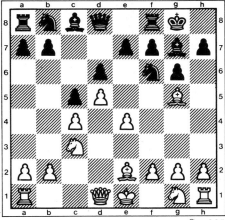

fig. 185

An illustration of Black's potential difficulties in this variation is the plausible

line **7. . . . e6** 8. Qd2 exd5 9. exd5 Re8 10. Nf3 Bg4 11. 0-0 Nbd7 12. h3 Bxf3 13. Bxf3 a6 14. a4 Qe7 15. Rae1 Qf8 16. Bd1 Rxe1 17. Rxe1 Re8 18. Rxe8. So, best for Black is: Qxe8 19. Bf4 and after an eventual queen exchange White's bishop pair are strong in the endgame.

7. . . .   h6!

Putting a question to the white bishop. If:

(a) **8. Bf4** e5! 9. dxe6 Bxe6 10. Bxd6 Re8 11. Nf3 Nc6 transposing into the Nf3/Be2 system with the difference that Black has played . . . h6 as a useful extra move.

(b) **8. Bh4** a6 9. a4 (*9. Nf3 b5*) Qa5 10. Qd2 b5 11. cxb5 axb5 12. Bxb5 Ba6 and Black has the initiative in return for the sacrificed pawn.

(c) **8. Be3** e6 9. Qd2 Kh7 10. dxe (better *10. h3 exd5 11. cxd5 Na6 12. Nf3 Bf5* but Black develops his pieces without problems) Bxe6 11. 0-0-0 Nc6 12. Qxd6? Qxd6 13. Rxd6 Nd4! (Uhlmann–Byrne, Hastings 1970–1). Black's last surprise move wins material, for if 14. Bxd4 cxd4 15. Rxd4 Ng4 when both Bxd4 and Nxf2 are threatened.

(d) Attacking lines where White plays f4

This is one of the most popular counters to the King's Indian Defence in amateur chess. Play goes (**1. d4 c5 2. d5 d6 3. c4 Nf6 4. Nc3 g6 5. e4 Bg7 6. f4 0-0 7. Nf3 e6 8. Be2 exd5.**

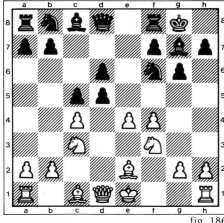

fig. 186

A critical position. This variation is full of tactical ideas and, although considered here from the defensive viewpoint of Black's 1. . . . c5 system, it is possible if you know it well enough to play it for either side with good effect.

9. cxd5

Natural and most popular. The other ideas are:

(a) **9. exd5** b5! (Tal's gambit idea) 10. Nxb5 (if *10. cxb5 a6* when the two open files, the pressure down the long dark diagonal and the loosened White centre give good compensation) Ne4 11. 0-0 a6 12. Nc3 (after *12. Na3* this knight is out of play as shown in Thorbergsson–Tal, Reykjavik 1964, which continued *12. . . .*

Ra7 13. Bd3 Re7 14. Nc2 Rfe8 15. Re1 Nd7 16. Ne3 Ndf6 17. Qc2 Nh5 18. g3 Bd4! with a strong attack) Nxc3 13. bxc3 Bxc3 14. Rb1 Bf5 15. Bd3 Qc8 16. Qc2 Bxd3 17. Qxd3 Bg7. White's K-side attack should be contained and Black has some play against the weak central pawns. This plan might be further improved by 11. .... Re8 at once, since the white knight has nowhere to go but homewards.

(b) **9. e5!?** (the Gunderam Gambit, dangerous to the inexperienced) dxe5 10. fxe5 Ng4 11. Bg5 Qa5 (best: many books give *11. .... f6 12. exf6 Bxf6* as equalizing but then comes *13. Bxf6 Nxf6 14. cxd5* with advantage *14. ... Ne8 15. Qd2 Nd6 16. h4* with a strong attack, Taylor–Smith, Sheffield 1962 or *14. ... Bg4 15. 0-0 a6 16. Ng5 Bf5 17. Rxf5 gxf5 18. Ne6* regaining the exchange and leaving Black a weak f pawn, Taylor–Skilliter, London 1966. Note that *11. ... Qb6*, the book move in similar positions in the 9. cxd5 variation is risky due to *12. Nxd5 Qxb2 13. 0-0*) 12. Qxd5 Nxe5 (winning the exchange by *12. ... c4?* turns out a blunder after *13. 0-0 Qc5+ 14. Kh1 Nf2+ 15. Rxf2 Qxf2 16. Ne4 Qb6 17. Nf6+ Kh8 18. Qc1* and wins) 13. 0-0 Nxf3+ (better than *13. ... Nbd7 14. d6!* or *13. ... Re8 14. Nxe5 Bxe5 15. Bc4 Nd7 16. d6*) 14. Rxf3 Nd7! (not *Bg4? 15. Rxf7! Rxf7 16. Bxg4* with more than enough for the exchange sacrificed). Following 14 ... Nd7 White still has some play, but Black has a pawn to console him and I don't think White's compensation (via d6 and Be7) is quite enough.

9. ... Bg4!
This should be the safest move. Formerly 9. .... b5 and 9. .... Re8 were usual, but then 10. e5, effectively a Gunderam Gambit with an extra weakening move for Black, has been shown to give good practical chances.
10. 0-0
10. e5 dxe5 11. fxe5 Nfd7 12. e6 fxe6 13. 0-0 Bxf3 14. Bxf3 Ne5 (Liptay–Geller, Prague 1966) is now unsound.
10. ... Nbd7
11. h3 Bxf3
12. Bxf3 c4!
followed by Rc8, a6, Nc5 and Nfd7, this gives Black enough chances with his Q-side 3–2 pawn majority to counter White's attacking prospects (g4, h4).

Gambit Defence to 1. d4
As in K-side openings where the French Defence is recommended as the main, solid line, backed up by little-known gambits and other offbeat lines to use against weaker opponents, so playing Black against 1. d4 needs the same twofold approach. As with the recommended lines in the Sicilian, Schliemann and Philidor Defences to 1. e4, you are recommended to build up a more detailed knowledge from specialist reference

books. This is best done gradually, by checking your play against master chess each time you come across a new variation of the system in question.

The Tarrasch Gambit
This active gambit is one of the best replies to 1. d4 when meeting a weaker player and particularly one who is defensively minded. For the system is only doubtful if White is primed in advance and reacts aggressively.

1.	d4	d5
2.	c4	e6
3.	Nc3	c5
4.	cxd5	cxd4

More usual replies until here are 3. .... Nf6, the orthodox Queen's Gambit Declined, and 4. .... **exd5**, the main line Tarrasch Defence.
5. Qa4+
5. Qxd4 Nc6 6. Qd1 exd5 7. Qxd5 Bd7 transposes to the column, while 5. dxe6? Bxe6 (but not *dxc3?? 6. exf7+ Ke7 7. fxg8=N+*) 6. Ne4 Nf6 gives Black a good development and a d4 wedge in return for the pawn.
5. ... Bd7
6. Qxd4 exd5

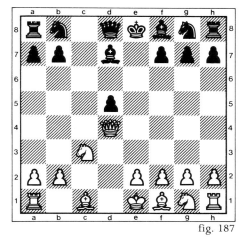
fig. 187

7. Qxd5
Cautious souls may decline the pawn with **7. e3**. Black can then continue to offer his gambit for a few more moves, and even if White continues to refuse the gift Black has free attacking play: 7. .... Nc6 8. Qd1 Nf6 9. Nf3 (*9. Nxd5 Qa5+* and *... 0-0-0 is strong*) Bd6 10. Be2 (*10. Nxd5? Nxd5 11. Qxd5 Qe7* and *... 0-0-0*) Bf5! 11. 0-0 Rc8.

Black's plan is simple: to line up his queen and bishop against h2 and then combine his other pieces in a direct attack. The game G.N. Stokes–A. Hall, York 1959 shows this succeeding: 12. Nb5 Bb8 13. Nbd4 Be4! 14. Nxc6 bxc6 15. Bd2 Qd6 16. g3 h5! 17. Bc3 Bxf3 18. Bxf3 h4 19. Rc1 hxg3 20. hxg3 Ne4 21. Bxe4 Qh6! 2. Re1 dxe4 23. Kf1 Qh1+ 24. Ke2 Qf3+ 25. Kd2 Rd8+ 26. Bd4 Rxd4+! and White resigned because of 27. exd4 Qd3 mate.

White can also try (from the diagram) **7. Nxd5** Nc6 8. Qd1 but then 8. .... Be6 9. Nc3 Qxd1+ 10. Kxd1 (*10. Nxd1 Nb4*) 0-0-0+ 11. Kc2 Bc5 12. Nf3 Nf6 regaining the pawn with advantage (*13. e3? Nb4+ 14. Kb1 Bf5+*).
7. ... Nc6
8. Nf3
Two weaker moves may be played:
(a) **8. Bg5** Nf6 9. Qd2 (*if 9. Bxf6? Qxf6 10. e3 0-0-0 11. 0-0-0 Bf5 12. Qf3 Qxc3+ 13. bxc3 Ba3 mate*) Qa5 10. Bxf6 gxf6 11. e3 0-0-0 12. Nf3 Bf5 13. Nd4 Nxd4 Nxd4 with a strong game.
(b) **8. e4?** (this makes f2 too weak) Nf6 9. Qd1 Bc5 10. Nh3 (or *10. Be2 Qb6 11. Nf3 Ng4 12. Nd5 Bb4+ 13. Nxb4 Qxf2+*) Qe7 11. Bb5 Bxh3 12. Bxh3 Nd4 13. gxh3 Rd4 14. Qb3 Rxe4+! with a winning attack (Winser–Sutton, Eastbourne 1963).
8. ... Nf6
9. Qd1
Best. 9. Qb3 Bc5 10. Bg5 (*10. Qxb7? Nb4* or *10. e3 Qe7 11. Be2 0-0-0* with an improved version for Black of the column since White no longer has the counter b4) h6 11. Bh4 g5 12. Bg3 Qa5 13. e3 (*13. Qb5 Bb4 14. Qxa5 Bxa5* also leaves Black an active position for his gambit pawn) 0-0-0 14. Be2 (*14. Qxf7 Ne4* is strong) Ne4 15. 0-0 Nxg3 16. hxg3 f6. Black's fine development and his threat to continue h5-h4 are worth more than a pawn.
9. ... Bc5
10. e3 Qe7

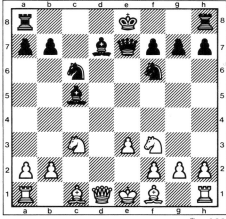
fig. 188

11. Be2
Natural and safest. Three other moves have been tried here unsuccessfully:
(a) **11. Bc4** 0-0-0 12. Qe2 g5 13. a3 g4 14. Nd2 Ne5 15. b4 Bb6 16. Bb2 Bc6 with strong pressure. B.H. Wood–Sutton, British Championship 1960, concluded 17. Rc1 Kb8 18. Rg1 Rhg8 19. Nb5? Nxc4 20. Qxc4 Bxe3! 21. Bxf6 Bxd2+ 22. Kf1 Qxf6 and White resigned.
(b) **11. a3** 0-0-0 12. Qc2 Kb8 13. Be2 (*13. b4 Nd4 14. Nxd4 Bxd4 15. Be2 Ba4! 16. Qb2 Be5 17. f4 Ne4!* with a winning attack) g5 14. 0-0 g4 15. Nd2 Rhe8 16. Nb3 Bb6 17. Bd2 Qe5 with strong threats (Gurevich–Safonov, Moscow 1960).

(c) **11. Bd2** 0-0-0 12. Qb3 Bf5 13. Rc1 Kb8 14. Na4 Bb4! 15. a3 Bxd2+ 16. Nxd2 Nd4 with a winning attack: Chanov–Gusev, USSR 1955 ended 17. Qc3 Rc8 18. Bc4 Rhd8 19. Nb3 Ne4 20. Qb4 Qxb4+ and White resigned (21. axb4 Nxb3).

11. ...   0-0-0

By castling QR Black opts for an all-or-nothing K-side attack. The attempted transposition **11. ... g5** is met by 12. Nd4 (not *12. Nxg5 Rg8 13. Nh3 Bxh3* or *13. Nf3 Rxg2*) g4 13. Nxc6 Bxc6 14. Bb5, but Black can instead build up his position more slowly by **11. ... 0-0** 12. 0-0 Rfd8 13. a3 Bf5 14. Qa4 Ng4 15. h3 N4e5 (Vladimirov–Ravinsky, USSR 1955).

12. 0-0

Active defence. In practice, many weaker players are overawed by the aggro of this type of attack and allow Black a fast K-side build-up. An example is **12. Bd2?** g5 13. Qc1? g4 14. Nd4 h5 15. Nxc6 Bxc6 16. 0-0 h4 17. Qc2 g3! 18. Rad1 h3! 19. fxg3 Rxd2 20. Rxd2 Qxe3+ and White resigned (D. Kerr–S. Fancy, London 1972).

12. ...   g5

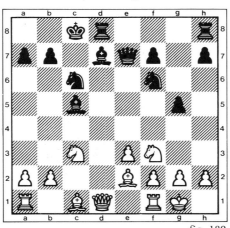

fig. 189

13. Nd4

Too slow is **13. a3** g4 14. Nd4 Qe5! 15. b4 Nxd4 16. bxc5 Nf3+! (Borisenko–Spassky, USSR 1959) with a winning attack.

The move **13. b4 Bxb4** transposes into the column after **14. Bb2** Rhg8 15. Nd4, while if instead **14. Qb3** Rhg8 15. Rb1 Bf5 16. Rb2 Be6! 17. Bc4 Bxc4 18. Qxc4 Qc5 keeps the game level (*19. Qxf7 Rd7*).

13. ...   Rhg8!

Most books give **13. ... g4** followed by h5 but this attack is too slow, *eg.* 14. b4 Bxb4 15. Bb2 h5 16. Ncb5 Kb8 17. Qb3 when Black's b4 bishop is hanging and White threatens 18. Nxc6+ Bxc6 19. Bxf6 Qxf6 20. Qxb4. One point of Rhg8 followed by Rg6 is to avoid this variation by enabling Black to recapture with the rook on move 19.

14. b4

If **14. a3** Qe5 intending Bd6 or Rg6-h6 with good play or **14. Bb5** Nxd4 15. exd4 Bxd4 16. Qxd4 Bxb5.

14. ...   Bxb4
15. Bb2   Rg6
16. Rc1   Kb8
17. Nxc6+

If **17. Qb3** Nxd4 followed by Bxc3 and the e2 bishop is hanging. If **17. Bf3** Nxd4 18. exd4 g4 19. Nd5 Qd6 20. Nxf6 gxf3! and wins. If **17. Ncb5** then either 17. ... a6 or 17. ... Ne5 intending a6 or g4.

17. ...   Bxc6
20. Qb3   g4

Black threatens Rh6 followed by Qe5 and then if g3 Rxh2! forcing mate. Undoubtedly White's moves can still be improved, but this gambit remains a promising idea for the attacking player. The success or failure of such a gambit depends in great measure not on the book analysis but on the tactical ability of those involved – particularly Black.

Mestel's Defence

Waiting tactics form an important aspect of contemporary opening strategy. The theme of defences like 1. ... g6 or 1. ... b6 is that Black only commits his central pawns after seeing how White will develop. These are slow, closed openings where a single tempo is less important than in the open game with an early clash in the centre, and ideas are current now which would have aroused horror among the theorists of half a century ago.

One example is the move (1. e4 g6 2. d4 Bg7 3. Nc3 d6 4. Be3) a6!? at first sight a beginner's push but in fact waiting to see whether White's formation is based on Nf3, f3, Qd2 or f4. If White's answer is an aggressive plan based on Q-side castling, then the a pawn is well posted to support the counter-attack ... b5, while if White prefers a calmer plan Black can himself continue ... b6 when the pawn has the function of stopping White bishop checks or pawn advances to b5.

One option which Black keeps in the 1. ... g6 Modern Defence is to retain for as long as possible the chance to bring his g8 knight into action at e7 or f6. This might seem just a psychological move, but the young British master Jonathan Mestel uses the system to reach a standard position in the better-known King's Indian Defence with two full moves in hand. Mestel's idea is not widely publicized and offers good prospects against opponents who develop in a routine way.

1. d4	d6
2. c4	g6
3. e4	e5
4. d5	

Exchanging pawns and queens gives White no advantage.

4. ...	Nd7
5. Nc3	Bg7

Mestel's Defence aims to set up a dark-square blockade on the queen's side and if possible to start K-side operations quickly by ... f5 if White allows. On the other hand, if White makes ... f5 unattractive Black can still switch into a normal King's Indian formation by ... Ngf6.

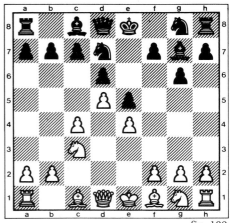

fig. 190

6. Be2

Van der Linde–Mestel, England v. Holland 1973, went **6. Nf3** Ne7 7. Be2 0-0 8. 0-0 f5 and Mestel won by a similar but more brilliant attack to the column: 9. exf5 gxf5 10. Ng5 Nf6 11. f4 e4 12. Be3 c6 13. Qd2 h6 14. Nh3 Kh8 15. Rac1 c5 16. a3 Ng4! (offering a pawn to open up squares and diagonals for the other pieces hidden behind the pawn chain) 17. Bxg4 fxg4 18. Nf2 Nf5 19. Nxg4 Qh4 20. Nf2 Nxe3 21. Qxe3 Bd4 22. Qxe4 Rxf4 23. Qe8+ Kg7 24. Rc2 Bh3! 25. g3 (*25. Qxa8 Rg4 26. Qxb7+ Kg6 27. g3 Rxg3+ wins*) Rxe8 26. gxh4 Rg4+ 27. Kh1 Bg2+ 28. Kg1 Bxd5 mate.

6. ...   a5

Black continues his Q-side play, waiting for White to develop his second knight. If at once **6. ... Ne7** White has attacking chances with 7. h4 followed by h5.

7. Nf3

Here the attacking **7. h4** is ineffective because of 7. ... h5 8. Nf3 Bh6! (Haygarth–Mestel, British championship play-off 1974–5) exchanging White's active bishop and thus helping Black's dark square play.

A superior plan is **7. a3** (planning a Q-side pawn advance and so depriving Black of waiting moves on that flank) Ngf6 (back into regular lines, but White is committed to the Q-side at an earlier stage than he would really like) 8. Bg5 0-0 9. Rb1 (White delays castling, intending to use the extra move for progress on both wings) h6 10. Be3 Nc5 11. Bf3! (*11. Bxc5 dxc5* followed by Ne8-d6 and *11. f3 Nh5* followed by ... f5 are both good for Black) Bd7 12. b4 axb4 13. axb4 Na4 14. Nge2 Ne8 (Speelman–Mestel, BBC Master Game 1976): White has more space, but Black has counter-play on the a and f files.

7. ...	Ne7
8. 0-0	0-0

A well-known variation of the King's Indian Defence runs 1. d4 Nf6 2. c4 g6 3. Nc3 Bg7 4. Nf3 0-0 5. e4 d6 6. Be2 e5 7. 0-0 Nc6 8. d5 Ne7 9. Ne1 Nd7; in comparison with this position, Mestel's Defence has gained Black two moves; he has played the useful . . . a5 while White has not yet prepared to meet the coming . . . f5 by Ne1 and f3.

9.	Qc2	f5
10.	exf5	gxf5
11.	Ng5	Nf6
12.	f4	e4
13.	Be3	h6
14.	Nh3	Ng4
15.	Nd1	Nxe3
16.	Nxe3	c6!

fig. 191

Black's last move stops any possible central blockade with the knights. If now 17. dxc6 Qb6 18. Kf2 bxc6 with Bd4 and d5 to follow. The game Vickery-Mestel, Jersey 1974, now concluded 17. Kh1 Qb6 18. Qd2 Qxb2 19. Qxb2 Bxb2 20. Rad1 Ba3 21. g4 Bc5! (preparing the decisive attack by the bishop pair) 22. Nxf5 Nxf5 23. gxf5 Bxf5 24. Nf2 e3 25. Nd3 Be4+ 26. Kh1 Kh8 and White resigned.

Defending flank openings

In recent years the non-committal first moves 1. c4, 1. Nf3 and even 1. g3 or 1. b3 have been gaining ground in club and tournament chess. Similarly in the Queen's Gambit Declined 1. d4 d5 2. c4 e6 Black may not get the opportunity to go into the Tarrasch Gambit if White adopts the solid Catalan Opening 3. g3. Another growing fashion is for White to choose a black opening to take advantage of his extra move, and the most popular method is the King's Indian Attack, analyzed on p. 104.

The simplest way for the ordinary player to meet these difficult and sophisticated openings is, as against 1. d4 and 1. e4, to have a solid line which will give a reasonable game against all of them while knowing some sharper tactical ideas for use particularly against weaker opponents.

The great German teacher Dr Tarrasch used to advise playing 1. . . . e6 and 2. . . . d5 against all these flank systems, and this does have the advantage of improving the chances of the game transposing into the Tarrasch Gambit which we examined earlier in the book. Here are some basic variations.

1.	c4	e6
2.	Nf3	

If White plays 2. Nc3 or 2 d4 then 2. . . . d5 with a likely transposition into the Queen's Gambit.

2.	. . .	d5
3.	g3	Nf6
4.	Bg2	Be7
5.	0-0	0-0

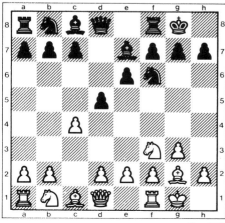

fig. 192

Jonathan Mestel – youngest British champion at 19, and an innovator in opening play.

Now there are three main lines of play:

(a) **6. d4 Nbd7** 7. Nc3 (an unclear pawn sacrifice) dxc4 8. e4 c6 9. a4 a5 10. Qe2 Nb6 11. Rd1 Bb4 12. Ne5 Qe7 13. Be3 Bd7 14. Nxc4 Nxc4 15. Qxc4 (Botvinnik-Lasker, Moscow 1936) e5 16. dxe5 Ng4 when Black has freed his position with a level game.

(b) **6. b3 b6** 7. Bb2 Bb7 8. e3 (*if 8. d4 Nbd7* followed by a centre strike with . . . c5) c5 9. Qe2 Nc6 10. Rd1 (*10 Nc3 dxc4 11. bxc4 Na5!* and the c pawn is a target for Black's pieces) Qc7 11. Nc3 Rad8 12. cxd5 (or *12. Rac1 Qb8 13. d3 a6* with the threat of . . . d4) Nxd5 13. Nxd5 Rxd5 14. d4 cxd4 15. Nxd4 Nxd4 16. Bxd4 (so far Vahanian-Karpov, USSR Championship 1971) Rd7 (in the game, Karpov blundered by *Rd6? 17. Rdc1! when after Qb8 18. Be5* wins the exchange) 17. Rac1 Qb8 with an even game.

(c) **6. d4 Nbd7** 7. Qc2 c6 8. Nbd2. This is the most popular line of play, where White guards his c pawn with a piece and then tries to gain space in the centre with e4. If Black reacts too cautiously, White carries out his plan and then his g2 bishop becomes effective on the long white diagonal while Black's c8 bishop is handicapped by its own light squared pawns.

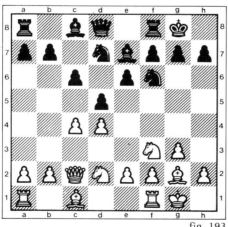

fig. 193

8. . . .   b5!

The most energetic continuation. A sequence like **8. . . . b6** 9. e4 dxe4 10. Nxe4 Nxe4 11. Qxe4 Qc7? 12. Bf4 Bd6 13. Bxd6 Qxd6 14. Rad1 Bb7 15. Ne5 Nxe5 16. dxe5 Qc7 17. Rd6, on the other hand, would give White everything he wants – command of central space, an open file, good against bad bishop, and no counterplay for Black.

9. c5

9. cxb5 cxb5 10. Qc6 looks menacing, but after 10. . . . Rb8 the queen will soon be driven back by Rb6 or even by a6 followed by Bb7. Equally White cannot take advantage of Black's pawn formation by 9. cxb5 cxb5 10. Nb3 because of Bb7 and the rook comes to c8 with gain of time.

9. . . .   a5

Necessary, else White might obtain a bind by b4 followed by Nb3–a5.

10. e4   e5!

This tactical stroke takes advantage of White's temporarily overstretched pawn formation to free Black's game completely. If 11. dxe5 Nxe4 12. Nxe4 dxe4 13. Qxe4 Nxc5 and 14. Qxc6?? would be a losing blunder because of 14. . . . Bb7 15. Qxb5 Ba6 16. Qc6 Rc8 trapping the queen.

The English King's Indian

Another good plan against 1. c4 which is effective against a cautious opponent is to set up a King's Indian formation with the bishop on g7 and then to attack the white king with a pawn advance. The great advantages of this system are that it is simpler to play than most of the subtle positional lines of the English Opening and that it takes a good defensive player to meet it successfully.

As an example of Black's strategy we analyze the game Isaksen–J. Kristiansen, North Sea Cup, Denmark 1977: 1. c4 g6 2. Nc3 Bg7 3. g3 d6 4. Bg2 e5 5. d3 f5 6. Nf3 Nf6 7. 0-0 0-0 8. Rb1 a5 9. a3 Nh5.

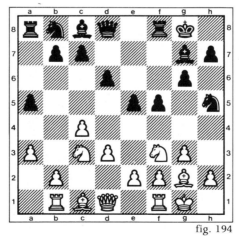

fig. 194

Black's basic plan here is to advance his pawn to f4, line up the QB and queen on the diagonal to h3 (*eg.* B at e6, f5 or g4 and Q at c8 or d7), play Bh3 to exchange the bishop which defends White's king, and then to work with such possibilities as a knight sacrifice on g3, f3 and Qh3, and if necessary doubling rooks on the f line. White's best chance to cross this plan is **10. Bg5** and if Bf6 11. Bh6 or if Qd7 11. Bd2 and in either case Black's plans are slowed down while White advances

on the other side with b4–b5. In practice, White often defends badly.

10. Qc2? f4 11. b4 (if 11. e3 the pin Bg4 is unpleasant) **axb4 12. axb4 Bg4** (note that Black postpones the decision whether to develop his QN at c6 or d7) **13. b5** (if 13. Nd2 Nc6! threatens Nd4) **Nd7** (now the knight has the c5 square) **14. Bb2 Nc5 15. Ra1 Rxa1 16. Rxa1 Qd7** (all in accordance with the master plan above. So White decides to centralize his knight at e4 and protect the g3 pawn) **17. Ng5 Bh6 18. Nge4 Nxe4 19. Nxe4 Qf7!** (threatening fxg3 followed by Nxg3 and hoping to provoke f3 which creates further holes) **20. Bc1 Nf6 21. Nc3 Bc8!** (otherwise White gets play on the white diagonal) **22. Ra8 g5 23. Nd5 Ng4! 24. Nxf4** (or 24. Rxc8 Rxc8 25. Nb6 cxb6 26. Bd5 Qxd5!) **gxf4 25. Rxc8 fxg3! 26. Rxf8+ Qxf8 27. Bd5+** (27. f3 Be3+ with a winning attack) **Kh8 28. f3 Ne3! 29. Qc3** (29. Qa4 Nxd5 30. Bxh6 Qxh6 threatens mate on h2) **gxh2+ 30. Kh1 Qg7 31. Bxe3 Bxe3 32. Kxh2 Bf4+ 33. Kh3 Qg3 mate.**

The King's Indian Attack

In the King's Indian Attack, White develops his KB at g2 then builds up his forces for a direct attack on the king. The importance of the opening is that it can be reached in several ways. It is achieved via the Sicilian Defence after the moves 1. e4 c5 2. Nf3 d6 (or Nc6 or e6) 3. d3 followed by Nbd2, g3, Bg2 and 0-0. It can also be reached from the French Defence via 1. e4 e6 2. d3, or directly via 1. Nf3 Nf6 2. g3 or even by 1. g3.

Having established this basic formation, White's intention is to develop his pieces, then advance his e pawn to e5 to drive a wedge in the black position. The QN is manoeuvred to the king's side from d2 via f1 and e3 or h2, while the e5 pawn is supported by Re1, Bf4, Qe2 and/or c3 and d4.

White can then proceed to direct attack if Black has castled king's side in the normal way. He advances his h pawn towards h6, perhaps regroups his knight from e3 or h2 to g4, and often exchanges the dark-squared bishops at g5. If all this is successful, there are chances of launching a direct checkmate attack on the black king by directing White's queen and knights against f6 and g7.

In practice there are many variations on this basic strategy, but many games have followed the above master plan. Here are two of them, showing White's attack succeeding with Black's defensive bishop first on e7 and then on g7.

White: Hulak. Black: Nonnenmacher
Yugoslavia v. West Germany, 1975
1. e4 c5 2. Nf3 e6 3. d3 d5 4. Nbd2 Nf6 5. g3 Be7 6. Bg2 0-0 7. 0-0 Nc6 8. Re1.

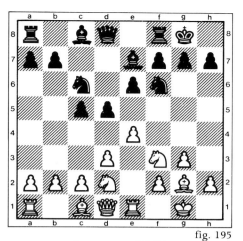

fig. 195

8. ...   Rb8?

Black should advance 8. ... b5 without delay, though even here there are problems. Bobby Fischer–Miagmasuren, Sousse 1967, continued 9. e5 Nd7 10. h4 a5 11. Nf1 b4 12. Bf4 a4 13. a3 (stopping Black's counterplay by ... a3) bxa3 14. bxa3 Na5 15. Ne3 Ba6 16. Bh3 d4 17. Nf1 Nb6 18. Ng5 Nd5 19. Bd2 Bxg5 20. Bxg5 Qd7 21. Qh5 Rfc8 22. Nd2 Nc3 23. Bf6! Qe8 24. Ne4 g6 25. Qg5 Nxe4 26. Rxe4 c4 27. h5 cxd3 28. Rh4! Ra7 29. Bg2 dxc2 30. Qh6 Qf8 31. Qxh7+! Resigns because of Kxh7 32. hxg6+ Kxg6 33. Be4 mate – one of the great Fischer wins.

9.	e5	Ne8
10.	Nf1	b5
11.	h4	a5
12.	c3	b4
13.	N1h2	Bd7
14.	c4!	

Because Black retreated his knight to d7 rather than the usual e8, his one chance of counterplay is Nc7-b5 followed by Nd4 or a3 and Nc3. White notices the difference and nips the plan in the bud.

14.	...	a4
15.	Bf4	Ra8

Admitting his eighth move was a mistake, but now White is two moves ahead of the usual KI Attack positions. ...

16.	Ng5	Nc7
17.	Qh5	

... and utilizes it for a direct piece attack rather than the slower h5-h6.

17.	...	h6
18.	Ng4	

Threatening to sacrifice at h6, so Black must take the other knight.

18.	...	hxg5
19.	hxg5	Rc8
20.	Nf6+!	gxf6
21.	Be4!	Resigns

A pyrotechnic finish, but easily foreseen by anyone familiar with KI Attack strategy. If 21. ... dxe4 22. Kg2 and Rh1 wins, or if 21. ... f5 22. g6 fxg6 23. Qxg6+ Kh8 24. Kg2 Bh4 25. Rh1 fxe4 26. Bg5 wins.

White: J. Anderson. Black: S. Spivack

Evening Standard junior championships, London 1975

1. e4 c5 2. Nf3 e6 3. d3 Nc6 4. Nbd2 d5 5. g3 g6 6. Bg2 Bg7 7. 0-0 Nf6 8. c3 0-0 9. e5 Nd7 10. d4.

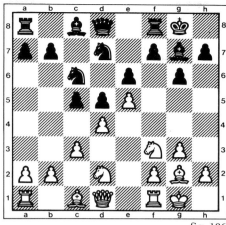

fig. 196

10. ... Qb6? (the source of Black's early defeat: correct is 10. ... cxd4 11. cxd4 f6 when White has just a slight edge) **11. Nb3** (stabilizing the centre before proceeding with the attack) **cxd4 12. cxd4 h6?** (another weakness) **13. h4 Qd8 14. Bf4 a5 15. Rc1 a4 16. Nc5 Nxc5 17. Rxc5 Bd7 18. Qd2 Kh7 19. Nh2 Na5 20. Ng4 Nc4 21. Rxc4!** (as in the two previous games freeing the e4 square for the bishop proves decisive) **dxc4 22. Bxh6 Rh8 23. Bg5 Qc7 24. Nf6+ Bxf6 25. Bxf6 Rhc8 26. Qg5 Rg8 and Black resigned** because of 27. Be4 and 28. Qh5+ mating.

Several reasonable counters have been worked out to the KI Attack. Prominent among these is for Black to simplify by exchanging his d5 pawn for White's at e4 and then develop his bishop at c5. A typical move order is 1. e4 e6 2. d3 d5 3. Nd2 Nf6 4. Ngf3 Nf6 5. g3 dxe4 6. dxe4 Bc5 when White can make little of his control of d5 and f5.

The drawback is that Black also has few prospects of winning play. Delaney–Nigel Short, Manchester Benedictine 1979, continued 7. Bg2 e5 8. 0-0 0-0 9. c3 a5 10. Qc2 Qe7 11. Nh4 Rfd8 12. Nc4 Be6 13. Ne3 Bxe3 14. Bxe3 Ng4 15. Nf5 Bxf5 16. exf5 Nxe3 17. fxe3 Rd6 and the game was soon drawn by rook exchanges on the d file. The outcome was not what Nigel Short was seeking – at the end of the tournament he missed a master result by half a point.

A little-known and more interesting answer to the KI Attack, suitable for attacking players, is where Black avoids castling and waits for White to commit his forces, particularly the queen and rook, to protection of the e5 pawn. Then Black counter-attacks against the white king by advancing his h and g pawns to open lines of attack.

White: Ajanski. Black: Dontschev Golden Sands, Bulgaria, 1978

1. e4 e6 2. d3 d5 3. Nd2 Nf6 4. Ngf3 b6 5. g3 Bb7 6. e5 Nfd7 7. Bg2 c5 8. 0-0 Nc6 9. Re1 Qc7 10. Qe2 Be7 11. c3? (better 11. Nf1, though Black could still play g5 as a pawn sacrifice) **g5!**

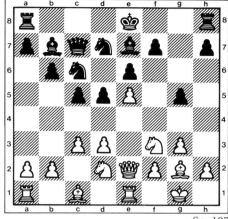

fig. 197

This surprise and original manoeuvre brought about the sudden collapse of White's game: **12. h3 h5 13. Nb3?** (he should at least safeguard e5 by 13. g4) **g4 14. hxg4 hxg4 15. Nh2 Qxe5 16. Nxg4 Qh5 17. Bf4 d4!** (opening up for the final attack and setting a trap into which which White falls) **18. cxd4? Nxd4 19. Nxd4 Qh1+! and White resigned.** If 20. Bxh1 Rxh1 mate.

A similar strategy won an important game at Hastings. The opening here deviates from a pure KI Attack when White advances c4 and Nc3, but although White creates more activity for his pieces than in the previous example the move g5 still proves the key.

White: Botterill. Black: Speelman Hastings 1978–9

1. e4 c5 2. Nf3 e6 3. d3 d5 4. Qe2 Be7 5. g3 Nf6 6. Bg2 Nc6 7. 0-0 b6 8. e5 Nd7 9. c4 Nf8 10. h4 (positionally threatening 11. Bg5, but weakening his own K) **h6 11. Nc3 Bb7 12. Re1** (better 12. Rd1 forcing Black to close the centre with ... d4) **Qd7 13. Bf4?** (the B becomes a target here) **d4 14. Nb5 a6 15. Na3 g5!** (if White's B was on d2 he could now keep the game closed by h5) **16. hxg5 Ng6 17. Bd2 hxg5 18. Bxg5 0-0-0!** (threat Bxg5 followed by Nxe5) **19. Bf6 Rh6 20. Nd2?** (20. Nb1 to bring this knight to e4 is the only chance) **Rg8!** (threatening Nf4) **21. Qg4 Ncxe5! 22. Bxe5 Bxg2** (the point: if 23. Kxg2 Nh4+) **23. f3 f5** (trapping the Q) **24. Resigns.**

Thus the KI Attack is a useful addition to the repertoire of a player prepared to take on the same line with both White and Black. On the one hand, the attacking ideas are clear-cut and easy to understand: while the little-known g5 counter will prove a strong psychological blow to unprepared opponents.

Winning Plans for White

White's extra move enhances the opportunities for directing openings into preferred channels, and for introducing sharp and unfamiliar complications. On the other hand, White's sheer multiplicity of choice creates its own problems. There are tales of grandmasters like Bronstein and Samisch agonizing for an hour on their first move, unable to come to a decision as to which of their many home-brewed variations to employ. Certainly in modern tournament play 1. d4, 1. e4 and 1. c4 all have their firm adherents.

The generally recommended pattern of openings with White should be similar to Black's. Above all, it is important to restrict yourself to lines which have a proven reasonable chance of occurring in practice. It can be infuriating to spend a couple of hours before the game looking at an interesting novelty on move ten, only to find your opponent upstage you with his own analysis at move six.

Within this pragmatic framework, the overall plan with White should be to strike a balance between solid and reliable systems where surprises are unlikely, and complex tactical ideas which are especially suitable when going for a quick kill against a weaker opponent. But because winning chess tournaments normally require a high percentage score with White, it is more important than with Black to have a number of systems in your armoury which are proven point scorers. They should be successful in the hands of experts and also give *you* good results. It is usual practice in chess instruction books to recommend variations which do well in grandmaster chess, but here the emphasis is different. Several of this chapter's systems are favourites of experts in the hurly-burly of weekend tournaments over a sprint distance, where hundreds of pounds or dollars are won by those who have mastered the necessary skills.

Vienna Gambit – a tricky tactical opening where White invites a queen check and aims for a fast king's side attack.

The Quiet Italian

An opening which used to be thought only good enough for routine equality is the calmest form of the Giuoco Piano or Italian Game. This opening is a sequence which many novices practice in their early games only to give it up for a less routine approach. Though it will surprise many to see it recommended as a winning weapon, its increasing popularity results from new ideas designed to give White overall space control.

The opening starts **1. e4 e5 2. Nf3 Nc6 3. Bc4.**

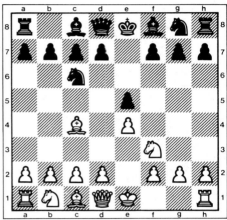

fig. 198

There now are two lines: (A) 3. . . . Bc5 (B) 3. . . . Nf6 followed by (C) Be7.

Line A

3. ...   Bc5
4. d3   Nf6
5. c3

In novice games, White automatically plays the symmetrical **5. Nc3** and the game proceeds something like 5. . . . d6 6. Bg5 Be6 7. Bxe6 fxe6 when victory goes to whoever makes the last-but-one blunder. Here White's plan is more definite: he intends a space-gaining Q-side advance with b4 and a4, and also prepares to bring his QN over via Q2 to the other flank to join in a K-side attack. Black has problems in creating room for his pieces to manoeuvre, so that White can gradually build up pressure without much risk.

5. ...   d6

The freeing **5. . . . d5** is met by 6. exd5 Nxd5 7. b4 Be7 8. 0-0 0-0 9. Bb2 Bf6 10. Nbd2 g6 11. Ne4 with a space advantage.

6. b4

Another good scheme is **6. Nbd2**, aiming to bring this knight to c4 where it eyes the centre and menaces the black KB, Bronstein-Ivkov, Amsterdam 1969, continued 6. . . . Bb6 7. Bb3 Be6? (*a6 is better to provide a bishop retreat*) 8. Nc4 h6 9. a4 0-0 10. 0-0 Re8 11. Bc2 Nd7 (*if Bxc4 12. dxc4* and White plays on the white squares by eventually bringing his knight to d5 or f5) 12. a5 Bxc4 13. axb6! Be6

14. bxc7 Qxc7 15. d4! and the delayed central advance, a theme of this opening, gives White the advantage. The game went on 15. . . . Bg4 16. d5 Bxf3 17. Qxf3 Nd4 18. cxd4 Qxc2 19. Bxh6! and White is well on top, for if gxh6 20. Qg4+ and 21. Qxd7.

6. ...   Bb6
7. a4

The logical follow-up to the last move. Now Black's bishop is threatened with 8. a5, and he has to make an escape square.

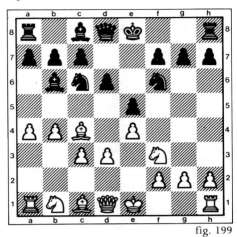

fig. 199

7. ...   a6

More flexible than **7. . . . a5 8. b5** when (a) **8. . . . Nb8** 9. 0-0 0-0 10. Bg5 h6 11. Bh4 g5 (*risky*) 12. Bg3 (also the sacrifice *12. Nxg5 hxg5 13. Bxg5 Nbd7 14. Kh1* followed by f4 gives a strong attack) Be6 13. Nbd2 Nbd7 14. Ba2 Kg7 15. d4! (Lutikov-van Scheltinga, Amsterdam 1969) and White has a fine game: he has carried out a delayed central push, and still has the c4 square for his knight and play on the K-side. The rest of the moves show the type of middle-game attack which can result from this opening: 15. . . . Bg4 16. Qc2 Nh5 17. h3 Bxf3 18. Nxf3 Nxg3 19. fxg3 Qe8 20. Kh2 Rc8 21. Rad1 c6 22. bxc6 Rxc6 23. Qb2 Bd8 24. Nd2! (the knight makes no more moves but its threat to march via c4 or f1 to e3 and d5 induces Black to compromise his position in a bid for counter-play) Nb6 25. Bg3 f6 26. Rf3 g4 27. hxg4 Qg6 28. Be6! h5 29. gxh5 Qxh5+ 30. Bh3 Nxa4 31. Qxb7+ Rc7 32. Qb3 Nxc3 33. g4! a4 34. Qxc3 Resigns.

(b) **8. . . . Ne7** 9. 0-0 0-0 10. Nbd2 Ng6 11. Bb3 c6 12. Nc4 Bc7 (Cafferty-Bryans, Manchester 1979) 13. Qc2 Nh5 14. d4! (the delayed central push) with advantage for White.

8. 0-0   0-0
9. Nbd2

Other good moves are **9. Na3** and **9. Bg5.**

9. ...   Qe7

Or **9. . . . h6** 10. Ba2 Ba7 11. b5 Na5 12. Ba3 Re8 13. Qc2 Be6 14. Bxe6 Rxe6 15. Rfb1 d5 (better *Bb6* though White is

still better after *16. Bb4*) 16. Bb4! c5 17. Bxa5 Qxa5 18. b6! wins material since if Bxb6 19. Nb3 (Miles-Sanz, Montilla 1978). In Ljubojevic-Furman, Portoroz 1975, 9. . . . Ne7 10. Bb3 Ng6 11. Nc4 Ba7 12. Ra2 (better 12. Qc2) h6 13. Re1 Re8 proved level, but White should have improvements.

10. Bb3   Ba7
11. Nc4   Nd8
12. Ra2   Kh8
13. Re1

Lutikov-Malisov, 1969. White's space advantage enables him to regroup his rooks while Black remains cramped. If now 13. . . . Ng8 14. d4! (the delayed central push) while the game went **13. . . . b5 14. axb5 axb5 15. Ne3 c6 16. Nf5 Bxf5 17. exf5** and White's light square control plus his attacking chances on both wings put him on top.

Line B (1. e4 e5 2. Nf3 Nc6 3. Bc4)
3. ...   Nf6

3. . . . Be7 will normally transpose into the column.

4. d3   Be7

4. . . . Bc5 transposes to Line A. A tricky but not quite sound pawn sacrifice is **4. . . . d5** 5. exd5 Nxd5 6. 0-0 Bg4 7. Re1 Be7 8. h3 Bh5 (*if Bxf3 9. Qxf3 Nd4 10. Qg4!* Larsen-Berger, Amsterdam 1964. favours White, since if *Nxc2 11. Rxe5 Nxa1 12. Rxd5 Qc8 13. Qxg7*) 9. g4 Bg6 10. Nxe5 Nxe5 11. Rxe5 Nb6 12. Bb3 0-0 13. Nc3 Kh8 14. Bd2 Bd6 15. Re2 and White can hold the attack (analysis by Marshall).

5. Nbd2   0-0
6. 0-0   d6
7. a4

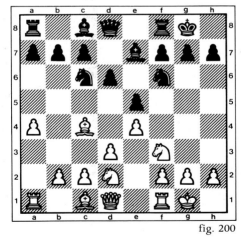

fig. 200

Black threatened to exchange the bishop by Na5.

7. ...   Be6

Other ideas are:

(a) **7. ... a5 8. c3 Nd7 9. Re1 Nb6 10. Bb3 Bf6 11. Nf1 Be6 12. Ng3 Qd7?** (*better g6*) **13. Bc2 Qd8 14. d4!** (the delayed advance) **exd4 15. Nxd4** with central control and a promising K-side attack (Cafferty-Pelitov, Albena 1971).

(b) **7. ... a6 8. c3 Na5 9. Ba2 c5 10. d4** (now the play is similar to the Ruy Lopez, and Black's best reply is 10. ... *cxd4*) **Nc6? 11. d5 Nb8 12. b4 N8d7 13. Qc2 b5 14. Bb1 Bb7 15. Nb3** with a useful Q-side space advantage (Harding-Kislov, postal game 1974–6).

(c) **7. ... Bg4?** (the pin merely helps a White K-side attack) **8. h3 Bh5 9. g4** followed by Nf1-g3-f5.

8. Re1

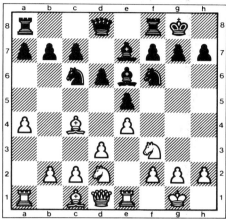

fig. 201

This position is similar to the closed Ruy Lopez where White also tries to gain space on the Q-side before switching to the other flank. White's bishops are more mobile and he has a straightforward attacking plan available in Nf1-g3-f5 along with g4, Kh2, Rg1 and attack down the g file. Black's central counterplay is hard to get going because his e pawn can easily become weak. Examples of play from the diagram are:

(a) **8. ... Nd7 9. c3 Bf6 10. b4** (*10. a5* is more precise) **a5 11. b5 Ncb8?** (since Black's bishop is not on the Q-side he can better regroup with *Na7-c8-b6*) **12. d4** (again this delayed advance) **Re8 13. Bxe6 Rxe6 14. Nc4 Re8 15. Ra2! Qc8 16. Ba3 Re6 17. Rd2 b6** (Botterill-Tatai, Middlesbrough 1978) and now according to Botterill White should consolidate his edge by **18. g3 h6 19. Rd3** intending exchanges at e5 followed by f4.

(b) **8. ... Qd7 9. a5 a6 10. h3 h6 11. Qe2 Rfe8 12. Bxe6 Qxe6 13. Nc4** and again White's superior minor pieces and space control give him the advantage (Cafferty-Pritchard, British championship 1971).

In summary, the Quiet Italian system gives White good chances if he can successfully blend the three underlying themes of Q-side bind, Ruy Lopez style K-side attack, and delayed central d4 push.

The Karpov Lopez

The Quiet Italian opening system discussed above has a double value: not only is it strong in itself, with good practical results, but its techniques and strategy are similar to, and thus a useful introductory course, before, the more complex ideas of the Ruy Lopez.

The drawback for the amateur player in taking up the Lopez is the wide range of defences at Black's disposal, ranging from tactical counters like the Bulgarian variation discussed in the previous chapter to the Marshall line with a d5 pawn sacrifice. Then there are the systems from Nxe4 which Korchnoi popularized in his world title match with Karpov as well as the closed variations which have been favourites of Capablanca, Karpov and Fischer as White and are illustrated in the Karpov biography (p. 78).

It is not possible or even desirable to deal with all these lines here. Rather the player who includes the Ruy Lopez in his repertoire with White should try to become familiar with them gradually, by checking out each one in a theory book after coming across it in actual play.

The Closed Defence is the most likely form of the Ruy Lopez to occur in practice, and the best way to absorb its ideas is to play over complete games by masters or strong amateurs in which White carries out the Karpov strategy shown in the two biography games.

White's basic idea in the Karpov Lopez is to plug the midfield by the advance d5, then advance his Q-side pawns to open lines for the rooks (as in Karpov-Westerinen, p. 78), gain space, and perhaps soften up the black game ready for a later switch to the K-side (as in Karpov-Unzicker, p. 78). Black can prevent or delay the queen's wing raid by himself countering in the centre, but this in turn opens up the board and creates chances for White's pieces with their greater room for manoeuvre. It is generally important for White to preserve his Ruy Lopez bishop – the white-squared one – since this can become very effective in an ending or if the board is opened up in the late middle game. Here is an example.

White: Unzicker. Black: Westerinen

Ruy Lopez (Haifa 1976)
1. e4 e5 2. Nf3 Nc6 3. Bb5 a6 4. Ba4 d6 5. 0-0 Bd7 6. c3 Nf6 7. d4 Be7 8. Nbd2 0-0 9. Re1 Re8 10. Nf1 h6 11. Ng3 Bf8 12. h3 g6 (if Na5 13. Bc2 keeps the key bishop) **13. Bc2 Bg7 14. Be3 a5** (holding up the Karpov-style pawn advance b4) **15. Qd2 Kh7 16. d5 Ne7 17. c4 Rf8 18. Rab1** (now a3, b4 and c5 cannot be directly stopped, so Black counters on the other flank) **N6g8 19. Nh2 f5 20. f4** (White looks for tactical chances based on the Lopez bishop's situation on the same diagonal as the black king) **fxe4**

21. fxe5 Bxe5 22. Nxe4 Nf5 23. Bf2 Nf6 24. Nf3 Nxe4 25. Rxe4 Bf6 26. Rae1 Rf7.

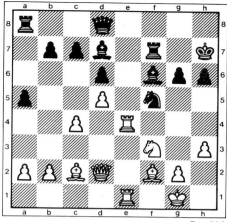

fig. 202

27. Qd3! (even with three men in the way, it is good technique to line up pieces on the same diagonal or file as the enemy king if there is reasonable prospect of opening the line. Black's position here is still defensible, though uncomfortable, but by gradually increasing the pressure White improves the chance of an unforced error) **Rg7 28. Rf4 Bg5 29. Nxg5+ Qxg5 30. Qf3 Rf8 31. Rf1 Re8?** (... which now occurs. After 31. ... h5, keeping the diagonal closed, there is nothing clear for White) **32. h4 Qf6 33. h5!** (now the Lopez bishop comes into its own and Black's game collapses) **Re5 34. hxg6+ Qxg6 35. Bd4 Rf7 36. Bxe5 dxe5 37. Rxf5 Resigns.**

Quite often in the Karpov Lopez Black defends inaccurately against the Q-side attack and White can establish a bind there while containing Black on the opposite wing. Here is a good example where White uses his d5 midfield plug to create an outpost square at c6. There his knight dominates the defences and shields the white rooks as they penetrate to the seventh.

White: R. Bellin. Black: A. Phillips
Ruy Lopez (Evening Standard congress, London 1973)
1. e4 e5 2. Nf3 Nc6 3. Bb5 a6 4. Ba4 Nf6 5. 0-0 b5 6. Bb3 Be7 7. Re1 0-0 8. c3 d6 9. h3 Nd7 10. d4 Bf6 11. a4 bxa4? (inconsistent with the strong-point defensive system of Black's moves 9-10: better is Bb7) **12. Bxa4 Bb7 13. d5!** (the midfield plug is particularly good here since it shuts out the black QB) **Ne7 14. b4 Nb6 15. Bb3 c6** (necessary to prevent White's c4-c5, but now the isolated a pawn becomes exposed and weak) **16. c4 cxd5 17. cxd5 g6** (the position is like some regular lines in the King's Indian Defence but more favourable to White. He has made fast progress on the Q-side, while Black's K-side counter has scarcely begun) **18. Be3 Bg7 19. Nfd2!** (to prepare the K-side pawn protection and switch the knight to the other wing) **f5**

109

20. f3 Kh8 21. Na3 Ng8 22. Ndc4 Nxc4 23. Nxc4 Bh6 24. Qd2 Kg7.

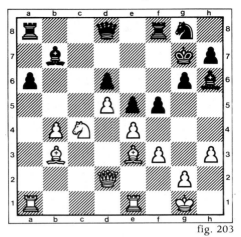

fig. 203

25. Na5! (strategically decisive; the white pieces take complete control of the Q-side) **Bc8 26. Nc6 Qh4 27. b5 fxe4 28. Bxh6+ Nxh6 29. Rxe4 Qg3 30. Qf2 Qg5 31. h4!** (completing the K-side guard) **Qf6 32. b6!** (32. Bc4 wins the a pawn but the white passed pawn could be blockaded. Now the knight controls the queening square b8) **Rf7** (if Ng4 33. Qe1) **33. Rc1 Bb7 34. Na5 Qd8 35. Rb4! Nf5 36. Rc7 Rb8 37. Nc6 Bxc6 38. Rxf7+ Resigns.** If Kxf7 39. dxc6+ wins.

Vienna Gambit

In contrast to the Quiet Italian and the closed Ruy Lopez, the Vienna is an attacking opening which gets particularly good results against weaker opponents. I have used it for many years in simultaneous displays at chess clubs and find that many average players go wrong in the early stages.

The opening starts **1. e4 e5 2. Nc3 Nf6 3. f4 d5** (for **3. . . . exf4?** see Novice Pitfall No. 7. Also inferior is **3. . . . d6 4. Nf3 Nc6 5. Bc4** when Black's KB has little scope within its own pawn chain) **4. fxe5 Nxe4 5. d3** (**5. Nf3** is also playable but less forcing).

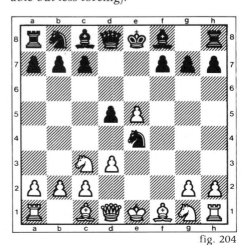

fig. 204

5. . . . Nxc3

5. . . . Qh4+ is analysed as Opening Trap No. 5 earlier in the book. Another line, complex though hardly ever encountered in amateur chess, is **5. . . . Bb4 6. dxe4 Qh4+ 7. Ke2 Bg4+ 8. Nf3 Bxc3 9. bxc3 dxe4 10. Qd4! Bh5!** (*exf3+ ? 11. gxf3* wins the bishop) **11. Ke3! Bxf3 12. Bb5+** (*12. gxf3 Qe1+ 13. Kf4 Qh5+* is a draw by perpetual check) **c6 13. gxf3 Qh6+** (if *cxb5 14. Qxe4 Qxe4+ 15. Kxe4 Nd7* with fair drawing chances for Black, though White's centralized K is strong) **14. Kxe4 Qg6+ 15. Ke3 cxb5 16. Qe4** (better than *16. Ba3 Nc6 17. Qe4 Qh6+ 18. f4 Na5!*) **Qh6+ 17. Kf2 Qa6 18. Rg1** with chances for both sides.

If you take up the Vienna and, rarely, your opponent chooses this line, look confident as you play the moves. In such a remarkable variation where the white king moves quickly to and fro over the central squares, a player's underlying confidence tends to become fragile and your opponent will be easily convinced you know it better than he does.

6. bxc3 d4

The alternative here is **6. . . . Be7** (6. . . . c5 probably transposes) **7. Nf3** (*also 7. d4 0-0 8. Bd3 f6? 9. Qh5 g6 10. Bxg6 hxg6 11. Qxg6+ Kh8 12. Nf3! Qe8 13. Qh6+ Kg8 14. 0-0 fxe5 15. Bg5* with a strong attack, analysis by Eales, but Black can stop the sacrifice by *8. . . . f5*) **0-0** (Black can also try *7. . . . c5* followed by c4 and castling long) **8. d4 c5 9. Be2 Nc6 10. 0-0 Bf5 11. Be3 Qa5** with complex play (Horseman-Gligoric, Hastings 1956–7).

7. Nf3

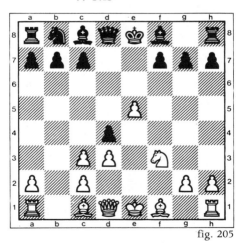

fig. 205

The most popular position for both sides in the Vienna Gambit, although it may prove to be better for White than the black alternatives analyzed earlier. Black can now choose among: **Line A 7. . . . c5** and **Line B 7. . . . Nc6**.

Line A 7. . . . c5

7. . . . dxc3 8. Be2 Nc6 9. 0-0 followed by Qe1-g3 gives a similar attack.

8. Be2 Be7

9. 0-0 0-0
10. Qe1 f6

Not **10. . . . Nc6 11. Qg3 Kh8 12. Ng5!** with a strong attack. Sax–Ciocaltea, Vrnjacka Banja 1974, concluded **12. . . . Bxg5 13. Bxg5 Qe8 14. Bh5 dxc3 15. Rae1 Nd4 16. Bf6 Rg8?** (*Ne6!*) **17. e6! Bxe6** (*gxf6 18. exf7*) **18. Bxd4 cxd4 19. Bxf7 Qxf7 20. Rxf7 Bxf7 21. Qf4 Bxa2 22. Qxd4** and a discouraged Black resigned.

11. Qg3

Better than **11. exf6 Bxf6 12. Qg3** when Black can reply **11. . . . Nc6 12. Bg5 Ne7.**

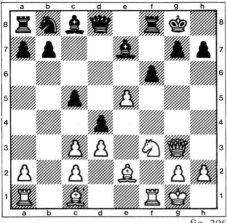

fig. 206

Figure 213 has occurred in several games and White's threat of Bh6 followed by exf6 and Ng5 has proved hard to parry. Some examples:

(a) **11. . . . fxe5 12. Bh6 Bf6 13. Nxe5! Bxe5** (or *dxc3 14. d4! Qxd4+ 15. Kh1 Bxe5 16. Bc4+* with a winning attack) **14. Qxe5 Rf6** (*gxh6 15. Rxf8+ Qxf8 16. Rf1 Qd8 17. Bf3*) **15. Bxg7!** and wins (Milner-Barry-Hanninen, Moscow 1956).

(b) **11. . . . Nc6 12. Bh6 Rf7 13. exf6 Bxf6 14. Ng5 Rf8 15. Ne4 Be5 16. Bf4** (Noskov-Stolyar, Leningrad 1966) and White should win.

(c) **11. . . . Kh8** is best but White keeps the advantage with **12. exf6 Bxf6 13. Bg5.**

Line B

7. . . . Nc6

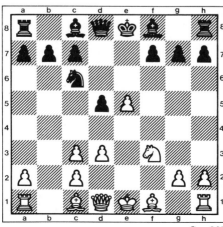

fig. 207

Now there are two promising approaches for White: (B1) the forcing 8. Be2 and (B2) the simplifying 8. cxd4.

Line B1

8.	Be2	Bc5
9.	0-0!	dxc3+
10.	Kh1	0-0
11.	Qe1	

Now White has the standard attacking position we already saw in line A. Black's game may still be defensible, but he has to be careful. The game Nunn-Hebden, London Lara 1979, continued **11. ... Nd4 12. Bd1 Nxf3+ 13. Bxf3 Be6 14. Qg3** (14. Bxb7 may be playable, but White logically continues to go for attack) **Kh8 15. Be4 Bd5?** (Be7! is necessary) **16. Bg5** (gaining a vital tempo, for if now f6? 17. exf6 gxf6 18. Bxd5 and Black cannot answer fxg5 because of 19. Qe5+) **Qd7 17. Bxh7! Kxh7 18. Bf6! g5** (if gxf6 19. Rf4! Be3 20. Rh4+ Bh6 21. Qf4 Bxg2+ 22. Kg1! forces mate) **19. Qxg5 Bxg2+ 20. Qxg2** (not 20. Kxg2? Rg8) **Rg8 21. Qe4+ Resigns.** If Rg6 22. Rf5 with a winning attack for White.

Line B2

8.	cxd4	Nxd4

Also playable is **8. ... Bb4+ 9. Bd2 Bxd2+ 10. Qxd2 Nxd4 11. c3 Nxf3+ 12. gxf3 Qh4+** (if *12. ... Qd5 13. Qe3* followed by Be2 and 0-0 and White keeps a space and development advantage) **13. Qf2 Qf4 14. Qg3 Qh6 15. Be2** (*Qe3 16. f4*) but White's command of central squares along with the open g and b files give him the edge.

9.	c3	Nxf3+
10.	Qxf3	Be7
11.	d4	c6

A better practical try is **11. ... Be6** but then 12. Qxb7 Bd5 13. Qb5+ c6 14. Qd3 Bh4+ 15. Ke2 leaves Black not quite enough for a pawn.

12.	Bd3	0-0
13.	0-0	Be6
14.	Qe4	g6
15.	Bh6	Re8
16.	Qe3	

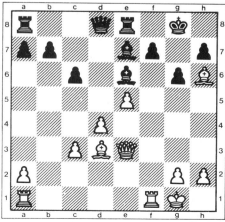

fig. 208

White now has good attacking chances

against the weakened K-side, while it is difficult for Black to organize central counterplay since his pieces, particularly the bishops, are needed for defence. Two illustrative games:

Barden-Andric, Cheltenham 1953: **16. ... Qd7 17. Rf4 c5 18. Raf1 cxd4 19. cxd4 Rac8 20. Qf2 Bd8 21. Kh1?** (missing the combination *21. Qb2! a6 22. d5 Qxd5 23. Rxf7 Bxf7 24. e6 and wins*) Rc3 22. Qe2 a6 23. h4 Bd5 24. Kh2 Qc6 25. R1f2 f5? 26. Bxf5! gxf5 27. Qg4+! Qg6 (*fxg4 28. Rf8+ mates*) 28. Rxf5! Be7 29. Qf4 Rec8 30. h5 Qxf5 31. Qxf5 Bf8 32. Qg5+ Kh8 33. Rxf8+ Resigns.

J. Allain-R. Drricott, postal game 1972-3: **16. ... Bf8** (the best chance is *c5 at once*) 17. Bg5 Qa5 18. Bc2 c5 19. Bb3 c4? 20. Bc2 Rac8 21. h4 h5 22. Rf6 Bg7 23. R1f1 Rc6 24. R6f2 (*24. Bxg6 bd5 25. Qf4 Rc7 26. Bf6 Bf8 27. Qg5 Qb5 28. g4 Qd7 (hxg4 29. h5) 29. gxh5 Qh3 30. Rh2 Qxc3 31. hxg6 Qxd4+ 32. R2f2 Bg7 33. e6! Resigns.* Black's defences are wrecked.

Meeting the French

The most promising line for the practical player against the French Defence 1. e4 e6 2. d4 d5 is to follow the world champion Anatoly Karpov who aims for a small but persistent advantage by the solid 3. Nd2. This move avoids the pin on the white QN which occurs in the popular variation 3. Nc3 Bb4 or in the system 3. Nc3 Nf6 4. Bg5 recommended in this book as a black formation.

There are two main lines of play after 3. Nd2. One is 3. Nd2 Nf6 which was analyzed in the previous chapter and where with the white pieces I recommend trying the Korchnoi Gambit (p. 94) which gives a nagging pressure difficult to counter. However the more popular variation in present-day chess is the system 3. Nd2 c5 which occurred in several games in the two Karpov-Korchnoi matches of 1974 and 1978. Although Korchnoi managed to hold his own with Black, he was often under pressure and unlike most players he is a superb defender. Few of your opponents are likely to have an equally resilient temperament and a much more likely course of the game at club and tournament level is that Black's game will become in-increasingly uncomfortable and passive as he defends the isolated queen's pawn which is the normal hallmark of this variation.

1.	e4	e6
2.	d4	d5
3.	Nd2	c5

Two other lines apart from Nf6 and Ne7, both analysed in the previous chapter, should be mentioned.

(a) **3. ... Nc6 4. c3** (simpler than the usual *4. Ngf3* because Black has less

choice of reply) e5 5. exd5 Qxd5 6. Ngf3 exd4 (if *Bg4 7. Bc4 Bxf3 8. Qb3! Qd7 9. Nxf3* – Keres-Botvinnik, Moscow 1955 – and White keeps the pair of bishops because if *9. ... Na5? 10. Bxf7+!* If *6. ... e4 7. Bc4* followed by *8. Qe2* and the e pawn is weak) 7. Bc4 Qf5 (after *Qh5 8. 0-0* is a promising gambit).

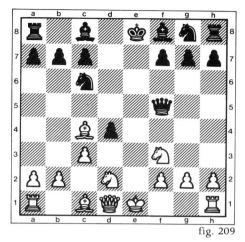

fig. 209

Now White can keep an edge by both:

(a1) **8. cxd4 Be6 9. 0-0 0-0-0 10. Bxe6+ Qxe6 11. Re1 Qd5 12. Qa4 f6** (or *Bd6 13. Nc4*) 13. Nb3 g5 14. Be3 Kb8 15. Rac1 Bd6 16. Nc5 followed by b4-b5 with attacking chances (Geller-Lein, Tiflis 1967) and

(a2) **8. Nxd4 Nxd4 9. cxd4 Be6?** (better *Bd6* followed by Ne7 and 0-0, though White keeps the initiative) 10. Qa4+! and Black's king position is unsafe (Korchnoi-Hug, Palma 1972).

(b) **3. ... dxe4 4. Nxe4 Nd7** is the Rubinstein variation, unpopular in present-day chess because Black concedes too much free space to his opponent: 5. Nf3 Ngf6 6. Nxf6+ Nxf6 7. Bd3 Be7 8. Qe2 0-0 9. 0-0 (*9. Bd2* followed by 0-0-0, intending a K-side attack, is also good) b6 10. c4 Bb7 11. Rd1 and Black remains cramped.

4.	exd5	

If you want to get out of the books quickly, an interesting idea is Cafferty's recommendation **4. dxc5 Bxc5 5. Bd3 Nc6 6. Ngf3 Nf6 7. 0-0 0-0 8. c3 Bb6 9. Qe2**, when White has a favourable form of what usually occurs from the Colle System in the queen's pawn opening (1. d4 d5 2. Nf3 Nf6 3. e3 e6 4. Nbd2 followed soon by dxc5 and e4).

4.	...	exd5

4. ... Qxd5 allows the black queen to be chased around too much after 5. Ngf3 cxd4 6. Bc4 Qd6 (or *Qc5 7. 0-0 Nc6 8. Qe2*) 7. 0-0 Nc6 8. Nb3 Nf6 (if Black tries to keep the pawn by *8. ... e5 then 9. Re1* is strong) 9. Nbxd4 Nxd4 10. Nxd4 a6 (too passive is *10. ... Be7 11. b3 0-0 12. Bb2 e5 13. Nb5 Qxd1 14. Rfxd1 Bf5 15. Rac1* and White's rooks control the open files, Tal-Uhlmann, Moscow 1967)

11. Bb3 Qc7 12. Qf3 Bd6 13. h3 0-0 14. Bg5 and White has the pressure (analysis by Keres).

5. Ngf3

This became the fashionable move after the 1974 Karpov-Korchnoi match where the former played it several times. But in the 1978 world title series Karpov, to general surprise, played **5. Bb5+ Bd7 6. Qe2+**.

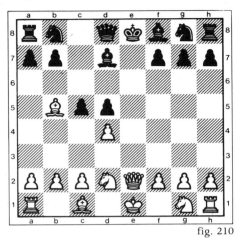

fig. 210

The diagram occurred in two games of the match; in the first Korchnoi drew after being under pressure, in the second he escaped from the jaws of defeat after amazing lapses by Karpov. Continuations were:

(a) 6. ... **Qe7** 7. Bxd7+ Nxd7 8. dxc5 Nxc5 9. Nb3 Qxe2+ 10. Nxe2 Nxb3 11. axb3 Bc5 12. Bd2 (maybe better still is *12. Nc3* which is favourable for White after either *12. ... Nf6 13. Na4* followed by *Be3* or *12. ... 0-0-0 13. Ra5*

as in Hort-Ivkov, Wijk aan Zee 1970) Ne7 13. Nf4 (also good is *13. Bc3*, Botvinnik–Euwe, world championship 1948) 0-0 14. 0-0 Rfd8 15. Nd3 (Karpov-Korchnoi, 16th game 1978). Black is uncomfortable because of the isolated QP: Korchnoi managed to draw but White has what chances there are.

(b) 6. ... **Be7** 7. dxc5 Nf6 8. Nb3 0-0 9. Be3 Re8 10. Nf3 Bxc5 (also good for White is *10. ... a6 11. Bd3 Ba4 12. Nfd4 Nbd7 13. 0-0-0 Nxc5 14. Nf5*, Tal-Portisch, Montreal 1979).

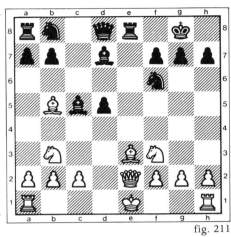

fig. 211

11. Nxc5 (unexpected: White can also play *11. Bxd7 Nbxd7 12. Nxc5 Nxc5 13. Qb5 Rc8 14. 0-0 a6 15. Qb4 Re4 16. Qd2 h6 17. Rad1* with a slight edge to White in the Larsen-Uhlmann match,

1971. The pressure in such positions is on Black since if the queens are exchanged his isolated pawn and dark squares are very weak) Qa5+ 12. Qd2 Qxb5 13. 0-0-0 b6 (the natural move is *13. ... Bg4* but then *14. Bd4 Ne4 15. Qf4 Bxf3 – or Nxc5 16. Qxg4* with advantage – *16. gxf3 Nxc5 17. Bxg7!* gives White a mating attack) 14. Nxd7 Nbxd7 15. Kb1 Ne4 (a sign of Korchnoi's dissatisfaction with his game; he seeks the queen swap he avoided on move six) 16. Qd3 Qxd3 17. Rxd3 with the better ending for White. The bishop is superior to the knight, and White can increase the pressure on the isolated d pawn by doubling rooks on the d file and then advancing the K-side pawns to undermine the defending knight. In the sequel, Karpov got a winning position.

5. ... Nc6

Not so good is *5. ... c4 6. b3 cxb3 (or b5 7. a4 Qa5 8. Ne5!)* 7. Bb5+ Bd7 8. Qe2+ when White is ahead in development and will have the use of the a file after recapturing axb3.

5. ... Nf6 looks natural, but the knight is really needed on e7: *6. Bb5+ Bd7 (or Nc6 7. 0-0 Be7 8. dxc5 Bxe5 9. Re1+ Be7 10. Qe2* with advantage) *7. Bxd7+ Nbxd7 8. 0-0 Be7 9. dxc5 Nxc5 10. Nb3 Nce4 11. Nfd4 Qd7 12. Qf3 0-0 13. Nf5 Rfe8 14. Nxe7+ Rxe7 15. Be3* and White is better with his strong bishop plus the usual play against the isolated pawn (Keres-Ivkov, Bamberg 1968).

6. Bb5	Bd6
7. 0-0	Ne7
8. dxc5	Bxc5
9. Nb3	Bd6

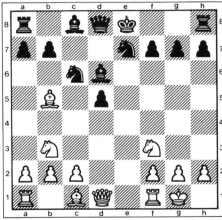

fig. 212

10. Bg5

This position produced a remarkable theoretical battle in the 1974 Karpov-Korchnoi match where the latter successfully parried Karpov's attempts to reach a position where Black would be left with either or both of a weak isolated pawn in a simplified position or a 'bad' white-squared bishop handicapped by the d and other pawns on light squares. Korchnoi managed to hold all these

games by active defence – but at more modest levels of chess Black's defence is more likely to falter than White's clear plan of strategy.

10. ... 0-0

Now there are two good ideas:

(a) **11. Bh4** and if **Qc7?** 12. Bg3 swapping off the dark-squared bishops or **11. ... Bg4** 12. Be2 Bh5 13. Re1 Qb6 14. Nfd4 Bg6 15. c3 Rfe8 16. Bf1 Be4 17. Bg3 Bxg3 18. hxg3 a5 19. a4 Nxd4 20. Nxd4 Nc6 21. Bb5 Rfd8 22. g4! Nxd4 23. Qxd4 Qxd4 24. cxd4 Rac8 25. f3 Bg6 26. Re7 (Karpov-Uhlmann, Madrid 1973) and White utilized the favourable factors in the position (out-of-play black B, rook on the seventh, and weak black b and d pawns) to win a fine ending.

Best against 11. Bh4 is the counter-attack **11. ... Qb6** when White can still try 12. a4 Bg4 13. Be2 (also interesting is *13. h3 Bh5 14. a5 Qc7 15. Be2*) Nf5 14. a5 Qc7 15. Bg3 Nxg3 16. hxg3 when Black has kept his more active bishop but White still has pressure against the Q-side and the isolated pawn.

(b) **11. Re1** Qc7 12. c3 Bg4 13. h3 Bh5 14. Be2 h6 15. Bxe7 Nxe7 16. Nfd4 Bxe2 17. Qxe2 (Karpov-Korchnoi, 18th match game 1974). A few moves later, Karpov exchanged a pair of knights to reach a knight *v.* bishop situation – but this time Korchnoi's bishop was the 'good', dark-squared one, while the queens also remained on the board. In the sequel, White's pressure against the d pawn proved insufficient for a win, but it took ingenious defence by Korchnoi to hold the game and in practical play the position gives good chances with White.

Sicilian Defence – the £3,000 Grand Prix Attack

One of the popular annual chess events in Britain is the Leigh Grand Prix which is decided on overall results of tournaments during the year. First prize is £3,000 and there is extra weighting for good results in the most important event.

Many qualifying tournaments on the Leigh circuit are weekend congresses where a large entry fights it out over five or six rounds of play. Under these conditions a high percentage is required to win and positive play is encouraged.

A frequent problem for the competitor in such tournaments is how to counter the Sicilian Defence 1. e4 c5, the most frequently met reply to 1. e4. David Rumens, who twice won the Grand Prix, relied on a little-known system aiming at sharp play and an early king's side attack. Tony Miles used the variation several times on the way to becoming Britain's first grandmaster and gaining the £5000 Slater award which went with the title. Other young experts were attracted by the success of Rumens and

Miles and the system has at the time of writing become one of the most popular and successful ways to counter the Sicilian on the British weekend circuit.

The overall ideas is not new; a similar plan with the black pieces was played by Bobby Fischer in 1969 and some of the variations also spring from the Dutch master Vinken. But given the many refinements and examples from English congresses, the name 'Cutty Sark Attack' seems an appropriate title for the system.

1. e4   c5
2. f4

Grandmaster Bent Larsen once made the provocative observation that 2. Nf3 and 3. d4 (the classical procedure against the Sicilian Defence) is 'something like a cheap trap' because it exchanges a central pawn for one on the flank. One very clear plus for 2. f4 against 2. Nf3 is that it drastically cuts down the amount of book theory you need to know in the highly analyzed Sicilian.

The white system can also be introduced by **2. Nc3** which cuts out Black's option of 2. ... d5 and after 2. ... Nc6 3. f4 d6 leads to positions analyzed below. However it has the drawback that Black need not play d6 and can instead adopt the formation (2. Nc3) Nc6 3. f4 g6 4. Nf3 Bg7 5. Bc4 (if 5. Bb5 Nd4) e6 6. f5 Nge7 which improves his chances of getting a good opening.

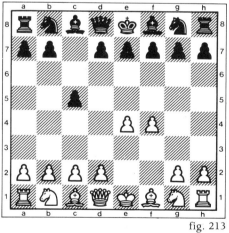

fig. 213

2. ...   Nc6

Several other moves are possible:

(a) **2. ... d5** 3. exd5 Qxd5 4. Nc3 Qd8 5. Nf3 Nf6 (better *5. ... Nc6 6. Bc4 Nf6 7. Ne5 Nxe5 8. fxe5 Qd4 9. Qe2* – 9. Bb5+ at once may improve – *Bg4 10. Bb5+ Nd7 11. Qe4 0-0-0* with level play, Hodgson–Franklin, Lloyds Bank 1977) 6. Ne5! e6 6. Qf3 Be7 7. b3 a6 8. Bb2 Nbd7 9. 0-0-0 with good attacking chances (Zinn–Minev, Halle 1967).

(b) **2. ... e6** 3. Nf3 d5 4. Bb5+ Bd7 5. Bxd7+ Qxd7 (better *Nxd7*) 6. Ne5 Qc7 7. exd5 exd5 8. Nc3 with a development lead for White. Larsen-Brinck–Claussen, Danish championship 1964, concluded 8. ... Nf6 9. Qf3 Qd8? (better *d4*) 10. Qe2

Be7 11. Qb5+ Nbd7 12. Qxb7 Rb8 13. Qxa7 Qc8 14. Qa4 0-0 15. 0-0 Nb6 16. Qb5 Nc4? 17. Nxd5! Resigns.

(c) **2. ... Nf6** 3. Nc3 d5 4. e5 d4 (if *Nfd7 5. Bb5*) 5. exf6 dxc3 6. fxg7 cxd2+ 7. Qxd2 Qxd2+ 8. Bxd2 Bxg7 9. 0-0-0 Bf5 10. Ne2 Nc6 11. Be3 with advantage, since Black's Q-side is weak. Miles-Plachetka, Dubna 1976, finished 11. ... Rc8? (better *b6* though this weakens the a6 and b5 squares; with his actual move Black sets the trap 12. Bxc5? Nb4!) 12. Ng3 Bg4 13. Rd5! Rd4 14. Bxd4 cxd4 15. Bb5 Bd7 16. Ne4 Rd8 17. Bxc6! bxc6 18. Rxd4 Bf5 19. Ra4 Rd7 20. Ng3 Be6 21. Rd1 Rc7 22. f5 Bc8 23. Rg4 e5? 24. Ne4 Ke7 25. f6+ Ke6 26. h3! Resigns because of Rd6+ and Ng3 mate.

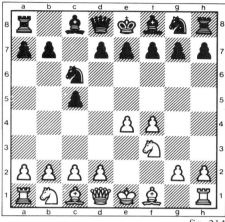

fig. 214

3. Nf3

This is again more flexible than 3. Nc3 because it leaves White the option to develop his bishop at c4 or b5, whereas the knight in this system rarely emerges at any square other than f3. This principle of maintaining your options is fundamental in accurate opening play.

3. ...   d6

Both 3. ... g6 and 3. ... Nf6 will normally transpose into lines considered later, but may develop differently. After **3. ... g6** 4. Nc3 Bg7 5. Bc4 Black can reply 5. ... e6! so as to advance ... d5 in one jump, but White can avoid this by (3. Nf3 g6) 4. Bb5! Bg7 5. Bxc6 bxc6 6. d3 and Black's pawn front lacks flexibility. An example is Hebd n–Leow, Lloyds Bank 1979, which continued 6. ... F b8 7. Nc3 d6 8. 0-0 Nh6? 9. Qe1 0-0 10. f5 e6?? 11. f6! and wins.

Another line is 3. ... **Nf6 4. Nc3 d5** 5. e5 d4 6. exf6 dxc3 7. fxg7 cxd2+ 8. Qxd2 Bxg7 9. Qxd8+ Nxd8 10. Bb5+ Bd7 11. Bxd7+ Kxd7 12. c3 f5 13. Be3 Kc6 14. 0-0-0 Nf7 15. Rhe1 Rad8? (*Rhe8* avoids the following tactic and keeps White's advantage minimal) 16. Rxd8 Rxd8? 17. Bxc5! Kxc5 18. Rxe7 Rf8 19. Rxb7 with a winning endgame for White (Miles–Gligoric, Tilburg 1977).

In this variation (**3. ... Nf6 4. Nc3**) **e6?** is dubious after 5. Bb5 Nd4 6. e5!

Nxb5 7. Nxb5 Nd5 8. c4! (an improvement on 8. *0-0? a6* when Black stands well. Hodgson–Waters, Lloyds Bank 1977) Nxf4 9. d4 Ng6 10. 0-0 cxd4 11. Ng5! with a winning attack. The game Hodgson–van Baarle, Lloyds Bank 1978, finished 11. ... f6 12. exf6 gxf6 13. Ne4 Be7 14. Nbd6+ Bxd6 15. Nxd6+ Ke7 16. Qxd4 Qa5 17. c5 e5 18. Qd5 Qa4 19. Qf7+ Kd8 20. Qxf6+ Kc7 21. Ne8+! Rxe8 22. Qd6+ Kd8 23. Bg5+ Ne7 24. Bxe7+ Rxe7 25. Rf8+ Re8 26. Rxe8+ Kxe8 27. Qxe5+ Kd8 28. Qf6+ Kc7 29. Qd6+ Resigns.

Finally there is the line (1. e4 c5 2. f4 Nc6 3. Nf3) **e6 4. Nc3 d5** (if **4. ... a6** White can switch to a different attack scheme by 5. g3! e.g. d6 6. Bg2 Be7 7. 0-0 Nf6 8. d3 0-0 9. h3 Qc7 10. g4, Hebden–Quinn, Lloyds Bank 1979). **5. Bb5.**

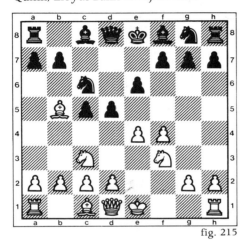

fig. 215

This is one of Black's better defensive ideas, though White retains good practical chances: **5. ... Nge7** (otherwise Bxc6 weakens the Q-side pawns) 6. exd5 exd5? (better *Nxd5*, Smyslov–Olafsson, 1959) 7. Qe2 (anticipating ... a6) Bg4 8. Bxc6+ bxc6 9. 0-0 Qd6 10. b3 Qe6 (if *10. ... Qxf4 11. Ba3*, while if *10. ... c4 11. bxc4 Qc5+ 12. Kh1* and Black's K was caught in the centre of the board in Zinn–Doda, Lugano 1968) 11. Qf2 Bxf3 12. Qxf3 Nf5 13. Ba3 with fine attacking chances. The finish of Rumens–J. Benjamin, Charlton 1976, was 13. ... Nd4 14. Qd3 Qf5 15. Rae1+ Kd7 16. Qa6 Kc7 17. Qa5+ Kd7 18. Na4 Qxc2 19. Nb6+ axb6 20. Qxa8 Ne6 21. Qb7+ Nc7 22. Re8! Kxe8 23. Qc8+ Ke7 24. Qxc7+ Ke6 25. Re1+ Kf5 26. Qe5+ Kg4 27. Qg5 mate.

4. Nc3

Once Black has committed himself to ... d6, White can continue with Nc3 and Bc4 confident that the counter ... d5 will not slow down his attack.

4. ...   g6

At this stage **4. ... e6** is rarely played and appears too slow: 5. Bc4 Nf6 6. 0-0 Be7 7. Qe1 0-0 8. d3 a6 9. a4 Bd7? 10. Kh1 Qc7 11. g4! with a powerful attack. Rumens–B. Valentine, Surrey Open 1978,

---

concluded 11. ... Nxg4 12. Rg1 Nf6 13. Be3 Rfe8 14. Qh4 g6 15. f5! exf5 16. Ng5 Ne5 17. Nd5 Qc6 18. Nxf6+ Bxf6 19. Bxf7+ Kf8 20. Bd5 Qc8 21. Nxh7+ Ke7 22. Qxf6 mate.

5. Bc4   Bg7
6. 0-0

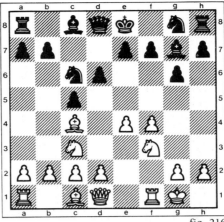

fig. 216

The diagram is a familiar position to specialists in the Grand Prix Attack. Black's two lines are (A) **6. ... e6**, normally associated with developing the KN at e7 and (B) **6. ... Nf6**.

Line A   6. ...   e6
7. Qe1

Once Black has advanced an early e6, this seems more precise than **7. f5 exf5 8. d3** and now:

(a) **8. ... Nf6?** 9. Qe1 0-0 10. Qh4 Nd4 (better *Be6*, but White keeps the edge by *11. exf5 Bxf5 12. Bg5 h6 13. Bxh6 Bxh6 14. Qxh6 Ng4 15. Qf4* according to the Dutch analyst van Wijgerden) 11. Bg5 Be6 (*Nxc2? 12. Nd5 Nxa1 13. Nxf6+ Bxf6 14. Bxf6 and 15. Qh6 forcing mate*. This dark-square attack on the black king forms the underlying strength of the Grand Prix system) 12. Nxd4! exd4 13. exf5! dxc3 (*Bxc4 14. Ne4 or gxf5 14. Nd5*) 14. fxe6 d5? (*cxb2 is a better chance*) 15. e7 Qxe7 16. Bb3 cxb2 17. Rae1 and White wins a piece and the game (Timman–Baljon, Dutch championship 1978).

(b) **8. ... Nge7!** 9. Qe1 h6 (also good is *Ne5*, as in van Wijgerden–Reshevsky, IBM 1977) 10. exf5 Bxf5 11. g4 Bc8! and White's attack is repulsed, says van Wijgerden.

7. ...   Nge7

7. ... Nf6 will probably transpose to the previous note.

8. Qh4

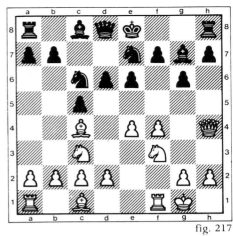

fig. 217

8. ...   a6

In the game Rumens–Rooney, Thanet Open 1978, Black tried 8. ... Nd4? and the result was another classic illustration of dark-square assault on the black king: 9. Nxd4 cxd4 10. Ne2 0-0 11. f5! exf5 12. d3! Nc6 13. Bg5 Qc7 14. Nf4 Ne5 15. Nd5 Qa5 16. b4 Qa3 17. Bf6 Be6 18. Qh6! Resigns. If Bxh6 19. Ne7 mate.

9. d3   b5
10. Bb3   Na5?
11. f5

Decentralizing the knight. Rumens prefers **Bd7** or **h6**.

Once again the familiar gambit. It is still strong here because, as the continuation shows, the BK is no safer in the centre than castled short.

11. ...   gxf5
12. Bg5   Qc7
13. Rae1   Nxb3
14. axb3   b4
15. Nd5!

Rumens–Whiteley, Nottingham 1978. The knight sacrifice shatters Black's position, for if 15. ... exd5 16. exd5 Be5 17. Nxe5 dxe5 18. Bf6! The game continued **15. ... Nxd5 16. exd5 e5 17. Bf6 Kf8 18. Bxg7+ Kxg7 19. Qg5+ Kf8 20. Qh6+ Ke7** and now **21. Qg7 Qd8 22. Nxe5 dxe5 23. Rxe5+** wins by destroying the BK's defensive cover.

Line B   6. ...   Nf6
7. f5!

In this line the pawn is best advanced at once before Black has the chance to go ... e6 and recapture with the e pawn. However **7. f5 0-0 8. f5** often transposes, while **7. d3 0-0 8. Qe1** did well in Rumens–M.L. Roberts, Thames Valley 1977: 8. ... a6? 9. Qh4 Nd4 10. f5 Nxf3+ 11. Rxf3 b5 12. Bb3 gxf5 13. Bg5 fxe4 14. Nxe4! Nxe4 15. Bxe7 Bd4+ 16. Kh1 Bf6? 17. Rxf6! Qxe7 18. Rg6+ hxg 19. Qxe7 and wins.

7. ...   0-0
8. d3   gxf5

If **8. ... Na5** 9. fxg6 hxg6 10. Qe1 a6 11. Qh4 threatening Bh6 followed by Ng5, or Ng5 at once, with a powerful attack.

9. Qe1

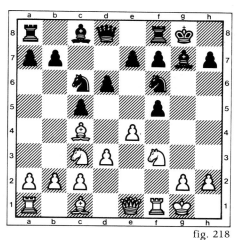

fig. 218

9. ... fxe4

Weak is **9. ... Na5?** since the knight is vulnerable after 10. Bd5! fxe4 (e6 11. Bg5 exd5 12. Nxd5 threatening 13. Nxf6+ Bxf6 14. Bxf6 Qxf6 15. Qxa5) 11. Ng5 e6 12. Rxf6! Qxf6 13. Be4 h6 14. Nh7 Qd8 15. Qg3 and White regains the sacrificed material with a continuing attack (Bellon–Merino, Orense 1974).

10. dxe4 Bg4

This plan was introduced by the English grandmaster John Nunn to blunt the impact of the Grand Prix Attack by piece exchanges. But his scheme was brilliantly refuted in Hodgson–Nunn, Aaronson Open 1978: **11. Qh4 Bxf3 12. Rxf3 Ne5 13. Rh3 Ng6** (Nxc4? 14. Nd5) **14. Qg3 Qd7 15. Nd5 Nxd5 16. Bxd5 e6 17. Bb3 d5 18. Qf3! c4 19. Ba4!** (sacrificing the bishop for a winning attack) **Qxa4 20. Qh5 Rfd8 21. Qxh7+ Kf8 22. Bh6 Bxh6 23. Rxh6 Rd7 24. Rf1 Ke8 25. Qg8+ Nf8 26. Rxe6+! Kd8** (fxe6 27. Qxf8 mate or Re7 27. Qxf7+) **27. Qxf8+ Kc7 28. Qc5+ Kd8 29. Rh6 Resigns.**

Summary: The Grand Prix Attack needs to be known by anybody who plays for or against the Sicilian Defence in congress or match play. It scores around 75 per cent for White on the British circuit and the basic plan (f4-f5, Qe1-h4, Bh6, Ng5, Nd5) is easy to understand and memorize. However there are a variety of plans for White and improvements are likely to be found in such a sharp and tactical line. Whether you take it on for White, Black, or both sides, detailed knowledge should prove very rewarding.

Against the Caro-Kann: the IQP system

The advantages and drawbacks of an isolated d or queen's pawn (IQP) have been keenly debated for many years among masters and tournament players, but the pros and cons still remain to a considerable extent a matter of taste. Following the principle of maximizing the chance of reaching the prepared sys-

tem, I recommend the IQP system against the Caro–Kann Defence 1. e4 c6.

The normal sequence of moves is **1. e4 c6 2. d4 d5 3. exd5 cxd5 4. c4 Nf6 5. Nc3 e6 6. Nf3 Be7 7. cxd5 Nxd5 8. Bd3 0-0 9. 0-0 Nc6 10. Re1.**

Some players prefer to meet the Caro–Kann by 1. e4 c6 2. c4 when after 2. ... d5 3. cxd5 exd5 4. exd5 Nf6 5. Nc3 Nxd5 6. d4 e6 7. Nf3 Be7 the same position occurs with less chance for Black to side-step.

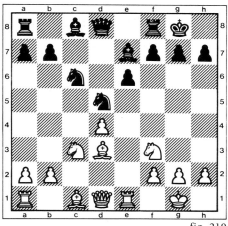

fig. 219

This is one of the key positions which can also occur by plausible moves from a Q-side opening. It is often reached via the Tarrasch Defence: 1. d4 d5 2. c4 e6 3. Nc3 c5 4. Nf3 Nf6 5. cxd5 Nxd5 6. e3 Nc6 7. Bd3 cxd4 8. cxd4 Be7 9. 0-0 0-0 10. Re1.

White strategy

The strategy for both sides from IQP positions is simple. White's assets are more space, chances for attack against the black king, the IQP's support for a knight outpost at e5, and the chance of a central break with d5.

The logic of this inventory of plus factors is that White should prepare for a mating attack against Black's K by deploying his Q at d3 and his king's bishop at c2 or b1, protected by the pawn at a3 from harassment by ... Nb4. White's king's rook belongs at e1, where it increases the power of a d5 central break, supports the knight outpost square e5, and can perhaps join in the K-side attack via e3 or e4. The queen's bishop normally goes to g5 with ideas of B(g5)xN (f6) and Qxh7 mate. White's knights find support from the IQP at e5 or perhaps c5.

Black strategy

While White thus goes for middle game attack, Black aims for the endgame. He tries to blockade the IQP with a knight at d5, which not only stops the pawn's advance but may also force piece exchanges to simplify the defender's task.

For example, if the white queen's bishop goes prematurely to g5, Black may be able to reply ... Nd5 swapping not only dark-squared bishops but also a pair of knights. Black can attack the IQP directly with pieces on the d file, and he can often start counterplay on the long black diagonal by ... Bb7.

Finally, if Black can reach the endgame, he can expose White's major liability. When few pieces remain on the board, White has to protect his weak IQP and stop the black men, led by the king, invading his position. Often he cannot manage both.

White's edge

Most masters at present prefer to play with, rather than against, the IQP in the particular setting of the last diagram. Many IQP games are decided by White breaking through in the centre before Black can prepare and execute his blockade.

The main line of the IQP system includes a promising trap featuring this central break. Black's moves are so natural that the trap caught out one international master and three grandmasters – among them the grandest of all, world champion Karpov – within the space of four years.

10. ... Nf6

Intending to protect the K-side and home in on the IQP. There are several alternatives:

(a) **10. ... Bd7** 11. a3 followed by Bc2 and Qd3 as in the column.

(b) **10. ... Bf6** 11. a3 (also **11. Ne4** going for the two bishops is worth trying) Nxc3 (Nxd4 12. Nxd4 Bxd4 13. Bxh7+ is a favourable pawn swap for White) 13. bxc3 b6 14. Qc2 with similar play to variation (c).

(c) **10. ... Nxc3** 11. bxc3 and now:

(c1) **11. ... b6** was refuted in Penrose–Nilsson, Varna, 1962 by 12. Qc2 g6 13. Bh6 Re8 14. h4 Bf8 (Bxh4? 15. Bb5 and Qe4 wins a piece) 15. Bg5 Be7 16. Bb5 Bd7 17. Qe4 Na5 18. Bxd7 Qxd7 19. Ne5 Qd8? (better Qd5 although 20. Qxd5 exd5 21. Nd7 wins at least a pawn) 20. Nxf7! Resigns. If 20. ... Kxf7 21. Qxe6+ Kf8 (Kg7 22. Bxe7) 22. Bh6 mate.

(c2) **11. ... Bf6** 12. Qc2 g6 13. Bh6 Re8 14. Rad1 also proved very strong for White in Hutchings–Solmundarsson, Haifa 1976: 14. ... Qc7 15. h4 Bg7 (if 15. ... e5 16. d5 or 15. ... b6 16. h5 Bb7 17. hxg6 hxg6 18. Bxg6 fxg6 19. Qxg6+ Bg7 20. Ng5) 16. Bxg7 Kxg7 17. d5! Ne7 18. d6 Qxd6 19. Bb5 and Black resigned.

(d) **10. ... Ncb4** 11. Bb1 b6 only helps White's attack after 12. a3 Nxc3 13. bxc3 Nd5 14. Qd3 Nf6 15. Ng5 g6 16. Qh3 (Szabo–Pogats, Kecskemet 1962).

11. a3

White intends to establish a battery of B at c2 and Q at d3, so stops Black's resource of exchanging by Nb4.

    11. ...   b6

The alternatives a6 and Bd7 are met in similar style.

    12. Bc2   Bb7
    13. Qd3

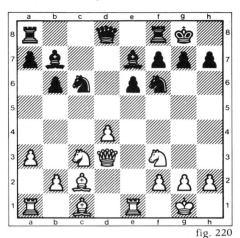

fig. 220

    13. ...   Re8?

This natural move is already a decisive mistake. A better plan is 13. ... g6 14. Bh6 Re8 15. Rad1 Rc8 although White still holds the initiative. Two examples:

(a) 16. Bb3 Na5 17. Ba2 Nd5 18. Ne4 Rc7 19. Ne5 Bf8 20. Bg5 Be7 21. Bxe7 Rexe7 22. Bxd5 exd5 23. Nf6+ Kg7 14. Qh3! with a strong attack (Christiansen–Gheorghiu, Malaga 1977).

(b) 16. h4 Nd5 17. Nxd5 Qxd5 18. Qd2 Qd6 19. Be4 Na5 20. Bxb7 Nxb7 21. Ng5 Na5 22. d5! (Ribli–Gheorghiu, Warsaw 1979) when White's active rooks made the defence difficult.

    14. d5!   exd5
    15. Bg5

An important finesse in White's overall plan has been to keep for as long as possible the option of developing this bishop at f4, g5 or g6. The point of the temporary pawn sacrifice is that 15. ... g6 loses to 16. Rxe7 Qxe7 17. Nxd5 – hence Black's answer is again forced.

    15. ...   Ne4
    16. Nxe4   dxe4
    17. Qxe4   g6
    18. Qh4

Until here, all the four master games were carbon copies except that in the other three Black had Rac8 thrown in as an extra move because the diagram occurred from a different opening on move 19.

The game Portisch–Karpov, Milan 1975, the most important for this open-

John Nunn concentrates at Hastings 1980. He believes in a regular rhythm, not more than five minutes a move, to avoid possible blunders due to time pressure. Karpov is also a quick mover, but Korchnoi and other world stars often have only seconds to beat the clock at the time control.

ing because it featured the world champion and one of his leading rivals, went 1. d4 Nf6 2. c4 e6 3. Nc3 Bb4 4. e3 c5 5. Bd3 d5 6. Nf3 0-0 7. 0-0 dxc4 8. Bxc4 cxd4 9. exd4 b6 10. Re1 Bb7 11. a3 Be7 12. Bd3 Nc6 13. Bc2 Re8 14. Qd3 Rc8 15. d5! and so on. It might be thought that the developing Rc8 would be a useful little extra for Black, but in fact the rook's different post does nothing to stop White's ensuing tactics.

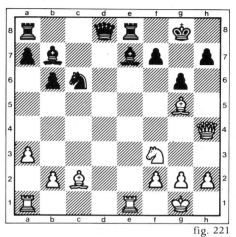

fig. 221

18. ...   Qc7

This was move 19 in all the other games. To Karpov's credit, he now realized the desperate nature of Black's position and played **19. ... h5** 20. Rad1 Qc7 to try and confuse the issue. The reply 21. Bb3 threatening 22. Qe4 should win the game (and in this case would have put Portisch in line for a $12,000 first prize) but White miscalculated with the sacrifice 21. Bxg6? and only drew. An expensive rush of blood to the head!

19. Bb3

Threatening 20. Bxf7+ Kxf7 21. Qxh7+ Kf8 22. Bh6 mate.

19. ...   h5
20. Qe4   Kg7

To stop 21. Qxg6+.

21. Bxf7!   Kxf7
22. Bh6

Threatening 23. Qe6 mate.

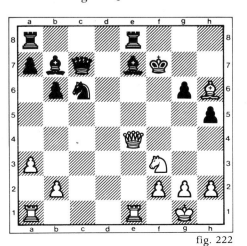

fig. 222

22. ...   Rh8

Creating a flight square for the king at e8. The other games also reached this position (with black rook at c8 instead of a8 and move 23 instead of 22). Black made different but equally hopeless attempts to rescue his trapped king.

Petrosian–Balashov, Moscow 1974, went **23. ... Qd6** 24. Qc4+ Kf6 25. Rad1 Nd4 26. Qxd4+ Qxd4 27. Rxd4 Rc5 28. h4 Resigns, while S. Garcia–Pomar, San Feliu 1975, finished **23. ... Bd6** 24. Ng5+ Kf6 25. Nh7+! Resigns because of Qxh7 26. Qf3+ and mate next move.

The game in the column is Wirtensohn–Pritchett, Cleveland 1979. Pritchett, Scotland's leading player, remembered none of the three precedents, and his rook move also led to a debacle for Black.

Wirtensohn–Pritchett ended **23. Qe6+ Ke8 24. Rad1 Nd8 25. Qxg6+ Nf7 26. Ng5 Qc4 27. Nxf7 Qxf7 28. Rxe7+! Kxe7 29. Qd6+ Resigns** because of Ke8 30. Re1+ and mates.

IQP system – other variations

Black's various methods of sidetracking White from the main line of the IQP system are discussed below. Chances for Black to diverge occur after the basic moves **1. e4 c6 2. d4 d5 3. exd5 cxd5 4. c4 Nf6 5. Nc3**.

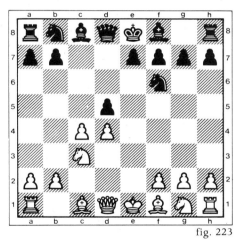

fig. 223

5. ...   g6

The most popular alternatives to 5. ... e6. Other ideas are:

(a) **5. ... Nc6** 6. Nf3 Bg4 aims at rapid development to undermine White's pawn centre, but White can keep the edge by forcing play: 7. cxd5 Nxd5 8. Qb3 Bxf3 9. gxf3 e6 (9. ... Nb6 10. Be3! e6 11. 0-0-0 Bb4 12. d5 Nxd5 13. Nxd5 exd5 14. Rxd5 Qc7 15. Kb1 0-0 16. Rg1 with a strong attack. Donaldson–Maddigan, USA 1978) 10. Qxb7 Nxd4 11. Bb5+ Nxb5 12. Qc6+ Ke7 13. Qxb5 Qd7 (Nxc3 14. bxc3 Qd7 15. Rb1! is still better for

White, Fischer-Euwe, Leipzig 1960) 14. Nxd5+ Qxd5 15. Qxd5 exd5 16. Be3 with endgame prospects due to the 2-1 Q-side pawn majority.

(b) **5. ... e6** 6. Nf3 Nc6 (6. ... Bb4 is also slightly favourable for White after 7. cxd5 Nxd5 8. Bd2 0-0 9. Bd3 b6 10. Nxd5 Bxd2+ 11. Nxd2 exd5 12. 0-0 Ba6 13. Nf3 Bxd3 14. Qxd3 Nc6 15. Rac1) 7. c5! (White aims to combine a Q-side majority with exchange of Black's QN and a dark-square bind) Ne4 (or 7. ... Be7 8. Bb5 0-0 9. 0-0 Bd7 10. a3) 8. Qc2 f5 9. Bb5 Bd7 10. 0-0 Be7 11. Bxc6 bxc6 12. Bf4 0-0 13. b4 (Vasyukov–Padevsky, Varna 1971). White has achieved his strategic objective, with the Q-side pawns mobile and Black's white-squared bishop trapped behind the pawn chain.

(c) **5. ... dxc4** 6. Bxc4 e6 7. Nf3 Be7 8. 0-0 Nbd7 directs Black's Q-side pieces on to the d5 outpost but gives White too much scope on the other wing: Barden–Brown, Oxford 1953 went 9. Bg5 Nb6 10. Bd3 0-0 11. Rc1 Bd7 12. Bb1 Bc6 13. Qd3 g6 14. Ne5 Rc8 15. Rad1 Bd5 16. Qh3! Nfd7 17. Bh6 Re8 18. f4 Bf6 19. Bg5 Bxg5 20. Nxf7! Kxf7 21. Qxh7+ Resigns.

6. Qb3   Bg7

Black allows his opponent an extra doubled pawn, hoping to regain it later. Instead **6. ... dxc4** 7. Bxc4 e6 8. d5 exd5 9. Nxd5 Nxd5 10. Bxd5 Qe7+ 11. Be3 Bg7 12. Nf3 followed by 0-0 and Rfe1 is favourable for White due to his active bishops.

7. cxd5   0-0
8. Be2

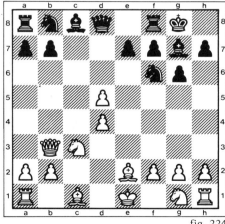

fig. 224

8. ...   Nbd7

White's plan is to use the time Black spends in regaining the pawn by speedy development and pressure down the e file. If Black plays **8. ... b6** 9. Bf3 Bb7 10. Nge2 Na6 11. 0-0 Qd7 12. Bg5 Rfd8 13. Rfe1 Nxd5 14. Bxd5 Bxd5 15. Qa3 wins the e7 pawn.

9. Bf3   Nb6
10. Bg5   a5

Other lines which show how White keeps up the pressure are **10. ... Bf5** 11.

Rd1 Qd7 12. h3 h5 13. Nge2 Rad8 14. d6 exd6 15. 0-0 d5 16. Ng3 and **10. ... Bg4** 11. Bxf6 Bxf3 12. Nxf3 Bxf6 13. a4 Qc7 14. 0-0 Rfd8 15. a5 Qc4 16. Ra3

	11. a4	Qd6
	12. Nge2	Rd8
	13. Bxf6	Bxf6
	14. Ne4	

Black can regain the pawn only at the price of weaknesses elsewhere. D. King-Hillyard, Lloyds Bank 1979, continued **14. ... Qb4** 15. Qxb4 axb4 16. Nxf6+ exf6 17. 0-0 Nxd5 18. Rfc1 Be6 19. Rc5 Nb6 20. Rb5 and White won the b pawn and the game.

Queen's Gambit Accepted

Players familiar with the ideas, plans and variations of the IQP system may have a chance to go into it from one or more of the standard queen's side openings such as the Tarrasch Defence or the Nimzo-Indian (1. d4 Nf6 2. c4 e6 3. Nc3 Bb4). Another such opening worth special note is the Queen's Gambit Accepted 1. d4 d5 2. c4 dxc4 – because it occurs as early as move two and because those who adopt this defence to 1. d4 tend to remain faithful to it over many games. Although 1. e4 is recommended here as the main standby for White, there can be occasions when strong players especially want to vary for a particular opponent or simply to widen their all-round experience.

The QGA begins **1. d4 d5 2. c4 dxc4 3. Nf3 Nf6 4. e3 e6** (the main alternative is **4. ... Bg4** when 5. Bxc4 e6 (but not **5. ... c5??** 6. Bxf7+! Kxf7 7. Ne5+) 6. 0-0 Nbd7 7. Nc3 Bd6 8. h3 Bh5 9. e4 e5 10. Be2 0-0 11. dxe5 Nxe5 12. Nd4 followed by Ndb5 or Nb3 is a system worked out by Hungary's leading grandmaster Portisch giving White a small advantage) **5. Bxc4 c5 6. 0-0 a6 7. a4.**

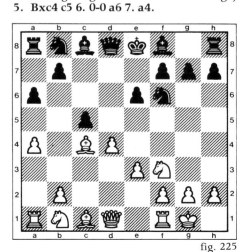

fig. 225

7. ... Nc6

Also possible is the immediate **7. ... cxd4** 8. exd4 Nc6 9. Nc3 Be7 when 10. Qe2 leaves the d pawn *en prise*. However, the pawn exchange seems premature since White can continue strongly. 10. Re1

e.g. Nb4 11. Bg5 0-0 12. Ne5 Re8 13. Re3! Bd7 (if *Nd5 14. Nxd5 Nxd5 15. Rh3 Bxg5 16. Qh5*) 14. Qb3 a5 15. Bxf6 Bxf6 16. Nxd7 Qxd7 17. Bb5 Nc6 18. d5! opening up the game for his better developed pieces (Miles–Clarke, BBC Master Game 1976).

	8. Qe2	cxd4
	9. Rd1	Be7

Black can't keep the pawn by **9. ... e5** because of 10. exd4 nor by **9. ... Bc5** because of 10. exd4 Nxd5 11. Nxd4 Bxd4 12. Be3.

	10. exd4	0-0
	11. Nc3	Nd5

It is wise to blockade the pawn, for if **11. ... Nb4** 12. Bg5 Bd7 13. d5! (Botvinnik–Petrosian, match 1963)

	12. Bd3	

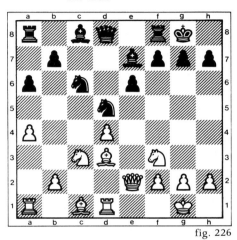

fig. 226

Compare this diagram with the normal IQP system; what's the difference? White's d1 rook is not quite so good as at e1 in the main line, but on the credit side his more advanced a pawn gives him a potential rook square at a3 plus possibilities of cramping the black Q-side. Black for his part can try to use the b4 square to create counterplay not available when the a pawn is at a3.

	12. ...	Ncb4
	13. Bb1	b6
	14. a5	bxa5

Or **14. ... Bd7** 15. Ne5 bxa5 16. Ra3 (threatening a snap mate attack by Nxd5 followed by Bxh7+, Rh3+ and Qh5) f5 17. Nxd5 Nxd5 18. Nxd7 Qxd7 19. Rxa5 with two bishops on open diagonals (Gligoric–Portisch, 1971).

	15. Ne5	Bb7
	16. Ne4	Rc8
	17. Ra3	

White has good attacking chances for his sacrificed pawn (Browne–Portisch, Lone Pine 1978).

Thus far we have looked at 1. e4 e5, 1. e4 e6, 1. e4 c5, and 1. e4 c6. There are three other principal defences to 1. e4 likely to be met in practical play – 1. ... d6, 1. ... g6 and 1. ... Nf6.

In countering 1. e4 d6 (Pirc Defence) and 1. e4 g6 (Modern Defence) I recom-

mend the 3. Nc3 and 4. Bc4 system analyzed in Trap Nine (Pieces beat the Queen), page 28. One advantage of this method is that, unlike some other variations, it can be used equally well against both 1. ... d6 and 1. ... g6, substantially reducing the amount of preparation required to counter this fashionable opening.

In addition to the sub-variations analyzed on page 29, Black can try to avoid the main line of the system by early QN development at c6: 1. e4 d6 2. d4 g6 3. Nc3 Bg7 4. Bc4 Nc6 (for 4. ... c6 see page 29).

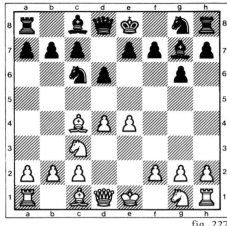

fig. 227

Play from the diagram again favours White:

(a) **5. Be3?** Nf6 6. f3 0-0 7. Nge2 e6 8. Bb3 b6 9. Qd2 Ba6 (Kristiansson–Keene, Reykjavik 1972) with probing attacks on the white centre.

(b) **5. Nf3** Nf6 (not *Bg4? 6. Bxf7+ Kxf7 7. Ng5+*) **6. d5** Ne5 7. Be2 or 6. ... Nb8 7. 0-0 gives White a freer game.

(c) **5. Nf3** Nf6 6. h3 0-0 7. Qe2 Nd7 8. Be3 Nb6 9. Bb3 Na5 10. 0-0 c6 11. Rae1 a6 12. Nd1 Nxb3 13. axb3 a5 14. c4 Nd7 15. Nc3 b5 16. d5 gives Black a passive, cramped game (Short–Ravikumar, Manchester Benedictine 1979).

Alekhine Defence

The defence 1. e4 Nf6, named after the great world champion Alekhine, aims to lure the white central pawns into a premature advance which can be exploited by counter-attack and rapid development of Black's pieces. White can fall in with Black's plan and hope to maintain his centre, thus permanently cramping Black's game, or he can try to exploit Black's unorthodox play by opening lines for his own pieces. It isn't clear which is really the better approach, but from the practical amateur's viewpoint piece development is easier to handle and also greatly reduces the number of variations you need to know.

	1. e4	Nf6
	2. e5	Nd5
	3. Nc3	

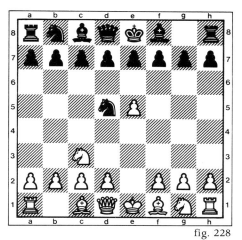

fig. 228

3. ...   Nxc3

If Black tries to keep his knight in the centre by **3. ... e6** then 4. d4 d6 5. Nf3 Nc6 (or *dxe5 6. Nxe5 Bb4 7. Qf3* followed by Bd2 and 0-0-0 with a promising attacking set-up) 6. Bb5! Nxc3 7. bxc3 dxe5 8. Nxe5 Bd7 9. Nxd7 Qxd7 10. Qf3 with pressure. If **3. ... c6** 4. d4, or if **3. ... Nb6** 4. a4 a5 5. f4 followed by Nf3 and d4.

4. dxc3

The normal rule of thumb is to make pawn captures towards the centre rather than away from it, but here taking with the d pawn is better in the context of rapid development. **4. bxc3** is playable but Black then has a good line in 4. ... c5 5. f4 d6 6. Nf3 g6 7. d4 Bg7 8. Be2 0-0 9. 0-0 dxe5 10. fxe5 Nc6 11. Bf4 Bg4 when White's weak central pawns pushed him on the defensive in Hennings–Gipslis, Havana 1971.

4. ...   d6

If **4. ... d5** White can dislocate Black's embryo pawn centre by 5. c4! d4 6. f4 Bf5 7. Ne2 Nc6 8. Ng3 e6 9. Nxf5 exf5 10. Bd3 g6 11. a3 a5 12. Qf3 (Ghizdavu–Torre, Nish 1972).

5. Nf3

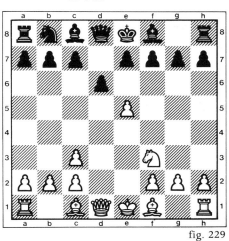

fig. 229

5. ...   Nc6

White's set-up looks at first sight rather harmless, but in practice Black finds difficulty in equalizing. One example of how Black can drift into a poor game is **5. ... Bg4** 6. Bc4 e6 7. Bf4 Nc6 8. Bb5 Be7 9. h3 Bxf3 10. Qxf3 d5 11. Qg3 Kf8 12. Rd1 a6 13. Be2 b5 14. Rd3 with a strong attack (Hutchings–Natt, Evening Standard 1972).

Other tries for Black are:

(a) **5. ... dxe5** 6. Qxd8+ Kxd8 7. Nxe5 Ke8 8. Be3 f6 9. Nd3 e5 10. 0-0-0 followed by f4 with some initiative.

(b) **5. ... g6** 6. Bc4 Nc6 7. Bf4 and now:

(b1) **7. ... Bg7** 8. exd6 cxd6 9. Qd2 followed by 0-0-0, Bh6 and h4 with attacking chances.

(b2) **7. ... e6?** 8. exd6 cxd6 9. Qe2 Be7 10. 0-0-0 a6 11. h4 also with attack (Keres–Westerinen, Tallinn 1971).

6. Bb5

Exchanging pawns at d6 would deprive White of all chances of advantage. However White can also support the e5 pawn directly by **6. Bf4**, a move which in Roos–W. Schmidt, Bagneux 1978, led to the defeat of Black (a grandmaster!) with remarkable rapidity: 6. ... dxe5 7. Qxd8+ Nxd8 8. Bxe5 c6 9. 0-0-0 f6 10. Bg3 e5? (*Be6*) 11. Bc4 Nf7 12. Rhe1 g6? 13. Bxe5 Resigns, for if 13. ... Nxe5 14. Nxe5 Bh6+ (*fxe5 15. Rxe5+ Be7 16. Rde1*) 15. Kb1 fxe5 16. Rxe5+ Kf8 17. Rd8+ Kg7 18. Re7+ Kf6 19. Rf7+ Kg5 20. Rxh8.

6. ...   Bd7
7. Qe2   Nxe5

7. ... a6 does not fully relieve the pressure after 8. Bc4 e6 9. Bf4 dxe5 10. Nxe5 Bd6 11. Bg3 followed by 0-0-0.

8. Nxe5   dxe5
9. Qxe5   f6

More accurate than **9. ... c6** played in Keres–Schmid, Zurich 1961, when Black became very cramped: 10. Bc4 Qb8 11. Qe4 e6 12. Bg5 h6 13. Bh4 Bd6 14. 0-0-0.

10. Qh5+   g6
11. Qe2   e5
12. Be3   Bd6
13. 0-0-0

White has the initiative and a freer game (Markland–Korchnoi, Bath 1973). Korchnoi managed to hold on and turn the tables, but at a less exalted level White has promising chances of attack, e.g. 13. ... 0-0 14. Bc4+ followed by h4–h5.

Minor defences

Three offbeat defences to 1. e4 are occasionally tried in tournament and match play.

The **Centre Counter 1. e4 d5 2. exd5 Qxd5** (if **2. ... Nf6** White can play for a slight edge by 3. d4 Nxd5 4. Nf3 g6 5. h3 or transpose into the IQP system by 3. c4 c6 4. d4 – it is risky to accept the pawn by 4. dxc6 – cxd5 5. Nc3) **3. Nc3 Qa5 4. d4 Nf6 5. Nf3 Bf5** (or Bg4 6. h3) **6. Bd2 Nbd7 7. Bc4 c6 8. Qe2 e6 9. d5! cxd5 10. Nxd5 Qc5 11. b4 Qc8 12. Nxf6+ gxf6 13. Nd4** (Spassky–Larsen, Montreal 1979) gives White control of the centre while Black's forces remain uncoordinated. That's the trouble with the Centre Counter – White cannot directly exploit the prematurely developed black queen but can drive it back while gaining time for his own attack.

The **Nimzovich Defence 1. e4 Nc6** should be favourable for White, but can be tricky in the hands of a player who knows it well even in the line **2. d4 d5** 3. Nc3 dxe4 4. d5 Ne5 5. Qd4.

I recommend instead the quiet (**1. e4 Nc6) 2. Nf3** when 2. ... e5 (probably best!) transposes into a normal 1. e4 e5 opening and thus thwarts Black's aim to escape from the books. Other possibilities are 2. ... d5? 3. exd5 Qxd5 4. Nc3 with a favourable form of the Centre Counter for White, or 2. ... d6 3. d4 Bg4 4. d5 Nb8 (not 4. ... Ne5? 5. Nxe5! Bxd1 6. Bb5+ c6 7. dxc6 Qa5+ 8. Nc3 and White emerges with too much material for the queen) 5. Be2 followed by h3 with a small but clear advantage in space.

The **English Defence 1. e4 b6 2. d4 Bb7 3. Bd3 e6** was a favourite with the English nineteenth-century player Owen, and has more recently been revived by the grandmasters Keene and Miles, also of England. White can develop normally by 4. Nf3 c5 5. 0-0 but a more interesting and crucial line is **4. c4** (threatening to shut both Black's bishops out of the game by a3 followed by d5) **f5 5. exf5 Bxg2 6. Qh5+ g6 7. fxg6 Bg7** (not Nf6? 8. g7+) **8. gxh7+ Kf8.**

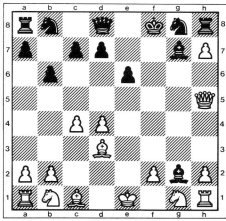

fig. 230

9. Ne2! (stronger than the obvious **9. hxg8(Q)+ Kxg8** when White's attack is not enough for the b1 rook) **Bxh1 10. Bg5!** (the point, forcing Black into an unwelcome pin) **Nf6 11. Qh4 Nc6 12. Nf4.** In this critical position White's main threat is not so much the obvious 13. Ng6+ as 13. Bg6 followed by Nh5 when the pinned knight falls and the black game collapses. Black can now try:

(a) **12. ... Nb4** 13. Bg6 Qe7 14. Nh5 Nc2+ 15. Bxc2 Qb4+ 16. Nd2 Nxh5 (if Qxb2 17. Nxg7! Qxa1+ 18. Ke2 wins) 17. 0-0-0! and a helpless Black resigned (Forintos–Fernandez, Cienfuegos 1979).

(b) **12. ... Kf7** 13. Bg6+ Ke7 14. Nh5 Qf8 (again Black is trapped in a permanent pin) 15. Nd2 e5 16. 0-0-0! Nxd4 17. Rxh1 Ne6 18. f4 d6 19. Ne4 Nxg5 20. Qxg5 Bh6 21. Qh4 (though material behind, White wins easily as he brings reinforcements to the pin) Bg7 22. fxe5 dxe5 23. Rf1 Kd7 24. N4xf6+ Bxf6 25. Nxf6+ Kc8 26. Be4 c6 27. Qh3+ Kb7 28. Bxc6+! Resigns (Browne–Miles, Tilburg 1978).

(c) **12. ... Nxd4** 13. Ng6+ Ke8 14. Qxd4 Rxh7 15. Ne5 Rh3 16. Bg6+ Kf8 17. Nc3 d6 18. 0-0-0 with a clear advantage.

(d) **12. ... e5** 13. Ng6+ Kf7 14. dxe5 Re8 15. f4! d6 16. Nc3 dxe5 17. 0-0-0 and White is on top (this and the last variation are analysis by Browne).

These fascinating variations illustrate how tactics can influence strategy at the chessboard. Because they are so favourable for White, few will care to risk them again with Black and this means that White can counter the English Defence with the centre-occupying c4, d4, e4 pawn formation without fearing that Black will undermine it. And this in turn reduces Black's willingness to venture the opening at all.

The £1,200 opening

Slightly offbeat but nevertheless sound and positive opening systems can sometimes have a remarkable temporary effect. Although in this chapter we are largely analysing 1. e4 openings, the story is worth recounting of how a quiet but specialized variation helped to win Britain's richest congress prize.

It happened at the London Evening Standard congress of 1979, where a young Yugoslav, Klaric, decided to use the Queen's Bishop Attack 1. Nf3, 2. d4 and 3. Bg5 in all his games with White. The intention is to follow up soon with Ne5 and K-side attacking piece play on similar lines to the Pillsbury Attack (page 58). This system is harmless enough if Black knows it well and is prepared in advance.

However, although Klaric played his system in the very first round of the tournament, later rivals neglected to check up on his play and emerged with poor games from the opening. Klaric used his system to win three games with White and then had good fortune, which tournament winners need, when he scored from a dubious position against the grandmaster favourite John Nunn. The net result – Klaric won the £1,200 prize awarded by the congress's major sponsor, the National Bank of Dubai.

1. Nf3   Nf6
2. d4   d5

The system is also playable against **2. ... g6** 3. Bg5 Bg7, although that is a simpler equalizing method for Black.

3. Bg5   e6

Klaric–Shallcross, Evening Standard 1979, went **3. ... c6** 4. e3 Bf5 5. Bd3 Bxd3 6. cxd3 Nbd7 7. 0-0 g6 8. Ne5 Bg7 9. Nd2 0-0 10. Rc1 Ne8 11. Nxd7 Qxd7 12. f4 Nd6 13. Bh4 Nf5 14. Bf2 e6 (Black has emerged quite well but should prefer *14. ... f6* intending e5 or else *... h5* safeguarding the knight) 15. Nf3 Rfe8 16. Ne5 Qe7 17. Qe1 Rac8 18. Kh1 f6 19. Nf3 Nh6 (e5 was still best) 20. e4 Qc7 21. e5 fxe5 22. fxe5 Rf8 23. Be3! (hoping for a tactical chance against the underguarded knight ...) Qb6? 24. Rc2 Qa6 25. Rc3! Qxa2?? 26. Qc1! (... which comes with the double threat of *27. Bxh6* and *27. Ra3*) Rxf3 27. gxf3 Resigns.

4. Nbd2   Be7
5. e3

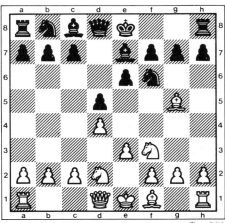

fig. 231

Here White is ready to set up the Pillsbury formation with Ne5, and Klaric's £1,200 games and others show how quickly his attack can develop:
Klaric–Flear, Evening Standard 1979:

(a) **5. ... c5** 6. c3 b6? 7. Bb5+ Nfd7 (more natural is *Bd7*) 8. Bf4 0-0 9. Ne5 Nxe5 10. dxe5 Nd7 11. Bxa6 Nxa6 12. Qg4 Kh8 13. Rd1 Qe8 14. 0-0 Qa4 15. e4 Nc7 16. a3 Rad8 17. b3 Qa5 18. Rae1 dxe4 19. Re3 Rd3 20. Nxe4 Rxe3 21. fxe3 c4 22. Bg5 Qxa3 23. b4 Nd5 24. h3 a5 25. Bxe7 Nxe7 26. Ng5 Nf5.

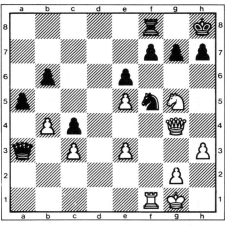

fig. 232

Black has tried to fight back from his poor opening: piece exchanges diminished the force of the Pillsbury formation, and the BQ has gone pawn hunting while the N barricades the other flank. But White's next move defeats the entire plan and finishes quickly.

27. Rxf5! exf5 28. Qxf5 g6 29. Qf6+ Kg8 30. e6 fxe6 31. Qxe6+ Kg7 32. Qe7+ Kh6 33. Ne6 Rf1+ 34. Kh2! Resigns because of the double threat Qh4+ and Qg7+.

(b) Klaric–Crouch, Evening Standard 1979: **5. ... h6** 6. Bh4 0-0 7. Bd3 Nbd7 8. c3 Re8 9. Ne5 Nxe5 10. dxe5 Nd7 11. Bg3 c5 12. 0-0 a6 13. Qh5! with a strong attack in Pillsbury style. Black now tried to create space for K-side defence but the white pieces exploited the resulting holes: 13. ... Bf8 14. Nf3 g6 15. Qh3 Bg7 16. Bf4 g5 17. Bg3 f5 18. exf6 Qxf6 19. Qh5 Rf8 20. h4!

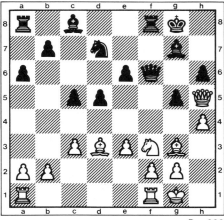

fig. 233

White cracks the defences. If now 20. ... gxh4 21. Bxh4 Qf7 22. Bg6 wins the queen. Instead Black surrenders a pawn but he cannot hold out long in such an open position: 20. ... g4 21. Qxg4 e5 22. Qh5 b5 23. e4 c4 24. Bc2 d4 25. cxd4 exd4 26. Qd5+ Kh8 27. e5 Qb6 28. Nxd4 Bb7 29. Qxd7 Rad8 30. Qe6 Qxd4 31. Qg6 Kg8 32. Qh7+ Kf7 33. Bg6+ Resigns.

(c) Fuller–Dankert, Esbjerg 1979: **5. ... 0-0** 6. Bd3 b6 7. Ne5 Bb7 8. Qf3 Nbd7 (a better chance is *Nfd7*) 9. Qh3 g6 (if *Ne4 10. Nxe4 dxe4 11. Ba6!*) 10. Qh4 Nb8 (or *Re8 11. Bb5*) 11. f4 c5 12. c3 Nc6 13. N2f3 Rc8 14. 0-0.

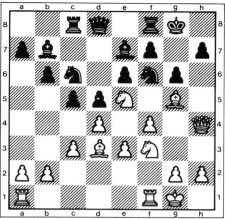

fig. 234

A classical attacking position for White in the Pillsbury system. The white queen and minor pieces are already directed at the king, the rooks can come into action via the f file, while black counterplay is far distant. Not surprisingly, the game ended quickly in White's favour: 14. . . . Rc7 15. Bh6 Nh5 16. Ng5 Nxe5 17. fxe5 Bc8 18. g4 Ng7 19. Rf6! Ne8 (or *Bxf6 20. exf6 Qxf6 21. Rf1*) 20. Bxf8 Bxf6 21. exf6 Qxf6 (*Nxf6 22. Nxh7!*) 22. Rf1 Qh8 23. Nxf7 Resigns.

(d) Spassky–Petrosian, 7th match game 1966: **5. . . . Nbd7** 6. Bd3 c5 7. c3 b6 8. 0-0 Bb7 (the right plan, demonstrated by Petrosian here, is to castle long and use White's K-side piece build-up as a target to aid a black pawn advance) 9. Ne5 Nxe5 10. dxe5 Nd7 11. Bf4 (better 11. *Bxe7 Qxe7 12. f4* with a level game) Qc7 12. Nf3 h6 13. b4 g5! 14. Bg3 h5 15. h4 gxh4 16. Bf4 0-0-0 17. a4 (better 17. *bxc5 bxc5 18. Rb1*).

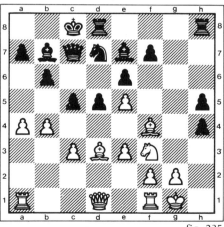

fig. 235

17. . . . c4! (a brilliant idea, conceding the d4 square but closing-up the Q-side) 18. Be2 (better *18. Bf5!* so that if exf5 19. e6 while otherwise the bishop can blockade the black pawns at h3) a6! 19. Kh1 Rdg8 20. Rg1 Rg4 21. Qd2 R8g8 22. a5 b5 23. Rad1 Bf8 (threat *f6* and if *exf6 e5*) 24. Nh2 Nxe5! 25. Nxg4 hxg4 26. e4 Bd6 27. Qe3 Nd7 28. Bxd6 Qxd6 29. Rd4 e5 30. Rd2 f5! (now the pawn phalanx

squashes White) 31. exd5 f4 32. Qe4 Nf6 33. Qf5+ Kb8 34. f3 Bc8 35. Qb1 g3 36. Re1 h3 37. Bf1 Rh8 38. gxh3 Bxh3 39. Kg1 Bxf1 40. Kxf1 e4 41. Qd1 Ng4! (the sealed move, and the prettiest and quickest way to win) 42. fxg4 f3 43. Rg2 fxg2+ 44. Resigns. If 44. Kxg2 Qf4 and finish.

Monkey business

The previous section on the Pillsbury formation and its contribution to a £1,200 prize is one suggestion for the club player who wants an easy-to-understand attacking method. However the Pillsbury system, like some others, has the drawback that it cannot be completely forced on an opponent.

The only way to be quite sure that chess opening homework will not be wasted is to have a system which begins on move one. A possible approach which used to be considered eccentric but is now treated with more respect is considered below.

The move 1. b4 was introduced into master play by Dr Tartakover in his game with Maroczy at New York 1924. Asked by reporters why he had considered such a strange move, the witty grandmaster replied that he had visited the New York zoo on the rest day and had 'fallen in love with the orang-outang enough to dedicate my next game to the animal.'

Tartakover had a reputation as a gambler both on and off the board. This, coupled with his self-mocking comment on the new move which became dubbed the Orang-Outang Opening, ensured that none of the other masters took the move 1. b4 seriously.

One player, however, did pay attention. The White Russian master, Alexei Sokolsky from Minsk, one of a school of original theorists, started to investigate 1. b4 in depth. He found that if Black defended with a cautious positional move like Nf6, d5 or e6 White could develop normally with his bishop well posted at b2 while in the middle game the b4 pawn could have a cramping effect on Black's queen's side.

Sokolsky made a further important discovery. He found that in many variations after 1. b4 e5 the advanced pawn at b4 could be offered as a gambit to lure Black's bishop from defence of the king's side. Further, after 1. b4 e5 there are also possibilities of playing a kind of delayed King's Gambit with f4 when the bishop at b2 forms an excellent back-up.

Sokolsky wrote a complete book in Russian describing his ideas and including many of his successful games. His personal results with 1. b4 were impressive and included wins or draws with grandmasters like Flohr and Geller.

Sokolsky's key variation of the opening runs **1. b4 e5 2. Bb2 f6 3. e4 Bxb4 4. Bc4.**

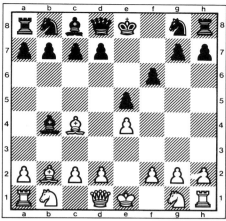

fig. 236

Here both bishops are on free diagonals and bear down on the squares surrounding the black king. There are possibilities to open the game up further by f4, or to bring the white queen into the attack by Qh5+.

Three continuations demonstrate the hidden strength of White's offbeat formation:

(a) **4. . . . Ne7** 5. Qh5+ Ng6 6. f4! exf4 7. a3 d5 8. Bxd5 c6 9. Bb3 Qa5 10. e5! Be7 11. Bf7+! Resigns (Katalimov–Ilvitsky). If 11. . . . Kxf7 12. e6+.

A still more convincing line after 6. . . . exf4 is 7. Nf3! which Bobby Fischer played in the only recorded instance where he chose the Orang-Outang (Fischer–Gloger, simultaneous, Cleveland 1964): 7. . . . Nc6 8. Nc3 (threat Nd5xf4) Bxc3 9. Bxc3 d6 10. Nh4 Ne7 11. Nf5 Kf8 12. 0-0 Qe8 13. Bxf6! Bxf5 14. gxf5 d5 15. fxg6 gxf6 (if dxc4 16. Bxe7+ Qxe7 17. Rxf4+ with a winning attack) 16. Qh6+ Kg8 17. g7 Resigns. After 17. . . . dxc4 18. gxh8=Q+ Kxh8 19. Qxf6+ White is winning on both material and position.

(b) **4. . . . Nc6** 5. f4 exf4 6. Nh3 Nge7 7. Nxf4 Na5 8. Bxf6! with a winning advantage (Sokolsky–Strugatsch). If 8. . . . gxf6 9. Qh5+ while if 8. . . . Nxc4 9. Bxg7 followed by 10. Qh5+

(c) **4. . . . Nc6** 5. f4 d6 6. f5 Nge7 7. Qh5+ g6 8. fxg6 Nxg6 9. Nf3 Na5 10. Nh4 (Sokolsky–Gurvitch). If 10. . . . Nxb3 11. Nxg6.

The Orang-Outang or Sokolsky Opening as many now call it, can thus be a useful surprise weapon. It is best to play such an opening rarely – but just enough to let the possibility of meeting it become known among regular opponents. Few relish the prospect of taking on a chess southpaw. Of course if Black plays sensibly there are several methods to secure a reasonable game. One logical approach is 1. b4 a5 2. b5 d6 followed by Nf6, g6 and a King's Indian Defence formation, followed later by manoeuvring Black's QN to a good square at b6 or c5 and/or using the advanced pawn as a target to open up the a file by . . . a6.

Pro Techniques for Amateurs

This chapter is intended for players who have learnt something about chess from this and other books, enjoyed social games with friends, and would now like to try their skill in competitions. However, while you expect to be reasonably successful, you don't want to spend months in advance preparation before you enter your first tournament.

In this chapter, the emphasis is on practical suggestions. Some are simple common-sense, others will involve work and study – how much depends on you – others are basic information to enable you to find your way round the chess club and the congress scene.

Elementary do's and don'ts

1 Successful opening play means centre control. At the start, advance either or both d or e pawns, two squares with white, one square with black. If you have a chance to get both central pawns in line abreast in the centre of the board, do it unless you spot some obvious snag.

2 Bring your pieces into action as fast as possible. This means a minimum of pawn moves. Three pawn moves should be your normal ration during the first ten moves of a game – the rest should be developing moves with pieces.

3 Bring knights and bishops into play before queen and rooks. In many openings the queen bishop is the last minor piece to develop. Early queen excursions are usually bad. Bring the knights and bishops to positions where they control or occupy a central square, or else restrict an enemy piece which attacks the centre. Castle early.

4 Avoid blunders! This golden rule of novice play separates the beginner from the first step up the chess ladder to weak club level. To avoid blunders and take advantage of those of your opponent, train yourself to look round the board before making any move. Look to see

(a) if your opponent's last move contained or uncovered any threats against which you must guard;

(b) if your opponent has left unguarded pieces you can take or attack;

(c) if your planned move will leave any of your pieces subject to capture.

5 When there are no obvious threats and you don't know what to do next, decide which of your pieces is worst placed and

least involved in the game. Then try to move this piece to a square where it plays a more active part.

6 Try to take the initiative, and pressure your opponent. Ways of doing this include:

(a) if there is an open file, occupy it with one or both rooks.

(b) direct your bishops on to diagonals leading to the enemy king.

(c) place knights on central squares where they can't be attacked by pawns.

7 In the early stages, avoid moving pawns in front of your castled king unless driving away an attacking piece. But when the game has gone 30–40 moves and many pieces have been swapped off, it usually pays to make a hole for your king by advancing one of the three pawns which protect the castled position.

8 Attack is easier than defence, and novices usually defend particularly badly. So keep pushing your forces towards the enemy king.

9 When many pieces, and particularly the queens, are exchanged the king is in little danger and must be used as an active

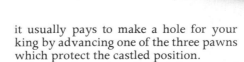

The Steinitz knight. White's Q6 knight dominates the black game, shields a rook build-up on the open line and prepares for a later attack on the king.

fighting piece. Other points for the end-game: use the rook as an attacker in enemy territory rather than in defending pawns; and keep most of your pawns on opposite coloured squares to your bishop. When down to a pawn ending, use the king to shepherd pawns through to queen.

General approach

Your attitude to chess can help significantly in deciding whether your play improves. That means treating all games, even friendly ones at home or in a club, with reasonable seriousness. As a start, never take back moves – this habit encourages sloppy thinking and blunders and is not allowed in serious matches.

Buy a score book (available from any chess equipment supplier) and take down the moves of every game. After the game, check to see where you went wrong (even if you won it's highly likely you made mistakes). If your opponent is a stronger player, the simplest way is to ask him to go over the game with you – most winners are happy to oblige and you get a free lesson.

Whether or not you and your opponent have a post-mortem, there is one further important technique you should practice after every game. Look up the opening in an openings book and the endgame (if there was one) in an endgame book and see how experts played similar positions to yours. This 'comparative learning' method is widely used in the USSR, the world's strongest chess country. Chess is above all a game to play, but immediately before and after each match or tournament the motivation for further study is at its strongest. That way you gradually acquire vital technical data even if you are not normally a bookish person.

Where to play

Most small towns have a chess club, major cities have several. Your local library will probably have information; if that fails, write to the national chess federation and they will advise you of local clubs (BCF, 9A Grand Parade, St Leonards on Sea, Sussex in England, and USCF, 1986 Route 9W, New Windsor, NY 12550 in the United States). Membership fees vary but are substantially less than for many outdoor sports: expect up to £5 a year in England and up to $20 a year in the US.

However, don't assume that your particular chess club will answer all your needs. Some small clubs can have memberships who play only among themselves and ignore newcomers not strong enough for the club team; others lack good facilities for coffee, sandwiches, or extra events beyond the club night. On the other hand, many strong clubs run several teams and make a special effort to make new members feel at home. You should be able to judge whether the atmosphere is forbidding or welcoming before parting with your subscription money.

Weekend congresses

If you are interested in chess competitions but are not interested in the idea of regular attendance at the local club, the best method of finding opponents of similar standard to your own is in the weekend congresses which are held regularly all over the US and Britain. In major cities such as London and New York there may be a dozen or more such events each year. Almost all such congresses cater for players of all standards and one of the features of the London Evening Standard event, the largest of its kind in Europe, is a special tournament for novices and beginners. Several hundred people will be taking part so you needn't fear that the experts will spend their time standing at your board sniggering at the blunders.

There is usually a friendly atmosphere at congresses and if by then you haven't found a club you would like to join there will quite likely be somebody at the event who can give you disinterested advice. Ask at the control desk or the bookstall, if they don't know themselves they can often put you on to the right person.

Congress technique

Most congress tournaments are organized on the Swiss system, an ingenious hybrid of all-play-all and knock-out. Players meet opponents with the same or similar scores, so that winners keep on meeting other winners until there are only one or two perfect or near-perfect scores after five or six rounds. Generally there are two or three games on Saturdays, two on Sunday, and perhaps one on Friday night – five or six games in all.

Prizes in the lowest section may be around £50 or $100, sometimes more or less depending on the number of entries and the status of the event. There is no difference in chess between professionals and amateurs as regards prizes: it is normal to award cash for at least first place in junior tournaments. Chess professionals are those who make a full-time living from the game, and this is rarely possible from weekend and other tournaments alone.

It is normal for all the adult events in a chess congress to be played with clocks. A chess clock consists of two clocks joined together; you push a button to stop one clock and start the other, so that each clock records the thinking time of one player. If you are a serious player, it is a good idea to buy your own clock (usually costing about £10–£15 or $25–30) which you can use for timed practice games.

Time limits in weekend congresses are normally something like 40 or so moves in 1¾ hours, followed (in British events) by a blitz finish where all the remaining moves have to be made in 15–20 minutes. Beginners normally play fast and don't make use of the available time. Later on you may find yourself one of the many who go too far in the other direction and run short of time near the finish. Chess clocks have a flag which falls on the hour and if you have failed to make the required moves by flagfall you automatically lose the game.

Time pressure

A simple technique if you get very short of time is to note subsidiary time limits on your score sheet. Normally the book opening moves, which may be anything from the first three on each side up to a dozen or 15, are made quickly. When you have reached the end of the opening and both players are thinking hard, work out the number of moves and time remaining and give yourself a schedule for each ten moves or so. For example you might find that you have reached the end of your book knowledge after move 10, with 30 more to go before the time control and 1½ hours left. Then, mark moves 20, 30 and 40 on the score sheet and note the clock time when you expect to reach these moves. Allow five or ten minutes extra for difficult situations.

Age and youth

Chess has become very much a young man's game in recent years, and this is particularly so in congress play. Even in a novice tournament, you may find that the unknown opponent on the other side of the board is a studious and ambitious-looking youngster clutching a tome of opening analysis. Whether you are also young or are a comparative veteran, the question is how should you tackle this type of person?

Young players at the chessboard have two assets. One is physical: in a four-hour tournament game it is hard for the older player to keep his energy and concentration at full pitch in that period when the game approaches its climax. In evening league games, when the older player has probably had a hard day at the office while the junior has been cramming current master variations, age is still more of a handicap.

Younger players are usually better at calculating tactics. The ability to see ahead at the board, to spot hidden traps and ideas in any position, declines after the age of 30.

But an older player has his assets too. A canny psychological approach, which is beyond many young players, can pay dividends. A mature attitude is valuable in defence, where a young attacker may overlook a key resource. If he over-reaches and the game starts to flow against him then his volatile emotions can make for dispirited resistance against a counter-attack.

When meeting a younger opponent try to stick to simple, strategic play, where judgment and general principles are more at a premium. In endgames, too, younger players sometimes lose interest because of the lessened chance of 'interesting' tactics.

Even Tal, renowned as a tactician, has used the simple approach against young players. Here is an example: meeting an opponent twenty years younger, Tal chose a simple variation of the Ruy Lopez, swapped off three sets of minor pieces to stop complications, drove his opponent on the defensive and quietly made sure of the win.

White: M. Tal. Black: R. Knaak
Opening: Ruy Lopez (Halle 1974)

1. e4 Nc6 2. Nf3 (following the recipe of Chapter 9 against Black's Nimzovich Defence) e5 3. Bb5 a6 4. Ba4 d6 5. 0-0 Bd7 6. d4 Nf6 7. Bxc6 Bxc6.

This recapture already shows Black has been psychologically thrown by Tal's unexpected swap. He heads for the old Steinitz Defence which is well-known to give Black a passive position (see Chapter 3, Trap 1). More active is bxc6.

8. Re1 Be7 9. Nc3 exd4 10. Nxd4 Bd7 11. Qf3 Bg4 (better 0-0, but Black is trying to be tactical) 12. Qg3 Qd7 13. h3 Bh5 14. Nf5 0-0-0 15. Bg5 Ng8 16. Bxe7 Nxe7.

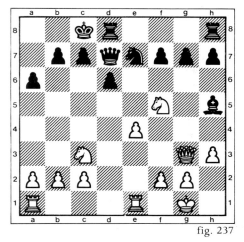

fig. 237

17. Qg5!
This drives Black completely on the defensive. The toughest way to resist now is 17. ... Nc6 18. Qxh5 g6, but Black, discouraged, overlooks this resource and Tal finishes neatly.

17. ... Nxf5? 18. exf5 g6 19. g4 Qc6 20. f6! (clearer than taking the bishop) d5 21. Re7 h6 22. Qe5 d4 23. Ne2 Rd5 24. Nxd4! Resigns. Neither Rxe5 25. Nxc6 nor Qc4 25. Rxc7+! gives Black any chance.

Choosing opponents

For purposes of rapid improvement, you should try to play with slightly stronger opponents: weak ones will teach you little, good ones will beat you too easily. Many people, however, cannot easily find such an ideal training partner; what alternatives are there apart from the club and the weekend congress?

Postal chess

One possibility, useful mainly for those who live far from major cities or who for other reasons cannot compete in weekend events, is to play postal chess. This will help to develop your analysis and strategy, though the fact that players can look up openings means that the games are sometimes unimaginative. International postal chess is at a high level but the general run of domestic competitions are weaker than over-the-board chess. Both the BCF and USCF can put you in touch with postal organizations in Britain and the US.

There is every possibility that the newcomer to postal play will be able to find opponents of a similar standard from beginner upwards. Two special pitfalls are present in this type of chess. One is the risk of blundering through setting up the wrong position. It is only too easy, after analyzing the consequences of the opponent's latest move in depth on a pocket board, to leave the position slightly altered with dire consequences a few moves later.

The recommended approach is to use at least two pocket sets for each game, one to show the actual position and the other for analysis.

Another risk to the postal player is a blunder through inattention or boredom during a protracted game.

Home computers

Computer chess programs have an excellent reputation, and the machines are versatile. Most models are of the sensory type where you make moves on a normal board, pressing the piece on to its new square to register the move with the computer. The computer indicates its own moves by lights on the board, and you move its piece for it.

Home chess computers can be set to make reasonable replies within a few seconds, or more considered replies after a couple of minutes. They have several levels of performance and skill, providing either a simple and encouraging game for a beginner, or a mind-stretching challenge for an expert. They can handle fine points of rules such as promotion to knight or draws by repetition, and they can give instruction.

The best machines play up to the standard of a strong county or chess club expert, and right at the top they can perform well against human masters. New models constantly appear on the market, and at writing the West German Mephisto Dallas seems to have the highest skills.

Others with superior achievements include the Novag Super Constellation and the Fidelity Excellent.

All these machines retail in the £100–£300 price range, but it is possible to buy a reasonable model for well under £100. Electronic equipment can develop faults, so it is important to establish guarantee and repair arrangements for the purchased machine. It is an asset if the machine can play a good game at its faster speeds, for time waiting for a computer drags more than against any human opponent.

Chess computers should never be underestimated, particularly when it comes to calculation. Major programs on powerful commercial machines are excellent at quick play and have already won several games against grandmasters. Then a US expert in a recent magazine article recounted his embarrassment at losing by a blunder to the 'Turbostar Kasparov' microcomputer in the US Open. 'Just tell people you lost to Gary's little brother Turbo' advised a friend.

Playing in simuls

Simultaneous displays where a master takes on twenty or more opponents at once are an interesting way to meet stronger players – there is a real thrill the first time you win or draw. What takes place is that the players sit round the outside of a circle while the expert moves from one board to another. About three hours is par for a 20-board exhibition and the simultaneous giver rarely scores less than 80 per cent.

One of the most remarkable such displays was set up at Emmen, Switzerland, in the summer of 1979. Werner Hug, Switzerland's best player, took 25 hours to meet 560 opponents, defeating 385, drawing with 126 and losing to only 49. Around 18,000 people watched, and Hug walked over twenty miles. I should be interested to know how he dealt with what I have found to be the main difficulty of very long displays – after some hours the expert is liable to develop cramp of the neck muscles through continual stooping down to the boards.

How should you beat the master in such an exhibition? Partly, it's luck – the expert usually makes one or two blunders and that can happen against the strongest player or the weakest. The technique for the master who commits a bad error in a simul is to race round the next move series so that the opponent concerned is pressurized into a quick decision on whether the move is brilliant or is a blunder. If you think the expert may have blundered watch to see whether he hastens to get round to your board again.

Roulette chess

Blunders apart, the most promising chance to beat a simul-giving master, or indeed to defeat any much stronger opponent, is by what is known as randomizing the position or roulette chess.

Roulette chess is a position which abounds in tactical chances and where neither player really knows what is happening. In such situations, the scientific precision of closed positions, strategic play against pawn weaknesses, technical know-how and book endgames all have less influence. Everything depends on tactics, and if the expert misses a check or a capture in the middle of a critical line you have the chance of an upset result.

How do you create roulette situations? Normally you do it by sacrificing a pawn or two so as to give the pieces attacking lines and chances for opportunist raids. Most defeats for the single player in simuls occur in middle game melees where the expert loses the thread because of the pressure of having to move quickly. On the other hand, let him have the initiative, a quiet position or an ending and his technical skill will outplay you even if his game is objectively worse. Grandmaster Bent Larsen says about rook endings in simuls that 'pawn down, I draw; level material, I win'.

Endgames in simuls should in fact be avoided at almost any price. Not only is the expert's technique superior to yours,

but by the time an ending is reached most games will be over and the final moves will be played at blitz speed to the benefit of the master's better sight of the board. Moreover, the pressure of being the last to finish watched by a crowd of spectators has caused many blunders by club players unused to being the focus of attention.

Chess may be a game of pure skill in theory, but in practice random chance is a factor in the form of unexpected tactical shots which even strong players can easily miss, and sometimes do. Thus practical advice on roulette chess is to encourage it when you meet a much stronger opponent. On the other hand you should minimize it against a weaker player whom you should beat on merit. Against him you aim for a routine, technical and positional game followed by simplification to an ending.

There are unkind ways for clubs to do well in simuls. One is to provide sets and boards of varying shapes and sizes and to use lighting whose quality varies in different parts of the room. You also have a better chance if you are on a corner table which juts out into the middle of the circle – simul players like to maintain a steady walking rhythm and the check to the master's stride will not help his game.

Simuls produce a quota of pretty and instructive wins as the master overcomes weak resistance. I've commented earlier

World champion Karpov takes on England's top ten juniors in a Lloyds Bank clock match, 1977, part of the Bank's £35,000 aid to school chess.

(see Chapters 2, 3 and 9) on the strength of the Vienna against inexperienced opponents; here is another example, won by Horowitz in a simul in 1941.

**White: Horowitz. Black: Amateur
Vienna Opening**
1. e4 e5 2. Nc3 Nc6 3. Bc4 Bc5 4. Qg4 Qf6? (best is Kf8) 5. Nd5! Qxf2+ 6. Kd1 Kf8 7. Nh3 Qd4 8. d3 Bb6 9. Rf1 Nf6 10. Rxf6! d6 (if gxf6 11. Bh6+ Ke8 12. Qg7 wins).

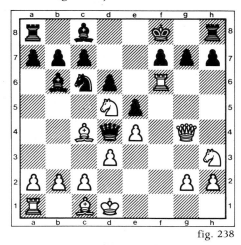

fig. 238

11. Qxg7+! Kxg7 12. Bh6+ Kg8 13. Rg6+ fxg6 14. Nf6 mate.

126

Chess books

There are hundreds of chess books in print, so any player who wishes to improve needs to be highly selective. Below is a list of those I think most useful – but if you browse at a congress bookstall you may find others you prefer.

General advice: *Think Like a Grandmaster* (A. Kotov); *Chess for Tigers* (S. Webb).

Openings: *Batsford Chess Openings* (G. Kasparov and R. Keene); *An Opening Repertoire for White* (R. Keene); *Openings for the Club Player* (L. Barden and T. Harding); *Chess Openings – Your Choice* (S. Reuben).

Middle Game: *Test Your Chess IQ* (A. Livshitz); *40 Lessons for the Club Player* (A. Kostyev); *The Middle Game in Chess* (L. Pachman).

Endgames: *Pocket Guide to Chess Endgames* (D. Hooper); *From the Opening to the Endgame* (E. Mednis); *How to Play the Endgame in Chess* (L. Barden).

Game collections: *My 60 Memorable Games* (R. Fischer); *Half a Century of Chess* (M. Botvinnik); *Fighting Chess Games* (G. Kasparov); *On the Road to the World Championship* (A. Alekhine); *Chess is My Life* (V. Korchnoi).

Puzzles and Problems: *Leonard Barden's Chess Puzzle Book* (L. Barden).

Reference: *The Oxford Companion to Chess* (D. Hooper and K. Whyld); *Chess, The Records* (K. Whyld); *Encyclopedia of Chess Openings* (Batsford/Chess Informant); *The Encyclopedia of Chess* (H. Golombek); *Kings of Chess* (W. Hartston).

Chess magazines: *Chess* (monthly, British, from Sutton Coldfield, West Midlands); *British Chess Magazine* (monthly, from 9 Market Street, St Leonards, East Sussex); *Chess Life* (monthly, US, from 186 Route 9W, New Windsor, NY 12550, United States).

Newspaper columns: Among the most interesting weekly columns are those in the *Spectator* (R. Keene), *New Statesman* (G. Botterill), *Sunday Today* (M. Pein), the *Guardian* (L. Barden) and the *New York Times* (R. Byrne). The *London Evening Standard* runs a daily chess puzzle.

Evening classes, individual tuition: Evening classes are available in London from Morley College, Westminster, SE1, while individual tuition by cassette is supplied by Audio Chess, 7 Billockby Close, Chessington, Surrey.

Coffee houses and pubs: You can play chess in London any day of the week at Chequers, 18 Chalk Farm Road, London NW1; the King's Head pub at Moscow Road, Bayswater; or at the Escape coffee house at 141 Greenwich South Street, London SE10.

Running commentaries on major games are a feature at many big international events, and a day spent in the audience at the annual tournaments like Hastings or the Lloyds Bank Masters in Britain or the US Open will be valuable experience.

Chess can be an exciting game to watch for two reasons: the knowledge that a single mistake can be fatal and the slow build-up towards the time control. As the game progresses the clock steadily increases the pressure and the tension for both players and spectators. The spectator can best share this excitement by watching a game where he has a partisan interest – for example a leading British or US player meeting a top Russian – and by working on the games himself.

This means taking along a pocket board and men and deciding on two or three games to watch seriously. Try to work out the best move on each turn, and then try to understand why the expert may do something quite different. Tackling the games this way, not knowing the result in advance, is more stimulating than playing over games from books.

If you are unable to attend a tournament, then the next best idea is to play over master games from books, covering up the next move and working it out. Time yourself with a clock as if you were one of the players. I used to find this valuable as a young player and recommend making it more interesting by marking yourself on a 5 point scale. You get 5 points for choosing the same move as the game winner or a move which the commentator says is just as good, 4 points for a move which (after the game) still seems as good as the one that was played, 3 points for a slightly inferior continuation, and so on down to 0 for an outright blunder. If you check your results over a period of weeks or months you can expect to record progressive improvement.

Points of technique

Successful middle game and endgame strategy and tactics is largely a matter of experience as well as recognizing the subtle differences in chess patterns – but some more general points will still be helpful.

Castling

Castling can sometimes be delayed with advantage, but the inexperienced player should castle rather than not if in doubt. The Yugoslav writer Vukovic once analyzed the results of a number of simultaneous displays by masters. He found one common feature in 'simultaneous massacres' where the expert won all or nearly all the games: late castling by the opponents.

While the beginner fails to castle quickly enough, the average player does so too mechanically. Vukovic quotes this diagram as a type-situation where club or county players castle unthinkingly for either side.

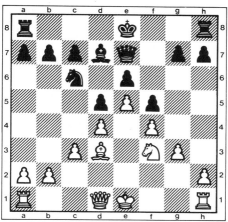

fig. 239

Here, if White castles KR, Black also castles short and White's obvious pawn attack with h3 and g4 will weaken his own king's defences. So White does better with the more subtle **1. Qe2** followed by long castling – **2. 0-0-0.** If Black thinks on routine lines and continues 1. Qe2 0-0? then 2. 0-0-0 followed by h3, Rdg1 and g4 is now very strong – White has a powerful attack, while his own king remains safe.

Thus a strong player with Black would spot White's intention and himself choose waiting tactics. After 1. Qe2 he could postpone the castling decision by **1. . . . a6.** Then if **2. 0-0-0 0-0-0!** Now the g4 attack is harmless, while if White advances on the other flank by b4–b5, his own king is exposed to the counter-attack Qa3+.

A still more sophisticated refinement after 1. Qe2 is for Black to regroup by **1. . . . Nd8 2. h3 Nf7 3. Qd2** (now both sides are jockeying for position) **0-0-0.** By now Black has sufficiently improved his position to castle long in safety, for if White castles short then the knight at f7 enables Black to play Rdg8 followed by g5 with a quick counter-strike. White would probably in turn avoid this line by **4. 0-0-0** after which the game proceeds along a calm positional course.

Pillsbury is said to have been the first to summarize the rule on castling for strong players, 'Castle because you must or because you want to, never just because you can.'

Planning and exchanging

Whether to complicate or exchange, and how to plan strategy, are common problems on the chessboard. There is no universal answer, but there are some guidelines. Here are a few:

(a) If you are short of time on the clock it is generally better to simplify; if your opponent is pressed for time then keep the attack going.

(b) If there is no definite plan, do not complicate but make a non-committal move which makes your position sounder – often a plan will suggest itself in the course of the next few moves.

(c) If you can gain material by exchanging, or if you are already ahead on material, then it generally pays to go for the endgame. It may not be the quickest or the prettiest win, but your aim once in a favourable position should be to safeguard the full point without letting your opponent back into the game.

(d) You should exchange if you are under attack or cramped, and avoid exchanges if you are attacking or command more space. This is particularly so if an exchange would swap one of your well-posted pieces and bring a poorly situated opposing piece into better play.

A typical situation: you have rooks at d1 and a1, your opponent rooks at d8 and f8. If you play R(d1) xd8 then the reply R(f8)xd8 changes a near-symmetrical situation to one where your opponent's rook is the better placed. Needless concession of an open line in this way can make the difference between victory and defeat. Better leave the opponent to exchange, or else look for an outpost square on the open file where your rook can be protected by a pawn. Then you have the chance to increase the advantage by doubling rooks.

Another frequent case: you have a bishop on g5 pinning a knight at f6 against a queen at d8. Your opponent attacks the bishop with pawn h7 to h6; should you swap bishop for knight?

Normally the answer is no. The bishop, a developed piece in good play, disappears, while the previously defensive queen comes into action. Usually in such cases it is better to retreat the bishop when the pawn advance will have weakened your opponent's king. But there are no absolute rules (bar checkmate); there are times when it is right to make the exchange because it gains a tempo or because it gives your remaining bishop and knights command of the light squares.

(e) If the game is being adjudicated (see page 132) you have to decide whether the simplified position after an exchange is more likely to be given a win.

Level positions, outposts and initiative chess

To become a successful match and tournament player it is essential to have the ability and determination to win positions that you shouldn't; to win from level positions and even bad ones. The art of swindling in bad positions is largely the ability to introduce unexpected complications: but what about when material and position is level (though the game is completely simplified) and your natural instinct is to offer a draw?

The first step is to follow a rule already mentioned to look for out-of-play pieces and switch them to more useful squares. One recurrent and practical theme in equal-looking middle games is to try and create outposts. This usually means a knight, rook, or bishop firmly established on a central square – it may not sound much, but a dominating outpost has the same effect as a tennis player in the net position or a soccer set-piece free-kick just outside the penalty box.

The special strength of an outpost is that it enables a player to switch to either side of the board for the most promising attack. The outpost cuts the defending forces in two, just as in the soccer set-piece where the attacking team has the option of a direct shot at the lone goal-keeper or going round the outside of the wall of defenders.

The square squeeze

A single square in a blocked position can be enough for a dominating outpost. The average chessplayer doesn't understand how such squares can dominate the entire game – witness the cool public response to the successes of Petrosian and Karpov who are essentially strategic, square control players.

As an example, here is a game beginning with a black defence – the Meran variation – which used to be a popular counter-attack line until White scored several successes with a Petrosian-style square squeeze.

Polugaevsky, the winner, is one of the world top ten, and his grand plan is based on the simple concept of settling a knight at the c4 outpost. The knight constantly threatens to help the d pawn advance, and Black's attempts to blockade this pawn are simply stopped by exchanges.

White: L. Polugaevsky. Black: P. Biyiasas

Opening: Queen's Gambit, Slav Meran (Petropolis 1973)

1. d4 Nf6 2. c4 e6 3. Nf3 d5 4. Nc3 c6 5. e3 Nbd7 6. Bd3 dxc4 7. Bxc4 b5 8. Bd3 a6 9. e4 c5 10. d5 e5 11. b3 Bd6 12. 0-0 0-0 13. Re1 Rb8 14. Bf1 Re8?

Black's last is the culprit which allows Black's pawn front to be immobilized and concedes White the vital c4 square. Black should have tried 14. . . . Ne8 15. a4 Nc7 keeping the Q-side pawns mobile. Spotting this, some experts claimed after the game that White should have played 13. a4, when Black in turn can try a square squeeze by 13. . . . c4 14. bxc4 b4 15. Ne2 Nc5 while White can aim to eliminate this blockade by Be3xc5. Who is really better is a matter of taste – but the real lesson is that the player who is familiar with square squeeze technique greatly improves his chances.

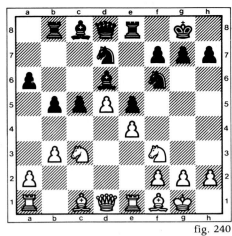

fig. 240

15. a4!

The key manoeuvre. The slight loss of time by the N regrouping from c3 to c4 via b1 and d2 counts for little beside the great value of controlling the c4 square. For the rest of the game, Black is always struggling.

15. . . . b4 16. Nb1 Nb6 17. Nbd2 Re7 18. Bb2 Ne8 19. Rc1 f6 20. a5 Na8 21. Nc4! (at last occupying the outpost) Rc7 22. Nfd2 (giving support to the first knight and preparing the advance of the central pawn roller) Bd7 23. f4 Qe7 24. fxe5 fxe5 25. Nxd6 Nxd6 26. Nc4 Nxc4 27. Bxc4 Resigns. If 27. . . . Qd6 28. Bxe5! Qxe5 29. d6+ wins.

The Steinitz knight

Steinitz once made the arresting observation that if you can plant your knight at d6 or e6 (d3 or e3 when playing Black) you can go to sleep and let the game win itself. The Steinitz knight is really an especially good form of the square squeeze; set far in the opponent's position, it paralyses his forces by denying them co-ordination.

The knight at e6 situation often comes about in the King's Indian or the Dutch (1. d4 f5) Defence in queen's side openings or in K-side openings with 1. e4 e5 where it is routine for Black to advance his f pawn for counterplay. If at that stage White has a pawn on d5 there may be a tactical chance to seize the e6 square by advancing the knight there via d4 or g5.

The knight at d6 situation comes about more often with support from a pawn at c5 rather than at e5. A typical preamble is a Sicilian or King's Indian Defence which Black has handled too cautiously and permitted White a space-gaining pawn advance. If the defender, trying for some active play, pushes his c and e pawns forward, then d6 is a natural target for a white knight.

There are three cautionary points to note before you establish a Steinitz knight. It is essential to check the knight can be adequately guarded should the opponent try to expel the unwelcome invader by a crossfire of bishops and rooks. Neglect of this precaution can lead to a Steinitz knight unable to move being pinned against its guarding rook or queen.

The Steinitz knight player also has to watch for defensive ideas based on sacrifice of a rook to eliminate the knight and its pawn guard. Thirdly, as Steinitz well knew despite his tongue-in-cheek aphorism, no chess game really wins itself. The Steinitz knight simply creates an opportunity for a winning attack elsewhere on the board. The game below is a good example of how to establish the knight and use it to force weaknesses around the enemy king.

White: Jansson. Black: Helmers
Opening: King's Indian (Sweden v. Norway 1976)

1. Nf3 Nf6 2. c4 g6 3. Nc3 Bg7 4. d4 0-0 5. Bg5 h6 6. Bh4 d7 7. e3 c6 8. Be2 Nbd7 9. Qc2 e5 (now the d6 square has no pawn guard and in the next phase of the game White aims to create his Steinitz knight) 10. Rd1 Qe7 11. 0-0 Re8 12. dxe5 dxe5 13. Nd2 Qf8 14. a3 a5 15. Na4 Nc5 16. Nxc5 Qxc5 17. Bxf6 Bxf6 18. Ne4 Qe7 19. Nd6 Rf8 20. c5.

The Steinitz knight is established. Now White backs it up with doubled rooks before advancing his h pawn to open up the black king.

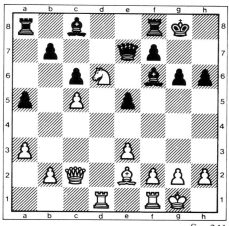
fig. 241

20. ... Be6 21. Bc4 Bxc4 22. Qxc4 Qc7 23. Rd2 Bg7 24. Rfd1 Kh7 25. h4! Rab8 26. h5 b6 27. cxb6 Rxb6 28. Qe4 R6b8 29. g3 Rad8? (Black blunders under pressure, but otherwise White could continue Kg2 and switch his rook attack to the h file) 30. Nxf7! Resigns. If Q or Rxf7 31. hxg6+ wins.

And now an even clearer example by the great Steinitz knight player Petrosian:
White: Petrosian. Black. I. Zaitsev
Opening: King's Indian (Moscow 1966)

1. c4 Nf6 2. Nc3 g6 3. e4 d6 4. d4 Bg7 5. Be2 0-0 6. Nf3 e5 7. d5 Nh5? (better Nbd7) 8. g3 f5? (better Nd7) 9. exf5 Qf6 (hoping for the gambit 10. fxg6 Bg4 11. gxh7+ Kh8 with attacking chances,

but after Petrosian's next move creating a Steinitz knight Black is already strategically lost) 10. Ng5! Qxf5 11. 0-0 Nf6 12. Bd3 Qg4 13. Be2 Qf5 14. f3 Bh6 15. Bd3 Qd7 16. Ne6!

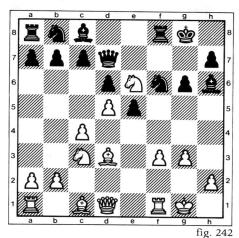
fig. 242

16. ... Bxc1 17. Qxc1 Rf7 18. f4! (threatening 19. f5 to make the knight impregnable) exf4 19. Qxf4 (threats Qg5 followed by Bxg6, or simply doubling rooks on the f file) Nxd5 20. Qxf7+ Qxf7 21. Rxf7 Bxe6 22. Nxd5 Bxd5 23. Rxc7 Na6 24. Rd7 Resigns.

Difficult positions

Most amateurs are scared by defensive positions, but experts treat them with resilience and patience. The important thing is not to make desperate or unsound moves to escape trouble – that is often the quickest way to lose. The way to play the defence is to reinforce weak points, especially around the king (Larsen once said 'with a knight on f1 or f8 you will never be mated'), watch out for direct threats, and look for weaknesses in the enemy camp created by his overstretched communication lines. It isn't always the obvious formations which are easiest to defend – thus bishops of opposite colour (one player with a bishop on light squares, his opponent with a bishop on dark squares) which amateurs think of as a drawing situation, is very favourable for the attacker in the middle game. But even here you can make the best of defence – think forward to the time when the attack fades, and then prepare for the endgame, for example by marching the king a little nearer the centre. Keep your pawns in compact groups: 'pawn islands' on their own are easy targets for rooks.

Endgame hints

The ending is the weakest part of many club players' game, and even reasonable technique is sure to reap dividends against many opponents. We have already stressed how essential it is to use the king and the rook as active fighting pieces in the endgame. A few more principles to remember:

(a) When you are one or two pawns ahead, exchange pieces but not pawns – your objective is to reach a pawn endgame without pieces, the easiest of all to win when you are material up.

(b) When you are one or two pawns down, exchange pawns but not pieces. If you reach an endgame with one piece against two they can be difficult or impossible to win when no pawns remain.

(c) Always use the rook actively. Here are two ideal rook situations for Black, with White's rook tied to passive defence:

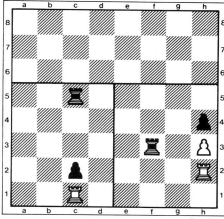
fig. 243

(d) Rook endgames are the most frequent in practical play, and there are two basic positions which it is essential to know. Many rook endings boil down to rook and pawn against rook. If the attacker's rook can then cut off the defender king, there is usually a win by Lucena's method; but if the defender's king can blockade the pawn he can normally draw by Philidor's technique. Both these positions are hundreds of years old but they remain valid.

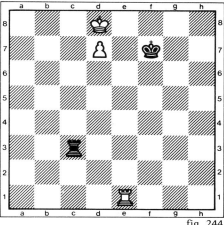
fig. 244

The Lucena position. White's rook makes a barrier which stops the black K approaching the pawn. The winning method is called 'building a bridge': 1. Re4 Rc1 (if Kf6 2. Ke8 wins) 2. Rf4+ Kg7 (if Kg6 3. Ke8 Re1+ 4. Kf8 Rd1 5. Rf7 wins)

3. Ke7 Re1+ 4. Kd6 Rd1+ 5. Kc6 Kg6 (if Rc1+ 6. Kd5 Rd1+ 7. Re4 completes the 'bridge' begun by 1. Re4, and White wins) **6. Rc4 Kf7 7. Kc7 Ke7 8. d8=Q+ Rxd8 9. Re4+ wins.**

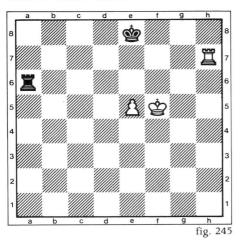

fig. 245

Philidor's draw. Black keeps his rook at a6 to hold back the white king. If the pawn advances, Black's rook goes to a1 to threaten checks on the files which White cannot escape with his pawn committed to the sixth: **1. e6 Ra1 2. Kf6 Rf1+ 3. Ke5 Re1+ 4. Kd6 Rd1+** with a draw.

(e) Passed pawns far from the opposing king are very strong, passed pawns in the centre can more easily be stopped.

(f) If you have the advantage, try to keep pawns on both sides of the board — it's easier to win if you can create threats on both flanks.

(g) Bishops are generally better than knights in the ending except where the bishop is blocked by its own pawn chain.

More advanced practical hints

This section of the chapter is intended for those who already have some experience in congress and match chess; well-routined club players who know what the game is about but are always on the lookout for methods to improve their results. For such players, a few small improvements here and there in practical technique and approach can spell a difference of five or ten grading points at the end of the season.

Chess pieces

Some players still make do with an ancient family wooden set whose knight heads have long since become detached from the body, or worse still with men designed in some unorthodox pattern. Nowadays virtually all major tournaments use plastic sets and roll-up boards available from any major chess supplier for a few pounds or dollars. It's a false economy not to possess one. The very design of such sets makes it easier to calculate ahead and can thus help your improvement; and it makes sense to keep your brain familiar with the exact set you will have in front of you for several hours when you try to win first prize in your next tournament.

Blunder avoidance

An increasing number of players in international chess write down their next move on the score sheet before making it on the board. Mikhail Tal set the world fashion for this technique and Tony Miles took it up for Britain, with the added personal touch that Miles writes his move in Russian notation and puts his watch on top of the score sheet to hide his move from the opponent.

The real point of writing down the move first is to reduce the ever-present risk of a blunder. Thus you should think out your move, write it down, and then spend another ten or twenty seconds just looking at it sceptically to see if you've missed anything obvious. There is no need to write down every single move in advance — for example it is pointless to do so in a routine book opening which you have decided on before the game, silly to do so when you are too short of time to keep score properly at all, and perhaps a good idea not to when your position is totally lost, just to try and make your opponent careless. But in ordinary circumstances this technique is recommended and will marginally improve your results — even if it only stops you blundering away one winning position a year that will be worth, for the average player, some two or three grading points in Britain or some 15–20 Elo points in the US.

Winning a won game

Failing to win won games is another common chessboard disease and is often another variation of blundering too often. Wins can also be missed by indecisiveness or by frittering away a big advantage.

The reason why some people are better than others at winning won games is rooted in chessboard psychology. It is only too easy during a game for a player to give himself credit for gaining an advantage. The temptation is to relax and to assume that the opponent's resistance will crumble. But relaxation in the expectation of an easy win communicates itself to the opponent and may well stiffen his determination to a rearguard fight action to the finish.

A Russian master, Romanovsky, once listed various psychological blocks to realizing an advantage. He noted excessive tension caused by the game, impatience in anticipation of an easy victory, the wish to finish the game quickly in a showy way, loss of interest in the technical phase of the game, and irrita-

tion at the opponent for his stubborn resistance.

The remedies? Romanovsky suggested several. Firstly, you must try to maintain your concentration right up to the moment of resignation. If the position gives a choice between a simple and a showy victory path, choose the simple one; from the practical viewpoint, you should reduce the risk of an analytical mistake. Keep the initiative, delay winning material if you can do it without permitting counter-chances.

If you constantly lose from winning positions, go over these games and look for a pattern in your errors. One strong player revealed that this search showed that several of his blunders arose through overlooking a double attack by the opponent's queen; another typical visual failing is to miss or underestimate backward captures, particularly on a diagonal. This is the classic instance:

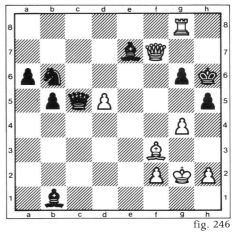

fig. 246

Reshevsky–Savon, Petropolis 1973. With only a few seconds to make his fortieth and final move before the time control, Reshevsky played 1. Qxg6 and announced 'Mate!' A fellow-grandmaster described Reshevsky's move as 'the blunder of five centuries' as Savon's bishop took the queen. The tragedy for Reshevsky was accentuated because White has a real mate by 1. g5+ Kxg5 (Bxg5 2. Rh8 mate) 2. h4+ Kxh4 3. Qf4 mate.

Self-knowledge of how you blunder can be very useful in avoiding the experience of losing several times by similar means.

Finally, a typical mistake when winning is to rush your moves. There are some occasions when 'blitzing' can be considered (see page 143) but a winning position is not one of them. You only risk your advantage. It pays to take your time working out a win. Two techniques which can help are writing down the move before you make it (see above) and the old-fashioned remedy advocated by Tarrasch of 'sit on your hands when the win is in sight'.

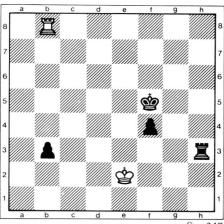

fig. 247

This ending from Bernstein–Smyslov, Groningen 1946, is a typical case of impatience jeopardizing a win, and the culprit was a future world champion. Black is two pawns up, and winning easily. He moved 1. ... b2 with the idea of 2. Rxb2 Rh2+ and 3. ... Rxb2 winning. No solution is given – you should be able to work out for yourself what Black missed.

Looking for peace

Probably well over half of all offers to draw a game are improper, that is made at the wrong time according to the laws of chess. The relevant rule in the FIDE (World Chess Federation) code requires a player to make his move, then propose the agreement to draw, and then start his opponent's clock so that the offer is considered in the opponent's thinking time. The opponent can decline the offer either verbally or by making a move. In the interval between the offer and the reply the offer cannot be retracted.

It is easy to make a draw offer at the wrong time in the heat of the moment. The most important and frequent case of improper draw offers occurs when a player makes a verbal draw proposal while it is his own turn to move instead of after making the move. If your opponent does this, it is important to remember you have the option of either accepting or refusing at once or of requiring him to make his move before you decide.

This means, from a practical player's viewpoint, that you should normally postpone the decision. If the move played is strong, you will still have the draw option; but sometimes your opponent will be thrown mentally off balance by the sudden requirement to find a move to justify his offer. If his move is unexpectedly weak, the draw can be refused with added psychological effect.

Repeated draw offers are bad etiquette and illegal, but people still make them and there is often no controller to rule that they are disturbing the other player. Two good verbal counters to the unwanted draw offer are 'Of course not!' (Fischer) and 'I'll say when it's a draw'.

Some players, particularly in master tournaments, do not offer a draw in so many words. A frequent euphemism is 'Are you playing to win?' At the 1953 world title candidates tournament in Zurich, Najdorf used this phrase to Boleslavsky. 'No!' replied the Soviet grandmaster. 'Are you playing to draw, then?' asked Najdorf hopefully. 'No!' 'What are you playing for, then?' 'Just to play', retorted Boleslavsky. The game continued, and was later agreed drawn – Boleslavsky had nevertheless out-talked his opponent.

Draws can, of course, occur in other ways besides mutual agreement, such as lack of mating material or perpetual check. An important draw for practical chess is by threefold repetition of the identical position with the same player to move each time. This exact definition is necessary since ignorance of it has cost even top grandmasters half a point.

Sometimes a threefold repetition occurs without the actual moves being the same – for example, when one player oscillated first a rook and then a bishop to and fro. It is only too easy for one side to check his score-sheet against repetition of moves and fail to notice that the position, though not the exact moves has been repeated.

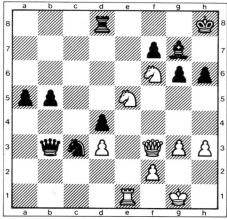

fig. 248

This diagram from Castro–Petrosian, Biel interzonal 1976 occurred just after Petrosian, playing Black, offered a draw which was turned down. The game continued 1. Qb7 Rf8 (Petrosian offered another draw) 2. N5d7 Rd8 3. Ne5 Rf8 4. N5d7 Rd8 (again Black suggested a draw) 5. Qc7 Ra8 6. Qb7 Rd8 7. Re7 and White's attack broke through to win. A remarkable lapse for a world champion –Petrosian should have *announced* that he was going to play 6. ... Rd8 and claimed a draw under the threefold repetition rule. Obviously both sides were here confused by the different order of moves which reached the same position. Note that the draw has to be claimed when it is your turn to move; once Rd8 was made on the board, Black

forfeited his right to claim.

The other typical error on threefold repetition is to forget that the same player has to be on move on each recurrence.

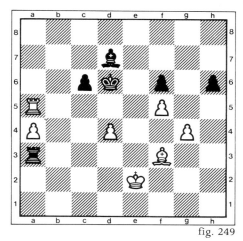

fig. 249

Keene v. Donoso, Haifa 1976, Keene needed to win this position to become a grandmaster, but though White is a pawn up it's difficult to make progress. Play continued 1. Ra6 Kc7 2. Ra7+ Kd6 3. Ra6 Kc7 4. Ra7+ Kd6 5. Ra8 Ke7 6. Ra6! Now Black should play Rc3, although he's still losing, but Donoso called over the controller, announced his intention of playing 6. ... Kd6, and claimed a draw by repetition since the same position occurred at moves 1 and 3.

His claim was at once dismissed by the arbiter, since a different player was to move on the third occasion. Moreover, by international rules, Black is committed to his announced move. The game ended 6. ... Kd6? 7. d5 Ke5 8. dxc6 Bc8 9. Ra8 Kf4 10. Bd5 Resigns.

Tactical offers of a draw are an important aspect of chess which few average players consider. If a poor position is starting to improve, or to become unclear; if the opponent, with an advantage, is getting short of time and starting to look anxiously at his clock; then a draw offer is good psychology. If it is accepted, you have escaped lightly from your troubles; if the opponent refuses and his position then deteriorates further the thought of the draw he turned down can demoralize him completely.

At the 1959 world title candidates, Olafsson offered Petrosian a draw. The Russian, who is deaf, failed to hear. He would have accepted if he had known about it, but instead played on and lost. Petrosian was leading the tournament, but never recovered from the upset.

At New York in 1949 there was a complete conversation among four people using only one word. Horowitz had a won game against Najdorf, then a world title contender, but the players had only a few seconds to reach the time control. Najdorf asked: 'Draw?' Horowitz (pleased not to lose to a stronger opponent) 'Draw!' Expert onlooker, noticing that Horowitz was a bishop up: 'Draw?!' Referee: 'Draw.'

Adjudications

Sometimes it is necessary to decide the result of a chess game before it has gone the full distance. This occurs particularly in inter-club matches which may not start until half-way through the evening and have to finish some two or three hours later. It is too awkward to arrange a second session and a normal arrangement is for the game to be stopped somewhere between moves 30 to 40 and for the result to be judged by an independent expert.

Adjudication is more prevalent in Britain than in other countries and has been harmful to the standard of play at club level. It means that many people never play an endgame and that games are often stopped just as the position is becoming critical.

The adjudicator's mandate is to decide the result with best play on both sides, something which would rarely occur if the game was played out. In my view there is no doubt that it would benefit British chess if the national federation took a lead and recommended that a three-hour club match session should consist not of 30 moves in an hour and a half followed by adjudication but of 30 in an hour and a quarter followed by a quick-play finish with 20 or more moves in 15 minutes on the clock. There would be blunders at the quick-play stage, true; but this would be a small drawback compared with the advantage that players would be responsible for their own game rather than relying on the adjudicator.

Meanwhile, adjudication is likely to continue for a while; how should you make the best of games under these conditions? Two special characteristics are that the game lasts fewer moves than in normal tournaments and that the position at the end will be judged, assuming the adjudicator knows his job, by the same highly objective standards as a master contest.

The implications of these parameters are that a strong player should avoid highly strategical openings or systems where the centre is likely to be blocked. The risk is too great that by move 30 any advantage gained will not be good enough for a win. For weaker players, the reverse applies – good openings for him in league chess are the solid defences to the Queen's Gambit such as the Lasker (with ... Ne4) and Tartakover (with ... b6); or the closed form of the Ruy López. Such openings enable the weaker player to progress a good part of the way towards move 30 adjudication while remaining in the shelter of the textbooks.

The other important factor in adjudication chess is that material advantage gains in significance. A pawn up without compensation would still be a tough fight in normal play, but on adjudication is worth the same as a rook. So the right styles for stronger players in local leagues are sharp tactical-style openings where the weaker opponent has plenty of problems to solve, and favourable variations where theory shows the stronger side gaining material.

Players involved in adjudication who really want to improve their win percentage must bear in mind that there is normally a right of appeal against a decision. Some positions are marginal and the adjudicator will normally settle them on general principles. If these general principles indicate a draw but your detailed analysis (or analysis in conjunction with the club top board) shows a win, then you have to set the analysis down on paper and be ready to send it off as the appeal as soon as the drawn verdict comes through.

Another useful tip when the game for adjudication shows chances for both sides: claim a win, even if you don't think you really have more than a draw. It is likely that the other team will put in for a win and the temptation is strong for the adjudicator, confronted with a tricky position and unsure who is really better, to award a draw in the hope this will make everybody happy.

What of adjudication when you have the edge on position but material is level? In this case the final few moves before adjudication are vital. The recommended technique is known as 'window-dressing': you put your pieces on the most active and impressive squares possible, knowing that in marginal situations adjudicators will be impressed by the general look of a position. If one side's pieces are on active squares while his opponent's are passive, you may sneak a win even though material is level. And it is harder to mount a successful appeal against such an adjudication than in positions capable of concrete analysis.

Too many average players assume that an adjudicator is infallible or that it isn't proper to appeal against decisions. But an ambitious player can make the best of adjudications by analyzing every position in depth. You should be highly motivated to do the work – it's your game – and hours spent examining the adjudication position can give you extra insight into chess. Write down your analysis and conclusions so that it is ready to send with the appeal against the verdict if needed. The technique of such analysis will be good experience for tournament adjournments or for postal games where players often analyse ten or fifteen moves ahead looking for chances to reach winning endings.

Gamesmanship

You don't have to be Bobby Fischer, turning up late to games, or Viktor Korchnoi, donning one-way mirror spectacles, to use offboard tactics. In theory the two protagonists in a game should be emotionless automata with impeccable behaviour; in practice some players adopt techniques designed to improve their own performance and mar the opponent's.

Stopping for tea or coffee is a frequent courtesy in friendly games or club chess, and it may help to suggest this break if you are surprised by some unexpected combination. If there is no tea or coffee handy, it is a good plan after an upset move to spend longer than usual on your reply, pondering till your calm is restored and you can view the position objectively. Offering to pay for tea or coffee can also be a subtle indication to your opponent that you like your position and feel ready to compensate him for impending defeat.

Mannerisms can be very distracting during a game and the problem is that the opponent never quite knows whether they are unconscious reactions or ploys designed to disturb him. You will certainly meet opponents with unpleasant mannerisms and it is difficult to aim for real chess success unless you can seal off your thinking enough to avoid breaks in your concentration.

Smoking is the most obvious form of disturbance to a sensitive opponent, and the US Chess Federation now restricts smokers to a separate room at several major tournaments. Lasker was one of the first great masters whose smoking habits aroused adverse comment, and some of his opponents argued seriously that the aroma of his pungent cigars was a factor in his successes. Later Botvinnik, a non-smoker, was bothered during tournaments by opponents who 'accidentally' blew cigarette smoke towards him; he overcame the problem by arranging a training match where his coach Ragozin was under orders to smoke heavily!

Some masters try to disguise a prepared opening by thinking long over the first few moves as if they faced unexpected difficulties. The same technique can be used after adjournment. Botvinnik on returning to finish an adjourned world championship game that everyone believed an easy win for his opponent, did not bring along his usual thermos of coffee. During his home analysis he had discovered some promising resources which could nevertheless be stopped if the opponent played precisely, and he wanted to give the impression that he expected the game to last only a few more moves. His opponent played carelessly and Botvinnik held on to a draw.

A common practice is symbolic physical aggression. My first experience of

this technique was at a Bognor congress in the mid-1950s where as a young player I had a winning position against a veteran master. While I pondered over the best way to win, the floor began to shake. It was my opponent marching up and down beside the board; the floor was uncarpeted and he was wearing hobnail boots. A more sophisticated version of this approach is described by Botvinnik who watched Alekhine play against Bogolyubov at Nottingham 1936. While Bogolyubov thought, Alekhine circled round the board like a kite, glaring at his opponent. When Bogolubov finally moved, Alekhine rushed to the board and, still standing banged down a surprise reply with such force that his opponent almost jumped out of his chair.

There are ploys, too, to impress your opponent with your own strength. The former world champion, Smyslov, has the habit when making a move of screwing down the piece into its new square with an air of finality as if no other move was reasonable. Fischer, and following him Nigel Short, has long arms and hands and stretches out to capture enemy pieces like a vulture seizing its prey. Botvinnik, and also Paul Keres who narrowly failed to become world champion, wrote down the moves slowly and exactly, as if the score sheet itself was part of a work of art. Petrosian has impressive eyebrows and frequently arches them as if amazed by his opponent's naive manoeuvres.

Karpov looks extremely cool and does not sweat even under television lights.

Grandmasters and masters in general are used to giving simultaneous displays and exhibitions, and acquire the flair of making moves and captures cleanly so that the taking piece operates with a kind of flick action. Even if you cannot always make good moves, you can train yourself to improve your physical presence at the board by watching the experts and copying them in these and other attitudes. Simply by acting like a good player, whether or not you really are one, will make some psychological impression on your opponent.

Problems

A problem is an artificial situation where White has to mate Black in a stipulated number of moves, usually two or three, against any defence. The positions bear little relation to practical play, but can have a charm of their own. The key move in a problem is seldom materialistic or obvious, and is rarely a check or a pawn promotion. There should normally be only one possible solution.

Specialized problems are based on the illustration of particular themes in the play or in 'tries' which nearly work. It is hard now to produce entirely original two-movers which the average solver enjoys, and largely for this reason many chess columns have gone over to game positions while others mainly publish the

World Champion, Karpov, confronts Kasparov at the 1986 World Championships. Kasparov wins and becomes the new world number one.
classical problems of past years.

From the viewpoint of the practical player who occasionally glances at a problem diagram, the most interesting challenges occur where only small forces remain, the position looks rather game-like, and the solution appears – but isn't – easy. As a brief introduction to this specialized world here are three problems whose answers can be found at the end of this chapter.

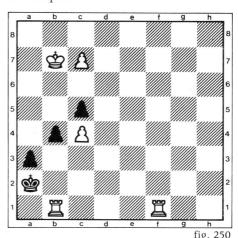

fig. 250

White mates in four moves at latest, against any defence (by O. von Krobshofer).

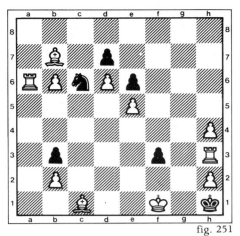

White mates in three moves at latest, against any defence (by T. and J. Warton).

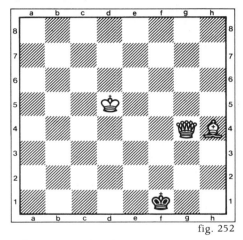

White mates in three moves at latest, against any defence. This puzzle defeats many solvers and can take a little of the credit for Russian chess successes – it was one of Lenin's favourites.

Women's chess

Women's chess has for years been the poor relation of the men's game in Western countries. At international level, the Russians and East Europeans are far ahead of everyone else. Within the USSR there is also the unique situation that the tiny republic of Georgia in the Caucasus produces more talented women players than the rest of the country put together. The last two world champions, and several title candidates, have all been Georgians.

The poor standards of women's chess in the West have been variously attributed to sex differences in spatial ability, related to hemispheric specialization in the brain, as well as to purely social causes such as the long tradition of chess as a male game. In contrast to bridge, a partner is not necessary to play chess and this often has the consequence that the interested woman or girl player has nobody to go with her to tournaments and clubs.

Despite this discouraging background, there are hopeful signs in recent years for women players. Both in the US and Britain, chess is gaining in popularity among women and girls. Lloyds Bank sponsorship of British chess includes a number of one-day ladies tournaments which are more practical for many competitors than longer congresses. Entries for some of these events have totalled nearly 100, a figure which would have been considered impossible for a women's tournament only a few years ago. Growing numbers will almost certainly mean rising standards, and we may yet see a Western challenge to the domination of the women's game by the girls from Georgia.

Grading and rating

Gradings (in Britain) and ratings (in the US and other countries) essentially mean the same thing – a way of measuring performances of players in a tournament or over a period.

The basic concept is simple. If you perform well against players better than yourself, your rating goes up; if you perform badly against players worse than yourself, your rating goes down. Rating is based only on results – wins, draws and losses – and no attempt is made to measure the quality of play or whether you won convincingly or only because of a blunder.

Some 10,000 British chessplayers have a published grade. A newcomer who takes part in a congress and meets graded players will have his grade calculated by totalling the grades of his opponents, adding 50 points for each game won and subtracting 50 for each loss, and averaging the total.

Example: Jones starts his chess career in a four-round tournament. He beats opponents graded 120 and 110, draws with a player graded 116, and loses to one graded 128. The total of his opponent's grades is 474, to which 100 is added for the two games won and 50 deducted for the loss, making 524. Divide by the number of games, four, and his grade based on his first event is 131.

Grades are normally published annually each autumn. They are based on at least 18 results to avoid distortion through too small samples. In calculating results against juniors aged under 18, ten points are added to the junior's grade to allow for improvement since the grade was calculated, while differences between players more than 40 grading points apart are calculated as if they were 40 points.

The system used in the United States, and in World Chess Federation ratings, takes a little longer to calculate but is more closely related to statistical probabilities. The formula as stated by Professor Elo is as follows:

$$Rn = Ro + K(W-We)$$

Rn is the new rating after a tournament.
Ro is your rating before the tournament.
W is the number of points scored.
We is the number of points he was expected to score, based on the difference between his rating and the average rating of his opponents.
K is a constant which is used to weight the most recent performance relative to past performance. This normally varies from 10 to 30 according to the strength of the players: the higher figure enables ratings to change more rapidly, and is useful in the case of juniors or of players who have competed in only one or two events. The number of expected points (We) is determined from a table, not shown here, which shows percentage expected against rating difference.

Personal chess audits

The stimulus of the grading/rating system is one of the most important assets in enabling a competition player to monitor his own improvement and spot weaknesses in his style. It is important to keep what I call a personal chess audit, for which essential equipment is a good quality scorebook and a copy of the latest grading list.

Rating lists contain published form assessments for active players. There is a single list for the United States while each major region of Britain – North, South, Midlands, West, Scotland, Ireland and Wales – has its own list. If you play in congresses or sufficient inter-club matches, your name should eventually appear on the list for your area. If you have difficulty in tracking down your local list, ask the BCF, a congress official, or the USCF.

In order to carry out your chess audit, make a provisional assessment of your own rating when starting match games by asking a couple of strong players to assess your standard, or find out the ratings of players above and below you in the club team and assume you are midway between them.

After each game, look up the opponent's rating in the list (in well-organized tournaments you will be able to find it directly from the pairings card or the wall chart) or ask him direct, then compare your results with the form expectation. You should score 60 per cent against players with British grades 10 points below yours, 70 per cent against those 20 points below, 90 per cent against those 40 points or more below, and so on. This should mean in practice that most of your drawn games will be against players whose grades are not too different from your own.

If you are improving, you should start to beat lower-graded opponents more regularly and take more frequent points and half points from higher graded ones.

Strength	British grade	British title	US rating	US title
International players	225 up	British Master	2400 up	Senior Master
Congress winners	213–224	Candidate Master	2300–2399	US Master
Strong national player	200–212	British Expert	2200–2299	US Master
County, club and state champions	175–199	Candidate Expert	2000–2199	Expert
Strong club players	150–174	Class A	1800–1999	Category I
Average club players	125–149	Class B	1600–1799	Category II
Lower board club players	100–124	Class C	1400–1599	Category III
Weak club players	75–99	Class D	1200–1399	Category IV
Novices	Below 75	Class D	Below 1200	Category V

The next step in your audit is when you have at least 20 results and can summarize what is happening. Are you doing a lot worse with Black than with White? You may not be scoring so well as you should against weaker opponents (overconfidence?) or stronger ones (scared of their reputations?) or it may be that you are performing below your grading expectation in particular openings, particular types of middle game, or endgames. You then have to try and isolate the recurrent errors in those games where your results are worse than they should be: the mistakes will exist as surely as a golf slice or a tendency to underbid at bridge, but in chess there is often a chance to avoid 'error-prone' situations by switching to a more suitable opening system.

Grading tournaments

In Britain it is perfectly possible to keep constant track of your grade and to check at the end of the year whether your calculations agree with those of the local or area grader (it is also possible to do this in the US, though with a slightly greater degree of approximation). The grading year is from 1 May to 30 April and the new lists are published between September and November.

In most British weekend tournaments there is not only an open tournament where leading players take part but where anyone can enter, but also lower sections limited to players below certain grades. If you take part in congresses, these events are another important reason for keeping exact track of your grade. The upper grading limits are often in the range 150–160 and 125–130. If you are a serious competitor, this is something which you should consider as you approach the end of the grading year. For example, if your grade is around 140 in March but you feel you can improve a lot on this, it will probably pay to drop out of tournaments for a couple of months and then concentrate your improvement

in the following grading year when you will be in contention to win the under-150 and under-160 tournaments. Of course the existence of such limits is a temptation to the really unscrupulous player to artificially deflate his grade by losing unimportant games, which is why in the USA rating limited prizes are confined to those who have not been rated above the figure in question for two years or more.

Prizewinning arithmetic

Masters and grandmasters often calculate the score required to win a tournament or finish among the prizes on the basis of percentages which have won in similar previous situations. The weekend congress player should do likewise. An overall score of 75 per cent in a master invitation guarantees a high prize in that type of event but would probably put a player out of the money in a weekend Swiss. This affects the strategy, for while international regulars often take energy-conserving draws when Black it is necessary to play for a win with both colours in a weekend domestic event.

The most common type of weekend Swiss runs for five or six rounds and has anything from 50 to 200 participants. It is likely that you will need at least $4\frac{1}{2}/5$ and $5/6$ to win substantial sums in smaller events while $5/5$ and $5\frac{1}{2}/6$ will be required if the entries approach 200. Assume for the moment that you are one of the stronger players in the tournament and have chances to win in your best form, how should you approach the tournament?

There are two especially promising ways of aiming to reach a score of 5/6 or better. One is by starting slowly with one or two draws in the early rounds (a bad start with a loss has a similar effect) and then coming from behind, meeting weaker opponents while avoiding the top players who are battling it out at the front. Whether this policy works really

depends on how many other strong players there are in the event. If there are quite a few, the odds are that you will meet one or two of them in the later rounds anyway when they too have dropped a draw or a loss. But if you are one of, say, half-a-dozen strong players in a field of a hundred, then the slow start method gives good chances of reaching a high score against fairly easy opposition.

The other method of improving your chances of becoming a consistent money-winner is if you can keep on winning for five of the six rounds. Paradoxically this may improve your chances of avoiding the strongest opposition in the middle and later rounds, when good players are paired together and may drop half a point. If you reach 5/5 in a six-round event you will be probably paired either with another player on maximum points – when in many cases the opponents agree a quick draw to make sure of a high prize – or with a player half a point behind who will also be tempted to accept a draw as it guarantees a reasonable prize. Only rarely does a player with 5/5 find himself a full point clear and paired with a 4/5 going all out for a win.

National titles

Another opportunity given to you by rated and graded chess in Britain and the US is to qualify for one of the national titles open to lower-ranked players. Of course at the lower and middle levels many other people will hold the same title and it will carry no great weight within chess; but outside the game non-players are impressed by such high-sounding names as 'candidate expert' and it may well gain you benefits in applying for a new job or a place at college.

Unfortunately the US and British national title systems are not standardized so that the same title refers to quite different levels of play in each country. Above is a comparative guide to the various rating and title equivalents.

These titles form a valuable target for all chessplayers of reasonable intelligence who are willing to work at the game. Even without any special talent for chess, a combination of learning from the masters, frequent play, and use of the many practical techniques recommended in this book should mean that the Class A/Category I level is a reasonable goal. If you have real ability, you can aim still higher.

Problem solutions (see page 133)

(a) 1. c8=B! b3 2. Bg4 b2 3. Bd1! Kxb1 4. Bb3 mate. If White's pawn had promoted to queen, his third move would draw by stalemate.
(b) 1. Ra3 f2 2. Rhxb3 Kxh2 3. Rh3 mate.
(c) 1. Qg7 Ke2 2. Qd4, and if Kf3 3. Qe4, or if Kf1 3. Qf2.

Chess for Champions

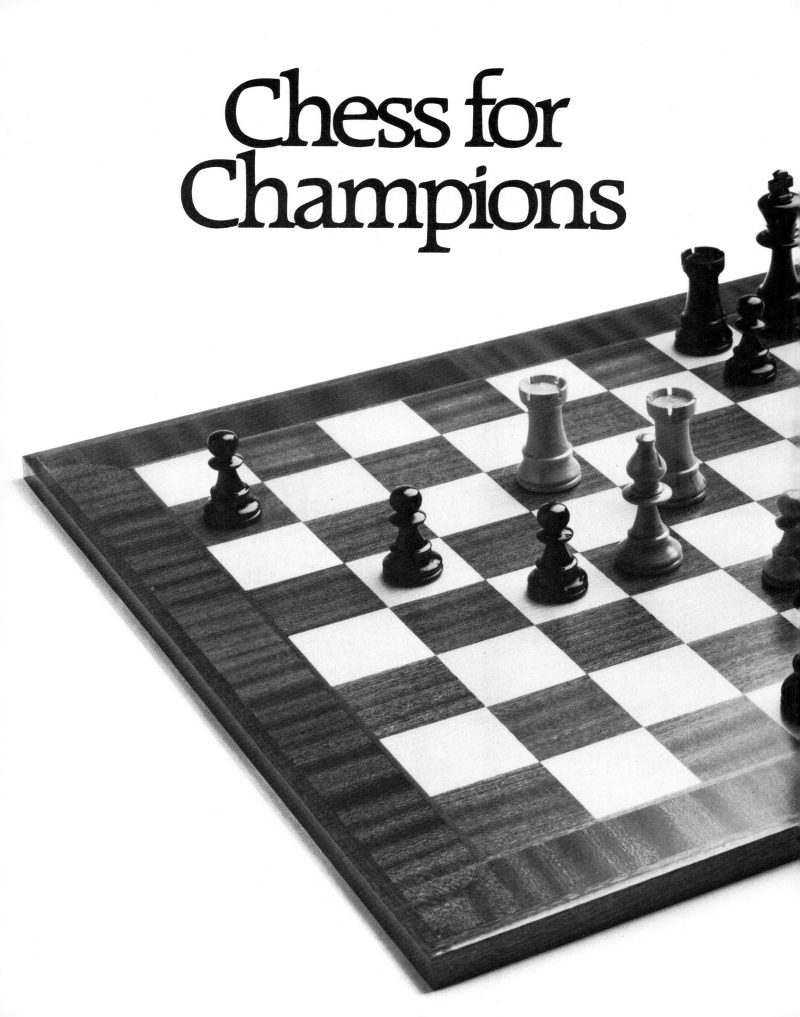

The final chapter of this book deals with the mechanics of getting on in the chess world for those readers who feel they have the talent, the ambition and the dedication to succeed at high levels of play. If you are able to treat chess as serious work and to harness your energies to an unremitting search for improvement, then you can start to think in terms of success in open competition, or international rankings and titles, and of the national championship of your country.

There are ultimately no barriers except ability and results, to becoming the heir to Bobby Fischer and Nigel Short and proving yourself the best player of the US or Britain. The national US magazine *Chess Life* periodically publishes ranking lists of the top 50 men, women and juniors based on performances in all rated events. Naturally you can only reach the top men's list if you do well in major events such as the US Open championship, the Eastern and Atlantic Opens, and the National Open. But if your results reach these exalted levels, the doors will open. Selection for the dozen or so players in the US closed championship is made on ratings as is the choice for the US team in the world olympics. Entry to the New York tournament, the most prestigious open in the world, is based on minimum ratings. All you have to do is prove yourself by your results.

In Britain, the national championship is open for anyone to enter on payment of a modest fee and joining the British Chess Federation (details from 9A Grand Parade, St Leonards on Sea). The preliminary stages of the event are organized in regional zonals, with qualifiers from these tournaments joining exempted players for the title during the annual congress in mid-August. About 60 players normally contest the final. Once there, you have the chance to defeat some of the leading masters and experts in the country, and the road to international chess opens both as a member of the England team and as an individual.

Some of the best English players are chosen every three years to compete in the world championship eliminators. Winning the national title along with other good results may well win one of these coveted nominations to a zonal tournament with representatives from the Netherlands and other West European countries. In the US, the national championship counts as an independent zonal.

A place in the top two or three of the zonal ensures a place in one of the two interzonals, contested between winners and high placers in worldwide zonal tournaments plus exempted masters from the previous world title series. With travel expenses paid by the national federation and hospitality provided by the organizers, you prepare to take on the celebrated Soviet grandmasters. You, they, and the rest of the field of around 18 players settle down for a month-long battle at the end of which you are again in the top three and qualify for a place among the eight world championship candidates.

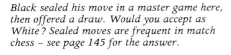

Black sealed his move in a master game here, then offered a draw. Would you accept as White? Sealed moves are frequent in match chess – see page 145 for the answer.

Candidates' matches last from ten to sixteen games against the same opponent. The prizes for winning are becoming more valuable but are still probably not more than £5,000 or $10,000. You win your quarter-final, semi-final and final matches, and you hit the jackpot – a series of perhaps 24 games against Gary Kasparov or whoever succeeds him as world champion.

You will now be the latest hope from the West whom chess fans everywhere want to see follow Bobby Fischer and challenge Soviet supremacy. There is intense interest in the match between the the reigning champion and the unknown from Britain or the US. Many cities bid to stage the match and you and the champion naturally choose the richest purse. Your payoff even if you lose the match is unlikely to be less than £50,000 or $100,000 . . .

Just a dream? Yes, but a dream every young and ambitious player should have. For to have the motivation to work at chess and to win monotonous rook and pawn endgames in unhelpful surroundings, you need to have a vision of reaching the top. Most chessplayers are too limited in their ambitions. Winning a club or area championship will not be a sufficient end in itself to stir your latent effort and talent; the effort of straining for 'impossible' targets brings out ability in players which they and their friends did not suspect.

Junior corner

Many chess players learn the moves and become interested in the game at primary or secondary school. At that age the possibilities of becoming a strong player are much better than for the adult beginner who, whatever his talent, finds it difficult to fit in enough time for the game because of job and family commitments.

Juniors have a great advantage in that they are the ideal age for absorbing the mass of detailed information that is contained in chess theory, generally have a highly developed desire for competition, and have the time to spend on chess until they get involved with the more difficult public examinations such as A-level or university entrance. Lower standard examinations such as the British O-level present few difficulties to most young chessplayers since they are normally academically bright and find the structure of chess tournaments similar to school tests. To make 40 moves in $1\frac{3}{4}$ hours is good training for writing four essay questions in the same period.

Junior events

Junior chess in the US is limited in scope. The US Chess Federation issues regular 'top 50' ranking lists for players under-21, 16 and 13 but apart from the annual

Schedule for grading performance

Age	International schedule	Age	International schedule	Age	International schedule
6.0	50	12.0	135	18.0	180.5
6.6	61	12.6	140	18.6	183
7.0	70	13.0	145	19.0	185.5
7.6	78	13.6	150	19.6	188
8.0	86	14.0	154	20.0	190
8.6	94	14.6	158	20.6	192
9.0	101	15.0	161.5	21.0	194
9.6	108	15.6	165	21.6	195.5
10.0	114	16.0	168.5	22.0	197
10.6	120	16.6	172	22.6	198.5
11.0	125	17.0	175	23.0	200
11.6	130	17.6	178		

US Junior Championship and the National High Schools Championship there are few chances for big all-junior competitions. This does not prevent the top players becoming very strong in their mid-teens but limits their strength in depth in comparison to their counterparts in England and Russia.

Junior chess in England starts with primary chess which includes team events for schools and areas, and a national championship for under-11s. At secondary level there is the *Sunday Times* national school championship, in which some 800 schools take part, as well as annual British and London age group championships, and the national junior squad.

The junior squad is unique to Britain and has had a marked influence on the development of a continual stream of talented young players. Grandmasters such as Petrosian, Hort and Spassky have all remarked that junior strength here is greater in depth than in the Soviet Union.

The main emphasis of the squad is to spot talented youngsters early, guide them into suitable tournaments, arrange coaching and give encouragement to ensure that they will gain opportunities as rapidly as their progress permits. Thus Nigel Short at the age of 9 was sent to play in the international open at Jersey with aid from the organizers and from the Slater Foundation, one of whose associates was co-sponsor of the tournament.

The squad emphasizes world performance and issues periodic ranking lists showing the best juniors in the world in each age group and how the most talented British youngsters compare with them. This immediately provides the 'world championship' motivation mentioned earlier in this chapter; the sight of his name up in lights as world no. 10 for his age immediately fires any youngster worth his salt to aim for the no. 1 spot.

Juniors are also encouraged to measure

their grading performance against a schedule designed to reach international standard by age 23. This schedule is revised from time to time in the light of experience but has proved to have good predictive value.

A junior who reaches any of these intermediate levels shows excellent promise. He has significant chances, if he maintains his interest, to reach 200 grading strength (2200 on the international scale) when he will be good enough to take part in international chess and will be among the top 100–150 players in the country. Girls who achieve these standards are potentially international women masters.

At the highest levels, world class players should be able to beat the schedule by a wide margin. Here are details of the ages at which outstanding players of the past, together with a few who may become outstanding players in the 1980s, reached various grading standards (Right).

Of those players listed who do not already appear in the biographies chapter, Maia Chiburdanidze is world woman champion, and has already won three grandmaster events ahead of men. Murray Chandler is a former New Zealander, now one of Britain's top internationals. Joel Benjamin is the rising star of American chess, already a grandmaster and runner-up in the US championship.

Two further policy planks of the successful British junior squad are also worth mentioning. The squad expects its players to compete wherever possible against older juniors and in adult events; regular practice against such hard opposition encourages a more controlled game with fewer of the errors through inattention which are frequent in all-junior tournaments. Squad players are also expected to take part in a lot of competitive games a year: the squad agrees with several leading grandmasters that frequent play is necessary for achieving results.

An improving and ambitious junior should play at least 80 competitive games a year and preferably 100 to 150. It is important to acquire as much chess information as possible while your memory is at its peak and your enthusiasm is at its maximum. *Chess Informant* and the *British Chess Magazine* are good reference sources. Later on in school years it becomes more difficult to play so frequently because of the increasing pressures of the school examination system. The break-through point for a junior is likely to come when he reaches around a 190 British grade or a 2100 international or US rating. This is the level for entry to major events such as the Hastings Challengers and international Swiss system tournaments, or to become a contender for a place in the national junior team. The IM schedule shows that the potential master needs to reach 190 strength by the age of 15 but this is also the time when examination pressures start to slow the natural rate of chess improvement.

Many parents of junior players ask about coaching. In Britain it is only rarely possible to arrange for regular master coaching for individual players, but this is by no means a major handicap. Such talented masters as Miles and Short became strong with little or no regular coaching. Now, backed by the National Westminster Bank, there is a nationwide programme which gives promising junior players weekend sessions with masters and grandmasters. The National organiser is Derek Evans, 47 Dalehouse Lane, Kenilworth, Warwickshire. Local chess officials also have details. Regular contact with a stronger player will help a novice improve quickly.

Simultaneous play against masters furnishes another incentive. Each year after the annual Hastings congress the England junior squad took on the Russian grandmasters. Later matches were at a higher level with squad teams challenging Karpov and Kasparov. The games varied in quality but they gave participants the vital motivating experience of meeting world-class competition. In his foreword to this book, Viktor Korchnoi describes his own match against the squad where Nigel Short was the only winner. Other grandmasters have found the going hard in similar matches. In 1978, Petrosian conceded nine losses and eleven draws in his 30-board Slater Foundation match against BCF squad and Central YMCA opponents – the best result ever against a world champion outside the USSR.

How does a keen youngster get to join the national squad? That's no real problem. All congress results and junior tournaments from everywhere in the country are scrutinized and youngsters who do well are given the opportunity at an early date to take part in a squad event. In consequence of this policy, little chess talent in England goes to waste or remains undiscovered, whereas in many other countries officials only start to take an interest when a junior has already reached international standard by his own efforts.

Junior games

A common characteristic of junior games as indeed of most chess below strong master level is that initiative counts for much and that players are relatively weak in defence. The overall standard in top junior chess is high, as shown by these two games which brought English victories in the world under-17 and European under-13 team championships.

White: J. M. Hodgson (England)
Black: L. Degerman (Sweden)
Opening: Sicilian, Grand Prix Attack (Viborg 1979)
1. e4 c5 2. f4 g6 3. Nf3 Bg7 4. Nc3 e6 5. d4 cxd4 6. Nxd4 Ne7 7. Be3 0-0 8. Be2 a6 9. 0-0 d6 10. Qd2 Qc7 11. Rad1 Rd8 12. f5 exf5 13. exf5 Bxf5 14. Nxf5 Nxf5 15. Nd5 Qd7 16. Rxf5! gxf5 17. Bg5 Nc6 18. Nf6+ Bxf6 19. Bxf6 Kf8 20. Bc4 Qc7 21. Qh6+ Ke8 22. Qxh7 Ne5 23. Be6 Ng6 24. Re1 Resigns

White: S. C. Conquest (England)
Black. P. Bezilko (France)
Opening: Reti (Eumig Children's Cup 1978)
1. Nf3 Nf6 2. c4 g6 3. b3 c5 4. Bb2 Bg7 5. g3 0-0 6. Bg2 Nc6 7. 0-0 d6 8. e3 Bf5 9. d3 Nb4 10. Ne1 Rb8 11. a3 Nc6 12. h3 Be6 13. Nc3 d5 14. Qe2 dxc4 15. dxc4 Qc8 16. Kh2 Rd8 17. Nd3 Na5 18. Nc1 a6 19. a4 Qc7 20. e4 Nc6 21. Nd5 Bxd5 22. cxd5 Nb4 23. f4 Nd7 24. Bxg7 Kxg7 25. Na2 Nxa2 26. Rxa2 e6 27. dxe6 fxe6 28. Qg4 Re8 29. e5 Rbd8 30. Qg5 Qb6 31. Rd2 Qc7 32. Rfd1 b5 33. axb5 axb5 34. f5 exf5 35. Rd6 c4 36. bxc4 bxc4 37. Bc6 Nxe5 38. Qf6+ Kg8 39. Bd5+ Resigns

International ratings and titles

One objective of every strong player should be to qualify for a World Chess Federation (FIDE) rating, opening up the possibility of obtaining international titles. Rating and title tournaments have to last at least nine rounds and more than half the players must have existing ratings or titles as appropriate. You can normally qualify for an international rating with nine games against players with existing FIDE ratings, provided that your performance in these games is better

Grading performance of outstanding players

	150 (1800)	175 (2000)	187.5 (2100)	200 (2200)	212.5 (2300)	225 (2400)	237.5 (2500)	250 (2600)
Alekhine	11	13	14	14	15	16	19	25
Capablanca	9	11	12	13	16	17	18	20
Reshevsky	7	7	8	9	11	19	23	24
Botvinnik	13	13	14	14	15	17	19	23
Spassky	9	11	12	12	14	15	16	18
Fischer	9	12	13	13	14	14	14	16
Karpov	8	10	11	12	14	15	19	20
Miles (b. 1955)	12	13	14	14	15	17	20	22
Seirawan (b. 1960)	12	12	13	14	14	17	19	23
Chandler (b. 1960)	11	13	14	15	16	19	20	26
Chiburdanidze (b. 1961)	11	12	13	14	16	17	22	
Kasparov (b. 1963)	9	10	11	12	13	15	15	16
Benjamin (b. 1964)	11	11	12	13	13	15		
Short (b. 1965)	9	10	11	12	12	14	17	21

than 2200 (equivalent to a 200 British grade). To convert a British grade to an international rating, multiply by 8 then add 600.

International titles are also awarded on the results of FIDE tournaments; to qualify for a title you have to perform at the stipulated level over 24 games and two or three tournaments, and to include among the opponents specified numbers of grandmasters, international masters or FIDE masters. In both England and the US there are normally several internationally rated Swiss system tournaments each year where anyone of 200 strength or slightly less can qualify for a rating.

Current men's titles are FIDE Master, for which the qualification is 24 games at a performance level of 2351 (219 British grade); International Master, with a performance level of 2451 (231 British); and Grandmaster (2601, 250 British). There are also women's master and grandmaster titles fixed at a lower level.

In countries where the state supports chess, notably Eastern Europe, possession of an international title confers an automatic salary and is therefore highly prized. The natural though unfortunate consequence of this over the years has been a rapid expansion of the number of titled players and devaluation of their importance. Only the title of world champion, because it is unique, has acquired progressively increased kudos.

In Western countries at the present time this has led to a strange contradiction: talented untitled players chase the IM title eagerly and are willing to take part in half-a-dozen tournaments a year to get it; but there is an increasingly high drop-out rate from regular tournament play among those who possess the master title and find it carries little financial value. The grandmaster title is

United States champion Yasser Seirawan works on his next move at Hastings to the sombre background of a black knight.

still rare. There are about 200 holders in the world, half of them players from the USSR who almost never compete in Western Europe. GMs have ample invitations to play in tournaments or give simultaneous exhibitions at tournaments at £50–£100 per session. But in relation to the time involved – around two to three weeks for a GM or IM tournament – competition prizes are poor, while events in Eastern Europe normally pay in unconvertible local currency.

Assuming that you are unlikely to become strong enough to be a grandmaster – or even if you are – it is better, in the context of world chess, to have as your main target a high rating rather than a title. As the IM title becomes devalued, ratings will become more important as the true index of strength.

From the practical viewpoint, it is easier to find events which help your rating rather than those which qualify for a title. Tournaments with two rounds every day can count for ratings but not for titles; you can also improve your rating at purely national events like the British Championship.

Rapid improvement can dramatically alter a player's rating. The formula for international rating, as explained on page 134, is $Rn = Ro + K(W-We)$. In mid-1971 Anatoly Karpov was, like several others, a promising young grandmaster and was considered a possible contender for the world title in the late 1970s. His rating was 2540.

In the 1971 USSR championship, which finished in mid-October, Karpov finished fourth with 13 out of 21. The average rating for the tournament was 2518, and by a table of percentage expected against rating difference (which I do not show) he was expected to score 53 per cent, that is 11.1 out of 21. The stabilising factor K counts as 10 for master players rated 2400 or higher, so FIDE, the World Chess Federation, assessed Karpov's performance as $2540 + 10(13-11.1) = 2559$, a rise of 19 points.

In the Alekhine Memorial tournament in Moscow from November to December 1971, Karpov scored 11 out of 17 and finished in a tie for first place. The average rating for the event, with Karpov still counting as 2540 (ratings only change from year to year), was 2586. As a result he was expected to score less than 44 per cent represented by a score of 7.4. $Rn = 2540 + 10(11-7.4) = 2576$, a rise of a further 36 points.

Karpov then went on to Hastings (December 1971-January 1972) where he shared first prize with Korchnoi, scoring 11 out of 15. The average rating of this event was 2498 and his expected score was 56 per cent, that is 8.4. Again using the table, his actual score gained a further 26 points. Thus at the end of the three events he had gained $19 + 36 + 26 = 81$

points and his rating had risen to 2621, well into the group of super grandmasters rated over 2600. Karpov's results in other events during this period meant that his rating in the next published FIDE list of July 1972 appeared as 2630.

There is an important practical application of this for the ordinary strong player who manages to acquire a FIDE rating and wants to go higher. The method of calculation, with the previous rating used as a constant, meant that Karpov's rating was 15 points higher than it would have been if adjusted after each event. The ratings are calculated once a year, with a cut-off at the end of October. If a player's results during the rating period are substantially better than his published rating, as was Karpov's, it will benefit him to play as much as possible because of the bonus effect of this calculation method. This fact is also relevant to the cluster technique for tournaments recommended on page 145. Many events take place during the summer when most players have extra free time and it is possible to make a decision on whether to step up your tournament programme in the light of your previous results during the FIDE rating year.

The basic mechanism of international chess, the system of title tournaments which has encouraged a rapid expansion of activity over the past decade, is approaching a crisis. There is no problem in making a living if you are Karpov, one of the top dozen grandmasters with a rating above 2600, or have regular newspaper writing commitments. But at lower levels the economics of inflation are rapidly overtaking the willingness of unsalaried chess masters in the West to continue on the European and US circuits. Chess tournaments attract little or no spectator income and, only world championships plus a few special events receive television coverage. Occasionally there is a genuine Maecenas like the patron Louis D. Statham who sponsored the annual Lone Pine international in California, but such wealthy and interested individuals are becoming rarer.

Small master events are usually dependent on business sponsors or on towns who value the publicity. The sponsor, however, sometimes does not get much in return: one or two professional GM and IM columnists report international events with hardly a mention of the people who put up the money. They may not cover some national tournaments at all unless they or their friends are personally involved in it. Thus the sponsor is only guaranteed a reasonable publicity return if he invites, say, Karpov, Korchnoi or Kasparov – and that becomes very expensive.

The conclusion? International titles are a nice tag to have before your name, but unless you are going a long way to-

wards the world championship or can combine mastery with some other allied ability such as chess journalism or authorship they are not likely to pay the mortgage. The talented player at national level will do better making his name on the weekend congress circuit, while testing his ability against the toughest opposition in one or two major tournaments a year. Weekend Swiss events have a friendly atmosphere but are highly competitive. They give the keen amateur a chance to try his skill against leading players, and are an excellent proving ground for young talent.

British and US events

If you are to make your name as a national chessplayer it helps to live in an area of major tournament activity. This means South-East England or the Manchester area in Britain, and New York or California in the US. Though it is possible to operate from other regions, the wear and tear of constant travel is a serious handicap.

The most important regular events in Britain are geared to school and university holidays. This is no accident. Younger players are a high proportion of tournament regulars, while schools and colleges are frequently used as playing sites. However, there is usually at least one congress somewhere in the country on almost every weekend of the year. The BCF publishes an annual tournament calendar.

Major British tournaments include Hastings (December-January), the British Championship (mid-August), the Lloyds Bank Masters (late August) and the ARC Young Masters (February). In all these except ARC there may be a chance to qualify for an international title. Prizes vary, but the top award is likely to be in the range of £800–£1500, and established international masters will often receive appearance money or a guarantee.

The most important US international is the annual New York Open (March–April) which has a generous prize fund of up to $50,000 and attracts grandmasters and masters from all over the world. But you have to be very strong already to qualify for this event, whereas the US Open in mid-August is still a prestigious tournament and allows anyone to take part. An unknown winner like Joe Bradford in 1978 will not immediately get on the national team, but his name is widely publicized in the media and he can expect to be offered places in other strong events. The World Open in July also has a big money prize fund, although its entry has never justified its high-sounding name. Other regular national and international tournaments are announced in advance in *Chess Life*.

Tournament technique

What kind of competitions should you enter if you are a strong player hoping for financial rewards on the weekend circuit? That will depend on how strong you are. At 190 strength, an upper board county team player, you are in the top 200 or so in Britain but you will normally find several better players at any congress. However one of the differences between US weekend tournaments and some British ones lies in the pairing system. In US events pairings are seeded according to ratings so that the favourites only meet after disposing of two or three lesser lights. Similar methods are used in the most important British events, but in some congresses, particularly outside south-east England, players may be paired by chance. Over a five-round course this makes for a reasonable possibility, that the strong players will knock each other out while a middle-rated player in the 180–200 range comes to the top against weaker opposition. Hence unseeded tournaments are your best bet at around 190 strength; but if you are say grade 210 or better you are better in tournaments with seeded pairings.

Both the British and US congress circuits have as their climax a Grand Prix, sponsored respectively by Leigh and Church's Fried Chicken. The Grand Prix, worth several thousand pounds or dollars, goes to the best overall congress performance with extra weighting for the strongest tournaments. To have a chance of winning, you need to be both a very strong player (say at least 220 or 2350 standard) and to be professional and organized not only on the chessboard but in your travel arrangements.

In the middle 1970s one of the sights of the British congress circuit was Gerald Bennett's Dormobile in which he travelled the country participating in a high proportion of the available congresses. David Rumens, who twice won the Grand Prix and popularized the Grand Prix Attack (see page 113) on the circuit, was a keen train-spotter as a child and used his knowledge of railway timetables and connections to be another active competitor.

Style for the weekend

A key factor in doing well in weekend events is to gear your play to the fast time limit and the long daily sessions which can be up to twelve hours when there are three games in a day. Fatigue or trouble with the clock are likely to bring their toll of blunders to knock you out of contention. The style for success in a sprint distance Swiss event of 5–6 rounds is similar to the method recommended against masters in simultaneous displays (see page 125).

Active, attacking chess with a simple plan reaps a high bonus. At 40 or 50 moves in two hours few opponents are capable of sustained precise defence. With two or three games in a day, you want to keep down the number of long endgames which leave little time for rest before the next round. A strong player should also be able to beat weaker opponents on technique without great mental exertion. One of the successful Swiss system players was Australian open champion Max Fuller, who commuted between the November–March circuit in his own country and the summer events in Europe. He derived a useful proportion of his weekend points from simple, direct king's side attacks which his opponent might be able to defend at a slower time limit. This win from the 1969 Athenaeum Open is a good example of the style which succeeds in a weekend Swiss.

White: M. L. Fuller. Black: R. F. Harman

Opening: Sicilian Defence

1. Nf3 g6 2. e4 c5 3. d4 Bg7 4. Nc3 cxd4 5. Nxd4 Nc6 6. Be3 Nf6 7. Bc4 Qa5 8. 0–0 (Black has geared his development to the theoretical line where White castles long, so White switches to a simpler line where he has a slight plus in the centre) 0–0 9. Bb3 d6 10. h3 Bd7 11. f4 Nxd4

12. Bxd4 Bc6 13. Qd3 Nd7? (a typical weekend imprecision. Better is 13. . . . Rad8 and if 14. Rad1 Nd7 15. Bxg7 Kxg7 16. Kh1 Nc5 17. Qd4+ e5! and if 18. fxe5 Nxb3 when Black stands well) **14. Bxg7 Kxg7 15. Rae1 Nc5 16. Qd4+ Kg8** (now e5 fails to 17. Qxd6. Consequently Black is unable to start the normal counterplay in the centre and for the rest of the game has to defend unsuccessfully against an easy-to-play king's side attack) **17. Bd5 Nd7 18. Kh1 Qb6 19. Qd2 Rad8 20. f5 Kg7 21. Rf4 Nf6 22. Rh4 h5 23. g4 Rh8 24. fxg6 fxg6 25. gxh5 Nxh5 26. Qg5 Nf6 27. Rg1 Be8 28. Rxh8 Kxh8 29. Qh6+ Nh7 30. Rf1 Bc6 31. Rf7 Resigns.**

Beating the clock

Handling the clock is important in weekend Swisses not only because the normal time limit is rather fast but because of the practice in British events of deciding the final moves over a 'blitz finish' where the game has to be completed after four hours or so with ten or fifteen minutes on each player's clock. Therefore points will be won and lost according to how well you handle your own time, can drive your opponent into severe time pressure, and exploit his time pressure when it occurs.

Techniques which can help if you are prone to time pressure include:

1 In less important games, make the clock the first consideration rather than the quality of the play: try to develop an inner control mechanism which stops you agonizing too long over a single move and keeps you aware of how the time is going.

2 If you cannot decide on any plan, or if you are in time pressure and your mind goes blank after an unexpected move, concentrate on improving the position of your worst posted piece.

3 If you have the chance to repeat moves any time once or twice during the game before time pressure comes along, do so – but make sure you understand the explanation of the threefold repetition rule on page 131.

4 Avoid repeated calculation of the same line of play – after two or three attempts assume you are not going to find significant improvements.

5 Use your opponent's time to keep track of general strategy, and your own time for concrete variations.

6 Look at the clock when it is your opponent's turn to move, not yours.

7 If the position is complicated and you don't have time to analyze, simply make the move which looks best on general principles.

8 Put ticks instead of writing down the moves – this will save precious seconds, although you must write up the score properly as soon as the time scramble is over.

Some players are notorious time pressure addicts. If you are a tournament regular you are likely to know some of them by repute or personal experience. When meeting such players, it is worth tempting them to go into the kind of trance which will produce time pressure later on; the same applies if you find during the game that your opponent is playing slowly.

Techniques which help:

1 If you know the opening well and your opponent clearly does not, try blitzing him. Make your moves fast, with an air of great confidence as if it was all analyzed at home for weeks ahead. I remember once using this technique against the late Hugh Alexander in the British Championship when after a dozen moves the clock showed Barden, 1 minute; Alexander, 1 hour. Later he fought back both on the board and the clock, but there was a delayed action effect when he made the decisive mistake later on during time pressure.

2 Try to create positions where your opponent will have no clear line of play but instead a choice between several apparently equal plans. If you can get him to spend half an hour deciding which rook to use to occupy an open file or which of four different pawn captures to make, you are doing almost as well as being a sound pawn up.

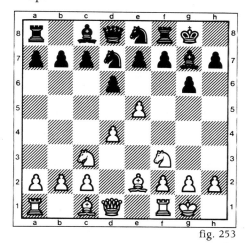

fig. 253

Botterill–Nunn, BBC Master Game 1975. Normal here is 1. Bf4, but White played 1. Bg5! a good example of a time-pressure inducing move. Black replied with the more-or-less forced 1. . . . f6 and then 2. exf6 leaves Black four plausible ways to recapture. Black settled for 2. . . . Ndxf6 – but the time spent put him later in clock pressure.

3 There may be a chance to repeat the blitzing technique in the opening if the game is adjourned, as happens in major tournaments lasting several days. Sometimes the player making the sealed move (see page 145) can do something unexpected; then that move

should be made quickly and confidently and the ensuing moves followed up in a barrage.

I was on the receiving end of this technique in the 1957 British Championship against R. G. Wade, when I adjourned with a good position and expecting to win and take a clear tournament lead. But the pressures of being blitzed with surprise moves after adjournment induced a losing blunder. A classic instance of this technique from world title play occurred in Korchnoi-Karpov, 5th game 1978.

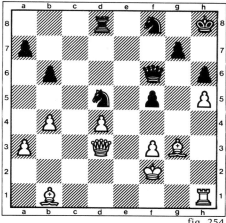

fig. 254

Black's game is probably lost, but Karpov sealed the unexpected 1. . . . Nh7! at adjournment which Korchnoi's team failed to analyze. Korchnoi eventually found the correct plan in reply (2. Be5 Qg5 3. Qxf5 Qd2+ 4. Kg3 N7f6 5. Rg1 Re8 6. Be4! followed by bringing the WK to h4 to clear the g file) but meanwhile he was getting into acute time trouble while Karpov replied quickly.

The consequence: some moves later, just before the next time control, Korchnoi missed an elementary mate. It shouldn't happen in a world championship, of course, but some of the credit must go to Karpov for his sealed move surprise/blitz technique.

4 Simon Webb in *Chess for Tigers* recommends walking away from the board when your time-trouble addict opponent is in a trance so as not to wake him up. Keep an eye on him from a distance and if he looks about to move (physical signs are shifting of position and flexing of the right arm muscles) then return to the board and appear to be concentrating hard again. This can have the effect of sending him into another long think – your action gives the impression that you have suddenly noticed a hidden resource, so of course he has to look for it too.

5 As time goes on and you get further ahead on the clock, try to make non-forcing moves which maintain the balance of the position. Pawn holes for

the king or 'mysterious' rook re-groupings are ideal.

6 When your opponent gets really short of time, say ten moves or so in a couple of minutes, then open up the game and if possible set him problems of exact calculation. At this stage, avoid positions where he can make non-forcing replies so as to reach the time control.

7 Use the *barrage technique*. This is another of Webb's suggestions, and has also been used effectively over the years by twice British champion Bob Wade in international play. The barrage technique consists of planning two or three moves ahead, then making them virtually instantaneously. If the second or third move is unexpected, the effect can be psychologically shattering to an opponent already worried about his clock.

8 If you are sufficiently ahead on time, combine the barrage technique with the *variable pace technique*. When a player is very short of time, he is mentally geared up for action, rather like a commuter rushing to finish his work before the last train or a journalist writing his piece before the copy deadline. But such a high pitch of mental energy cannot be sustained for long and is biologically followed by a let-down. Therefore, the experienced pro will use his long lead on the clock to shoot off a series of moves on the barrage technique, and will not move then at all for five or ten minutes.

Wade tells of a tournament game where he met the German grandmaster Samisch, for years the most notorious time pressure player in the world who once went through an entire tournament losing every game on the clock. Wade was an hour and a half ahead on time, and Samisch was sitting at the board with his clock flag already starting to rise and 25 moves to go before the control. The position was level, an expectant crowd gathered round the board waiting for a scramble to start. Wade made a three-move barrage and then, as his opponent sat poised and expectant, got up with his own clock ticking and . . . went off to buy a coffee. He brought it back and sat slowly stirring and sipping while his opponent wilted. Some moves later Samisch's clock duly fell.

9 If your opponent has stopped taking score due to his time pressure, cover up your own sheet. Neither you nor the controller has any obligation to tell him how many moves remain until the control, and if he has allocated his time so that he has hardly any left for the last few moves, that's his fault.

All these time-pressure techniques only apply as major weapons when the position on the board remains unclear or is at best only slightly in your favour. But if you are winning hands down, ignore your opponent's clock, concentrate on the most accurate method to victory and avoid his traps. Some experts will deliberately get themselves short of time, in a really poor position, with the object of heightening the nervous tension and increasing the chance of the player on top blowing the game. It isn't easy to deal with such tactics and you may have to consciously work to keep your cool.

Dirty tricks

There is a narrow and often unclear dividing line between legitimate tactics in order to wear down your opponent's psychological resistance and other practices which many would consider unethical. The laws of chess give controllers power to award penalties up to loss of the game for infractions of 'moral principles', and a player's position in the tournament will not survive being caught in the toilet with a copy of an openings manual and a pocket set. But in many other cases distrubance to the opponent when both sides are under tension due to clock pressure is difficult to rule on. Here are some items you may meet in the dirty tricks department.

1 Saying 'j'adoube' as often as possible in time pressure, and adjusting several pieces so that they are centred exactly on their squares. The opponent, geared up to reply immediately to any move, gets understandably rattled but there is often too little time left for him to protest.

2 Continually leaning over the board to look at the clock while the opponent is thinking, thus obstructing his view of the board; picking up the clock to look at the time just as the opponent is ready to move and press the clock button.

3 Writing down an extra move for each side, then letting the opponent see the score sheet so that he thinks he has reached the control when there is still a move to go.

4 Leaning right over the board so that the head is over the central squares – even more effective if the player is tall with long hair.

5 Hovering near the edge of the board within the edge of the opponent's field of vision. This form of symbolic physical aggression is unpleasant for an opponent in time pressure or when he is trying to rescue a bad position.

6 Making an illegal move in the opponent's time pressure; the illegality is naturally of the sort where the prescribed penalty is only to make a legal move with the same piece: Ray Keene describes one incident where his opponent's 'move' was to place his king off the board in an ashtray. The correct counter to this ploy is to react immediately, without making a counter-move or protest, and simply to restart your opponent's clock: you are not obliged to have time recorded against you unless presented with a legal position. The same counter is available when your opponent knocks over several pieces, spills coffee, etc.

Chess swindling

Contrary to first impressions, swindling at chess is more ethical and normal than the dirty tricks described above. Swindling means recognizing that the position is lost and making the decision to look for active resources rather than just get ground down. Swindle technique normally applies in defensive positions and recognizes that the only real chance to fight back is to gain an initiative or counter-attack even at the price of more material.

To set up a possible swindle means abandoning to their fate one or two weak pawns which tie your pieces to passive defence; perhaps giving up a rook, which is most useful in the endgame, for a bishop or knight, more valuable in a middle-game counter-attack, and also to use what Webb calls 'controlled desperation'. If you see several moves, most of which give your opponent a clear win, then choose the one plausible move left without deep analysis. This method enables complicated moves to be made quickly and places the onus on your opponent of trying to work them out.

The psychology of swindling favours the swindler – it is unpleasant for the opponent to have to adjust from a solid positional plus to a war of movement and confusion where the chance of a decisive mistake is much greater.

Webb recommends swindlers to heighten the effect of the change of the board by facial expression: to look completely downcast and beaten when on the defensive in the hope that the winning player becomes careless; then, once the pieces get into action and the position becomes complex and unclear, to look as confident as possible to scare the opponent. If you are setting a tactical trap however, the correct facial impression is either a normal one or one that is a little nervous. It is important not to overact but if possible to feel the emotions you are trying to convey across the board; this is not too difficult because any chess game approaching its climax arouses powerful tensions.

Finally, if despite your efforts, your position remains considerably worse approaching the time control, you can try (since you will undoubtedly be starting to feel nervous yourself) communicating this feeling to the opponent. Such body gestures as rocking, glancing at the clock and back to the board, hovering over the piece as you are about to make a move, can be infectious and increase your opponent's tension to the extent where he starts to make errors. Of course the position on the board has to be such that there is tension to communicate: you will feel and look utterly ridiculous if you try these techniques when a piece down in a simple ending without compensation. But when you have the right occasion, chess swindling works.

Sealed move and adjournments

In major tournaments at international time limits it is normal for unfinished games to be adjourned after four or five hours and resumed either later the same day or, more rarely, the next morning or another day. The final move of the session is not played on the board but written down on the score sheet and placed in a sealed move envelope for reopening when the game resumes. Often the players reach the first time control right at the end of the session and the side with White has to readjust his thoughts and emotions from the battle with the clock to finding the best and most precise sealed move while his opponent goes off to analyze.

The period between the time control and the sealed move is a tricky one because tiredness can impair both sides' judgment. One of the classic mistakes is to reach a won game at the time control and then go on blitzing moves instead of sealing. Even world champions are not immune.

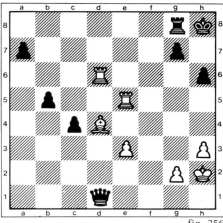

fig. 255

Karpov-Korchnoi, 22nd match game 1978. This was the position after Korchnoi's 40th move as Black Rxd6. Now White should surely win by the obvious 1. Rxd6 Nxd6 2. Rxa4. Black has some chances by 2. ... h5 but they shouldn't be enough: the white Q-side pawns aided by the wide-ranging bishop run faster than Black's pawns on the other wing.

All this was unimportant beside the fact that the world champion had the chance to adjourn and work out a win at leisure. Karpov was tiring in the later stages of the match and this must have affected his normally sound judgment, for play continued **1. Rxd6?** (the ? is because this was White's ideal oppor-

tunity to seal) **Nxd6 2. Bc7??** (an 'improvement' . . .) **Re1+ 3. Kc2 Ne8!** (. . . which misses this resource. Now demoralized by his oversight, Karpov continued at blitz speed although he could still probably win by adjourning: **4. Ba5 a3 5. Rb8 Re7** and now **5. Bb4?** (5. bxa3!) **Re2+ 6. Kd3 axb2** drew for Korchnoi. A remarkable escape, with a clear moral.

Another practical lesson was given by the following position from Knaak-Zilberstein, Tallinn 1979.

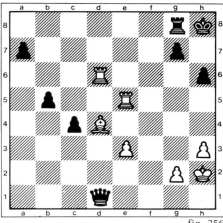

fig. 256

The diagram arose immediately before adjournment, and Black had to seal his move. He is material up with queen and two pawns against rook and bishop, but White has some counterplay. Knaak, a grandmaster, analyzed the position and decided that after 1. . . . Kh7 2. Rxb5 he had good chances to draw.

He was nevertheless relieved when Zilberstein, champion of the Russian republic, came to him and offered a draw straightaway. Knaak agreed. But then he found that Zilberstein had sealed the dreadful blunder **1. . . . Qb1??** after which White wins at once by 2. Rxh6+ gxh6 3. Rxb5+ and 4. Rxd1.

Thus you normally never accept a draw during the adjournment without seeing the opponent's sealed move first. It might be a blunder, as here, or it could be inferior or even illegal, the latter costing the game. Remember that your opponent's draw offer after a sealed move cannot be retracted until you have replied to it or made your next move on the board.

I have written 'normally never accept a draw' because you have to consider the physical conditions of the tournament. If the event is in a small town or resumption of play is later the same day then there's no doubt you should insist on inspecting the sealed move. But in some very big events like the world team championship the players stay a lengthy bus journey from the playing site: at Buenos Aires 1978 the unlucky masters resuming adjournments had to rise at

7 a.m. following a hard late night match the previous evening. Under conditions like that, the experienced pro has to judge whether the possibility of finding a bad sealed move is worth the absolute certainty of extra fatigue in the next round.

Cluster technique

If you do unexpectedly well in any tournament and feel you are in good form, consider *cluster technique*, which means concentrating your play so that you enter a number of other events in a short period. The rationale for this approach lies in the mechanics of chess improvement demonstrated by Professor Elo's work on performance measurement. Deeper understanding of new strategies and ideas in chess comes not in a steady flow but in quantum jumps mixed with long periods of steady consolidation where the player may not seem to be getting better.

At the most elementary level, quantum jumps can be demonstrated by the improvement a beginner makes when he understands scholar's mate or how to mate with a king and rook. At a higher and more complex level, the comprehension of various chess attacking and defensive patterns often seems to 'click' into place. The player has probably read the correct approach or technique in a book but due to his limited experiences his first few attempts to apply it in his own games are unsuccessful. Then, rather in the way that a novice cyclist suddenly stops falling off his machine, acquires balance and co-ordination, and in most cases never loses it, so the chessplayer suddenly succeeds in incorporating the new technique into his existing game.

Thus the unexpectedly good tournament result can be a sign of a personal quantum jump, and it is important to take advantage of it. In England and the US there are plenty of matches and tournaments offering competitive chess, and the quantum jump can be exploited by concentrated play – the cluster technique – in order to boost a player's rating. The converse of the cluster technique is that after an unexpectedly poor result you should take a break, analyze the defeats, and restructure your game and opening repertoire as necessary.

How many games?

The Soviet grandmaster Geller used to say he felt rusty and out of practice if he played fewer than 80 tournament and match games a year. Korchnoi has gone on record with similar comments. Such a level of activity is not for everybody – for example, Botvinnik kept at his peak with a much lower output of games which he compensated for by especially meticulous preparation. But for most strong players, particularly if aged under 30, a total of

80 – 150 games a year is needed to give the concentrated experience which will help improvement.

With such numbers of games, cluster technique can be used to real effect. In the summer of 1979, for example, Wales's leading player Botterill began the British circuit after a fallow period of two years following a previous success run when he became an international master. The 1979 circuit included the National Bank of Dubai Open, the British Championship, the Lloyds Bank and Benedictine Masters, and the Aaronson Open – a total of 51 games in seven weeks and a gruelling schedule. But Botterill started well in the first event and kept going as long as his good form lasted, which was the full period of the circuit. At the end of it all he had tied for first prize in the Manchester Benedictine event and had been in the running for a grandmaster result in the earlier Lloyds Bank tournament. Until then no-one had considered him a potential GM prospect – the cluster technique helped to make the quantum jump.

Act like a grandmaster

Two popular books by Alexander Kotov are *Think like a grandmaster* and *Play like a grandmaster*. Both are informative on aspects of GM thinking and in particular how to settle an individual move by a logical step-by-step process. But there are also grandmaster approaches to the broader mechanics of success in all-play-all and tournament play.

The normal strong expert thinks of his progressive score in a tournament in the obvious terms of points scored relative to rounds played, such as 2½ out of 3 or 5 out of 7. But in events longer than a weekend it is more useful to adopt the master approach of thinking of a target score in terms of the number of wins relative to losses. The GM thinks of 2½/3 as 'plus two' (ie. two more victories than defeats), 5/7 as 'plus three' and so on.

The next step is to check on the target score for various events and plan the playing campaign beforehand in terms of what you can reasonably expect. In the British Championship a player aiming to win the event will plan for plus five or plus six (8 or 8½/11) and a player hoping to finish in the prize list at plus three (7/11). At a higher level, grandmasters aiming to be one of the three qualifiers to the world championship candidates aim for plus five or plus six in a 17-round tournament. How you reach such scores (always assuming you are good enough) is a matter of style and approach: somebody like Petrosian will try to avoid losses and beat all the tail-enders, a more enterprising player will reckon on a couple of losses but will aim to beat one or two of his rivals.

In a Swiss system event, unlike an all-play-all, you don't know in advance exactly who you will meet, but it is still possible to map out a schedule. For example leading contenders in the British Championship try to reach at least plus two by the end of the first week, remembering that the hardest games are in the middle rounds.

The final round

Another characteristic where the Swiss may differ from the all-play-all is the importance of later rounds and especially the final one. The section on Lasker (page 55) drew attention to his strength as a last round player, and to be a good finisher is even more important in a short five or six-round Swiss. It is far from easy to ensure this since playing two or three rounds the previous day is very tiring.

However, the sensible pro will take some precautions – for a weekend event:

1 Get a good night's sleep on the Thursday before the tournament.

2 If the event is not within easy travelling distance of your home (don't forget to allow for fewer trains and buses at weekends) it is worth considering a stay at a hotel near the event. Of course it adds to your costs even if you do well, but it may be essential if you continually find you flag on the final day.

3 Be firm with yourself and take a ten-minute walk between rounds to clear your brain.

4 Watch for Sunday morning: the most frequent cause of drop-outs from weekend events is oversleeping on Sunday, and this quite often occurs to players who are still in contention for a prize.

5 Remember that your opponents will also be feeling varying degrees of tiredness, and adapt your technique accordingly: avoid very highly-analyzed variations against young opponents with their absorbent memory banks, and sharpen up the play against older opponents who will be relying on strategy and feeling the pace on the Sunday.

6 Try to keep control of the position against weaker opponents, winning if possible by technique. Kotov advises strong players even to go for simplified endings, since the nuances of such positions are harder for the weaker player to spot.

Fast chess

Fast chess is a technique for improvement whose value has been greatly underestimated. Good speed players can easily adapt their game to slower time limits. It is no mere coincidence that Lasker, Capablanca, Fischer, Tal, Karpov and Korchnoi were all among the best fast players of their time, and at the Leipzig olympics of 1960 where Fischer, Tal and Korchnoi all played they had blitz sessions in the hotel lobby almost every evening. After the final round Tal played all day in an officially organized

ten-minute tournament and then all night five-minute games in his hotel room with Fischer. Abstainers from blitz among the top GMs, for instance Botvinnik and Portisch, are in a minority.

From fast chess one learns tactical awareness, and ability to play fast under pressure is essential for good results near the time control at slower rates.

Prolonged experience of fast chess helped improve my own playing standard from promising junior to British championship competitor. During the middle 1940s when organized chess in London began to revive at the tail-end of the war, the Lud Eagle club in the West End staged weekly five-minute tournaments. Competition was fierce. After a few visits the masters kindly accepted me into the top group where, on penalty of losing my small pocket money in losing stakes, I had to learn to play well at speed. The continuous experience against these international elders proved an excellent chess education and in today's terms I improved around 20 grading points or 150 rating points in about a year.

The most popular current form of fast chess is the quickplay tournament, at time limits ranging from twenty minutes up to one hour per player for the entire game. Thirty minutes per player per game seems the most successful. Like it or not, this type of event seems destined to gain ground in the 1980s. Strong economic forces favour the one-day Saturday tournament. These include the narrow cost margins of many weekend congresses, the prohibitive costs of organizing a master tournament without a major sponsor or spectator income, the difficulties with Sunday venues and travel, and the awkwardness of overnight stays for out-of-town entrants.

Rapid sight of the board, evidenced by unusual ability at lightning and five-minute chess, can be an early sign of mastery. Olafsson, Iceland's best-ever player, won a blitz tournament ahead of many GMs at the Staunton Centenary in England in 1951 while he was still an unknown junior. David Bronstein, an incessant five-minute player in the Moscow clubs, surprised everyone the same year when he came through the world title eliminators at the first attempt and nearly took the championship from Botvinnik.

Special rules for quickplay and five minute games are that each player must tap his clock with the hand he uses to make his moves. Opinion is divided on whether a player who makes an illegal move loses automatically. Since games often continue till mate, there are various provisions to avoid ridiculous results. In

Tension at Hastings as, left to right, Michael Stean and I. Zilber ponder while Nigel Short writes his move on the score sheet.

147

most quickplay tournaments a draw is declared when a player with a clearly winning position on the board finds his flag go down.

Quickplay tournaments had a boost in the 1980s when FIDE decided that they could be internationally rated. Kasparov and Short played a quickplay match for television, and the first British Open quickplay championship was held at Leeds with £1000 for the winner – who turned out to be Nigel Short, triumphant in all eleven games.

In London, there are two regular quickplays a month, run by the Civil Service Chess Association (details from 903 Longbridge Road, Dagenham, Essex) and by City Chess of 5 Carlisle Road, N4. Anyone can enter, with or without previous experience, and all competitors play the full six games.

There is normally a first prize of around £100, with many lesser awards. Opponents are likely to be of varying standards, ranging from top London masters to novices and beginners.

If you are absolutely new to competitive chess, I recommend a quickplay as your first step even before joining a chess club. The events have an informal camaraderie, if you lose you will meet fellow losers, while the surroundings are pleasant with canteen facilities and space for post-mortem analysis.

I expect quickplay, rather than five-minute or ten-minute games, to prove the boom form of chess in the 1980s and 1990s. It is slow enough for even average players to turn in a fair game and for clock wear and tear to be limited, yet fast enough for a one-day tournament.

Advice on how to play it must include emphasis on the danger of lagging too far behind on the clock. Even in a strong position on the board, ten minutes in a half-hour game is a big handicap. Initiative chess pays off, since it's hard to defend well when moving fast. Generally the best players will still win – few people remember that Bobby Fischer's final tournament before he gave up chess was a 22-round blitz event in New York in 1971 which he won with 21 wins and a draw. That was his last public training before beating Spassky.

The inhibitions which affect some chess organizers about quickplay events damaging the clocks do not seem to affect their counterparts in Russia where five-minute championships are held on the highest level with the top grandmasters taking part. The Soviet controllers cheerfully accept that there will be occasional flare-ups. One year there was a bitter dispute between grandmasters Kotov (a senior chess establishment member and Communist Party dignitary) and Karpov (then a young newcomer to the top flight) over whose flag had gone down first; excited spectators joined in the dispute.

The best known Soviet fast event is the annual Moscow five minute championship which has often been won by outstanding players such as Tal, Bronstein and Vasyukov. Here is a quick victory from the 1978 event where Black tries a new move 8. . . . Nf6 only to find that it weakens the c6 knight and the f3-a8 diagonal too much.

The pin on the e file proved decisive (14. . . . Qxc6 15. Rxe7+ winning the game) so Black resigns early.

White: E. Vasyukov. Black: A. Suetin

Opening: Ruy Lopez (Moscow 5-minute 1978)

1. e4 e5 2. Nf3 Nc6 3. Bb5 a6 4. Ba4 d6 5. c3 f5 6. exf5 Bxf5 7. 0–0 Bd3 8. Re1 Nf6 9. Nd4 Qd7 10. Qf3 Bxb1 11. Nxc6 e4 12. Rxb1 bxc6 13. Rxe4+ Be7 14. Bxc6! Nxe4 15. Qxe4 Rd8 16. d4 d5 17. Qxd5 Resigns

How well Bobby Fischer played at five-minute speed can be judged by this game from the Manhattan blitz event of 1971. Fischer was an expert on the black side of a King's Indian Defence and here the only discernible blemish in his play is the slight loss of time with the queen on moves 21–22. If you didn't know the circumstances, it would be easy to credit this as a normal slow rate tournament game.

White: P. Brandts. Black: R. J. Fischer

Opening: King's Indian (Manhattan 1971)

1. d4 g6 2. c4 Bg7 3. Nc3 Nf6 4. e4 d6 5. Be2 0-0 6. Nf3 e5 7. 0-0 Nc6 8. d5 Ne7 9. Ne1 Nd7 10. Nd3 f5 11. exf5 gxf5 12. f4 Ng6 13. Be3 Nf6 14. Qc2 Re8 15. fxe5 dxe5 16. Bg5 h6 17. Bxf6 Qxf6 18. Qb3 e4 19. Nf4 Nxf4 20. Rxf4 Qg5 21. R4f1 Qe3+ 22. Kh1 Qg5 23. c5 Kh8 24. Rad1 Be5 25. g3 Rg8 26. Nb1 f4 27. Rg1 f3 28. Bc4 Qh5 29. Qe3 Rxg3 30. Qxe4

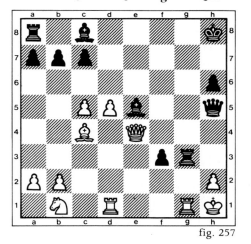

fig. 257

30. . . . Qxh2+! and White resigned because of 31. Kxh2 Rh3 mate.

An illustration of ten seconds a move chess is this game from the 1977 British lightning championship. Nigel Short here loses to one of the country's leading masters, but the following year the youngster won the lightning title outright. The game shows the theme emphasized often in this book that you have to take your chances for initiative chess. Short made an automatic pawn recapture on move 20 and lost without a real fight: instead 20. . . . Nfe4! would have brought him out of defence into active play.

White: J. Speelman. Black: N. D. Short

English Opening (British lightning 1977)

1. c4 c5 2. Nf3 Nc6 3. Nc3 g6 4. e3 Bg7 5. d4 cxd4 6. exd4 d6 7. Be2 Nf6 8. 0-0 0-0 9. d5 Nb8 10. Nd4 Nbd7 11. Re1 a6 12. Be3 Ne5 13. h3 Qc7 14. b3 N5d7 15. Rc1 Nc5 16. Bf1 b6 17. Bg5 Re8 18. Qd2 Bb7 19. Re2 e5 20. dxe6 e.p.

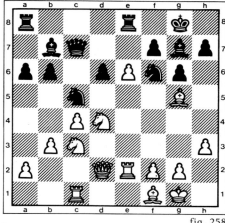

fig. 258

20. . . . fxe6? 21. Bxf6 Bxf6 22. b4 e5 23. Nf3 Ne6? 24. Nd5! Bxd5 25. cxd5 Resigns.

The practical master

If you ask amateur chessplayers what books and magazines they read regularly, you will get a great variety of answers. Most of them will rely for their openings knowledge on a long-possessed and outdated manual such as the eleventh edition of 'Modern Chess Openings' or some pocket compendium. For the middle game some will swear by Nimzovich, others like the collected games of such as Larsen and Fischer, most will have a store of well-known opening traps.

Masters and grandmasters tend to be more standardized in their choice. If you are a very strong player you will already have a wide corpus of knowledge at your fingertips and the problem is to keep abreast of new ideas in popular openings and to get to know the repertoires of future rivals.

Practically all masters will use the five-volume Yugoslav-written *Encyclopaedia of Chess Openings* (ECO) as their basic reference source. The books are packed with data from games of the 1980s and contributors include many leading grand-masters. But the five volumes cost around £100 or $200 and such expenditure can only be logically justified for a player who is already strong and who intends to be an active tournament competitor.

In order to supplement ECO most GMs and IMs will take at least one of these theoretical journals:

Chess Informant (twice a year)
New in Chess (four times a year)

Taking suitcases of chess books on the tournament circuit can result in both armache and airline excess luggage charges. Many international players therefore prefer to pick up further information as they go along, looking at ideas gleaned from the postmortems of their own games and those of rivals. If they specialize in a particular opening, they will probably have the relevant Batsford monograph or the loose-leaf section of the RHM openings survey.

Players who enjoy reading and keeping abreast with ideas may also take one or more of such chess journals as *64* (Russian fortnightly), *Chess* and *British Chess Magazine* (both English) and *Chess Life* (US). It is also possible to keep ahead of those who only read the theory journals if you go directly to the primary sources, the bulletins with all the games of particular tournaments. In Britain for example, Hastings, the Lloyds Bank Masters, and the British Championship all issue bulletins.

However much or little he reads, the would-be pro will find it a useful exercise to keep his own game files in which to note variations played by regular opponents and novelties in his own favourite systems. The point is not to have easily accessible reference material, though this is important, but to gain sufficient feeling for a system of play that you start to develop your own ideas and innovations.

One example: the young New Zealand champion Murray Chandler played a lot of games with the Grunfeld Defence **1. d4 Nf6 2. c4 g6 3. Nc3 d5.** Some of his opponents replied with the quiet system **4. Nf3 Bg7 5. Bg5 Ne4 6. cxd5 Nxg5 7. Nxg5 e6 8. Nf3 exd5 9. e3 c6 10. b4.**

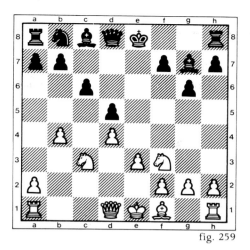

fig. 259

This position is harder than it looks for Black. White plans the minority pawn attack where his a and b pawns run at the black Q-side trio with the object of creating a weak isolated or backward pawn which the white rooks and minor pieces can then attack. The conventional reply manoeuvre is 0–0 followed by Re8 and Bf8-d6, regrouping the black forces in the hope of a K-side counter-attack. But the rook is not so well placed on f8: Black's counterplay often requires the pawn advance f7-f5 followed either by f5-f4 to open the f file or by Ne4 and if White takes the knight to recapture with the f pawn.

From his experiences with this problem Chandler hit upon his new idea: he played at once **10. . . . Bf8!** with the intention of first regrouping the bishop, only then castling, and playing the K-side attack with the rook employed on its best square at f8. When Chandler introduced his novelty in the Philadelphia international of 1979, his opponent burst into laughter. Not for too long: Chandler won the game and his innovation was widely praised in the theory journals. This type of creative thinking is applicable to many opening situations.

Results analysis

At the USSR Championship final of 1978, Gary Kasparov scored 50 per cent in his first attempt on the title at the age of 15, a result acclaimed round the world. However at his next tournament a few months later at Banja Luka, Kasparov did even better, outclassing a star field of grandmasters. What had occurred in the meantime?

Something which clearly happened was that Kasparov and his teacher Bot-vinnik reviewed the results of Kas-parov's openings in the championship and discovered that he didn't win a single game with Black. Careful not to do badly on his debut, Kasparov stuck to solid defences like the Caro-Kann and aimed simply for equality from the openings. But such ultra-positional systems did not

really suit his style – a cross between Fischer and Tal with White, vigorous and active and generally striving for open play.

At Banja Luka Kasparov revised his repertoire and chose more positive systems with Black. He was rewarded with several fine victories and evidently bene-fitted from his homework.

Such constant checking on opening systems to weed out those whose results are below par is a necessary exercise for any strong player. Just before writing this chapter I happened to be talking to the English grandmaster Dr John Nunn, who told me that he had diagnosed the weakness in his own repertoire as the Tarrasch Defence to 1. d4. Nunn did not use the gambit analyzed on page 101, instead playing the more classical system where Black accepts an isolated queen's pawn in return for piece play. For some time this gave him good results but Nunn's opponents gradually came to expect it and in international games he had to contend continually with home-brewed attempts at refutation. The young GM told me he was going to include a more solid defence. Coincidentally or not, a few months later he became the first British winner at Hastings for 26 years. The point is to demonstrate the import-ance of keeping tabs on your results and finding the systems which suit you best against opponents of similar or superior rating.

The best way to analyze your results and style is to consider all your games for the last year or two and assess them in terms of openings, middle game stra-tegy and tactics, time trouble and endings. Try to pick up situations where you did well, i.e. got results above your grading expectation, and put more em-phasis on openings which lead to the positions you like. If there are openings doing badly, phase them out of your repertoire.

Conclusion

All the hints in this chapter and through-out this book are designed to have a cumulative effect. One becomes a strong chessplayer, as Viktor Korchnoi says in his foreword, by treating each event and the preparation for it as serious work. Chess is such a complex and many-sided game that any individual piece of advice, no matter how faithfully you follow it, will only apply to a small percentage of your games and tournaments. A working knowledge of a wide variety of strategic patterns and of their subtle differences takes years to acquire. What can make it all possible is your dedication and desire to become a master or expert. In the pro-cess you will discover that the subtleties of chess and the comradeship of fellow-players add an extra dimension to your cultural and sporting life.

Glossary of chess terms

Accelerated Swiss
Swiss tournament pairing method for large numbers where strongest players are paired with close rivals in opening round.

Adjourned game
Tournament game not completed in one session.

Algebraic notation
Co-ordinate system for game recording.

BCF
British Chess Federation.

Blitz finish
Final moves of game are decided by clock flagfall.

Castle
Non-chessplayer's name for rook; experienced players use the word only to describe the castling process.

Castling long
Castling on the queen's side (0-0-0).

Castling short
Castling on the king's side (0-0).

Cheapo
A trap.

Check
Attack on the king, which need not be verbally announced. A player whose king is in check must get out of check at once.

Checkmate
When a king cannot escape from check.

Clock
Chess clocks are used for timing games. They have two faces, one for each player. Buttons at the top enable a player to stop his own clock after moving and to start his opponent's.

Combination
Forcing sequence, often involving sacrifice(s) to gain material or other advantage.

Congress
Gathering of chessplayers for tournaments. To use 'conference' gives away that you are a non-player.

Descriptive notation
System of move recording where squares are named according to where the pieces stand at the start of the game: thus the king's starting square is K1, the next square in front of the king K2, and so on.

Development
Bringing pieces from their starting position to squares where they are more active.

Diagonal
Slanting row of squares of the same colour.

Discovered check
When one piece moves to uncover check by another piece.

Double check
Where the king is in check from two pieces at once.

Doubled pawns
Two pawns of the same colour standing on the same file.

Draw
Position where neither side can force mate; where the players agree a drawn result; where one side has perpetual check, stalemate, or can repeat the identical position three times with the same player to move. A draw counts half a point in chess scoring.

Elo rating
A rating on the international scale, whose statistical principles were worked out by Professor Arpad E. Elo of Milwaukee.

Endgame (or ending)
When few pieces remain on the board.

En passant
Special move where one pawn captures an opposing pawn. See page 14.

En prise
An attacked piece is said to be en prise.

Exchange
Sequence where each side captures a man or men.

Exchange, win the
Win rook for bishop or knight.

Fianchetto
Developing a bishop on b2, g2, b7 or g7 after advancing the b or g pawn one square.

FIDE
Federation Internationale des Echecs, the world chess ruling body to which over 100 countries are affiliated.

File
Line of squares running directly from one player's side of the board to his opponent's side.

Forced move
No other move possible.

Fork
Double attack by one piece on two others, normally resulting in material gain.

Gambit
Opening where material (usually one or two pawns) is sacrificed in return for quick development.

Game
Single encounter between two players.

GM
Grandmaster; title awarded by FIDE for very good international results, and currently held by about 150 players.

Grade
Performance figures based on results in the previous year.

Hanging pawns
Pawns line abreast on adjacent files in the centre (normally at c4 and d4) without pawns of the same colour on the two adjacent files.

Heavy piece
See major piece.

Illegal move
Move which breaks the rules of the game.

IM
International Master; title awarded by FIDE on the basis of international results and held by about 500 players.

Interpose
To move a piece between an attacked piece and its attacker.

Isolated pawn
A pawn with no pawn of the same colour on either adjacent file, hence often vulnerable to attack by opposing pieces.

J'adoube
'I adjust'. Spoken by a player when he does not wish to move but merely to stand a piece correctly on its square.

Line
File, rank or diagonal.

Major (or heavy) piece
Queen or rook.

Maroczy bind
Control of the centre squares with pawns at c4 and e4 against an opposing pawn at d6; named after the Hungarian champion Geza Maroczy.

Master
Shortened form of 'international master' (q.v.) or of 'national master' which has less stringent requirements.

Match
Series of games between two players.

Middle game
Stage of game after both sides complete opening development.

Minor piece
Bishop or knight.

Norm
Required points for grandmaster or international master tournament result.

Open file
File with no pawns.

Opening
First few moves of the game.

Opposition, the
When two kings face each other with one square intervening; one king has to retreat so that the other, which 'has the opposition' can then advance.

Passed pawn
Pawn with no opposing pawn in front of it or on the adjoining files which can prevent it promoting.

Patzer
Derogatory term for weak player.

Perpetual check
Continued, inescapable series of checks resulting in drawn game.

Pin
When a piece cannot move without exposing a more valuable man to attack.

Plus two
When a player has two more wins than losses during a tournament.

Point
Synonym for square; alternatively, one point is scored for winning the game.

Problem
Artificial position where White has to checkmate Black in stipulated number of moves.

Promotion
Pawn reaching the most distant rank and substituted by any piece of its own colour bar a king. Usually the queen, the most powerful piece, is chosen.

Rabbit
English term for weak player.

Rank
Row of squares from left to right across the board.

Repetition of position
Method of drawing a game: when the same position occurs three times with the same player to move each time, then the player about to move can claim a draw.

Resignation
Conceding defeat in a hopeless position.

Sacrifice
Deliberate loss of material.

Score
Written down moves of the game; in tournaments it is compulsory to keep score.

Sealed move
Move written down when the game is adjourned, and revealed to the opponent when play resumes.

Seeded Swiss
Swiss system tournament where pairings are based on grades or ratings.

Semi-open (or half-open) file
File with pawns of only one colour on it; these pawns may become a target for the opposing attack.

Skewer
Attack on two pieces on the same line. When the front piece moves away, the second piece is captured.

Stalemate
Drawn position, where a player is not in check but has no legal move.

Strategy
Overall plan of campaign.

Strong player
Chess idiom for good player.

Study
Composed situation where White wins or draws.

Swiss system
Tournament pairing system where players with similar points totals meet each other.

Tactics
Detailed execution of strategy.

Tempo
Time taken to move pieces into required positions. If a player takes a move longer than necessary, he is said to lose a tempo.

Time limit
Used in tournament play. Common time limits are 40–50 moves in 2–2½ hours for international chess; 24 moves an hour in local leagues; 40–48 moves in 1½–2 hours in weekend congresses; 40–50 moves in ¾–1 hour for young juniors; the whole game in 30 minutes per player in quick play tournaments.

Tournament
Set contest among a number of players.

Under-promotion
Promoting a pawn to rook, bishop or knight.

USCF
United States Chess Federation.

Weakie
Shortened form of 'weak player', word popularized by Bobby Fischer.

Win
Worth one point in chess scoring. A comment 'White wins' means that White is sure to win with correct play, although there is no immediate checkmate.

Zugzwang
Compulsion to move; a player is said to be in zugzwang when any move he makes will seriously weaken his position, though the opponent has no concrete threat.

Zwischenzug
A move that interrupts an apparently forced sequence; a common example is when a player checks before capturing an opposing piece which is en prise.

! and ?
'Good move' and 'bad move'.

Index

Index of Complete Games

Acknowledgments

The publishers would like to thank the following individuals and organisations for their kind permission to reproduce the photographs in this book.
Camera Press 67, 74; Cleveland Public Library 57; Mary Evans Picture Library 52, 55; Courtesy Lloyds Bank 130; Novosti Press Agency 63, 69, 70–71, 73, 78, 85; BBC Hulton Picture Library 59, 60; Rex Features 75, (Sipa) 89; Malcolm Robertson Endpapers 1, 2–3, 4–5, 8–9, 16–17, 18–19, 21, 22–23, 25, 27, 30–31, 33, 35, 38–39, 41, 42, 43, 46–47, 50–51, 82, 91, 92–93, 99, 103, 106–107, 112, 116, 122–123, 136–137, 140, 142, 146–147, 151; Frank Spooner Pictures (Gamma) 133; Uitgeverij Andriessen, Amsterdam 7.